Fr

C. Anne Wilson

FOOD & DRINK IN BRITAIN

From the Stone Age
to the 19th Century

ACADEMY
CHICAGO

Academy Chicago Publishers

Published in 1991
First US paperback edition 2003
Academy Chicago Publishers
363 West Erie Street
Chicago, Illinois 60610

Printed and bound in Canada

Library of Congress Cataloging-in-Publication Data
Wilson, C. Anne
Food and drink in Britain: from the Stone Age to the 19th century / C. Anne Wilson.
p. cm.
Originally published: Food & drink in Britain from the Stone Age to recent times. London: Constable, 1973. With new introd. and bibliography.
Includes bibliographical references and index.
ISBN 0-89733-364-0 (hc.)
ISBN 0-89733-487-6 (pbk.)
1. Dinners and dining—Great Britain—History. 2. Cookery, British—History. 3. Gastronomy—History. I. Wilson, C. Anne. Food & drink in Britain from the Stone Age to recent times. II. Title.
GT2853.G7W54 1991
641.3'00942—dc20 91-29559
CIP

Contents

A Note to the First American Edition

It is a pleasure to introduce *Food and Drink in Britain* to a new generation of American readers. Although the United States is today a land of many different food traditions, the cuisine imported by the earliest settlers came with them from Britain. They had to make some changes, to add New World ingredients where necessary in place of Old World ones. But the framework was British, and it survived for a very long time among their successors.

It is not surprising, therefore, that the earliest cookbooks published in North America were editions of books originally brought out in London, such as Eliza Smith's *The Compleat Housewife* (first London edition 1727; first American edition, Williamsburg 1742), and Hannah Glasse's *The Art of Cookery* (first London edition 1747; first American edition, New York 1760). Even when Amelia Simmons compiled *American Cookery... adapted to this Country and all Grades of Life* (Hartford, Conn. 1796), the basic ideas for the "Pastes, Puffs, Pies, Tarts, Puddings, Custards and Preserves" listed came from the British mode of cookery and food presentation.

Meanwhile, back in Britain itself, cookery did not stand still. Turkeys, green beans, chocolate (cacao), vanilla, allspice and other new food finds from the Americas had made the reverse journey across the Atlantic from west to east, to be drawn into the British cuisine. So in matters of food and cookery, Britain and America enjoyed what was very much a two-way relationship during the seventeenth and eighteenth centuries.

Since *Food and Drink in Britain* was first published in 1973, more and more people on both sides of the Atlantic have become interested in food history. One important reason for this must surely be the great advances made in methods of food processing and food preservation. As we get further away from traditional ways of cooking and conserving, so we become more eager to find out about our lost food heritage. People collect early cookbooks, either originals (which have become very expensive as demand for them has increased) or modern reprints. Scholars discuss the results of their researches into food history at Symposium meetings, and publish their findings in journals such as the American *Food and Foodways* (New York 1986–) and the English *Petits Propos Culinaires* (London, 1979–), which has an English-language text despite its French title. Many books are published which touch on food history. Among the books on national and regional cookery published in Britain in recent years, several have included not only early recipes for traditional dishes, but also modernised versions that can be reproduced in the kitchens of today.

To update *Food and Drink in Britain*, more might be said about the coloured Anglo-Norman pottages, influenced by Saracen cuisine and recipes and brought back by crusaders and others who visited the medieval Frankish kingdoms at the eastern end of the Mediterranean. The gold-coloured confections had a special significance for the promotion of good health and longevity. More might be said about the origins of marmalade, and fruit preserves; and about the influence of Portuguese quince marmalade which was already arriving in England by the later fifteenth century. Much more might be said about all aspects of food in Britain in the nineteenth century.

But these and the other additions that might be made would together result in a very long book indeed. I hope, therefore, that American readers will enjoy the present version, and that it will whet their appetite and encourage them to sample some of the other books listed under the headings: "Suggestions for Further Reading" and "Bibliography", at the end of the book.

C. Anne Wilson
Leeds, England
May, 1991

About the Author

C. Anne Wilson is an Assistant Librarian at the University of Leeds's Brotherton Library. Her appetite for the history of food was whetted when she catalogued John F. Preston's collection of ancient English cookery books, which were presented to the library in 1962. She is also Editor of the *Food and Society* series published by Edinburgh University Press. The first two volumes of the series, published in 1991, include papers Ms Wilson presented at the annual Leeds Symposium on Food History, which she founded in 1986 and which she continues to organize. In her spare time, Ms Wilson writes books and articles on the history of food and related subjects.

Illustrations

Preface

In this book I have tried to present an outline of the gradual changes and developments in the preparation of foodstuffs in Britain from the days of the hunters and food gatherers until the period of the industrial revolution. Most of the story relates to Great Britain, although references to food in Ireland appear from time to time.

This is a history book, but it is also a recipe book, so that those who have a practical interest in historical cookery can try their hands at some of the dishes eaten by their more remote ancestors. Spelling has been modernized, but otherwise the recipes are printed as they first appeared. For those who wish to research further in this field, a list of cookery books of many periods appears as part of the bibliography on pages 457–9.

Our earliest written recipes date from Roman times, and the English translation of Apicius' *Artis Magiricae Libri X* by Flower and Rosenbaum (Professor Alföldi) gives a most valuable insight not only into Roman, but also into medieval cookery; for many Roman practices survived in France to be reintroduced into England under Norman influence. For a later period, English household and cookery books reflect the gradual changes that took place. Many of the books were reissued several times, and innovations in contemporary eating habits can be traced from one edition to another, as for example in the inclusion of a new section of pudding recipes in the 1631 issue of Gervase Markham's *The English House-wife*, or the ways of dealing with turtle which were added to the fourth (1751) edition of Hannah Glasse's *The Art of Cookery*.

My interest in the history of food in Britain was aroused when Mr John F. Preston presented his collection of English cookery books from 1584 to 1861 to the Brotherton Library of the University of Leeds, which already housed the cookery collection of the late Mrs Blanche L. Leigh. I had the task of cataloguing the Preston books for the library.

Early recipe books make fascinating reading, and in noticing some of the modifications that have taken place in the way we eat during the past four hundred years, I began to wonder about the still greater changes that preceded them. The vast resources of the Brotherton Library allowed me to trace a part of the picture, inevitably incomplete, of eating and drinking in prehistoric times; and also to build up the historic background which provides a context for the later recipes. Of these, by far the greatest number came from the two collections already named, but, where there were gaps, extra material was found in the British Museum Library.

I should like to express my gratitude to the University of Leeds for granting me study leave from my duties in the Brotherton Library for three separate periods of two weeks and one of three months between the years 1966 and 1969 for work on this book. My thanks are also due to Mr G. C. F. Forster of the School of History, University of Leeds, who kindly criticized the first draft; to Mrs P. A. Dulling for her able typing of the final draft; and to Miss E. M. Read for her useful assistance with the checking of typescript.

It would have been pleasing to have re-used the title of the earliest book in the Preston collection for the present volume; but it was not quite appropriate. So I place it here instead, to form, as it were, a second sub-title:

A Booke of Cookry Very Necessary for All Such as Delight Therein, Gathered by A.W.

Leeds 1973

Chapter 1

Introduction

Although the Shortness of Man's Life is imputed by some Persons, to his departure from the simple and frugal Manner of Living of our first Parents, and to the vast Quantities of exquisite Ragoo's and Sauces that are continually coveted; it is certain, That this Practice cannot be justly censur'd, at least without calling in Question the Conduct of Divine Providence, that has ordain'd so great a Variety of Things for the Use of Man. . . .

F. MASSIALOT
The Court and Country Cook 1702

Between the fifth and the fourth millennium BC Britain became an island, isolated to the far north-west of the European land mass. Henceforth new ideas and objects, plants and animals, could reach it only if they were brought in by outsiders. The sea was a barrier to casual movement, but for the adventurous it was also a means of communication. And the continent from which Britain had been severed was still aware of its existence.

For Britain was a land where a living could be made. Wave

after wave of settlers arrived from western Europe all through the neolithic period and the Bronze and Iron Ages. In historic times the sporadic land-hungry settlers were succeeded by more purposeful colonists, their eyes fixed firmly upon the exploitation of Britain's riches: the Romans, the Vikings and the Normans. Lastly Britain itself became a colonizer, vying with other European countries for a share in the newly discovered wealth of the Far East and the Americas.

Not all the new objects that reached the British Isles were brought by settlers. Far back in the prehistoric period Britain was involved in trade with other regions of Europe. It had raw materials to offer, tin, copper and jet in the Bronze Age, later supplemented by such natural products as cattle, corn and wool. In return came the luxury goods of southern Europe. Even before the Roman occupation these included foodstuffs such as wine and savoury herbs. With the Romans fresh varieties of plants and animals arrived which had evolved in the kinder climate of the Mediterranean basin; and small quantities of exotic spices from the still more distant lands of subtropical and tropical Asia.

Britain now learned something of a cuisine more complex than its own. Roman cookery was based inevitably upon the foods of southern Europe. That of France, which was to influence Britain repeatedly from Norman times onwards, followed Roman antecedents, with a bias towards the plants and animals of France's Mediterranean territory.

Other influences came from the Vikings in the centuries before the Norman conquest of Britain; from the Arabs after they had naturalized some of the economic crops of the east in southern Europe; and from the new world at the end of the Middle Ages. All left their mark on British food and cookery.

New foodstuffs were accepted most readily by the wealthy, for the sake of their novelty and interest, and by those who had travelled and had already encountered them elsewhere. Back at home, the Romano-Briton who had seen something of southern Europe, the crusader who had journeyed to the east Mediterranean, and the nabob who had voyaged still further east alike encouraged the eating of new foods and the preparation of strange dishes which they had enjoyed in foreign lands.

In the more remote parts of Britain ancient cooking practices prevailed longer, especially in the northern and western highland zone, where the climate made it difficult to grow new tender plants, and poor communications with the rest of the country hindered the spread of imported foodstuffs, even when these had become well known in the south. During the eighteenth century the cooks of the southern gentry followed recipes for curries and pickles from east Asia, or soup made with West Indian turtles, while at the same time the inhabitants of remote Scottish islands were boiling their beef in the hide, or casing unplucked fowls in clay to roast them in the embers as their forebears had done in prehistoric times.

The chapters that follow have been divided into broad periods for the more convenient marshalling of their contents. But the reader should never forget that at any given period part of the diet of an earlier era still survived somewhere in Britain, while elsewhere the food pioneers were already introducing a foretaste of a future cuisine.

Chapter 2

Seafish, freshwater fish and salt

Prehistoric period

When the land bridge between Britain and continental Europe was first breached the dividing channel towards the French side was no more than a narrow strait of water. Behind the English shore lay vast tracts of fenland that extended far beyond the boundaries of present-day East Anglia. There, and in streams and rivers, pools and lakes throughout Britain, freshwater fish abounded, offering nourishment to the prehistoric Britons wily enough to capture them. Around the coasts seafish were plentiful, and shellfish and crustaceans could be found.

The art of fishing was already well developed in western Europe. Fish were taken by means of lines and hooks, lines and gorges, funnel-shaped basketwork weels or traps, and drag-nets of lime-bast or nettle fibre which were held between two boats or two groups of men. Contemporary evidence for fishing in Britain is tantalizingly scarce. But from mesolithic times pike were speared with leisters (primitive fish-spears made from barbed prongs of bone lashed in pairs or three or more together to a stick: they were the forerunners of the later metal tridents). And a salmon weir which was in operation on the river Bann in Ireland in the neolithic period suggests another early method of trapping fish.

Crabs are thought to have been taken from the deep waters off Oronsay and Oban by means of plaited baskets. The inhabitants of Oronsay also ate conger, haddock, sea bream, ballan wrasse, thornback ray, skate and sharks, for which they must have fished from coracles with lines in their inshore waters. Bones from all these species were found on an occupation site of the pre-neolithic period. It is rare for tangible evidence of fish to survive from such early times, for fishbones dissolve easily in acid conditions. But similar small fishing communities must have existed at innumerable places around Britain's coastline all through the prehistoric era. Shellfish are more easily traced, and the shells of limpets, mussels and whelks taken on rocky shores, and of oysters from river estuaries, show that all were eaten at an early date. But except among very poor and backward groups of people shellfish were usually only a subsidiary source of food.

Early cooking methods, too, are elusive. Small fish and steaks from larger ones could have been spitted on green sticks and roasted, or broiled on hot stones, or stewed in wooden or leather containers heated by potboilers. Shellfish were sometimes consumed raw, but were often roasted in their shells.

Summer was the usual fishing season, for it was the most favourable time of year for taking many species. A few successful expeditions must often have produced a glut, so ways of preserving the catch were devised. Prior to the discovery of free salt, the most obvious means was by wind drying. It was, however, dependent upon the weather and could only be effective if the fish could be brought to a certain point of desiccation before they began to putrefy. But at an early stage the smoking process was invented, possibly by people who had tried to hasten wind drying by hanging up their fish close to the fire.

Wood or peat smoke was much more than a simple aid to drying. It introduced a preservative, formaldehyde, into the fish or meat that was exposed to it; it lessened the chances of insect infestation, and it added interesting new flavours, which were probably quite welcome in the case of rather insipid freshwater fish. Last but not least, fish thus treated could be kept for consumption in the lean seasons of the year.

An early fish-curing industry may have existed in Ireland beside the river Bann. About the beginning of the second millennium BC a group of people were making regular seasonal visits to the area. But although they did some flint working there, probably in order to make prongs for leisters, and also had many hearths with successive layers of ash, they left no domestic debris. The most likely explanation is that they made a summer camp beside the river and built a weir in order to take salmon. They then dried and smoked the fish over smudge fires.

A windfall from the sea in prehistoric times was a stranded whale, and strandings were not infrequent. Even in recent years, between 1913 and 1926, no fewer than 407 whales have been stranded around the coasts of Britain; and when estuaries were much broader and shallower it must have been still easier for the huge creatures to be cut off from the open sea by a falling tide. Their carcases were stripped of meat and blubber with the help of tools such as the axe blade of perforated antler found still leaning against the skull of a rorqual at Meiklewood near Stirling. In the case of whale meat drying and smoking would have been very necessary skills to preserve the massive quantities of flesh for use as food.

There was but little change in techniques of fishing during the later prehistoric period. Inland a farming economy replaced the earlier one based upon hunting. But fishing remained a seasonal occupation for the early summer before the crops had ripened. Only in the Iron Age when cod was being caught to a much greater extent, is there a suggestion of longer lines and more offshore fishing.[1]

Cooking methods were advanced by the introduction of pottery among the neolithic farmers who began to arrive from continental Europe towards the end of the fourth millennium BC. Thereafter fish could be stewed in cooking pots along with cereals and herbs. Much later, bronze and iron cauldrons came into use: these, however, did not produce any innovation in the manner of fish preparation.

One important new discovery reached Britain during the later centuries of the prehistoric period. Throughout Europe the spread of agriculture meant that people were living more and more on cereal foods, supplemented only occasionally by meat and fish. Such a diet was lacking in salt; and it was the craving for salt which led to the opening up of salt mines in the eastern Alps, perhaps as early as the second millennium BC followed by a trade in this highly valued commodity along routes that stretched north to the Baltic and south to the Mediterranean.

Knowledge of the techniques of salt mining and of the extraction of salt from brine springs by evaporation likewise travelled slowly through Europe. But although several different groups of invaders reached Britain from the continent during the neolithic and Bronze Ages, the first known to have practised salt winning here were the Celts of the early Iron Age, who began to enter the country about 600 BC. Their raw material was seawater, and their salt workings have been found along the east coast. The method used at several sites in Lincolnshire was to evaporate brine in shallow pottery dishes set on brick stands over fires. In Norfolk, Essex and Kent the salt was won in a different way by pouring brine over baked clay bars, heating them until all the water was evaporated, and then scraping off the salt. Both techniques must have required much fuel and much patience, owing to the extremely low salt content of seawater.[2]

The size of the industry suggests that the salt was traded on a more than local scale, and that it probably reached the east midlands and the fens. Not only did salt add savour to cereal foods and provide the sodium chloride necessary for health; it was also a most useful preservative for meat and fish. Because it helped to dehydrate fleshy tissues through osmosis, salt could speed up the drying process.

It was introduced into Britain at an opportune moment. In the early Iron Age, and perhaps even before, the climate of the country began to deteriorate. The weather became cooler and wetter, not unlike that of today, and the air more humid. The wind drying of food became a slower and more difficult business with a greater risk of loss through the growth of bacteria and moulds. Salting, either alone or in conjunction with smoking, provided a solution to the problem.

During the next few centuries salted foods were produced on a very large scale in the countries of western Europe. Spain exported salt fish to the Romans in Italy, and Gaul sent salt pork and bacon. Neither product is mentioned by classical authors as a British export; but salt appears to have been used quite considerably to preserve meat and fish for home use. Fish salted at the seashore may well have been traded far inland along land and river routes. We may assume that the dried, salted fish was prepared for eating by being first soaked in water, and then slowly stewed in a cooking pot in liquid, usually with pottage cereals and herbs.

Roman period

In AD 43 the Roman army made its successful invasion of Britain, and within four years had reached the line of the Fosse Way, extending from Exeter to Lincoln. In the wake of the army arrived Roman traders and civilian officials. Roman buildings were constructed in new towns on the sites of the old tribal capitals in lowland Britain; and native farmhouses began to be transformed into Roman villas. Among other aspects of classical life which now reached Britain were Roman ideas of food and cookery.

In Italy the Romans had an amazing enthusiasm for eating fish. They had come late to the idea of fish as food, for they had been inland farmers for centuries before military expansion into south Italy brought them into contact with the Greeks of Magna Graecia and the Greek way of life. From the third century BC there were Greek cooks at Rome who taught the Romans to enjoy Greek dishes. Seafish, always an important part of Greek diet, became immensely popular, and those Romans who could afford to do so spent huge sums on mullet, sturgeon, turbot and many other varieties.

So the Romans who came to Britain and who lived within reach of the sea must have been happy to enjoy the local seafish, and British fishermen would have had a good market for their catches. Fishing in Britain still followed the traditional pattern. The chief innovation was the use of more sophisticated materials for equipment. Barbed hooks for line fishing and spears or tridents were now of bronze, and net-sinkers of fired clay or lead. Cod, ling, haddock and other bottom feeders were fished by lines from boats. Nearer inshore, seafoods such as crab and lobster were taken.

Shellfish of many kinds became very popular. The shells of oysters, whelks, cockles, mussels and limpets are found extensively on the sites of Roman towns, villas and forts at least as far north as Hadrian's wall, not only near the coast but also at great distances from the sea. They must have been transported alive in water-tanks (as they were to be again in medieval and later times). But as yet no archaeological evidence has been found to show how the shellfish trade was organized.

Oysters were the particular glory of Britain. They were marketed widely within the country, and were even sent as far as Rome itself. The shells of a variety from the mouth of the river Colne are still sometimes found on the sites of the ancient capital.

The Romans regarded freshwater fish less highly than seafish. Under Diocletian's price edict of AD 301 the former were rated at little more than half the value of the latter. Nevertheless the owners of inland villas in some provinces thought it worth while to have their own fishponds (*vivaria*) on their estates where spawn and young fish could be reared for table use. There is little trace of such arrangements in Roman Britain; or of the fishpools (*piscinae*), percolated by the tides, that were built near some Mediterranean coastal villas so that seafish could be fattened up close at hand. Fresh fish in Britain were perhaps plentiful and plump enough to make fish farming unnecessary.

But there was now a new gulf in the country's eating habits. Hitherto differences in diet had depended on local variations in natural resources, and the only distinction between the princeling and the poor relation, servant or slave had been one of quantity: the rich ate more of the best of what was available. Now an entirely new cuisine was introduced from the Mediterranean world, and soon the richest and most Romanized Britons were learning to enjoy elegant feasts prepared in the Roman manner.[3]

The Greco-Roman cuisine which now reached Britain had been evolved in Greece as early as the sixth century BC. It comprised a subtle mingling of native and imported flavouring herbs with small amounts of meat or fish, cereals, nuts, vegetables, eggs, oil and wine in a great variety of ways. Recipe books were produced, some of them by medical men who were interested in the effect of nutrition upon health. The views of Greek physicians, formulated in their writings from the fourth century BC onwards, were later developed and handed down through the works of Celsus and Galen into the medical lore of the Middle Ages. The medieval theory of the four humours, with its emphasis on the degrees of heat or coldness, dryness or moisture inherent in every food, went back through Rome to fourth-century Greece.

Of the many cookery books of the Roman imperial period only one has survived to our own day. This is Apicius' *Artis Magiricae Libri X*. Although it bears the name of Apicius, a famous gourmet of the first century AD who wrote a general cookery book and another entirely devoted to sauces, it is in fact a compilation of the fourth century AD. Recipes from several Greek books on cookery, dietetics and domestic science were added to original Apician items, and in order to ensure its success the compiler launched his collection under the name of the master.[4]

The Greek-inspired recipes of Roman times needed more careful cooking than primitive stews or roasts, and appropriate vessels had already been invented. Some were particularly well suited for fish, among them a shallow round pan with a long handle, thought to be a *patella*; a rather deeper two-handled dish (perhaps a *patina*); and the round or oval Roman frying pan, *sartago* or *fretale*, which sometimes had a collapsible handle so that it could be used inside an oven as well as over direct heat. The first two were either of bronze or earthenware; the last of bronze or iron.

Metal gridirons (*craticulae*) or tripods were used to support pans over a small charcoal fire or brazier, invaluable for the many thickened sauces which needed to be cooked over controlled heat. They could also serve to grill meat or fish: shellfish in their shells were cooked on a gridiron.

Eating was carried on by means of knives, fingers and spoons: iron-bladed knives and fingers for foods stiff enough to be cut and conveyed to the mouth in slices; and spoons for sauces, pottage and foods of a softer consistency. Spoons were made of bone, bronze or silver, with round or oval bowls. A small spoon known as the *cocleare* was used at the bowl end for eating eggs, and had a pointed handle convenient for picking shellfish out of their shells.

But before the Romano-Britons could eat their meals in true Roman style they had to acquire not only Roman cooking utensils and fine pottery vessels (and a Greek cook, if possible, to supervise their use), but also some of the Roman speciality foods. Apart from the wine, oil and Mediterranean herbs that were basic to the new cuisine, there was the important condiment *liquamen* which took the place of salt in the majority of dishes.

Liquamen, also known as *garum*, was adopted from the Greeks, who made it out of a fish they called *garos*. But the Romans prepared it from small red mullet, sprats, anchovies, mackerel and the like which were mixed with the entrails of other, larger fish, salted, and put in a vessel to lie in the sun. After a time the concentrated juice was removed with the aid of a sieve and stored in earthenware amphorae. It was produced on a commercial scale at several places around the Mediterranean; and the *garum sociorum* supplied by a trading company called the *socii* or 'allies' at Carthago Nova on the river Ebro in Spain was sent all over the western Roman empire.[5]

Apicius' book included many recipes for fish preparation, most of them apparently drawn from his original compilation on sauces. A typical sauce for boiled fish contained pepper, lovage, parsley, origan, dried onion, honey, vinegar, *liquamen*, wine, a little oil, and was thickened when boiling with *amulum* (wheat starch). Alternatively the fish could be simmered in a *court bouillon* of water containing dill and coriander seed and sprinkled with vinegar before serving. Oysters were given a dressing: 'pepper, lovage, yolk of egg, vinegar, *liquamen*, oil and wine; if you wish, add honey also'.[6]

Salt-pickled Mediterranean fish, sturgeon, tunny and swordfish from the Black Sea, and tunny hearts from southern Spain and southern Italy were a luxury food at Rome, and must have been rare imports into Roman Britain.[7] Possibly the Britons already salted their own fish for long keeping, for salt winning was still an important activity. Brine was heated in evaporating vessels of baked clay supported over fires on clay bars and handbricks, not unlike the apparatus formerly used during the Iron Age. The debris left from the industry has been found on many Roman sites in the Fens and around the coasts of Lincolnshire, Essex, Kent and Sussex; and it is likely that salt was also extracted at the brine springs of Droitwich and at a place in Cheshire, probably Nantwich. Both were called *Salinae* (salterns), the Roman name for places where a salt industry was carried on.

Salt may also have been shipped to Britain from the Atlantic coast of Gaul, where it was possible to evaporate sea-water by solar heat alone. That region was a great supplier of salt to the more northerly countries during the Middle Ages.

The impact of Roman eating habits on landowners and town dwellers in lowland Britain during nearly four centuries of imperial dominion was considerable. But it was far weaker upon the peasants and the Britons of the north and west. They continued to boil their fish or bake it in the embers in traditional fashion, and only the gradual spread of a few Mediterranean flavouring herbs brought a new fillip to the peasants' fish stew.

Early medieval period

The sophisticated Roman cookery of fish and its appropriate sauces fell into disuse when Romano-British town and villa life died away at the beginning of the fifth century AD. In the period immediately following the Roman withdrawal fish was at a low ebb of popularity in Britain. In the Celtic parts of the country seafish were looked upon with disfavour by the early Christian church: they were sacred to Venus, a pagan goddess whom the church particularly disliked because of her other connections.

Eastern Britain was gradually occupied by Germanic settlers who were farmers. Their primary interest was in crops and livestock. Though they made use of such fish as they could easily catch inland or on the coast (five salmon and one hundred eels appear as part of a food rent in the laws of Ine AD 690–3), their main concerns were not those of seafarers.[8]

The situation began to change when the rites of the Roman church were brought to England at the end of the sixth century AD, and the heathen Saxons were gradually converted to Christianity. Unlike the Celtic church that of Rome did not look askance at fish. Roman policy was ever to replace a pagan observance by a Christian one. If fish had formerly been eaten on Friday (*dies Veneris*) by the devotees of Venus, it was now to be eaten on the same day by good Christians in memory of the events of Good Friday.

The eating of fish on fixed days was not a new idea. Fish days had been kept by command of the Emperor Licinius early in the fourth century AD, probably on economic grounds in order to save meat. The economic aspect may have had some influence on the fasting arrangements of the early church, too. At any rate, Lent fell conveniently towards the end of winter, when most domestic animals, other than those kept for breeding purposes, had already been killed off for lack of winter fodder; and meatless meals were a necessity as well as a virtue.

And if lay people now came to rely on fish as a regular part of their diet, the members of the monastic orders of the new church did so still more. The rule of St Benedict demanded that his monks should abstain altogether from fleshmeat, or more exactly from 'the meat of quadrupeds' except in time of sickness. This ordinance was maintained in monasteries throughout Britain from 960–1216. Thereafter by gradual degrees meat eating crept in, initially for the abbot and his guests, and finally for all the monks at certain times of the year.

Even in the earlier period there were backsliders. 'At Winchester', it is reported, 'the first Norman prior, Simeon, found the brethren eating meat and weaned them from it by exquisitely prepared dishes of fish. The monks were delighted with these, and asked that they should always be given such food, and then they would willingly abstain from meat.'[9]

Elsewhere, however, the meatless diet of the monks was strictly adhered to, even before Norman times. This is made clear in Aelfric's *Colloquy*, an early eleventh-century schoolbook, from which we learn that schoolboy novices at the monastery were still allowed to eat meat, which was forbidden to their elders in full orders.

The religious fast days gave a new impetus to fish consumption, and the fishing industry expanded to meet it. Fishermen ventured further out to sea, and with bigger boats and longer lines angled for the white fish that lived at the sea bottom. There was no question of deep-sea fishermen confining their activities to territorial waters. '*Piscatores Angliae, Galli et Belgae*' are said to have been active at the mouth of the Yare in the sixth century AD, and this state of affairs continued through most of the medieval period, when Hollanders and Zeelanders fished on the English side of the channel and sold their catches at English ports.[10]

A new kind of fishery was the taking of herrings in nets, which seems to have been beyond the skill of prehistoric fishermen, perhaps because of the difficulty of making drift-nets large and strong enough to bear the weight of the catch. Such nets could easily have been made in Roman times, and either in the late Roman period or not long afterwards the herring fishery began. It expanded and grew, receiving fresh impetus from the Viking invaders during the ninth and tenth centuries AD. It has even been claimed that their arrival in Britain was connected with the temporary disappearance of herrings from their own home waters. At all events, having taken possession of large stretches of the British coastline, they continued to go out and fish for both the herrings and white fish which, according to the sagas, they had formerly caught in more northerly fishing grounds.

By the time of the Norman Conquest the herring fishery was an important factor in the economy of Britain. Several east and south coast fishing ports paid rents in the form of huge numbers of salted herrings, and the famous Yarmouth herring fair, held each year from Michaelmas to Martinmas (29 September to 11 November) was already established.[11]

Nets were not only used to take herring: they also became important adjuncts to coastal fishing. They were employed in a manner that was not dissimilar to their use on land in hunting game. A curved hedge of nets and stakes, known as a sea-hedge (*heia maris*), was set up on the beach at a point where it would be completely covered by the sea at high tide. As the water receded, the fish which had swum over the top and round the edges of the barrier were cut off and trapped. By the time of Domesday there were many such sea-hedges attached to seaside manors, especially along the southern and eastern coasts of England; and fishing in this fashion has continued until modern times.

The nets took mackerel and other small fish. They were in use in Wales, too, where under the Laws of Hywel Dda seaside landowners could build a 'weir' on the foreshore bordering their lands; 'but if the sea throw any things upon the land, or upon that beach, they belong to the king: for the sea is a pack-horse to the king'. In English law, as well as in Welsh, whales which came aground were crown property, though several charters from the period following the Norman Conquest show that, except for the tongue (regarded as the special delicacy) or occasionally the whole head including the tongue, the whale was usually granted to the tenant upon whose shore it was marooned.

Whale meat was salted, which both preserved and tenderized it; and in this form it was kept to eat as Lenten food. It was perhaps valued more in France than in England, where salted herring became the great standby for Lent. But in the tenth century the salted whale of France, known as *craspois*, was imported regularly from Rouen, along with the wine of the country. In 982 King Aethelred laid down the tolls payable on both commodities at London Bridge; this suggests that *craspois* may at that time have been nearly as much of a luxury as wine.[12]

Shellfish lost their status as a delicacy during the first few centuries after the end of Roman rule. They were rarely eaten, for instance, at the prosperous early dark-age settlement of Dinas Powys in Glamorgan, although whelks, cockles, mussels, limpets and especially oysters had formerly been a considerable feature of the diet at the Roman villa of Llantwit Major which was only slightly nearer to the sea. Later they returned to favour and in the early eighth century Bede listed shellfish among the outstanding natural riches of Britain. Well before the Norman Conquest the old Roman practice of transporting shellfish inland was revived. At Thetford, a populous Anglo-Danish town, archaeologists found plentiful remains of oysters, cockles, mussels and winkles which had been brought forty miles from the coast. These must have been favourites of the period, for all are named among the fisherman's 'catch' in Aelfric's *Colloquy*.[13]

Rivers and inland waters yielded freshwater fish, and fishing, like farming, was made to take its place in the feudal system.

The larger fish weirs became the property of the manor, and their use had to be paid for by a rental in kind from the fish they caught. The manor of Tiddenham in Gloucestershire, lying in the triangle formed by the Wye and the Severn, drew a great part of its income in the late Anglo-Saxon period from basket weirs and hackle weirs on the two rivers. According to a contemporary survey, every alternate fish and all rare fishes belonged to the owner of the estate. Elsewhere fishermen worked the rivers from boats, and they had little difficulty in selling their catches in local towns and villages.[14]

The eel and salmon fisheries of Britain were noted by Bede, and rents in both commodities were being paid at the time of the Norman Conquest. Eel rents were common particularly in the East Anglian fens. Much of the region had been drained and turned over to corn growing during the Roman occupation, but a fall in the land level before the middle of the fifth century AD had led to flooding and thereafter its principal products for many centuries were fish and waterfowl. Some manors paid many thousands of eels each year in rents to the Abbot of Ely.

Watermills became widespread in lowland Britain from the eighth century onwards. Under the feudal system both the mill and the millpond were the property of the lord of the manor, and the fish in the millpond belonged to him too. Eels were taken in wickerwork traps in the millstream above the water-wheel; and several mills rendered eel rents rather than corn rents.

As both river fish and seafish were caught in ever greater numbers salt became increasingly important as a means of preserving them. Salt was still won in many of the places that had been worked in Roman times. But a new and quicker way of evaporating it had been found, well before the Norman Conquest, which used up less fuel than earlier methods. In Lincolnshire the salter worked on the 'mould' or 'muldefang' which was the sand from the upper part of the shore, above the usual tide-line, but covered several days a year by the spring tides. Such sand acquired a high salt content. The salt was dissolved out of it into sea or fresh water, which was drawn off into a wooden vessel over a filterbed of peats and sods. When sufficiently concentrated (an egg floating on the surface was the gauge), the brine was boiled and evaporated in leaden pans. Turves fed the fires; but elsewhere around the coast wood was burned for the purpose.

The brine springs of Worcestershire and Cheshire also yielded salt, much of which was traded into Wales. The *salinae* at Droitwich, which were active in AD 691, had probably been worked more or less continuously from Roman times. Like other sources of natural wealth, salt pans and brine springs usually belonged to manors or monasteries, and were let out to tenants.[15]

Salt was now in general use in the drying of fish. But Egil's *Saga* records that in the ninth century the dried fish of western Norway was also imported into England, to be traded there for cloth and metal.[16] This was the beginning of the traffic in stockfish, which was to become such a staple of poor man's fare. The early spring shoals of cod were caught along Norway's western seaboard, and were dehydrated in the cold, dry, sunny air to a point at which they would keep almost indefinitely. Viking settlers in northern Britain no doubt encouraged the trade in a foodstuff already well known to them. Stockfish was notoriously hard, and had to be both beaten and soaked to make it edible again. It then required stewing, and may have been eaten, as in later days, with butter.

But fresh fish could be broiled, fried or simmered in broth in the *cytel*, which was the Anglo-Saxon version of the iron cooking cauldron. The proverbial 'kettle of fish' may go back as far as this.

Later medieval period

Fasting days continued after the Norman Conquest, and even increased in number. The fasts of the church had a two-fold object: to mortify the flesh by removing the immediate pleasure of meat eating; and to reduce carnal passions, which were held to be inflamed by too meaty a diet. Fish foods, however, were lowering. 'All manner of fish is cold of nature and doth ingender phlegm; it doth little nourish', according to medieval medical lore.

Fish days may have achieved the second aim, but they soon ceased to fulfil the first one. A very large number of days was involved, for Lent and all Fridays and Saturdays were kept as fish days until late in the Middle Ages; and Wednesdays were likewise observed until the early fifteenth century. This meant that on about half the days of the year meat could not be eaten, and some of those days could not fail to coincide with occasions for celebration or special hospitality. 'Upon fasting days, salt fish, and two dishes of fresh fish; if there come a principal feast, it is served like unto the feast honourably' was the rule in the household of Princess Cecil, mother of King Edward IV, and such was the general practice.[17]

Fish was cooked in the same rich spicy pottages as meat, was baked in pies, and was turned into blancmange or jelly. The venison and frumenty of ordinary days were replaced by porpoise and frumenty on fish days, and the porpoise was carved 'after ye form of venison'. At some great feasts the most prominent abbots and prelates of the church were present, and when this happened on a flesh day, it was customary to offer two separate menus. Two or even three courses of butcher's meat, poultry and game were served to the lay guests, and were paralleled by two or three equally magnificent fish courses of as many dishes for the religious men.[18]

People outside the church, who were free to eat flesh on all permitted days, were warned by the physicians that 'fish and flesh ought not to be eaten together at one meal'. With so many compulsory fish days, it can have been little hardship to forgo fish on days when meat was permitted.

The rich fared perhaps not too badly. They could afford the more expensive varieties of fresh fish, and could conceal the flavour of other kinds with rich, spicy sauces. For the poor, fish days meant salt fish, and more salt fish. 'Thou will not believe how weary I am of fish, and how much I desire that flesh were come in again, for I have ate none other but salt fish this Lent, and it hath engendered so much phlegm within me that it stoppeth my pipes that I can neither speak nor breathe', ran a passage in a schoolbook of the fifteenth century, that must have wakened an echo in the mind of many a schoolboy. It is hardly surprising that first the Wednesday and then the Saturday fish day fell into disuse; though Fridays and Lent were observed continuously until the seventeenth century.[19]

To provide so many fish meals in a year the fishing industry was fully extended. The herring fishery prospered. The season began in early June off the Shetland Isles where the shoals first appeared, small, lean fish, less oily than those caught in later months. All through the summer the herrings were taken off the coasts of Scotland, the north of England and Ireland, as the shoals divided in their southward migration.

Then the herrings, grown large, fat and oily, reached the seas off East Anglia, where the fishing was at its most intensive. Men of Sussex, Kent and even Cornwall came over to join the native fishermen. Their presence was not always welcome and led to skirmishing and the 'herring wars' at Yarmouth during the thirteenth and fourteenth centuries. The Dutch who fished the same waters and brought their catches to the ports of Norfolk and Suffolk seem to have fared better, at least until the end of the fifteenth century; and periodically they received encouragement in the form of remission of customs dues, and protection in time of war.[20]

Finally the herrings reached the south coast, and the men of Sussex were again active in taking them. Further west pilchards, smaller oily fish related to herrings, and likewise appearing in seasonal shoals, were caught and salted by Cornish and Devonshire fishermen.

The west of England received its herrings from Ireland, and Bristol was the chief centre for their distribution. But in the east, the great herring city was Yarmouth with its regular autumn fair. Here were purchased the pickled herrings that were to be eaten during the following winter, and especially through Lent.

Whale stranded at Tynemouth, 1532

From Olaus Magnus: *Historiae de gentibus septentrionalibus*, 1555

Catching and smoking salmon

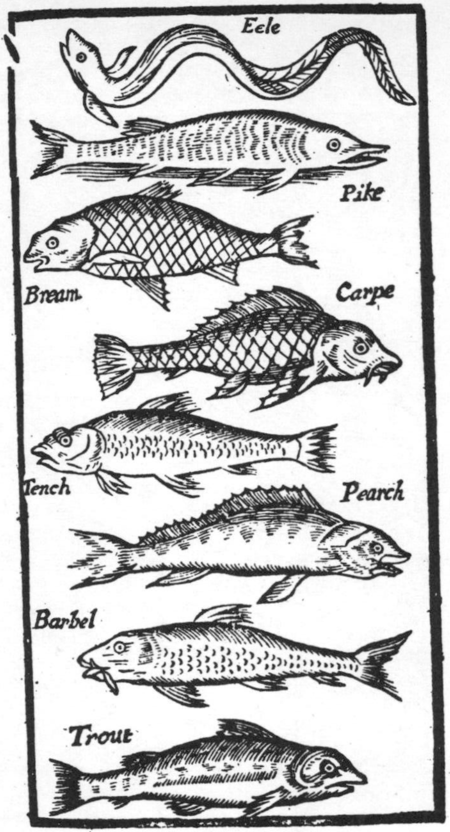

Several fishes
From H. Wooley:
The accomplish'd ladies delight, 1686

Man fishing
From W. de Worde: *Boke of S. Albans*, 1496

At first the fish were preserved in a very primitive fashion, salted in heaps on the shore without even being gutted, and they can hardly have been fit for long keeping. Later the methods of the fourteenth-century Dutchman, William Beukels or Beukelzoon, were adopted. The herrings were gutted and soaked for fourteen or fifteen hours in brine, before being barrelled up in rows between layers of salt. It was important to keep the air from them, for it caused their fat to oxidize, so that they became rancid. For this reason it was virtually impossible to preserve them by drying; though the lean young fish that were caught off Scotland in early summer were apparently being dried about 1240.

The smoking of herrings was a development of the late thirteenth century. The fish were first given a long soaking in heavy brine, then strung up and smoked in special chimneys for many more hours and finally they, too, were barrelled. 'Their goodness consists in their being large, fresh, fat, soft and pliable, well salted and barrelled; their roes safe within them, and their outside of a yellow gold colour.' Thomas Nashe in his *Lenten stuffe*, 1599, described the excellent keeping properties of red herrings. 'The poorer sort', he claimed, 'make it three parts of their sustenance.'[21]

Unlike herring white fish lived permanently on the sea bed, and fishermen could go out and angle for them at any time of the year. These fish were taken with hook and line, and in the course of the Middle Ages longer and longer lines came into use, equipped with many hooks, so that fishing could be carried on at greater distances from the shore. Much of the catch was salted and sold for despatch inland, or for keeping against future fast days and Lent. In the case of distant water fishery, salting was often done on shipboard. Otherwise it was carried out in port immediately after the fish was landed.

Particular ports had their own specialities. Plaice and merling or whiting were caught off the Sussex coast. 'Playz de Wychelsee [Winchelsea]' and 'Merlying de Rye' were both esteemed in the fourteenth century, and appear in a number of household accounts, including those of the royal household. 'Morue [cod] de Grymsby' was equally famed. Like the east-coast herrings, the more northerly cod attracted fishing boats from the south coast, as well as those of the local fishermen.

Fishing arrangements were always seasonal. The inshore fishermen of Scarborough in the first part of the fifteenth century, for instance, fished for plaice in winter, for lobsters and cod in Lent, for skate and more lobsters in the summer. The distant water fishermen of the region, who had larger boats, pursued herrings in east-coast waters in the autumn and further north in the winter; haddock and cod off eastern Scotland and on the Dogger Bank in spring; while in summer some of them sailed towards Iceland for the cod fishery.[22]

The 'Icelandic fare' began early in the fifteenth century. Two- and three-masted ketches with rudders, larger and more sophisticated than earlier fishing boats, had been developed during the previous hundred years. Lodestones were already known, and the use of the compass was spreading from the Mediterranean to northern seas.

The English mariners set out in February or March, at first mainly from east-coast ports, though later Bristol men were much involved. They took with them provisions for the summer, and salt. When they reached Icelandic waters they caught cod, salted it on board before drying it (the summer climate being too warm and humid for successful wind drying); and at the end of summer when all their salt had been absorbed, they sailed for home and the autumn markets. Some crews went less far and fished for cod off the Shetland and Faroe islands.

Not all the fish were salted and dried. Some were barrelled in salt, and left in their own pickle until the ship came home. Fish in this state were known as green fish. Sometimes they were taken out and dried at the end of the voyage, after spending several weeks in brine.

The degree of hardness and dryness finally obtained varied with the method of curing. The names given to salt fish also varied, and it is not always easy now to tell what they originally meant. The term 'stockfish' was applied to several members of the cod family, such as pollack, scalpin (whiting) and milwell; and was given to salt fish as well as to that which was wind cured without salt.

'Ling' often meant dried cod in general. It is, in fact, a separate species, but seems not always to have been recognized as such. Fifteenth- and sixteenth-century records show that stockfish was only about half the price of salted ling; so whatever meaning was attached to the latter name, it clearly denoted preserved fish of a finer quality.[23]

Coastal fishing by sea-hedges or with hook and line brought in the smaller fish which were sold fresh at or near the place where they were landed. And shellfish were gathered in great quantity for sale in towns near the coast. All through the Middle Ages they were one of the few seafish which poorer people in London could afford. Various prices shown in contemporary documents, such as oysters at twopence a gallon in 1298 or fourpence a bushel in 1491, were very low in relation to the cost of other kinds of fresh fish.

Whales, porpoises and sturgeon were all royal fish, not only when they came aground but also if they were taken at sea. But since the fisherman, or the tenant on whose foreshore a whale was stranded, was usually granted the carcase apart from the head or tongue, he could make a good profit. Much salted whale found its way on to the market. Pieces were often bought for the Countess of Leicester and her household, according to her household roll of 1265. At the end of the thirteenth century whale 'of this year's salting' sold at twopence a pound in London while if it was more than a year old (*superannuata*), it fetched only half the price.[24]

Seals were still eaten in medieval Britain. Like porpoises they went into pottages for fish days; and twelve porpoises and seals appeared among the provisions for Archbishop Nevill's great enthronement feast at York in 1467. Within the next two hundred years they dropped out of the British diet except on some remote northern islands. On Heisker in the 1690s the natives still salted seals with the ashes of burnt seaweed, and ate them in springtime 'with a long pointed stick instead of a fork, to prevent the strong smell which their hands would otherwise have for several hours after'.[25]

Away from the coasts freshwater fish were much in demand; for the carriage of goods by river or road was very slow, and seafish deteriorated too quickly to be brought far. Millponds continued to be a reservoir of fish for their manorial or monastic owners. Artificial ponds or stews were also constructed, in the tradition of the Roman *vivaria*.

From time to time the ponds were broken, the fish sorted out and some removed.

> The mill pond. And in the seven year of the king, twenty-eight day of January [1467/8], I brake mine greatest pond in the park, and out of that I took in great breams, sixty-five. And put them in to the mill pond, the which is new made; and I put the same day in to the same pond six great carps; and the same day I put in to the same pond in little carps, twelve score. And in great tenches the same time, forty-three. In small tenches, twenty. In little breamets sixty-six. In roaches thirteen score. In perches, six score. All these is at this hour and day in the mill pond.[26]

Very large households, like that of the Countess of Leicester, included a fisherman as a permanent member of the staff, and it was his job to catch fish from the ponds as they were needed. For the less exalted there was free fishing on navigable rivers as far upstream as the tide ebbed and flowed, in certain streams and in the 'town ditches' surrounding boroughs to which free fishing rights had been granted by royal charter.

Fishing rights in private waters were also allowed at times to poor tenants and other humble persons, perhaps in return for services rendered. The fifteenth-century *Treatyse of Fysshynge with an Angle*, which has been attributed to Dame Juliana Berners, abbess of Sopwith, charged all noblemen to refrain from fishing in poor men's private waters, and from breaking the gins in their weirs so as to steal the fish caught in them. Dame Juliana's list of the fish caught includes salmon ('the most stately fish that any man may angle to in fresh water'), trout, grayling, barbel ('a sweet fish, but it is a queasy meat and a perilous for man's body. For commonly he giveth an introduction to ye fevers'), carp, chevin or chub, bream, tench, perch, roach, dace, bleak, ruff, flounder, minnow, eel and pike. In connection with the last-named fish she noted an example of the animal-baiting sports so well loved in her day. You had first to get your pike firmly hooked on your line. 'And if ye list to have a good sport, then tie the cord to a goose foot: and ye shall see good haling, whether the goose or the pike shall have the better.'[27]

Eels were found in many rivers, notably in the Fens; but were also imported in great numbers from the Netherlands all through the Middle Ages. They were cheaper than most fish, and were probably the only fresh variety, other than shellfish, bought by poor people.

'The carp is a dainteous fish; but there be but few in England', wrote Dame Juliana Berners in 1496. Carp had been introduced from the continent (they are native to the Danube region), and since they do not breed easily in northern Europe, they never became plentiful in Britain. Sir John Howard presented friends with some from his greatest pond in September 1465, described as 'carps for store'. They were perhaps well wrapped in moss to be hung in a net in a cellar and fattened on bread and milk. They could thus be preserved alive for as long as a fortnight, according to an eighteenth-century author.[28]

Salmon from the river Bann and other Irish rivers was still in demand, no longer smoked as it had been three thousand years earlier, but barrelled in brine and sent to west England ports.[29] Scottish salmon likewise pickled was transported by sea to London and other southern markets.

Lastly, a few medieval delicacies were regarded as fish which would hardly fall into that category today. The barnacle goose was one. 'It has its wings, feathers, neck and feet. It lays eggs and tastes like a wild duck. We had to eat it as a fish, but in my mouth it turned to meat, although they say it is indeed a fish because it grows at first out of a worm in the sea. . . ,'

Puffins were classified in the same manner, and roasted puffins were part of the fish feast held for the enthronement of the Archbishop of Canterbury in March 1504/5.[30]

Beaver's tail owed its designation to Pliny, whose *Natural History* was a treasure house of knowledge for medieval Europe. He had written: 'The beaver has a fish's tail, while the rest of its conformation resembles an otter's'; and this piece of lore was largely responsible for the extinction of the beaver in Britain at the hands of those in search of lawful meat for fish days.

> There have been taken of them whose tails have weighed four pound weight. . . . The manner of their dressing is, first roasting, and afterward seething in an open pot, that so the evil vapour may go away, and some in pottage made with saffron; other with ginger, and many with brine; it is certain that the tail and forefeet taste very sweet. . . .[31]

The distribution of the more usual forms of fish was carried out mainly by the fishmongers, who had their own guild in London by the middle of the twelfth century. The varied range of their merchandise can be gathered from the accounts of Daniel Rough, who was the common clerk of Romney, Kent from 1353 to 1380, and a fishermonger as well. His stock included 'oysters, crabs, trout, sprats, porpoise, salmon, haddock, lampreys, mackerel, codling, conger eel, shrimps, red and white herrings, whiting, "pickerelle" [young pike], stock-fish, gurnards, whelks, tench and "strikes of pimpernelle" [small eels]'.[32]

Except at the seaside fresh fish sold for more than salt fish because of its perishability. In London it was not only offered in open markets and at the fishmonger's stalls, but was also hawked through the streets to ensure quick disposal. But in Lent so pressing was the demand for fish of all sorts that the chandlers and salters, as well as the fishmongers, were officially licensed to sell it. Traders were subject to many regulations, which were not always observed. For instance, they were forbidden to offer unsalted fish for sale after the second day; and they were not allowed to water fish more than twice. Mackerel, being oily and particularly perishable, could be sold on Sundays, before and after divine service.

But the quantity of salt fish passing through the bigger ports was far greater than that of fresh fish, and for a time separate guilds of saltfishmongers and stockfishmongers existed side by side to undertake its distribution. The two merged in 1536 to become the Worshipful Company of Fishmongers, still in existence today.[33]

The salt industry became more indispensable than ever. The Lincolnshire salterns were active all through the medieval period, but met their doom in the great flood of 1571. Elsewhere around the coasts similar methods survived longer. John Leland described salt winning on the shores of north Lancashire; while along the Northumberland and Durham coast sea-coal, washed out of underwater surface seams and brought in by the tide, served to heat the evaporating pans of the salt-makers.[34]

The salt produced in Britain could not, in the end, keep up with an ever-increasing demand, and by the beginning of the thirteenth century it became necessary to import French salt. 'Bay salt', as it was called, was produced in the Bay of Bourgneuf, and the same name was carried by salt made all along the French Atlantic coast and on the beaches of north Spain and Portugal. It was prepared from seawater drawn off into huge basins on the long, level beaches, and such was the efficacy of the summer sun that no other source of heat was needed to evaporate the seawater and crystallize out the salt. It was a coarse, dark salt, full of impurities which found their way into the open basins on the foreshore and were not removed.

In the fourteenth and fifteenth centuries Bay salt cost between half and two-thirds as much as the more carefully prepared white salt. The Dutch bought it, refined it by boiling it in seawater, and resold it as 'salt upon salt'. Nevertheless Bay salt with its large grains and sharp sweet taste came to be preferred to finer salts for preserving purposes. The technical reason was that it could penetrate flesh more completely and thus produce a better cure, whereas fine salt tended to seal the surface tissues, but not to enter further. It is clear from many household accounts which have survived from the fourteenth to the seventeenth centuries that families regularly purchased both sorts, the Bay salt for preserving and the white varieties for the table. In noble households the white salt was placed upon the table in large very ornate salt cellars of silver or even gold plate.[35]

The wide range of fish dishes in the contemporary cookery repertoire varied from the simple to the unrecognizably complex. Alexander Neckam, writing in the twelfth century, said that fish should be boiled either in salted water, or in a mixture of wine and water. Several recipes exist, too, for fish stewed in ale and water: 'Plaice boiled. Take a plaice, and draw him in the side by the head; And make sauce of water, parsley, salt, and a little ale; and when it beginneth to boil, skim it clean, and cast it thereto, and let seeth.'

The association of parsley with fish began early. Alexander Neckam recommended that 'green sauce' should be served with all fish. Its ingredients were to be sage, parsley, costmary, dittany, thyme, garlic and pepper; and 'let not the benefit of salt be overlooked'. Medieval green sauce was thickened with breadcrumbs and tempered with vinegar or ale. It might include several green herbs such as mints, pellitory, and those already named; or it might be a simple parsley sauce. 'Take parsley and grind it with vinegar and a little bread and salt, and strain it through a strainer, and serve it forth.'[36]

The herbs often came from the herb garden. But the Countess of Leicester during her stay at Dover Castle purchased two-pennyworth of parsley on Tuesday 16 June 1265. It is tempting to believe that it made the parsley sauce for the plaice, breams and soles eaten on the following day.

Later in the Middle Ages green sauce was appropriated to 'green fish', which was newly salted white fish, probably through an association between the two names; but it was also recommended for fresh turbot. Foils (leaves) of parsley, often wetted in vinegar, were used as a garnish for such freshwater fish as salmon, trout and perch.[37]

Fish was incorporated into pottages, not only the great Anglo-Norman spiced pottages, but also the peasant stews of barley or oatmeal and herbs. Although fish and meat were regarded as interchangeable in many of these dishes there were a few speciality pottages, proper only to particular fish. Such a one was 'balloc' or 'balourgly' broth, made from pike and eels cut into gobbets and stewed in wine and water which was afterwards spiced and poured over the fish as a sauce.[38]

Alexander Neckam singled out two items of equipment as being specially connected with fish cookery. One was knives, employed for gutting. The other was a stock of wheat starch (*amulum*) or finely grated breadcrumbs, to be kept hidden away along with the spices in the cook's own little storeroom and used to 'consolidate' small fish before cooking. These would have been the fish that were fried in butter or oil – olive oil in the rich man's kitchen, and rape oil in the poor man's. Butter was much in demand for fish frying, and people bought in an extra supply of it just before Lent. Plaice, whiting, flounders and gudgeon were among the fish for frying. So were loaches, roaches, tenches and soles, often eaten with sweet-sour egerdouce sauce. As a garnish, fried parsley became popular.[39]

The gridiron was another necessary utensil of the medieval cook. Before being laid upon it, fish were often given a preliminary scalding or boiling.

> Another diting of a tench. Take a quart of wine and a little vinegar, and tender bread, and steep all together, and draw it through a strainer; and let it boil; and cast thereto powdered pepper; and take a tench, and split him, and rest him on a gridiron, and cast his sauce upon him in the dish; and then serve it forth hot.[40]

Freshwater fish, less well liked than seafish, were also less esteemed among medical men. River varieties were preferred by them to fish from stagnant ponds or moats, for 'fish the which liveth and doth feed on the mud . . . doth savour of the mud'. These last must have been the 'mudfish' which appear so frequently on fish days in the accounts of the Petre family of Ingatestone Hall in Essex.[41]

Fish were baked in pies to eat both hot and cold. The pastry 'coffin' or shell seems to have been regarded merely as a means of cooking the fish, and was not always eaten. Baked lampreys were cooked in a syrup inside the pie. When the crust was opened, the liquid was mixed with wine and spice and spooned on to slices of white bread in a dish warming over a 'chafer hot' or hotplate. The lamprey was then cut into 'gobbets as thin as a groat', and placed on top of the bread and sauce.

A cold pie was a means of preserving fish, for such pies were filled up with clarified butter which set and excluded the air. Medieval rents were sometimes paid in eel pies; and twenty-four herring pies made of the first fresh herrings of the season, each pie containing five herrings flavoured with spices, were rendered annually to the king by the city of Norwich.

Fish pies often contained not only spices, but also dried fruit, wine and sugar, all of which made them distinctly sweet to the taste. One pie that was made to mark the midpoint of Lent had a filling of figs, raisins, apples and pears, all ground up and cooked with wine and sugar to which was added boiled fish – calver salmon, codling or haddock – brayed with spices. The mixture was placed in its pastry coffin, and 'planted' on top with stoned prunes and quartered dates.[42]

Fish jelly was a favourite feast dish, eaten in the second course or the third, if the occasion was grand enough to demand three. Tenches, pikes, eels, turbot and plaice were considered suitable for the purpose. They were cut up and boiled well in wine or wine and vinegar. Then the fish pieces were removed and laid in dishes, while the broth was spiced and coloured with saffron or other dye, further reduced and skimmed. It was strained through a cloth, poured over the fish and left to set.

In recipes of the mid-fifteenth century the liquor was based upon fresh pike, and if it would not jell, 'sounds [swimming bladders] of watered stockfish' were added, precursors of the later isinglass. Jellies were brightly coloured, and it was not unusual for two colours to be served together as 'jelly departed'. But 'crystal jelly' could also be made by boiling the fish in 'white wine that will hold its colour'.[43]

Shellfish were popular with rich and poor alike. For a large household several hundred were bought at a time, especially as a treat during Lent. Dame Alice de Bryene of Acton Hall, Suffolk, for her Sunday dinner on 19 March 1413, paid for 'four wash [a measure of an eighth of a bushel] of oysters, one wash of mussels bought at Colchester, together with the expenses of a groom of the kitchen and his two horses fetching the same 13d.; three hundred whelks 9d.' Her groom was sent to Colchester every Sunday throughout Lent to make a similar purchase.

Shellfish were cooked either in a simple broth of their own juice with perhaps a little ale and pepper; or more elaborately in 'gravey' or 'civey', or the spicy 'potage wauter', a confection of whelks with, among other things, almond milk, cloves, maces and sugar. The fish were usually removed from their shells at an early stage of the operation. But one recipe for mussels had them stewed in wine with pepper and minced onions until 'they beginneth to gape'. They were then served up in their shells, as happens with some Mediterranean fish soups today.[44]

Whelks were also boiled in water and eaten cold with vinegar and parsley leaves. At the enthronement feast of William Warham as Archbishop of Canterbury on Passion Sunday 1504/5, four thousand whelks were proffered to the more distinguished of the guests in the form of a garnish for salted sturgeon.[45]

Lobster, crayfish and crab were greatly enjoyed, though they seldom reached the inland eater. At formal meals they presented difficulties. 'Crab is a slut to carve and a wrawde wight [perverse creature].' By the time the carver in a noble household had finished picking the meat out of every claw with a knife-point, had piled it all into the 'broadshell', and had added vinegar and mixed spices, the tepid crab had to be sent back again to the kitchen to be reheated before he could offer it to his lord. Crab and lobster were also boiled and eaten cold with vinegar, as were shrimps.[46]

The royal fish – sturgeon, porpoise and whale – appear in the menus for royal feasts, but they were on the king's table at other times; and on other tables too, since they reached the open market. Five barrels of salted sturgeon supplied the guests at the enthronement feast at Canterbury in 1505; but it was something of a luxury for the average manorial family. Dame Alice de Bryene bought a quarter of a barrel to last a year, whereas she had four barrels of white herrings over the same period. Salting not only preserved but also tenderized the sturgeon. In its fresh form it had to be 'shorn in pieces, and steeped overnight, and sodden long as flesh: and he shall be eaten in vinegar'.[47]

Porpoise, the venison of fish day, was boiled and served with frumenty, or was baked with spices in a pasty, made in the manner of venison pasty. Fresh whale meat, swordfish and porpoise, if roasted, needed to be very well done. Salted sturgeon, swordfish and porpoise were sauced with vinegar, and whale with sour wine. An alternative for salted whale, according to a French source, was to be cut raw into strips, boiled like bacon and eaten with peas.[48]

Stockfish, salt fish and red and white herrings were the staple Lenten and fasting day foods for the majority of people in Britain. In most years all were fairly cheap, and they were still cheaper if they were bought at the end of the summer and stored until needed.[49]

The medieval stockfish required drastic treatment to make it edible. 'And when . . . it is desired to eat it, it behoves to beat it with a wooden hammer for a full hour, and then set it to soak in warm water for a full two hours or more, then cook and scour it very well like beef; then eat it with mustard or soaked in butter.' The stockfish hammer was a regular kitchen item, even in Elizabeth's reign.[50] The fish could also be boiled and soaked in hot water, and then simmered in spiced stock from fresh fish, or put into pies like the one for mid-Lent already described. The sounds of stockfish helped to set jelly in the fifteenth century; but a hundred years later were ousted by isinglass, derived from sturgeons' sounds and brought by Dutch traders from Russia to Britain.

Salt fish, like stockfish, was eaten more for necessity than pleasure. Too much was thought unwholesome, for, as Andrew Boorde said, 'the quality doth not hurt but the quantity, specially such salt fishes as will cleave to the fingers when a man doth eat it'. But its exceptional keeping properties made it invaluable for provisioning army garrisons and ships' crews; and Elizabethan mariners took prodigious quantities of salt fish as well as salted meat with them on their voyages of discovery.

At home salt fish, like stockfish, was boiled and eaten with mustard or butter. Fresh white herrings were served in a dish with salt and wine, and salted ones with mustard. And both salt fish and herrings were put into pies with fruit.[51]

The substantial nature of a sixteenth-century Lenten breakfast can be seen in the *Northumberland Household Book*, which lists the provisions appointed for some of the meals for members of the family of Henry Algernon Percy, fifth Earl of Northumberland, about the year 1512. 'My lord and my lady' had: 'First a loaf of bread in trenchers, 2 manchets, a quart of beer, a quart of wine, 2 pieces of salt fish, 6 baconned herring, 4 white herring or a dish of sprats.' These provisions were slightly reduced in the breakfast given to the two older children, while the two still in the nursery got 'a manchet, a quart of beer, a dish of butter, a piece of salt fish, a dish of sprats or 3 white herring'. Red herring were not thought suitable food for any of the children. The sprats, like the white herring, were pickled in brine. Nine barrels of the former had been laid in for Lent, and five casks of white herring. And no fewer than 2,080 salt salmon were put into store to last the Percy family from Shrovetide to Whitsuntide.[52]

Early modern period

By Elizabeth I's reign, the nature of fish days was changing. Hitherto they had been kept for religious reasons; now economic and political considerations also lent their weight. In the first place, meat animals in Britain had become scarce and dear. In the second, the English government wished to encourage the building of ships as a safeguard against possible Spanish attacks; and more fishermen in peace time meant more reserves to be called into service with the navy should need arise. Nevertheless the act of Parliament by which the Saturday fish day was reintroduced in 1548 claimed firstly that 'due and godly abstinence is a means to virtue and to subdue men's bodies to their soul and spirit', before adding the two political reasons already given. Fifteen years later, as a result of proposals by Secretary William Cecil, Wednesday was also made a statutory fish day.[53]

The sick could obtain a licence from their priest or bishop permitting them to eat meat during Lent and on other fasting days. Contrary to modern opinion, meat was considered more suitable than the little-nourishing fish as a food for invalids, though it was usually given to them in the form of meaty broths. The household accounts of Sir William Petre of Ingatestone Hall, Essex, for 1551/2 show that he strictly observed the Saturday fish day imposed three years earlier. But a special note on his Lenten expenditure records: 'Spent this Lent two lambs, three capons, four partridges, six chickens on the children and them that were sick'.

After 1585 attempts to enforce fish days were abandoned for a time, but there were further proclamations against eating meat in Lent and on other fasting days during the reign of James I. Under the Commonwealth fish days were abolished as a Popish institution. After the Restoration efforts were again made to revive them with a view to encouraging the fishing industry. But fish was too scarce and expensive; and people who had enjoyed freedom from obligatory fish meals during the previous years were most unwilling to go back to them.[54]

Nevertheless the concept of fasting-day food survived, even through an era when Roman Catholic practices were not officially condoned. The largest section in Hannah Glasse's *The Art of Cookery*, 1747, is entitled: 'For a fast-dinner, a number of good dishes, which you may make use of for a table at any other time', and the chapter is a curious conglomeration of dishes based on fish, vegetables and eggs: soups, fritters, puddings and pies, the only common factor being the absence of meat.[55]

The abolition of compulsory fast days affected the fishing industry in a number of ways. The rich still ate fish often enough to provide a market for the choicer sea and freshwater species. But the poor and the frugal no longer cared either for the coarser types of freshwater fish or for the endless salt fish of an earlier era.

Red and white herrings remained in demand, but the herring fishery itself underwent some vicissitudes. From the fifteenth century onwards the fleets which sailed out from the eastern coasts of England and Scotland were in constant competition with the Dutch, who fished openly on the British side of the channel, selling their catches at British ports. It was only in the eighteenth century that the Hollanders became careless about the curing of their fish, so that their trade declined, and the British seamen won back the right to provide their own countrymen with herrings. And then they found that their profits were less than they should have been because of the government tax on the salt with which the fish were preserved.

Herrings were usually salted at sea, even before they were landed. But as salt fish became increasingly unpopular, more effort was made to try to bring white fish to the markets in a fresh condition. During the seventeenth century ships carried tanks in their hold in which the catch could be conveyed back alive. The tanks were also used to bring expensive varieties of fish from distant coasts to London. Turbot and lobsters taken near Tynemouth were kept alive there in rockpools until they could be transferred to the 'wells', as they were called, inside the ships which would carry them to the London market. In the eighteenth century well-vessels, which had been invented by the Dutch, came into regular use. In them the well ran from wall to wall across the ship, and its sides were perforated so that the seawater could circulate among the fish put to swim inside. Well-vessels fished on the Dogger Bank and in the North Sea. The fish they brought back was, of course, sold at high prices.

Cod and other white fish were taken in the North Sea and off Iceland. During the reign of Elizabeth I, west country seamen began fishing the seas off Newfoundland, and somewhat later off Nova Scotia and New England. The winter climate there was well suited for dry curing fish with a minimum of salt. But such hard, dry fish was no longer welcome in Britain, and the market for it there declined steadily. Eventually most of it was sold in the Catholic countries of southern Europe, where it was popular because it kept well in hot weather.[56]

Some other contributors to the former fish day diet of Britain were now abandoned. Whales virtually ceased to be eaten, and were no longer salted for Lenten food. Porpoises went more gradually out of favour, and for a time a few of the gentry still cultivated a taste for baked porpoise, prepared in the manner of a venison pasty. Sturgeon, the other royal fish of earlier times, were occasionally caught in the Severn, Thames or Tyne. Since royalty often waived its ancient claim to them, they could be enjoyed by commoners and several recipes for their preparation are to be found in seventeenth- and eighteenth-century cookery books.[57]

Shellfish lost none of their attraction. Oysters were the favourites, eaten by rich and poor alike. They could be kept alive in brackish water for as long as twelve days; so they were carried long distances, and frugal housewives in such inland parts as Hertfordshire pickled them in vinegar to last for several weeks.

During the eighteenth century there was a vogue for green oysters. In Essex around Mersea and the rivers Crouch and Roach the oysters developed green beards about September, which were caused by the growth of harmless algae. When these shellfish became fashionable, local purveyors collected oysters and put them into pits in the salt marshes for six or eight weeks, which greatly increased the coloration and turned them a dark green, much admired in London. Not surprisingly, in view of the frequent adulteration of other foods of the time, there were those who hinted that the colour of the oysters had been produced by copperas or other poisonous mineral dyes.[58]

Lobsters, crabs, shrimps and prawns continued to be enjoyed. And a new fish that came to be much used as a garnish and condiment was the anchovy. Mediterranean anchovies, pickled in brine, were occasionally imported during Elizabeth's reign, and their primary function was to stimulate the thirsts of wine-bibbers at their drinking sessions. Botargo, a relish made from salted mullet or tunny roes, was also brought from southern Europe, and was sold for the same purpose. Anchovies, however, were very soon taken into the sphere of cookery, where they were added to sauces or made dishes not only of fish (they were a piquant accompaniment to insipid freshwater fish), but in due course of meat as well.

With the end of compulsory fish days, freshwater fish went out of favour, except for the choicest varieties. For a time some of the gentry kept the stews on their estates in operation as reservoirs of such fish. In the 1690s the Earl of Bedford had live pike and perch sent regularly by barge from Thorney in the Fens to stock his ponds at Woburn in Bedfordshire. But during the eighteenth century most landowners allowed their lakes to lapse into ornamental waters.

Improved methods of transport made it less necessary for fish to be stored live upon the estate. Before 1724 a direct trade had been established between Whittlesey and Ramsey in the Fens and London in 'tench and pike, perch and eels, but especially tench and pike, of which here are some of the largest in England'. They were carried alive in water butts on wagons; and the water was drawn off and changed each evening during the journey.[59]

Otherwise newly caught fish despatched overland still travelled in luggage vans, horse drawn and slow moving, which made the enterprise a risky one, especially in warm weather.

Land carriage was more successful later in the century, after the road system had been improved.

And in the closing years of the eighteenth century a new venture was just beginning: that of packing fish in ice in order to transport them over long distances. It was first practised on Scotch salmon. These fish had been well known in London for some hundreds of years. They had arrived salted, or dried, or smoked (with a hard, salty cure, quite unlike modern mild smoked salmon), or pickled in vinegar with or without the spices that were added to make 'Newcastle salmon'. In the eighteenth century fresh or would-be fresh salmon were brought to London by land carriage from as far north as Cumberland; but that style of transport made them extremely expensive.

Once it had been discovered how to preserve salmon in boxes of ice (an idea originally suggested by a member of the East India Company, who had seen fish conveyed long distances in China encased in snow), the method was quickly developed. Ice-houses were built on all the principal salmon rivers; and early in the nineteenth century Londoners were receiving quantities of ice-packed salmon despatched by sea which, it was claimed, were 'as fresh as when they were taken out of the water'.[60]

But salt was still the principal preserving agent for pickled salmon, herrings and other oily fish, and there was no diminution in the trade in Portuguese and Bay salt, the preferred type for the purpose. Britain's own salt industry continued and prospered, too. On the coasts of Northumberland and Durham coal-pit coal now heated the evaporating pans formerly fired with sea-coal. The Firth of Forth, also conveniently close to coal fields, was another area with an active salt industry. The Scottish salt was very fine and rather bitter from the calcium and magnesium salts precipitated in it by rapid boiling after little or no prior evaporation in the sun. It was suitable for table use, but not for curing fish since it produced saltburn on the surface tissues.

Coal from north-eastern England was shipped to the south

to stoke furnaces at such places as Lymington in Hampshire. There Celia Fiennes watched the process in the later seventeenth century. Seawater was drawn into a series of ponds and allowed to evaporate for a time in each before being led on into the next. When sufficiently concentrated, the brine was brought through pipes into

> a house full of large square iron and copper pans, they are shallow but they are a yard or two if not more square, these are fixed in rows one by another, it may be twenty on a side, in a house under which is the furnace that burns fiercely to keep these pans boiling apace and as it candies about the edges or bottom so they shovel it up and fill it in great baskets. . . . Their season for making salt is not above four or five months in the year and that only in a dry summer.

The brine springs of Worcestershire and Cheshire were, of course, still active; and in 1670 rock salt was discovered near Northwich, and was quickly exploited. It was made into strong brine with fresh water, and then taken to the river mouths of North Wales to be reboiled with seawater, 'which produces as strong and good salt as the others', explained Celia Fiennes. She herself invested in the new industry by taking out a mortgage on some land near Marbury. The rock salt was even sent by sea to Bideford and Barnstaple where it was reboiled with seawater to make 'salt upon salt' that was employed with great success (exceptionally for British salt) in curing herrings.[61]

The herring fisheries were hard hit when salt was subjected to taxation. After one or two earlier attempts to raise revenue by this means, a salt duty was imposed in 1643 which remained in force, with periodic increases, until 1825. The bounties offered in the later eighteenth century to encourage fisheries partly offset the effects of the tax. But it was claimed that great quantities of herrings were thrown back regularly into the sea by fishermen who found it more profitable to take only such fish as they could bring alive, or at least newly caught, to the market.

London's fish market was Billingsgate, close to the river and its wharves. From medieval times tolls had been charged on the cargoes of fish, but in 1699 an act of Parliament declared Billingsgate a free and open market for the sale of fish six days a week, and of mackerel, only, on Sundays, before and after divine service. The exceptionally perishable mackerel required special treatment. In the eighteenth century they were brought up the Thames from Folkestone by the London and Barking mackerel smacks which 'fly up to market with them, with such a cloud of canvas, and up so high that one would wonder their small boats could bear it and should not overset'.[62]

When buying fish at Billingsgate or any other market, the purchaser had to be wary. Advice was given in late seventeenth- and eighteenth-century cookery books on the distinguishing marks that showed whether fish was newly caught, fresh and firm, or flabby, sunken eyed and already beginning to decay. Even pickled fish were suspect. Anchovies and herrings which had grown rusty might have been rebarrelled in new brine; pickled salmon might be fish which had been 'made up again when damaged'. Lobsters' claws were filled with water and plugged to make them more weighty, and careful buyers looked for the telltale plugs and removed them. If, despite all warnings, a customer acquired fish that was 'near tainting', he was recommended to gut them, and lay them on dry rushes with hyssop or winter savory over them.[63]

Fresh or otherwise, fish was always well seasoned. The standard Elizabethan broth for a carp or pike was made thus: 'Take water and yeast, and boil them together, then take whole mace, currants, prunes, pepper and salt, parsley, thyme and rosemary bound together, with a little verjuice and vinegar, and a good piece of sweet butter, and boil them all together. To all kind of fish the same broth, excepting prunes.' More ambitiously a pike could be boiled in wine with oranges, dates and spices. It was neatly dissected first, and was reassembled for serving, when its head was placed upright with an orange in its mouth.[64]

The basic broth for fish was subsequently modified, yeast

being dropped, and wine or vinegar alone replacing the verjuice. Currants and prunes were abandoned in favour of gooseberries, grapes or barberries, added towards the end of the cooking time, or orange or lemon zest or juice. Sometimes, instead, the stock was turned into a sauce with anchovies or shellfish.

During the seventeenth century more solid stews in the form of hashes, bisks and fricassees began to replace the earlier pottages. The fork came into regular use later in the century. Hitherto forks had been rare possessions of the gentry, employed for eating pears or ginger in syrup; while country people had felt no need of 'little forks to make hay with our mouths, to throw our meat into them'.[65] Thereafter diners found a fork easier to convey into their mouths those foods which were intermediate in consistency between the liquid spoonmeats and the firm lechemeats of medieval days. The fork was an excellent utensil for the eating of crumbly cooked fish, and together with the sharp-pointed knife of the period was helpful in the prior discovery and removal of fish bones.

Fish were not always stewed. Stuffed pike were tied to spits between wooden lathes, and roasted before the fire. Eels were spitted direct 'like an S', or were stuffed and attached to the spit with packthread; while oysters were spiked upon small wooden spits tied to the usual iron one, and were dredged with flour or breadcrumbs and basted with butter or anchovy sauce as they roasted. Pieces of sturgeon were toasted in front of the fire. Smaller fish could be broiled on a gridiron or fried in butter (Sir Kenelm Digby advocated a mixture of oil and butter).[66]

During the sixteenth and seventeenth centuries fish were still served upon sops, and it became customary to run warm melted butter over them before they came to table. At the same time a garnish was added, which now took the form of gooseberries, grapes, fresh or pickled barberries or red currants, or orange or lemon slices.

For a time Seville oranges were the favourite fruit garnish, but in the eighteenth century lemons prevailed. Barberries became an occasional alternative for boiled pike, mackerel, skate or ray; and scalded gooseberries were sometimes served with mackerel, which might also be garnished with parsley and fennel.

Parsley chopped into melted butter slightly thickened with flour was a usual sauce to accompany white fish in eighteenth-century cookery books. Horseradish was now often scraped over the oilier fish such as mackerel, herrings or salmon. Mustard was still much in favour with herrings. Anchovies, shrimps, prawns or mussels went into sauces for other seafish.[67]

Shellfish were always popular. In the era of compulsory meatless days they adorned the Elizabethan fish day salad, which might be made according to one of the following recipes: 'First a salad of green fine herbs, putting periwinkles among them with oil and vinegar. . . . An other. White endive in a dish with periwinkles upon it. . . . Another. Alexander buds cut long ways, garnished with whelks.'[68]

The next century saw a new departure. The rigid demarcation between fish and meat meals was becoming blurred, and shellfish, especially oysters, began to be prominent in the latter. Cookery books now gave instructions on how 'to boil a capon with oysters and pickled lemons', 'to fry mussels, periwinkles or oysters to serve with a duck or single by themselves', and 'to roast a capon [stuffed] with oysters and chestnuts'. Oysters were added to hashed mutton, or used to force a leg of mutton. Oyster stuffing for domestic fowls, especially turkey (which was eaten with oyster sauce for good measure) continued in fashion all through the eighteenth century. There was even a vogue for mutton or pork and oyster sausages.

Oysters were still eaten on their own, of course, either fresh or pickled. In the seventeenth century they were often taken as an *hors d'oeuvre*; otherwise pickled oysters or other shellfish appeared as a second course dish. There were dozens of recipes for the pickle which supplied 'an excellent means to convey oysters unto dry towns, or to carry them in long voyages'.[69]

Little fresh oysters were eaten raw; while large ones were stewed with herbs and spices, or together with other fish, or were roasted or baked in pies. A suggested menu for a large fish day feast in the 1630s has stewed oysters in the first course, and oysters in three states – fried, pickled and baked in a pie – in the second. Bills of fare some thirty years later show meals made up mainly of meat dishes, with oysters either as *hors d'oeuvre* or *finale* during the months with an R in their name.[70]

The liberal use of oysters in cookery continued into Victorian times, while pickled oysters were a regular food of the poor in London and other towns. Then quite suddenly the oyster beds became exhausted, partly through over-exploitation and partly perhaps already from the effects of pollution; and it was only by deliberate artificial breeding that they were saved from complete extinction.

Anchovies were made to fill the same role in meat dishes and sauces as *liquamen* had done in Roman cookery. Mid-seventeenth-century recipes show them boiled with a neat's tongue or beef palates, or in a salad with slices of cold breast of hen or capon. A hundred years later they were being added to jugged pigeons, or a sauce to eat with veal, or a stuffing for a sirloin of beef. And throughout the period they appeared in many other equally diverse dishes.

They were still eaten as appetizers; and sprats and spurlings from home waters were 'pickled for anchovies', crowded close in a barrel or deep glazed pot with salt, saltpetre and bayleaves sandwiched between the layers. 'In three months they'll be fit to eat as anchovies raw, but they will not dissolve.' It was the solubility of true anchovies, when they had lain long in brine, that made them so useful for sauces and pickles.[71]

Lobsters, crabs, shrimps and prawns could be dressed in many ways, but the commonest was to boil them to eat cold. After being simmered in a brine of water and Bay salt in a fish kettle, lobsters could either be eaten immediately, or kept as long as a quarter of a year, wrapped in brine-soaked rags and buried deep in sea-sand.

Shrimps were seethed in equal parts of water and ale or beer 'and some salt good and savoury' in Elizabethan times. The ale motif persisted into the eighteenth century, when they could be preserved in a simple pickle of alegar and salt. For special occasions, lobsters, crayfish, prawns or shrimps were set in jelly.[72]

Fish pies were a welcome part of Lenten fare as long as meatless meals were obligatory at that season. They were rich food, filled with the oilier species, such as white herrings, eels, salmon or sturgeon (drier fish like carp had to be larded with pieces of eel); and until late in the seventeenth century they were still made with much butter, spices, and raisins or currants. Minced pies of fish and dried fruit had their lids iced. The Lenten ling or salt fish pie was somewhat less sweet, the fish being mingled with egg yolks, herbs, spices and butter; but even this had its cover adorned with 'good store of sugar' before it came to table.[73]

In due course new methods of baking fish were evolved, which no longer depended upon the traditional standing coffin of strong paste. Its place was now often taken by a patty-pan lined with richer, shorter pastry. In the next phase the pastry was dropped altogether, the fish being baked direct in an open dish, sometimes covered by a protective layer of breadcrumbs dotted with butter. Hot fish pies were still made on occasion, but the seasonings had taken a more savoury turn, with herbs or anchovies predominating.[74]

The cold pie of preserved fish changed more drastically. A method of conserving fowls or pieces of fleshmeat already practised in Elizabeth I's reign was to parboil them, dip them in hog's lard or clarified butter 'till they have gotten a new garment over them', and pack them in stoneware pots that were filled up with more spiced lard or butter. Sir Hugh Platt claimed that meat so protected would keep 'sound and sweet for three weeks or one whole month together, notwithstanding the contagiousness of the weather'.

The same idea was adopted by the people of Gloucester in order to preserve the long-celebrated Severn lampreys (Henry III had considered all other fish to be insipid by comparison). Hitherto cold butter-sealed pies had been the vehicle in which the lampreys had travelled to other parts of the country. Now there was a gradual changeover to pot-baking. Gutted and well seasoned, the lampreys were baked in butter, drained, and then sealed under more butter 'to fill up the pot at least three fingers breadth above the fish', when they would keep for up to a year.[75]

The lampreys in their pots were sent as far as London, to be sold by the fishmongers there. So too were the char from the upland lakes of northern and western Britain. Celia Fiennes described their dappled skin with reddish spots, and said that 'if they are in season their taste is very rich and fat, though not so strong and clogging as the lampreys are, but it is as fat and rich a food'. The season of the Westmorland char was between Michaelmas and Christmas, and many were then potted in spiced butter for despatch to distant parts.[76]

During the seventeenth century potted fish, like potted meat, became a fashionable dish at the tables of the well-to-do, served among the lighter fare of the second course. Recipes abounded for the potting of eels, lampreys, salmon, smelts, mackerel, lobsters, shrimps and any fish that was regarded as particularly desirable. They continued to be enjoyed in this guise throughout the eighteenth century, and some are still potted as delicacies today. But cold fish pies, their preservative function superseded by potting, disappeared from the mainstream of cookery, and only survived in a few regional versions.

The other usual way to conserve fish was to pickle it. Sides of salmon, sturgeon or pike, and large eels and congers split lengthways were rolled in collars and soused like brawn. Cutlets of salmon were put into liquid pickles based upon wine, vinegar and water, or beer. 'Some will boil in the liquor some rosemary bound up in a bundle hard, two or three cloves, two races of sliced ginger, three or four blades of large mace, and a lemon-peel', wrote Robert May.

Beer was the secret of the famous Newcastle salmon, which came not from Newcastle at all, but from the River Tweed. The fish were carried sixty miles by pack-horse to Shields and were there simmered in the characteristic pickle before being despatched by sea to London and other ports. When the recipe for Newcastle salmon was finally revealed, it consisted in stewing the fish in two quarts of water, with three of strong beer, half a pound of Bay salt and half a pound common salt; and next day putting it in pots and making up the pickle with strong alegar and several spices. Salmon treated thus would keep, it was claimed, for a whole year.

A different type of pickling was applied to flat fish, smaller white fish and pieces from larger ones. Sir Hugh Platt in 1605 advised: 'Fry your fish in oil, some commend rape oil and some the sweetest Seville oil that you can get, for the fish will not taste at all of the oil because it hath a waterish body, and oil and water make no true unity, then put your fish in white wine vinegar, and so you may keep it for the use of your table any reasonable time.' The method had been known to the Romans, and Sir Hugh could have borrowed it from Apicius' cookery book, which had been published on the continent in four or five different editions during the previous century. 'Marinating' and later 'caveaching' were the names given to the process in Britain; and marinated or caveached fish, like pickled and potted fish, was served as a side-dish for the second course.[77]

Pickled sprats, herrings and oysters were popular among poorer people, who gradually ceased to buy the salt fish on which they had been so dependent in former times. Salt fish and even stockfish were still an occasional food among those of the middling sort. Hannah Glasse recommended that stockfish should be beaten almost to atoms with a sledgehammer, softened in milk and warm water, and then simmered with new milk and spices and served up in place of a pudding.

Softer salt fish were steeped in milk and water, or water with a glass of vinegar in it. The larger ones were then boiled, while the smaller were grilled and basted with oil. Cooked salt cod was served with a sauce of hard boiled eggs chopped in melted butter, and its proper vegetable accompaniment was 'parsnips boiled and beat fine, with butter and cream'.[78]

Some local dried and salted fish from northern Britain became more widely known during the eighteenth century. 'Newcastle is a famous place for salted haddocks', wrote Hannah Glasse in 1747. 'They come in barrels, and keep a great while.'

Speldings – wind-dried whitings wetted as they cured with sea-water to give them their own special taste – were made along the Scottish coast to the north of Aberdeen, and were on sale in London during the 1770s. A few miles to the south of Aberdeen, haddocks were dried on the seashore and then smoked over peat or seaweed fires by the wives of the fishermen of Findon. They became well known in Edinburgh, where they were sent by stage coach in the later eighteenth century, and were the ancestors, albeit harder, drier and more salty, of the modern finnan haddock. Shetlanders salted and dried haddock, coal-fish and cod for their own winter use, and the Faroese were still living on stockfish and dried whale in the early years of Victoria's reign; but these products were for home consumption only, and were not exported to other parts of Britain.[79]

But Scottish-dried salmon, hard and salty, was shipped to southern ports. 'Though a large fish, they do not require more steeping than a whiting, and when laid on the grid-iron, should be moderately peppered', claimed Hannah Glasse. Salmon pickled in vinegar was also sent to the south, and was very much a food of the London poor, like pickled oysters, even in the 1830s. The coming of the railways, which allowed fresh salmon to be transported long distances within a short time, finally ended the trade in dried, salted and vinegar-pickled salmon.

And the town poor soon acquired another cheap fish food. A few fried fish shops were in existence by 1851, where fried cod or flat fish could be bought, along with a slice of bread or a baked potato. Chipped potatoes were introduced from France about twenty years later. This new complete meal had an enormous success among the working poor in London and the industrial towns of northern England. As a result, fish consumption in Britain increased vastly; and fish assumed an importance in the country's diet which it had not had since the days of Elizabeth I.[80]

Chapter 3

Game beasts and tame beasts

Prehistoric period

The meat eaters of Britain in about 5000 BC were in most cases the same people as the fishermen. Hunting and fishing were seasonal occupations, the former for winter and the latter for summer. The animals caught were red deer, roe deer, elk, wild ox and wild pig, with an occasional hare, beaver or other small creature when bigger quarry was elusive. The climate of the time was moist and had become warm enough for the growth of mixed forest trees, such as oak, alder, elm, lime; and their leaves provided fodder for the larger animals that roamed among them.

The hunters camped near lakes and rivers on the edge of the forest, and pursued their prey with bows and arrows and barbed spears. Other means of capture may have included nooses hung from tree branches to trap unwary creatures as they went by; and the hounding of animals into gullies and down precipices. At Star Carr settlement in Yorkshire were found stag frontlets of red deer, with horns still attached, worked into the form of masks which the hunters could wear. Thus attired they must have felt that they had magically acquired the strength and swiftness of the deer themselves, and the masks could also have camouflaged the men as they stalked the forest.

Implements of the period included deer-antler mattocks with which to gouge meat off the carcase, and flint blades to cut it up. At Star Carr cooking fires were kindled with stripped bracket fungus for tinder, and flint and iron pyrites to create the initial spark.

But mesolithic Britons had neither pottery nor metal vessels in which to cook their meat. Roasting was their simplest mode of preparation, and spits could easily have been contrived from green forest branches. The flesh would have had to be cooked warm from the kill, as was the practice among German tribes of the first century AD. When this was not possible, long hanging would have been necessary to break down the connective tissue and tenderize the meat, and it would have been eaten high, as is still the case with game.

Animal heads, offal and blood would not have been wasted. The gut, used as a container for liver, lights and brains, cut up and mixed with fat, could be roasted slowly in the embers. Homer described this type of cookery in the *Odyssey*, and it is found almost universally among primitive peoples. In Britain the haggis was still a regular food in the Middle Ages; and in remote highland areas it survived until modern times.

Another byproduct of early meat animals was the remains of leaves and grass contained in their stomachs. British hunters at the stage of the Star Carr people were poorly provided with plant foods, and may have eaten the partially digested contents of the game they killed. Finally the bones were stripped and broken to extract the marrow. The fatty tissue within the bone cavities was then, as later, prized as a nourishing food. To primitive hunting people, the marrow must have represented the very core of the animal and the carrier of its virtue.[1]

One constant problem of early hunters was that of scarcity, when animals were elusive, and roots, grasses, nuts and berries made an unsatisfying diet. At other times luck in the hunt produced excessive abundance, and more flesh was available than the small groups could eat before it decayed. The solution lay at first in air drying, a technique which survived until comparatively recently in St Kilda and the Shetland and Faroe islands. Visitors there reported that the meat initially underwent an unpleasant change, but after some months of hanging was cured and fit to eat.[2]

The next development was smoking, which protected flesh against decay, and helped to ward off insects. In a future lean period, it could be reconstituted with water, cooked and eaten.

The mesolithic hunters had reached Britain by an overland route, or at most had made short canoe hops across shallow broads between Flanders and East Anglia. But by the time the next settlers arrived, during the fourth millennium BC, Britain was already an island. They came from northern France and Belgium; they brought with them seed corn and domesticated animals, and they were our first farmers. Their continental homes were on chalklands, and they chose to live on similar terrain in south and south-west England. Later, when they spread to other parts of the country, it was to the sandy soils of Suffolk, the limestone plateaux of Somerset and Gloucestershire, and the wolds of Lincolnshire and east Yorkshire. Those areas were no less heavily wooded than other parts of the country. But their soils were lighter and drier, and they yielded more easily to the slash and burn technique of cultivation. The farmers cleared and fired a small piece of woodland, raked the ashes into the earth, planted their corn among the charred tree stumps, and for a year or two it grew well enough. As soon as the soil began to lose its fertility they moved on, and the forest took over again.

Their main meat animals were cattle, pigs, sheep and goats.

The two last named were indigenous in their wild form to parts of the Near East; and it was there that they were first herded, perhaps as early as 9000 BC in Iraq, by hunters who conceived the idea of having their meat and milk supply ready at hand.[3] Thereafter both creatures moved very gradually westwards, bound to man by the new links of domestication. Subsequently cattle and pigs, which were feral in most areas of Europe, were also herded.

Sheep and goats were introduced into Britain by the first farmers. They may have brought cows and pigs with them as well, and in any case they must soon have begun to tame the native wild stock. Cattle were the most important animals in neolithic Britain, and their bones are far more numerous than those of other livestock on contemporary habitation sites. In later years cattle owners in southern England built large enclosures surrounded by banks and ditches, such as those at the Trundle and Windmill Hill, where their beasts could be rounded up for sorting and branding, and fed in winter on leaf-fodder, and where cows with calves could be milked. At other times the animals browsed among the forest trees, their stock being constantly crossed with that of the indigenous wild cattle of the same breed (*bos primigenius*).

About 2500 BC Britain's climate became drier and warmer, and animals could survive more easily in the open. But winter feeding remained a problem, and where fodder was hard to obtain, as for instance at Skara Brae, a large proportion of animals was killed off in autumn, a practice that continued until late in the Middle Ages.

Cows supplied milk as well as meat, though the lactation period was much shorter then than now. They were probably bled, too, in the hard months at the end of winter when all food was scarce. The practice is common among primitive peoples, and was still extant in Scotland in the eighteenth century. The blood could be made into pottage, or formed into cakes with ground cereals.[4]

The pigs of neolithic times were given less attention than cattle, and were left to forage for themselves in the forest.

They were not milked, and were therefore caught and brought in only when pork was required. Sheep and goats were few at first, since they had difficulty in subsisting upon leaf-fodder. They were more frequent where grassland had already developed, as on Orkney and other Scottish islands. There too domestic animals could obtain extra food by browsing on seaweed along the beaches.

The older hunting communities of Britain did not intermingle with the immigrant farmers. For some centuries they continued their way of life in the forests of the hinterland. But subsequent arrivals in eastern and south-eastern England, farmers of the 'Peterborough culture' who lived in river valleys or along the coasts, combined a hunting with a farming economy.

Horses were still among the game of the forest, for the practice of breaking them in for riding and drawing vehicles does not seem to have reached Britain from continental Europe until about 700 BC. Their bones have been found on many prehistoric sites in England and Wales, often cracked open for the extraction of the marrow.[5]

Meat was still prepared by the time-honoured method of roasting. But the neolithic farmers and their families made a significant contribution to the progress of cookery by introducing pottery vessels. Within them meat could be stewed in water at the edge of the fire. Tough portions were made tender by the breaking down of the connective tissue, and more edible protein was thus obtained from each carcase. Moreover stewed flesh, sealed under the layer of fat that formed on its surface during cooking, remained fresh for a longer time than cooked meat exposed to the air. Nevertheless the use of pottery spread slowly, and in some places an earlier style of cookery by potboilers survived until very late.

A piece of flesh was placed in water within a wooden or leather container, and stones heated by fire were dropped in beside it. The meat itself survived the treatment quite well, but the broth, scummy with ash from the potboiler stones, cannot have been very appetizing.

An experiment in potboiler cookery was made by Professor

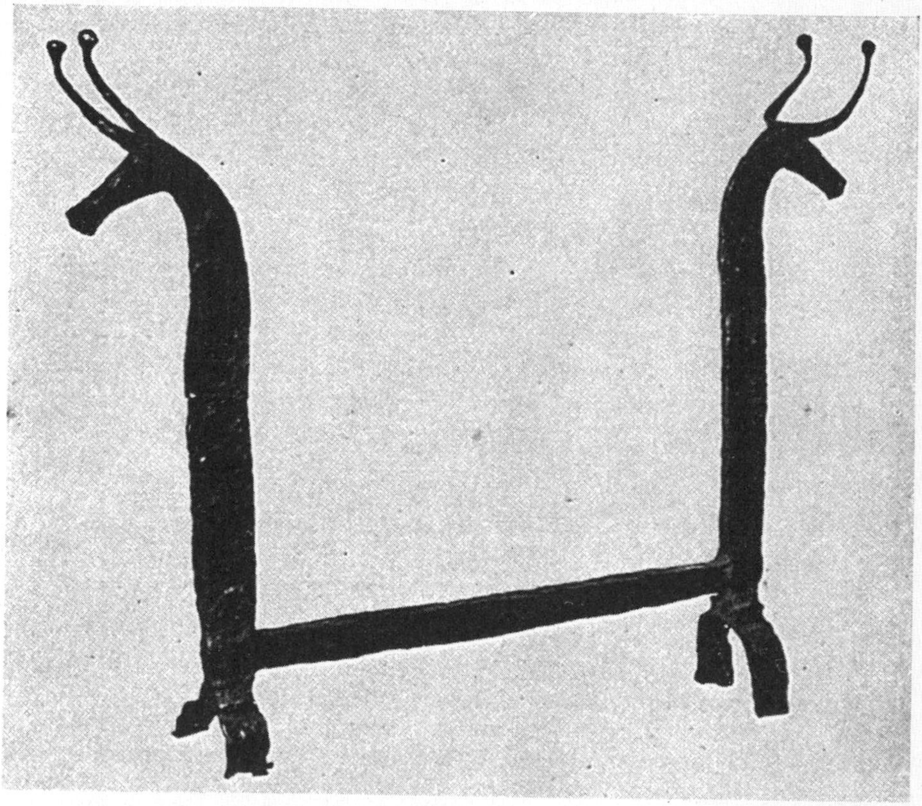

Wrought-iron fire-dog from Lord's Bridge, Cambridgeshire. Probably 1st century BC

Spit. 14th century AD

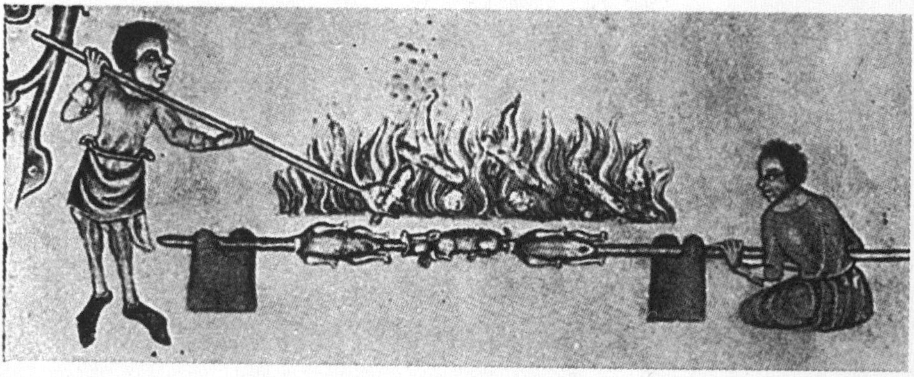

Three harts

From G. Tubervile: *Boke of hunting*, 1576

Hunting the hart

M. J. O'Kelly and his fellow archaeologists at an ancient cooking site at Ballyvourney, County Cork, in 1952. There, at some time in the second millennium BC a trough had been sunk into a boggy part of the peat, where the water-table was high enough to keep water within from seeping away; and it had been lined with timber and stones. At either end an arc-shaped hearth had been constructed.

The archaeologists restored both pit and hearths to their original form, and broke up the local sandstone to make new potboilers resembling those they had found on the site. These they stacked with wood along the length of one hearth, firing them from one end so that a succession of well-heated stones was produced. The stones, transferred to the water trough with a dampened wooden shovel, brought the water within to the boil in little over half an hour, and an additional red-hot stone dropped in at a different point every few minutes kept it simmering.

Following the practice described in early Irish literature, a leg of mutton weighing about ten pounds was wrapped in clean straw, tied with a twisted straw rope, and lowered into the boiling water. After three hours and forty minutes (twenty minutes to the pound and twenty minutes over) the meat was cooked through to the bone, and quite uncontaminated by ash from the potboilers or mud churned up into the water. But the trough was already two-thirds filled with stones, so the original cooks cannot have used it for joints of much larger size.

Also on the Ballyvourney site was a second pit, stone lined and thought to have been employed as an oven. The archaeologists preheated it with brushwood, which they then drew out through a gap apparently left for the purpose at one end. Another ten-pound leg of mutton was placed inside and surrounded by a rough dome of red-hot stones heated on one of the arc-shaped hearths. Within twenty minutes the joint was sealed with a crisp brown crust that kept in its juices and made basting unnecessary. The covering of stones was changed seven times in the course of three hours and forty minutes, and at the end the meat was 'excellently cooked and most tasty'.

The two processes evidently made up 'a roasting and a boiling', a double operation several times referred to in early Irish poems. Many similar cooking sites have been discovered in Scotland, Ireland and Wales, and a few are known in England. They range in date from perhaps 2000 BC down to the Viking period, and some Irish examples may be as late as the sixteenth century AD. An accompanying feature, according to the poems, was a hut roofed with sedge for use as a meat store, and traces of such a hut, complete with postholes for a meat-rack and a butcher's block, were found at Ballyvourney. The quantity of broken stone remaining around the cooking site there and at Killeens, County Cork, suggested to the excavators that both were occupied as hunting camps for a short period only. Thus we have the survival of a primitive type of cooking as a temporary arrangement long after the time when pottery and metal vessels were in use in more permanent settlements.

The boiling of beef in the hide by potboilers still continued in the 1720s in some remote Scottish islands. 'Otherwise', wrote Captain Edward Burt, 'being destitute of vessels of metal or earth, they put water into a block of wood, made hollow with the help of the dirk and burning; and then with pretty large stones heated red-hot, and successively quenched in that vessel, they keep the water boiling, till they have dressed their food.'[6]

About the middle of the first millennium BC there were further changes in Britain's economy, many of them due to a recent deterioration in the climate. Its effects extended to the continent, where floods and waterlogged land caused folk migrations, and eventually led to the arrival in England of groups of Celtic tribesmen, users of iron artefacts and the last newcomers before the Roman invasion.

The final deforestation of the lighter soils, coupled with the colder, damper weather, caused Britain's farmers to settle down with permanent houses and fixed fields. Cattle were stalled in winter and fed on hay, first harvested early in the Iron Age. Their dung was collected to manure the fields, and they themselves grazed the corn stubble in autumn and fertilized the soil. Only Ireland retained a mild climate where the old nomadic life continued.

Immigrants of Bronze Age times had already introduced into Britain a new breed of cattle, *bos longifrons*, progenitor of later dairy types. The constant browsing and rooting of cattle and pigs over many centuries had checked the regrowth of the forest, and as more open country emerged, sheep and goats were kept in increasing numbers.

The nature of the terrain decided the principal domestic animals of each area. Among the Celts the differences were reflected in the meats which were placed with the dead as sustenance for their final journey. At Maiden Castle in Dorset, after the Roman assault of about AD 47, the victims were buried with joints of mutton beside them. In contemporary Belgic tombs of the Hertfordshire region, and in those of the Yorkshire Parisi some two centuries earlier, the meat among the grave goods was pork.[7]

The Celts, like their predecessors, prepared their meat by roasting or stewing. Both methods became easier after the introduction of metal utensils. Bronze, known in Britain from the middle of the second millennium BC, was for a long time used sparingly for weapons, knives or jewelry. The inspiration for cauldrons of the metal came from the Greek trading colonies on the French Mediterranean coasts. Their vessels of riveted sheet bronze were seen and copied by itinerant Irish smiths about the eighth or seventh century BC. Soon cauldrons began to be made in Britain too, though they were rare at first and were probably reserved for ritual meals rather than everyday ones.

Metal had many practical advantages over pottery. The new containers could be placed directly over the flames of a fire. They were not liable to be broken through over-heating or by being accidentally dropped. They were even more hygienic, for they could be cleaned with sand or ash and water more thoroughly than earthenware pots. The latter must soon have become fouled, with adverse effects on the food they held.

Bronze and, later, iron equipment gradually became more common. Iron was still difficult to work, and the prehistoric smith had to heat his iron ore into blooms and then hammer it into shape; for melting and casting techniques were not developed until the end of the Middle Ages. But by the time the Belgae arrived both metals were in widespread use in Britain.

The Belgae, the most sophisticated of the pre-Roman Iron Age peoples to reach Britain, came from the region bounded by the rivers Seine, Marne and Rhine during the first century BC, and settled in southern and south-eastern England. Their metalware included tripods and chains with pothooks to suspend their cauldrons above the flames, and firedogs to facilitate the roasting of meat. The earliest firedogs had bull-head finials, drawing attention to the importance of cattle in their owners' lives and diet. They were used singly, placed before or over a central hearth with the spit held transversely by hooks or loops on the uprights.[8]

Alternatively meat was stewed. When ready to eat, it could be lifted from the cauldron with a metal flesh-hook, an invention which went back to the Bronze Age.

Mealtimes among the Celts in Gaul were described by Posidonius (135–51 BC), and the picture in Britain must have been similar. The diners sat on the ground on straw or hides, and ate their meat with their fingers 'in a cleanly but leonine fashion, raising up whole limbs in both hands and biting off the meat, while any part that is hard to tear off they cut through with a small dagger which hangs attached to their sword-sheath in its own scabbard'.

They were waited upon by their older sons and daughters. 'Beside them are hearths blazing with fire, with cauldrons and spits containing large pieces of meat. Brave warriors they honour with the finest portions of the meat.'

The Celtic Iron Age saw the establishment of salt working around British coasts. The salt helped to preserve meat for winter use, and especially the pork so well loved by the Celts. The hams prepared by their neighbours in Gaul were exported to Rome as a delicacy; but we know no details about the salted meats of Britain.

According to an Italian recipe of the mid-second century BC, hams had to be covered with salt and steeped in their own brine for seventeen days, dried in a draught for two, rubbed over with oil and vinegar, and then smoked for a further two days. It is likely that Celtic Britons followed similar practices, barring the oil and vinegar dressing. English recipes many hundreds of years later show that the method had hardly changed.[9]

Roman period

The arrival of the Romans in AD 43 and their rapid occupation of lowland Britain soon brought Roman farming practices to the country. Villas of Italian type were built on British farms both by foreign settlers and native landowners, new animals were introduced, and the existing domestic livestock cared for more scientifically.

In Italy animal husbandry had become an important part of farming economy. Successful landowners read – and wrote – treatises on the management of livestock, and game parks were constructed where selected wild creatures were preserved. The main object was to secure a better supply of meat, though additional profit was made from milk, hides and wool.

The Roman farming methods which now reached Britain were hardly improved upon until the end of the Middle Ages. The larger, heavier cattle which began to appear in the country may have been bred from imported stock, but they also owed much to improved feeding. Turnips were used as winter fodder in Gaul in Roman times, and perhaps in Britain too. Chickpeas, vetches and beans, recommended for the purpose by Columella, may have been employed on the more advanced farms.

British cattle were exported to the continent even before the Romans arrived, and beef was probably the favourite meat of Roman Britain. In the lowland zone beasts were raised on the villa estates; in the upland north and west the Iron Age tribesmen continued their traditional pastoral way of life. To protect their cattle, their most valued possessions, they had formerly constructed combined fortifications and cattle enclosures: those in the west country and south Wales of about the first century BC recall the multivallate arrangements of the neolithic period. At Stanwick in Yorkshire a hill fort was extended between AD 50 and 72 into a 730 acre fortified pasture, where a large number of Brigantian tribesmen with their herds and flocks vainly defied the Roman army.[10]

But once drawn within the bounds of the Roman empire, the cattle owning Britons found they could enjoy both peace and prosperity. Beef was the preferred meat ration of the Roman army in Britain, and their forts and fortresses were mostly in or near the highland zone, providing the tribesmen with a market for their beasts. Even in the south and east, there is evidence for increased cattle rearing in the third and fourth centuries AD, so there was no diminution in the taste for beef.

Sheep and goats were also common in those parts of upland Britain where there was open grazing ground. They were already numerous on the Wessex downs by the first century AD, and continued to be bred there on a considerable scale, especially in the later Roman period. Both sheep and goats were milked; and sheep also supplied wool for British textiles, some of which were exported to other provinces.

A fair amount of mutton was consumed by the Roman soldiery, though it was never as popular as beef or pork. But two places – Barr Hill fort on the Antonine Wall and Corbridge in Northumberland – have provided an unexpected sidelight on Roman military diet. At both sites an exceptionally high proportion of mutton bones was found. Barr Hill was held by a Syrian unit; and Corbridge appears from other evidence to have had an oriental element in its population. So some homesick foreigners during their sojourn in Britain clung to the fleshmeat they had once lived on in far-distant homelands.

Two varieties of goat were kept in Britain during Roman times. Columella recommended employing an agile and energetic goatherd to follow these creatures around. He supplied some folk remedies for diseases of goats, adding after one that if it did not cure their sickness, they must be sold; failing that, they should be slaughtered and their flesh salted. The salting of the meat of unfit animals for human consumption was a practice which survived in some parts of Britain until a comparatively recent date.

Pigs were already plentiful, especially in the south and east of the country, where the Belgae had begun to cultivate the heavier soils, and the surrounding woodland supplied the necessary pannage. Pork was an important foodstuff in the Roman army, and lard was part of the men's daily rations. Following Roman procedure, some British farmers now began to pen their pigs in sties and fatten them on grain. Two who did so farmed at Pitney, Somerset, and Woolaston Pill in Gloucestershire, both within reach of the great legionary fortress at Caerleon where pork played a part in the soldiers' diet second only to that of beef.[11]

Careful feeding of farm stock enabled the more enlightened Romano-British landowners to raise animals that were bigger and better fleshed than those of prehistoric days. Nevertheless they were still smaller, tougher and more sinewy, with thicker hides and less meat on their bones than their modern counterparts. As for the gourmet foods of Roman Italy, such as wombs from splayed sows and the exquisitely flavoured livers of pigs specially nourished before slaughter on dried figs, they must have had few adherents in Britain. Figs there were a luxury food for humans, hardly to be cast before swine.

One former game animal had now changed its status. By the end of the Bronze Age (*c.* 700 BC) horses were being tamed and broken in for riding and for drawing wagons and chariots. Thereafter wild horses, never as numerous in Britain as wild cattle or pigs, were gradually brought into captivity. Celtic warriors rode and drove them, and in death were buried alongside their chariots and steeds in full harness ready for the longest journey. Horse meat became rarer as a food, although still eaten here and there, as at the first-century-BC settlement at Glastonbury where the stripped horse bones were cracked to release their marrow.[12] The coming of the Romans further influenced opinion away from the eating of horse meat, which was not a usual practice elsewhere in the empire.

Some new smaller food animals were now introduced from southern Europe. There they were to be found in the *leporaria* or hare gardens attached to the villas of well-to-do Romans, who thus had them quickly available for cooking and eating.

Rabbits were confined in this manner. Native to the Spanish peninsula, they were first spread through Europe by the Roman conquerors. Then it was discovered that, once established, they were almost impossible to get rid of (the people of the Balearic islands had to beg the emperor Augustus for military aid to deal with the problem). So rabbits were bred more carefully inside *leporaria* for the sake of their meat; their young, cut from the womb of the mother before birth or taken new-born from the breast, were regarded as a special delicacy (*laurices*). Britain's earliest rabbits must have been raised within such enclosures.

Two other food animals beloved by Roman epicures were kept in close captivity. Dormice of the continental European species known as the 'fat dormouse', larger than the native British variety, were enclosed and fed upon acorns and chestnuts. Finally they were fitted into tiny earthenware pots to be plied with more nuts until they became exceedingly plump. They were eaten at Roman banquets, after being stuffed with a mixture of minced pork and dormouse meat and baked in the oven. The evidence for these dormice in Britain is unfortunately very slender, and even in other provinces the taste for them died out at the end of the Roman empire and was never later recovered.[13]

Also bred as a table delicacy was the snail. Several varieties were eaten, including the large Roman snail (*helix pomatia*) which is still popular in France and Italy. Snails had to be kept on land entirely surrounded by water, to prevent them wandering away and disappearing. They were fed on milk or wine-must and spelt, and were put into jars containing airholes for the final plumping-up. When so much fattened that they could no longer get back into their shells, they were fried in oil and served with *oenogarum* (*liquamen* mixed with wine).[14] Shells from Roman snails have been found on many Romano-British villa sites, testifying to local enjoyment of this food.

To enclose the larger game animals, Roman landowners in the western provinces fenced in vast tracts of woodland. In such game parks fallow deer, introduced from Asia Minor into Europe, would have first been bred in Britain. Great areas of the country were still covered in woodland, where roamed the indigenous red and roe deer, wild oxen and pigs. Bears lived in the Caledonian forest and in parts of Wales, and were sometimes transported all the way to Rome to engage in wild beast shows.

Although farmyard animals were the main source of meat, hunting brought in additional supplies, and trained hunting dogs were exported from Britain to the continent even before the Roman occupation. The hunt scenes on Castorware pottery, with running figures of dogs, hares and deer in low relief, reflect the continuing popularity of the sport in the third and fourth centuries AD. The Nene valley potteries, where Castorware was made, were on the edge of thickly wooded hunting country.

The cookery of meat in Roman Britain benefited from the introduction of new kitchen equipment. Roasting was carried out over a low fire or brazier either on a gridiron or in a small portable oven (*clibanus*) with double walls, between which the heat rose to surround the food inside. Neck of mutton, sucking kid or lamb, kidneys and stuffed dormice were cooked in the *clibanus*, according to Apicius. A bigger kid or lamb was roasted in a larger fixed oven like a baker's oven, or on a spit before the fire.

Meat was stewed in iron cauldrons hung by chains above the flames, similar to those already in use in Britain. Sometimes an animal such as a stuffed sucking pig was suspended within a basket in the water that simmered in the stewpan. Poorer people now began to acquire metal cooking vessels, for under Roman rule small round-bellied iron cauldrons were mass produced, which were less costly than individually wrought ironware.

Roman cookery added sauces to meat no less than to fish.

Sauces helped to disguise off-flavours in flesh foods which developed quickly in the climate of southern Europe. So dependent were the Romans on aromatic flavourings that they introduced into Britain a wide range of Mediterranean herbs with which to enliven their cooked dishes.

Sucking pig roasted in the oven was served 'à la Flaccus' under a thickened sauce which contained pepper, lovage, caraway, celery seed, asafoetida root, rue, *liquamen*, wine-must and oil; and was then sprinkled with powdered celery seed. Beef or veal was roasted, sliced, and the slices covered with another sauce. Fried veal was given a sweet-sour sauce, with raisins, honey and vinegar in its composition, as well as pepper, dried onions and several other aromatics.[15]

Game was either roasted or boiled (for variety, boar could be boiled in seawater, real or artificially concocted), and served with similar highly flavoured sauces. Two suggested for venison by Apicius have Jericho dates as an ingredient, and a third dried damsons or prunes, so the preference for a sweet, fruity sauce with deer meat goes back to at least the first century AD.

Sow's udder was put into a mixed *patina*, along with fish, chicken meat and small birds. A recipe for kid's or lamb's liver ran: 'Make honey-water and mix into it eggs and some milk, and make incisions in the liver and let it absorb the liquid. Then cook it in wine and *garum*, sprinkle with pepper, and serve.'

Hams and bacon were either dry-salted or barrelled in their own brine. The Romans recognized ham (*perna*) and shoulder bacon (*petaso*) as two separate meats, and had different recipes for preparing them for the table. According to Apicius both were to be first boiled with dried figs, but ham could then be baked in a flour and oil paste, while bacon was to be browned and served with a wine and pepper sauce.[16]

The spiced and seasoned dishes were eaten in Britain by well-to-do settlers and the more Romanized Britons, who abandoned native fare in favour of the 'elegant feasts' of Roman civilization. Other Britons prepared their meat by the traditional methods of their forefathers.

In the highland zone the chief point of contact between

Roman and native was the military camp with its civilian settlements of traders and camp followers outside the walls; and by the fourth century AD the distinction between Roman and non-Roman had blurred. The domestic equipment of the camps included tripods to support pans over charcoal fires, like the one found in Carlingswark Loch and now in the National Museum of Antiquities in Edinburgh. In the late Roman era, or soon afterwards, local smiths had the idea of combining the principle of the tripod with the round-bellied cooking pan, and thus created the three-legged cauldron that has continued as the main cooking vessel of the Celtic regions almost to the present day.

Early medieval period

In the ensuing centuries there were few innovations in meat cookery either in highland or lowland Britain. The same farmyard animals were kept, and the same forest game hunted to supplement home-killed meat. One creature which disappeared temporarily was the rabbit. The *leporaria* were lost when the villas decayed, and escapers were unable to withstand the many predators in the vast forest tracts of early medieval Britain.

In eastern counties of England, after their settlement by Saxon farmers, sheep, pigs and goats came to predominate over cattle, which were raised mainly as draught and plough beasts. At the time of the Domesday survey there were almost 130,000 sheep in Norfolk, Sussex and Essex, as against 31,000 pigs, nearly 11,000 goats and under 9,000 cattle and oxen.

Sheep were popular because they were highly economic creatures, supplying wool and milk as well as meat. But the poor man's animal was the pig, which could be turned out to feed on the waste or in the woodlands beyond the arable land, under the eye of the communally supported village swineherd. When slaughtered, the pig became the source of bacon, a favourite food among the Anglo-Saxons.

Pigs were important too in western Britain. They were the preponderant food animal at the early dark-age settlement of

Dinas Powys in Glamorgan, their bones accounting for sixty-one per cent of all the bones found on the kitchen midden there. Much later the large herds of swine kept in the Exe and Creedy valleys in Devon were recorded in the Exon Domesday.[17]

The tribesmen of the Celtic north and west counted their wealth in cattle. In Wales white beasts with red or black ears were greatly prized, descendants, perhaps, of white cattle introduced from Italy in Roman times. Further north animals of similar ancestry may have become feral, and lived thus for centuries before the survivors were enclosed in such parks as Chillingham, Northumberland, and Cadzow Castle, Lanarkshire.

There was a temporary return to the horse as a provider of fleshmeat in the Anglo-Saxon domains, for horse meat was eaten in the Germanic homelands and for a time the practice was continued in England. It was on the decline in Bede's day, and a hundred years later was discountenanced at two great councils of the church. Thereafter public opinion influenced most people against it. Only the 'wild Irish', as reported by Fynes Moryson in 1617, 'will feed upon horses dying of themselves, not only upon small want of flesh, but even for pleasure'.[18]

The breakdown of ordered life at the time of the Roman withdrawal affected farming in some areas, and led to a greater dependence on game animals. Latimer villa in the Chilterns was one such place, where the fifth-century inhabitants caught and consumed deer in far greater numbers than their predecessors had done during the heyday of Roman prosperity.

Anglo-Saxon farmers who settled in eastern and central England hunted in the forest too, to keep down the predators that destroyed their crops and even their stock, as well as for the sake of extra food. The flesh of boars and deer was highly esteemed, but wolves were not normally eaten, although occasionally parts were incorporated into folk medicine.

Hunting became a major sport among the Saxon aristocracy, and in later centuries game parks were made, modelled on those of western Europe; for the Gothic and Frankish nobility had kept up the Roman practice of creating such enclosures. By the time of Domesday there were thirty-one parks and seventy hays in the lowland zone of Britain. Hays, also inherited from the hunting techniques of imperial Rome, were places where nets were set up into which the hunters and their dogs endeavoured to drive their quarry.

In Celtic areas too hunting was a special pastime of the nobility, a tradition that almost certainly went back to the horse-riding aristocracy of the pre-Roman Iron Age. From the laws of Hywel Dda we learn that Welsh kings had a staff of professional hunters to assist them, who were allowed more than two-thirds of all the meat, hides, bones and horns from the kills. Special seasons were assigned to particular species. Stags could be hunted from midsummer to the beginning of winter; thereafter a short period was devoted to wild swine; and from February to midsummer hinds were taken.

For a time bears were still trapped in the remote north and west, and the trained animals exhibited by Anglo-Saxon gleemen may have been native cubs taken young and tamed. But the success of the hunters led to the extinction of British bears before the time of the Norman Conquest.[19]

The cookery of meat was on traditional lines. The tender cuts were roasted upon spits, and the tougher meat stewed with herbs and cereals. The Anglo-Saxons had, in addition to their iron stewing kettles, at least two types of open pan, the *braedepanne* in which meat was spread and grilled before the fire, and the *hyrsting panne* in which it was fried.[20]

In both Saxon and Celtic Britain meat was salted, and salt tubs are mentioned among the household goods of both peoples. Sides and hams of swine were the favourite meats for the purpose, but oxen were salted too (they are sometimes listed in Anglo-Saxon food rents); and in Wales and on the borders it is likely that goat hams, a noted speciality of later times, were already being prepared.

Bacon fat or lard was in particular favour among the Anglo-Saxons who used it for cooking and also as a dressing for vegetables. Bone marrow was well regarded too. The springtime bleeding of cattle probably took place in the highland zone. But in the Anglo-Saxon domains, oxen and cows were working animals. Their winter feeding was poor, and had they been bled in addition, they would have been too weak to perform their normal duties.

Later medieval period

The pattern of animal husbandry changed only very slowly through the years following the Norman Conquest. But eventually the number of cattle on the manors rose as cows' milk came to be preferred to ewes' milk. In the thirteenth and fourteenth centuries many farmers in Lincolnshire, Yorkshire and the midlands switched from cereal growing to sheep farming, so that they could share in the expanding English wool trade. And there was a gradual diminution in the number of pigs kept as the woods were lopped away to create arable land, and less pannage was available. In meat terms this spelt out more beef and mutton, and eventually less pork and ham.

During the summer all animals had to forage for themselves, under the guidance of neatherd, shepherd, swineherd or goatherd. In winter horses might receive oats, but cattle had to make to do with hay or straw, sometimes supplemented with pease or vetches; and other animals were usually underfed. For fodder was costly, and only the biggest landowners could afford proper nourishment for their livestock.

The great autumn slaughter of stock helped to save the price of winter feeding; 'for stall-fed and pease-fed play pick-purse the thief'. Many cattle, sheep, pigs and even deer were then killed and salted. But some were spared, among them the milch and breeding animals, working beasts and those destined to provide fresh meat from autumn until the beginning of Lent, and again after Easter.

At Hallowmas [1 November] slaughter time soon cometh in:
  and then doth the husbandman's feasting begin,
From that time to Candlemas [2 February] weekly kill some:
  their offal for household the better shall come,

wrote Thomas Tusser. Hams and sides of beef could be salted, smoked and kept; but offal, blood and marrow had to be eaten fresh, and it was more economical to kill the animals off week by week. And in a mild winter and a sheltered place, they could be grazed out of doors until Christmas or later.[21]

Beef soon emerged as the Englishman's favourite fleshmeat. Not enough could be produced in the arable southern and eastern counties, and cattle owners in the pastoral north and west found it profitable to drive their beasts long distances to the lowland markets. In the mid-thirteenth century drovers were taking cattle from south Wales to Gloucester and beyond. In northern England a similar trade developed. By Tudor times a system had grown up whereby beasts were driven to the midlands, East Anglia or even the home counties, and were there grazed and fattened up to be resold to the butchers of London and other towns.

Cattle were also fattened locally. Thirty-four 'lean beefs', half-starved on their winter diet, were purchased for the Earl of Northumberland on St Helen's day (21 May) and fed in his pastures to supply his households in Yorkshire from midsummer to Michaelmas, when a further hundred fat cattle were acquired to last until the following midsummer.[22]

Pork was almost as well liked as beef, and pigs were plentiful especially in the first centuries after the Norman Conquest. There are frequent references in Domesday to places where 'there is woodland for *x* swine'. They were of a long-legged, razor-backed, long-snouted variety differing little from wild swine. 'And let them be able to dig', wrote Walter of Henley, 'They have need of help in three months, in February, March and April.' For the rest of the year they rooted about in the woods and on the waste and fended for themselves.

Sheep were raised in ever-increasing numbers. In common with other farm animals they were culled periodically, and the weaker stock was fattened up for the table. Sheep that ailed, and even those that had died a natural death, were occasionally pressed into service, but there were some misgivings about the practice.

> Some men replace others for those which died of murrain. How? I will tell you. If a sheep die suddenly they put the flesh in water for as many hours as there are between midday and three o'clock, and then hang it up, and when the water is drained off they salt it and then dry it. And if any sheep begin to fall ill they see if it be because the teeth drop, and if the teeth do not fall out they cause it to be killed and salted and dried like the others, and then they cut it up and distribute it in the household among the servants and labourers. . . . But I do not wish you to do this.[23]

Drovers brought sheep as well as cattle from more distant pastures into south-eastern England. Thomas Moufet, the Elizabethan physician, wrote:

> The best mutton is not above four years old, or rather not much above three; that which is taken from a short, hilly and dry feeding is more sweet, short and wholesome than that which is either fed in rank grounds or with pease-straw (as we perceive by the taste); great, fat and rank fed sheep, such as Somersetshire and Lincolnshire sendeth up to London, are nothing so short and pleasant in eating as the Norfolk, Wiltshire, and Welch mutton; which being very young, are best roasted; the elder sort are not so ill being sodden [boiled] with bugloss, borage and parsley roots.

Goats could be kept on steep, scrubby land, and the nannies, like ewes, were suppliers of milk. Old goats were tough, and Moufet maintained that they should be baited to death like bulls; 'and when he is dead, you must beat the flesh in the skin, after the French fashion of beating a cow'.

But tender young kids, roasted or stewed, were a favourite springtime dish when Lent was over. Kid was eaten in the households of such thirteenth-century personages as Eleanor, Countess of Leicester, and Richard de Swinfield, Bishop of Hereford. It was still popular in Tudor times. Two kids were among the meats at dinner and one among those at supper at a wedding feast at the home of Sir William Petre in June 1552; and six months earlier his family consumed several kid pasties during the twelve days of Christmas.[24]

Game animals supplied a greater part of the fleshmeat of medieval Britain than they do today. In Saxon times hunting had been a pastime shared by rich and poor alike, each man having the right to hunt on his own land, and to allow others to do the same. But the Norman kings and their successors enforced their personal ownership of all forest lands and game, and debarred the commoners therefrom. When poachers were caught they were blinded or otherwise maimed in punishment; and ordinary folk had no redress when deer and boars emerged from the woods and trampled their crops in the open fields.

Then occasional days of hunting were conceded, like the annual day in Epping Forest granted by Henry I to the citizens of London, and the day at Easter subsequently allowed to them by Henry III, on which they were permitted to hunt within twenty miles of the capital. And in 1217 the most stringent of the game laws were repealed, and villagers and others concerned could again pursue the destructive forest animals.

The aristocracy, of course, hunted regularly. Moreover many of them sought, and gained, royal permission to empark areas of waste land for the sport. By the later sixteenth century there were said to be a hundred parks in Kent and Essex alone, and twenty in the bishopric of Durham 'wherein great plenty of fallow deer is cherished and kept. As for warrens of coneys, I judge them almost innumerable, and daily likely to increase'. For rabbits had been reintroduced from France, and their earliest settlement on islands such as Lundy and the Scillies towards the end of the twelfth century was followed in due course by the establishment of coneygarths on the mainland. As the forest receded and beasts of prey became rarer, escapers from the rabbit warrens bred more readily outside, and eventually there was a large wild population to supplement the enclosed groups. In Scotland, too, every burgh soon had its rabbit warren and warrener. But highlanders had no truck with coneys, and instead coursed the native mountain hare.

The status of large wild animals in Britain had undergone a transformation. Prehistoric man had pitted his wits against them in order to survive and win a livelihood. Now some were extinct, or nearly so, while the rest escaped that fate mainly through being preserved in parks and protected by keepers.

Although the British bear had already disappeared, bear meat was still occasionally consumed during the later medieval period. Continental bears were imported for that well-loved sport, bear baiting, and those that were done to death in the ring were subsequently eaten. Some members of the nobility even kept bears on their estates, for baiting and to take part in artificial bear hunts. Turbervile wrote briefly about bear hunting in his *Booke of Hunting*, 1576. Of bear meat he said: 'Their flesh is delicate to some men's tooth; but in mine opinion it is rammish and unsavoury. . . . Their feet are the best morsel of them, for they be delicate meat.'

Wild cattle survived longer. Forest bulls (*tauri sylvestres*) lived in the woods around London in the twelfth century. Mention was made of the wild and vicious cattle abroad in Knaresborough Forest in Yorkshire about 1200; and six wild bulls (descendants, perhaps, of the aforementioned cattle) were among the provisions for the great feast given when George Nevill was installed as Archbishop at York in 1466. By Elizabeth's reign forest cattle had retreated from lowland Britain, but were still to be found in remote parts of Wales and Scotland.

Wild boars were common until the fifteenth century, and the brawn made from their heads and shoulders became a part of traditional Christmas fare. Turbervile thought the boar should not be hunted with hounds, 'for he is the proper prey of a mastiff and such like dogs'. He was already rare in Turbervile's day, and became extinct in the seventeenth century. But for some time before that, most of the Christmas brawn had been made from tame boars.

The hart or red deer stag was accounted 'the most noble game, the fallow deer is the next, then the roe, whereof we have indifferent store, and last of all the hare, not least in estimation'. Some of the herds of fallow deer which roamed the medieval forests and parks were of great antiquity, and may well have continued to renew themselves since Roman times.[25]

Hares and coneys were the poor man's game, coursed on foot with dogs. Greyhounds were used to pursue hares, and spaniels or small greyhounds to chase coneys, though these were also often taken in hays, or with ferrets. Hunting hares in the snow was a popular pastime, because they were then much easier to trace to their forms. But Henry VIII had to forbid the sport for a time, for hares in the snow were too easy a prey, and in his day they had become 'decayed and almost destroyed' at the hands of the hunters.

Coneys too had to be protected in Henry's reign, with a close season for selling them proclaimed in 1529 and again in 1551, which coincided with their spring breeding season. Both hares and coneys recovered, and became again a valuable source of fresh meat for poorer people.

Until well into the seventeenth century the name rabbit was used only of a young coney of less than a year old. These creatures were sometimes distinguished as 'rabbit suckers' and 'rabbit runners' according to their stage of development. They were particularly well regarded. 'Coneys' flesh is good, but rabbits' flesh is best of all wild beasts, for it is temperate and doth nourish, and is singularly praised in physic; for all things the which doth suck, is nutritive.'[26]

Coneys had continued in France from Roman days, and *laurices* became a special luxury of the monks because it was decided that they need not be regarded as a meat food at religious fasts. By the sixth century AD domestic rabbits were being bred for their litters in French monastic courtyards. But when they eventually reached England again, they were usually enclosed in warrens, and their young were eaten as fleshmeat.

One further small wild food animal deserves mention. The red squirrel was a dish for a lord. 'Browet farsure' was an early fifteenth-century pottage which contained the meat of partridges and coneys 'or else rabbits for they are better for a lord. . . . And for a great lord, take squirrels instead of coneys.'

By Tudor times they were going out of favour. Dr Moufet wrote, 'Squirrels are much troubled with two diseases, choler and the falling-sickness; yet their hinder-parts are indifferent good whilst they are young, fried with parsley and butter: but being no usual nor warrantable good meat, let me skip with them and over them to another tree. . . .'[27]

Meat was cooked by roasting, broiling on a gridiron, frying and stewing. In addition, the pie was developed, which allowed meat to be sealed within a strong crust and baked, often accompanied by several other ingredients.[28]

Large-scale roasting in medieval times, whether for feasts or for the meals of great households, often took place out of doors, where there was more space and fire risks were fewer. For a time, indoor roasting was still done on a spit carried by a single firedog over a central hearth. A turnspit scullion or other menial was in attendance to rotate the spit and baste the meat. During the twelfth century fireplaces began to be built into sidewalls, though it was to be another four hundred years before wall fireplaces were constructed in every home. The new fireplaces were wide and shallow with huge chimneys, and often in a large household two were ranged side by side or in adjacent walls of the kitchen. The firedogs, sometimes called andirons, were increased to two, and were placed at right angles to the hearth, bearing the spit or spits between them.

Joints from the larger meat animals were carried on the spit, but sucking pig, kid, lamb, hare or coney were spitted whole, often with their heads left on. Sometimes they were parboiled before roasting, to ensure tenderness. Coney, kid, breast of veal and other dry flesh was larded; and meat was basted as it cooked with the fat that fell from it into the dripping pan placed below. Fatty meat ('the side of high grease') was scored with a knife, and basted with red wine, pepper and salt.

Kids and young pigs were stuffed. A pig might contain a forcemeat of figs, raisins, sugar, saffron, salt fat pork and bread-crumbs, ground together and mixed with cream and egg yolks. When the meat was ready, the animal was endored or glazed on the outside with egg yolks.

A similar finishing touch was given to 'pommes dorres', which were meat balls of pork, or sometimes beef, mingled with currants and spices. They were threaded on to the spit, well roasted and then dredged with a mixture of shredded parsley, flour and beaten egg to give a greenish apple-like effect. They could be made purely golden by replacing the parsley with saffron.

A still more exotic set-piece was 'urchins' or hedgehogs. Pigs' maws were stuffed, sewn up and spitted, pricked all over with holes which were stuck with split blanched almonds. After roasting, the hedgehogs were endored in a like manner, some golden, some green and some black with blood (the favourite black food colorant of medieval times).

Roast meat in a great household was cut up by the carver. He also had to make sure that the correct sauces were at hand: mustard for brawn, beef or salted mutton, verjuice for veal and bacon, ginger sauce for lamb, kid, piglet or fawn.[29]

Tender cuts of meat were grilled. Pork, either spit-roasted or broiled on a gridiron before the fire, needed no sauce but pure salt or a simple garlic dressing, according to Alexander Neckam. Beef or venison steak in the fifteenth century was sliced and 'griddled up brown', sprinkled liberally with cinnamon at the dresser, and then served with a little sharp sauce.

Veal olives were a seventeenth-century variant of the much older beef or mutton olives, originally called 'allowes' or 'alaunder' of beef or mutton. A seasoning of suet, shred onion, egg yolks, parsley and spices was laid upon slices of meat which were then rolled up and roasted either on a spit or a gridiron.[30]

Roasting joints and juicy steaks came from young beasts, chosen for slaughter because they were barren or unsuitable to work on the farm. As for worn-out plough animals, 'when the ox is old, with ten penny-worth of grass he shall be fit for the larder'.[31] The flesh was tough, and those who could afford better things used it to make strong broth (in one recipe called 'mighty broth of beef') in which to cook other meats or roots.

Poor people, and household servants who received 'livery pieces' of ox flesh as part of their daily food allowance, stewed such meat well with herbs or onions and spices. It might be beaten first, or chopped into gobbets and fried, to tenderize it; or it could be pounded in the mortar and made into a thick standing pottage.

By the fifteenth century braising had been developed. To make 'a dry stew for beef', the flesh with minced onions, cloves, maces and currants was enclosed in a glass vessel which was suspended inside a cauldron of boiling water over a low fire.

Entrails were put into pottages. The umbles of calf, swine or sheep were stewed in good broth with herbs and cibols (Welsh onions). Other recipes have the umbles of pork cooked in broth and wine with the white of leeks, and those of deer in their own broth with onions. The umbles comprised more than just the liver, kidney and heart which are accepted as human food today. Lung, spleen and gut were also eaten. Their flavour could be strong, even rank, and powerful seasonings were needed as a counterpoise. The tradition survives in the modern liver and onions.

Whole heads or palates, tongues, udders and stones were also eaten. Some tasty recipes were created for neats' tongues. One of the late fourteenth-century ran: 'Take the tongue of the rether [ox or cow] and scald and shave [scrape] it well and right clean, and seeth it and seeth. Take a broach [larding-pin] and lard it with lardons and with cloves and gilliflower and do it roasting, and drop it while it roasteth with yolks of eggs, and dress it forth.'

Pig's liver, together with that of hens and capons, was sometimes cut into pieces, fried in lard and put into little pies with yolks of hard-boiled eggs and ginger. More usual were pies of pork or veal fleshmeat, minced or pounded in the mortar and mingled with dried fruits, powdered spices and strained eggs.[32]

The preservation of meat was a matter of great importance. Long-term methods were required at the time of the autumn slaughter of stock. But there was also need for short-term conservation during hot weather. The first problem was met by heavy dry-salting, barrelling in brine, or immersion in a 'sousing drink'; the second by lighter salting or by dipping the meat in a brine and vinegar pickle.

The old Roman idea of using honey as a preservative was revived, but was never seriously taken up, partly no doubt because honey was far more expensive than other preservatives, but chiefly, one suspects, because the principle of the total exclusion of air was at that stage insufficiently understood and applied. In the late fifteenth century the author of the *Liber Cure Cocorum* argued that if the blood was pressed out, one could 'save venison fresh over the year' sealed under honey in a pot. A hundred years later the recipe was still appearing in cookery books. It can never have worked really satisfactorily; but the idea behind it was developed more successfully in the 'potting' techniques of the seventeenth and eighteenth centuries.[33]

Dry-salting was the most general method of preserving meat. The process had changed little since the Iron Age. The chief advance was the introduction of saltpetre (potassium nitrate) which had a more penetrating and drying effect on the tissues of the flesh than had the Bay salt usually employed for salting. But only a small proportion of saltpetre could be used along with the ordinary salt, as too much gave the meat a rank and nauseous flavour.

Beef could be green-salted in brine in a single night, and treated thus would last for a few days in summer or a week or two in winter. For longer keeping it was steeped in brine for several days and then hung up in a dry or smoky atmosphere, usually in the kitchen or living-room rafters. It was in low esteem among the physicians. 'Martinmas beef, which is called "hanged beef" in the roof of the smoky house, is not laudable; it may fill the belly and cause a man to drink, but it is evil for the stone, and evil of digestion, and maketh no good juice.' When the time came to eat it, the hard salt-beef had to be simmered long in water with hay or bran to get rid of some of the salt. It was generally made into pottage with plenty of herbs.

Mutton and goat meat were also salted or 'powdered'. Goat hams came to be known in Wales as 'hung venison'. But the favourite salting animal was the pig; for even the peasant could usually keep two or three hogs, and could afford to kill one at least once a year. The flesh salted well, requiring less salt than any other meat, and remaining more succulent.[34]

Country folk ate their bacon with pease or bean pottage or with 'joutes'. The well-to-do could enjoy a 'bruet' consisting of half a dozen stuffed chickens stewed with 'a good gobbet of fresh beef' and some herbs, and then served in with bacon. Kept on one side through Lent, bacon was brought out again at Easter and eaten with veal to celebrate the end of the long meatless fast.[35]

But in times of dearth the poor peasant lacked even bacon. In such a period Piers Plowman exclaimed:

> And yet I say, by my soul, I have no salt bacon
> Nor no cook, by Christ, collops for to maken.

Collops were a peculiarly British fashion of eating bacon, not known elsewhere in Europe. Rashers were sliced from a side of salt bacon and fried, often together with eggs. The result was viewed by the physicians as an unwholesome food; nevertheless among ordinary folk fried collops and eggs were 'a usual dish toward Shrovetide'.[36]

Another British speciality was the brawn made of the head and foreparts of a boar or pig. Richer and fattier than the hams, it was regarded as a delicacy for the medieval feast, and by Tudor times had become fare for the twelve days of Christmas. In the thirteenth century it appeared in the last course of the feast, along with the game birds and spicery. It was also sometimes incorporated with vinegar, pepper and other spices in a rich pottage called 'brawn en peverade'; or was sliced and served in a thick spiced syrup of wine with honey or sugar as 'brawn in comfyte', or with ground almonds and sugar as 'blanche brawn'.

By the end of the fourteenth century 'brawn en peverade'

or simple brawn with mustard had become first-course dishes; and some fifty years later it was being eaten still earlier in the meal. 'First brawn and mustard out of course, served with malmsey' opened the feast given for the enthronement of Archbishop Nevill (1467). Thereafter brawn was nearly always offered in the position of an *hors d'oeuvre*.

The time soon came when it could no longer be made as formerly from 'boar, the wild swine'. That creature had to be replaced by his tame cousin, who was specially prepared for his fate.

> At Michaelmas safely go sty up thy boar,
> Lest straying abroad ye do see him no more

advised Thomas Tusser; while Thomas Moufet wrote, 'Shut up a young boar, of a year and a half old, in a little room in harvest-time, feeding him with nothing but sweet whey, and giving him every morning clean straw to lie upon, but lay it not thick; so before Christmas he will be sufficiently brawned with continual lying, and prove exceedingly fat, wholesome and sweet.'

Clearly factory farming is no new idea. But humane slaughtering methods had not been thought of in Moufet's time. His account continues: 'And after he [the boar] is brawned for your turn, thrust a knife into one of his flanks, and let him run with it till he die: others gently bait him with muzzled dogs.'[37]

The details of brawn preparation were first made public in Elizabeth's reign by William Harrison. He described brawn as

> a great piece of service at the table from November until February be ended, but chiefly in the Christmas time. With the same also we begin our dinners each day after other; and, because it is somewhat hard of digestion, a draught of malvesey, bastard or muscadel, is usually drank after it . . . . It is made commonly of the forepart of a tame boar . . . the rest is nothing so fat, and therefore it beareth the name of souse only, and is commonly reserved for the serving-man

and hind. . . . When the boar [i.e. his foreparts] is thus cut out, each piece is wrapped up, either with bulrushes, ozier, peels, tape inkle [broad tape] or such like, and then sodden in a lead or cauldron together, till they be so tender that a man may thrust a bruised rush or straw clean through the fat: which being done, they take it up and lay it abroad to cool. Afterward, putting it into close vessels, they pour either good small ale or beer mingled with verjuice and salt thereto till it be covered, and so let it lie (now and then altering the sousing drink lest it should wax sour) till occasion serve to spend it out of the way.[38]

Not only were the hindparts of a hog or boar put into pickle on occasion, but also its ears, cheeks, snout and trotters, the whole mixture being known under the general name of souse. For the small Elizabethan farmer, souse no less than brawn was a part of the good fare of Christmastide. The sousing drink could include wine, ale or verjuice, salt and spices; or could be simple strong brine.

Beef, too, was salted and barrelled to keep in brine of its own making. Thus preserved it was a standby for soldiers under siege, and for ships' crews bound on long voyages.[39]

The byproducts of slaughtertime, blood, fat and marrow, were all utilized. Blood and suet or lard went into black puddings; the pale fats alone into white puddings. Blood also coloured dark pottages and sauces, while white grease or lard was added to pale ones thickened with cereal flour. Suet made the strong paste for standing pies, and lard was an alternative to butter for the pastry of more delicate pies and tarts. The meat content of the pie, too, if at all dry, was well larded.

Finally the marrow was extracted from the cracked bones. Pliny had written: 'All marrow is emollient, filling, drying and warming', and his influence ensured its continued popularity all through the Middle Ages and beyond. Marrow bones were used to make broth and pottage, and the marrow was sometimes served separately, as in the recipe for cabbages boiled in broth. 'And when thou servest it in, knock out the marrow of the bones, and lay the marrow two gobbets or three in a dish, as thee seemeth best, and serve forth.'[40]

Gobbets of marrow were put into pies, too, especially those that contained fresh or dried fruit, such as pear pie, or 'crustard lumbard' (Lombard tart) with its filling of strained eggs and cream with sliced dates, prunes and marrow. Marrow was added to stuffings, and the contents of 'alaunder of beef'. It had a traditional association with puddings, and when these became more common in the sixteenth and seventeenth centuries, marrow was often an ingredient. Eaten alone, marrow was rather unctuous, 'and doth mollify the stomach, and doth take away a man's appetite; wherefore let a man eat pepper with it'.[41]

A highly esteemed confection with a meat basis was 'jelly of flesh', which, like fish jelly, was a speciality of Norman cookery, made for feasts and other celebrations. Jelly of flesh in the fourteenth century comprised 'swine's feet, and snouts, and the ears, capons, coneys, calves feet', washed and seethed in equal parts of wine, vinegar and water. The mixture was boiled and the liquor was strained through a cloth into an earthenware pot, was spiced with pepper and yellowed with saffron, simmered and scummed, and poured over the meat pieces. When it had set, it could be decorated with laurel leaves.

The colouring of the jelly was an important part of the preparation. 'Colour it with turnsole', says one recipe, 'or with indigo, or with alkanet, or sanders, or saffron. . . . And if thou will make it of two manner of colours in a dish take and make a round of paste, and lay it in the midward of the charger, and pour in the jelly; and when it is cold, take out the paste, and pour together of another colour, and serve it forth cold.'

Jelly-making methods were unhygienic, but effective. In one recipe small chickens and sides of pork were set to stew in a broth made from calves' feet and wine. 'And let a man evermore keep it and blow off the gravy; and in case that the liquor waste away, cast more of the same wine thereto; and put thy hand thereto, and if thy hand be clammy, it is a sign that it is good; and let not the flesh be so much sodden [stewed] that it may bear no cutting.' The liquid was well seasoned with salt, pepper, saffron and vinegar, and poured over the meat to set, when blanched almonds and pieces of pared ginger were scattered upon it.[42]

There was no lack of recipes for preparing game animals for the table. But first catch your game. Hares, coneys and the destructive boars could be pursued by all, once the most stringent forest laws had been repealed. But deer and venison remained the prerogative of landowners, their friends and protégés. Huntsmen and keepers, who assisted at the chase, received a substantial share. The king's hunter went home joyfully at the end of the day, according to the early fifteenth-century *The Master of Game*, and ordered his supper well 'with worts and the neck of the hart and other good meats, and good wine or ale'. The Elizabethan gamekeeper 'beside three shillings four pence or five shillings in money, hath the skin, head, umbles, chine, and shoulders: whereby he that hath the warrant for a whole buck hath in the end little more than half.'

For other folk venison was a more chancy business, for whether hunted by the landowning gentry, or trapped illegally by poachers (who in medieval times might come from any class: the nobility kept up their family feuds by this means), it had the peculiar characteristic that it was not bought or sold in the open market. But once killed, it had to be disposed of, sometimes with the utmost speed. And so it came as a gift to many people who might otherwise never have tasted it.

Andrew Boorde must sometimes have been the recipient of presents of venison, for he wrote very longingly of it:

> I have gone round about Christendom, and overthwart Christendom, and a thousand or two and more miles out of Christendom, yet there is not so much pleasure for hart and hind, buck, and doe, and for roe buck and doe, as is in England; and although the flesh be dispraised in physic I pray God to send me part of the flesh to eat, physic notwithstanding. . . . I am sure it is a lord's dish, and I am sure it is good for an English man, for it doth animate him to be as he is, which is, strong and hardy but I do advertise every

man, for all my words, not to kill, and so to eat of it, except it be lawfully, for it is a meat for great men. And great men do not set so much by the meat, as they do by the pastime of killing it.[43]

Nevertheless some great men had venison salted in the autumn, along with the flesh of the farm stock. Many carcases of deer were brought in and preserved thus on the estate of Richard de Swinfield at Martinmas in 1289; and salt venison was often on his menu in the following May and June before the midsummer opening of the new hunting season brought in fresh game. To prevent its decay over so many months, the deer meat had to be soaked for half a day in clean water, dried, salted, boiled in brine and then left to soak in the brine for three days, when it was salted again and barrelled up.

If gifts of fresh venison were delayed in transit, or poachers were obliged to hide their kill in the forest for later retrieval, tainting could result. The remedy was burial in the ground for three days and nights. 'And after take it up and spot it well with great saltpetre, there where the reesting is, and after let it hang in rain water all night or more.'[44]

Fresh venison was of course eaten high, since it had to be hung for several days to tenderize its tough sinews. Roast venison was accompanied by the strong pepper and vinegar sauce 'peverade', or salt and cinnamon, or powdered ginger. With boiled venison, frumenty was almost inevitable. 'Fat venison with frumenty, it is a gay pleasure.' The two dishes were prepared separately, and brought to the sideboard where the meat was carved ceremoniously before being offered to a great lord. 'Touch not the venison with no bare hand', was the instruction to the carver. He had to pare it with the forepart of his knife, to score it twelve times across with the knife edge, and then to cut out a section with the forepart and convey it into the frumenty.[45]

The less desirable parts of the meat, such as the ribs and the umbles, and also salt venison that had first been parboiled in fresh water, were cut up and stewed in well-spiced broth with wine, vinegar or ale. The blood was often reserved and used with brown bread to darken the pottage.

Both fresh and salt venison, again highly seasoned with pepper and ginger, were put into pasties. Umble pie in medieval times was a confection for gamekeepers and other lesser folk, and it did not reach the cookery books. The earliest surviving recipe is Elizabethan and suggests a form of mince pie of umbles shredded with suet and seasoned with wine, spices and currants.[46]

Hares and coneys were enjoyed by high and low alike. A roasted coney was fit for a feast, but roasted hare was more of an everyday dish which did not appear on festal menus. This accorded with the tradition whereby coneys were kept in warrens (even though there was an ever-growing population of escapers), and were the property of the lord of the manor; while the native hares ran free.

The coney was prepared as follows: 'Take a coney, flay him, and draw him above and beneath, and parboil him, and lard him and roast him, and let the head be on; and undo him [the official carver's term was "unlace that coney"] and sauce him with sauce ginger, and verjuice and powder of ginger, and then serve it forth.' Rabbits, though named separately, were roasted in a similar fashion to the adult animal.

Both hares and coneys went into such typical Anglo-Norman pottages as 'civey' and 'gravey'; and coneys were also cooked in 'egerdouce', in the similar 'syrip' and in 'brewet of Almaynne'. 'Hare in worts' was a simple stew, with green herbs and aromatics added to the hare meat. 'Hares in talbotays' had the animal 'hewn in gobbets and sodden with all the blood'. The broth was thickened with bread, pepper and ale.

Until wild boar became rare in the sixteenth century, it was almost synonymous with brawn, and recipes carrying the word 'boar' in their title usually refer to brawn in their text. However, boar's ribs were chopped up and the meat incorporated with spices, pine kernels, currants and onions in broth and wine to make a pottage called 'boor in brasey'; although this too was dressed up with little slices of brawn before serving. Boar hams could be baked in a pasty in the manner of venison.[47]

Early modern period

The goat was still an accepted meat animal at the end of the Middle Ages, along with sheep, swine and cattle. Roast kid was a dish of the early seventeenth century, and soused kid is mentioned fifty years later; but goat meat was by then going out of fashion in lowland Britain. It lingered on later in Wales. Thomas Pennant reported in 1776 that kids there were 'a cheap and plentiful provision in the winter months'; while dried and salted goat haunches, known as 'hung venison' were eaten in place of bacon.

> The meat of a splayed goat of six or seven years is reckoned the best; being generally very sweet and fat. This makes an excellent pasty; goes under the name of rock venison, and is little inferior to that of the deer. Thus nature provides even on the tops of high and craggy mountains, not only necessaries, but delicacies for the inhabitants.[48]

The cattle, sheep and pigs of Tudor and early Stuart times were of stock which had hardly been improved since the days of the Romans. They received inadequate winter feeding, and in the case of oxen and of milch animals had a long working life before they were butchered. So although they were culled and fattened before slaughter, their meat must often have been dry and of poor quality. Not until new fodder crops had been introduced was it possible to achieve the tender, well-flavoured meat for which Britain was to become famous.

Winter feeding of stock upon turnips was developed from about 1650 onwards, and a little later cabbages were first used for the same purpose. During the seventeenth century too, new grasses including Dutch clover, trefoil, sanfoin and lucerne were introduced from the Netherlands. All contributed to make the animals stronger, better-fleshed and quicker to mature than their medieval counterparts. The same period saw the growth of large country estates, increased often by the enclosure of common land, so that landowners had space in which to nurture meat animals in greater numbers than before.

In the next century experiments were made to improve stock further by breeding. The best local animals were selected for the purpose, and some people purchased fresh strong breeding stock from a considerable distance. Cattle were even brought over from Holland into eastern England. Pigs changed in build more dramatically than any of the other farm animals when, during the eighteenth century, they were cross-bred with imported Chinese pigs. As a result the native types, descendants of the medieval pigs, were gradually replaced by new varieties, which differed from region to region but no longer bore much resemblance to wild swine.

The long-distance trade in meat animals between upland and lowland Britain, already a feature of medieval marketing, continued and grew. In the seventeenth century Scotland too was sending cattle to the south, to be fattened up for slaughter in the home counties. By the Georgian period the system had developed into an industry. Graziers in the counties around London devoted themselves entirely to improving their pastures, so that they could buy the beasts that had been raised far away, feed them up and resell them to the town butchers. For now distinctive breeds of cattle had emerged which were meat-producers as opposed to other varieties raised for dairying purposes. The droving of sheep and cattle for the meat market (they were often sold at fairs on the way, and rested for a time before continuing their long journeys) was a part of the country's economic life until the middle of the nineteenth century. Thereafter it became more profitable to transport animals quickly by rail or steamship.

For the well-to-do, the farm animals gradually replaced much of the game, wildfowl and small birds which had provided a big part of the meat diet of the Middle Ages. Fish days were never successfully re-established after the Commonwealth, and freedom from the old obligation to eat only fish during nearly half the year meant a further rise in the demand for farm livestock. During the prosperous decades of the early eighteenth century, when a series of good harvests reduced the cost of all foodstuffs, even the poor in towns could often afford to buy butchers' meat. Country labourers returned to the old practice of keeping animals, and they were able once more to rear pigs to provide themselves with bacon, or a cow or poultry to supply milk or eggs, though they generally ate less butchers' meat than did the townspeople.

The quantity of fleshmeat consumed in Britain in the late seventeenth and early eighteenth century struck visitors from Europe as quite remarkable. M. Misson, after travelling in England in the 1690s, wrote:

> I always heard that they [thc English] were great flesh-eaters, and I found it true. I have known people in England that never eat any bread, and universally they eat very little: they nibble a few crumbs, while they chew the meat by whole mouthfuls. . . . Among the middling sort of people they have ten or twelve sorts of common meats which infallibly take their turns at their tables, and two dishes are their dinners: a pudding, for instance, and a piece of roast beef.[49]

He also observed that the English dressed their meat more plainly than the French. The latter had not moved very far away from the medieval tradition, but in England a change towards simpler and less highly seasoned cookery had already begun.

Per Kalm confirmed this view after his visit of 1748, and he stressed the excellent quality of the meat then available.

> Roast meat is the Englishman's *delice* and principal dish. The English roasts are particularly remarkable for two things. 1. All English meat, whether it is of ox, calf, sheep, or swine, has a fatness and a delicious taste, either because of the excellent pasture, which consists of such nourishing and sweet-scented kinds of hay as there are in this country,

where the cultivation of meadows has been brought to such high perfection, or some way of fattening the cattle known to the butchers alone, or for some other reason. 2. The English men understand almost better than any other people the art of properly roasting a joint, which also is not to be wondered at; because the art of cooking as practised by most Englishmen does not extend much beyond roast beef and plum pudding. *Pudding* in the same way is much eaten by Englishmen, yet not so often as butchers' meat, for there are many meals without pudding. I do not believe that any Englishman who is his own master has ever eaten a dinner without meat.[50]

Meat was still spit-roasted. The turnspit boy was replaced in Tudor times by the turnspit dog. A pulley system linked the spit with a hollow wheel-shaped structure above, and a small dog was trained to tread continuously within, thus turning both wheel and spit. An alternative device was the gravity spit. It was operated by a cord, with a heavy weight attached at one end, which was wound round a cylinder above the hearth. As the weight slowly descended, cogged wheels transmitted the motion of the cylinder to another which was connected via a grooved disc with the end of the spit. Then it was rewound and the process began again. Both varieties of spit were in use all through the seventeenth and eighteenth centuries.

A third type was the smoke-jack, worked by a fan fixed into the chimney and turned by the updraught from the fire. Its main disadvantage was that a large fire had always to be kept up in order to produce sufficient draught. Poor people, who could not afford a spit and its accompanying tackle, hung their pieces of meat from a string in front of the fire, and turned them by hand.[51]

The details of successful roasting remained the private lore of cook or housewife, passed on by word of mouth from generation to generation, until 1615, when Gervase Markham published instructions for a wider audience. He described the qualities of fire required for different types of meat; how to spit the pieces economically; the best basting material, which could be butter, oil, fine suet rendered up with cinnamon, cloves and mace, or simple salt and water; and the best dredging, of fine white breadcrumbs or oatmeal. The object of dredging was to protect the surface layer of the meat from drying too much as it roasted.

In addition to the joints and fillets of beef, veal, mutton or pork which were roasted alone, mutton could be stuffed with oysters, a young pig with forcemeat, and slices of veal with herbs and egg yolks to form veal olives. The last were the descendants of the medieval 'allowes' of beef.

Mutton was still eaten at three or four years old, and was much stronger in flavour than the young sheep of between nine and eighteen months which are today sold as 'lamb'. House-lamb, often hand reared, came to table when still very young. It could be boiled in water or milk and water, or roasted with a quick fire, when it had to be protected by sheets of buttered paper so that it did not shrivel and dry. It was in season at Christmas and through the winter months.

During much of the seventeenth century the roasted meats were served with a wide range of pungent sauces. Thereafter, as the quality of meat improved, sauces became simpler. Dredging of meat as it roasted was reduced to a light sprinkling of flour. Often it was added at the end, and was immediately frothed with butter, so as to plump up the skin of the joint. Butter and dripping were the most usual bastings as the meat roasted.[52]

When wheat flour had come into common use for cakes and puddings, some economically minded cooks in the north of England devised a means of utilizing the fat that dropped into the dripping pan to cook a batter pudding while the meat roasted. In 1737 the recipe for 'A dripping pudding' was published in *The Whole Duty of a Woman.*

> Make a good batter as for pancakes; put it in a hot toss-pan over the fire with a bit of butter to fry the bottom a little, then put the pan and butter under a shoulder of mutton, instead of a dripping-pan, keeping frequently shaking it by

the handle and it will be light and savoury, and fit to take up when your mutton is enough; then turn it in a dish and serve it hot.

Similar instructions were reproduced by Hannah Glasse eight years later under the title of 'Yorkshire pudding'. 'It is an excellent good pudding; the gravy of the meat eats well with it', she observed.[53]

In private households meat was seldom oven-roasted. A recipe of 1655 suggests that a leg of mutton to eat cold might be roasted thus if well larded all over to obviate the need for basting, and laid upon two crossed sticks in a silver dish to prevent it from sopping in its own fat and gravy.[54] But this is an exception, and oven-roasting in the home did not become usual until the nineteenth century.

The roasting of meat in the ovens of the public baker was an earlier development. For a small charge, those who lacked spits or fuel to roast at home could have their meat cooked by the common baker. In southern England, where by the later eighteenth century such bakers operated even in quite small villages, labourers' families often carried both their bread dough and their weekly joint to the bakehouse.

Broiled or grilled steaks, already an established dish in medieval times, became very popular in the sixteenth and seventeenth centuries under the name of 'carbonadoes'. Elizabethan carbonadoes of mutton were made thus: 'Cut a leg of mutton in thin fillets and to make it tender: chop it on both the sides with the back of the knife so that they be not chopped through. Then salt them well and lay them on a gridiron and broil them till they be enough, and with vinegar and minced onions serve them forth.'

The chopping or scotching of the meat, which was typical of this style of cookery, served to tenderize it. An alternative was to pre-cook it. 'For there is no meat either boiled or roasted whatsoever', claimed Gervase Markham, 'but may afterwards be broiled.' The better-fed farm animals of the eighteenth century produced juicier steaks, and carbonado-ing gave way to simple broiling or grilling, often carried out over a small chafing dish filled with hot coals to supply a source of controlled heat.[55]

In the later sixteenth century the thick medieval pottages of meat began to yield to fricassees, hashes and similar made dishes, often of French origin. To make a 'fricassee of cold mutton or veal' in 1584, 'Chop flesh small and fry it in sweet butter. And then put thereto a little white wine, salt, and ginger, and serve it forth in fair dishes.' In the next century the fricassee was started with the frying of small pieces of meat, but a thickened sauce was then made in the same pan, to envelop the meat.

Hashes were at first prepared from sliced fresh meat, stewed with herbs, spices, broth and often wine. They took their name from the French *hachir* to chop, and early recipes were apt to begin: 'Take a couple of legs of lamb, or a leg of young mutton; hash it exceeding thin with your knife'; or, 'Take your calf's head and . . . hash it in slices as thin as you can.' Hashes were for some time served upon sops of bread or toast, but these were replaced in the eighteenth century by sippets of toast laid around the edge of the serving bowl. At that period too the recipes began to suggest using pre-cooked meat for a hash, and thereafter the dish became a useful way of producing left-over meat on a second occasion.

Other confections introduced into Stuart England were olios from Spain and bisks from France, made dishes which contained a large number of separate ingredients, wild and tame fowl of different breeds, pieces of pork, beef, veal, and bacon with sweetbreads, palates and so forth, piled up to form a magnificent pyramid. Part of the broth in which they had stewed was poured over all; the rest was strained and offered separately in a silver cup or china basin. For bisks, the larger fleshmeats usually supplied only the broth, while pigeons or other small birds formed the solid part; and bisks were also made of fish, especially crustaceans.[56]

The *daube* and the *casserole*, meat stews adopted from France later in the century, allowed fleshmeat to cook slowly in its own juice or a little wine, with accompanying herbs and roots. The meat cookery of Georgian times included also *braises* and *ragouts*, both again of French origin, and both based on the principle of stewing meat slowly in good broth, and then adding a more highly seasoned sauce towards the end of the cooking time. The meat thus kept its own flavour to supply a contrast to that of the sauce, instead of being absorbed into the aroma of more strongly tasting seasonings which had been present throughout the period of cooking.

One eighteenth-century speciality which recalls certain medieval dishes was the 'surprize'. The skin of a calf's head, with the meat, was raised carefully from the bones, stuffed with forcemeat, stewed, and served up in its original shape. Or cooked rabbits were stripped, and the flesh mixed with forcemeat fitted neatly back over their skeletons and browned with a salamander. They were carried to the table with their jaw-bones stuck into their eyes, and bunches of myrtle in their mouths, looking very surprised indeed.

Another medieval dish in a slightly changed guise was the 'porcupine'. It comprised a breast of veal stuffed, larded all over with small strips of red lean ham, white fat bacon and green pickled cucumber, and slowly stewed, so that its appearance when it reached the table recalled that of the earlier 'urchins'.[57]

Such elaborate confections were prepared for the meals of the English gentry, and those of middling rank who aspired to gracious living. But others simply boiled their meat in water with seasonings, and served it at table either in the middle of a bowlful of its own broth, or on a plate surrounded with vegetables, the broth being offered separately.

Simpler still were the eating habits of some remote parts of Britain where customs had hardly changed since prehistoric times. Beef was boiled in the hide in certain Scottish islands even in the eighteenth century; and 'the lower orders of Highlanders' bled their cattle in springtime and boiled the blood 'into cakes, which together with a little milk and a short allowance of oatmeal, is their food'.[58]

In lowland Britain the improvements in winter feeding of stock meant that there came to be less need for a vast autumn and early winter slaughter of meat animals. But the short-term preservation of fleshmeat was still an essential domestic craft. By the eighteenth century ice-houses had been devised in which a few of the well-to-do could achieve some degree of refrigeration for their meat. Nevertheless most people continued to rely on salting. The ever-increasing salt taxes from 1643 onwards made the process more expensive than it had formerly been. But country folk who could afford to keep a pig or cow usually managed to salt sides of bacon or prepare hung beef, even though they sometimes had to sell a part of the meat at slaughtertime to pay for the salt.

Hams and bacon were cured by several methods. Some people put brown sugar as well as salt, saltpetre and sal prunella in the preliminary pickle; and smoking over a wood or sawdust fire was often recommended.

The common use of coal as a fuel among south-country people became a hazard in the preparation of hung beef. William Ellis advocated laying the pieces of meat in boiled brine, with saltpetre and a little vinegar in it, for a week or a fortnight, then hanging them in the chimney defended by four or five sheets of brown paper from the fumes of the sea-coal. 'If you hang it by a wood fire, it needs no paper. . . . But we in the southern parts of England do not prepare hung beef as well as they do in Lancashire and the north; because they dry it there with the smoke of turf, which gives the beef such a very pleasant tang, that it is much coveted and sent for to considerable distances.'

Cooked beef could be pickled in vinegar – one of the culinary secrets unveiled by Sir Hugh Platt in 1605. By the middle of the eighteenth century beef barrelled in vinegar with herbs and spices was said to 'go good to the West-Indies, and keep a year good in the pickle, and with care, will go to the East-Indies'.[59]

Brawn, preserved in its sousing drink, was still eaten in the time around Christmas. Those who did not wish to make their own could buy it from the butchers, and Hannah Glasse explained how to distinguish between true boar pig's brawn and that of a barrow-hog or sow, by the thickness of the rind. A certain falling off in standards is reflected in Elizabeth Raffald's recipe for making mock brawn from the belly and head of a young porker interlarded not with its own fine fat, but with oxfeet boiled tender and sliced. The decline in the quality of brawn, whether made by the butcher or at home, finally led to its disappearance from the traditional Yuletide fare.

But during the seventeenth and eighteenth centuries many other kinds of meat were preserved in wet pickle, and sousing and collaring were among the skills that the compleat housewife was expected to be able to employ in her home. A whole pig might be tied up in collars, like brawn, and so might a boned leg or breast of veal or mutton or a piece of beef. They were rolled up tightly, bound fast with tape, boiled tender and left to cool in the salted cooking liquor. White wine or vinegar was often added to the 'drink' for veal or pork, along with a few herbs or spices (bay leaves were popular with pork during the seventeenth century). Claret wine could be put to beef, but if the original brine contained saltpetre as well as salt, that was often enough to produce the desired red colour without the addition of red wine.

The well-to-do and people of the middling sort had the soused and collared meats as side dishes at their tables, usually served in the second course. The meat pieces could be made more decorative if they were first scored with wide nicks which were filled, in the case of one recipe for flat ribs of beef, with chopped parsley, fat pork, and spiced breadcrumbs alternately. On serving, the roll of beef was to be cut at either end, when 'it will be in diamonds of different colours, and look very pretty'.[60]

The poorer country people also ate soused meat, very often made from the head, feet, ears and chitterlings of the pig which was their most usual meat animal. Country housewives made their sousing drink from salt and water boiled with bran or oatmeal, and they prepared and kept their pork in it during the winter months when 'the weather is generally cold enough to agree with sousing-drink for preserving pork in sweetness a month or more together'. Larger pieces of pork were barrelled in brine to which a little saltpetre was added to give them a pink colour. They had to be soaked in several fresh waters when the time came to eat them.

In Scotland in the 1720s, 'there is hardly any such thing as mutton to be had till August, or beef till September; that is to say, in quality fit to be eaten; and both go out about Christmas. And therefore at or about Martinmas [11 November], such of the inhabitants who are anything beforehand with the world, salt up a quantity of beef, as if they were going on a voyage.' The Martinmas 'mart' and the occasional 'braxy' (a sheep which had died naturally, often of braxy, a form of colic, and thereafter been salted) were said to be the only butchers' meat eaten by the poor of Scotland at that period.[61]

The method of preserving cooked meat under a layer of butter was known in Elizabeth's reign. It grew in popularity, and recipes for potting meat delicacies proliferated, as well as for potting fish and fowls. To make potted brawn in 1655 the buttocks of the hog, spiced with pepper, cloves, mace, nutmeg and salt, were put into claret wine in an earthenware pot sealed with a pastry lid, and were baked for seven hours. The cover was removed, all liquor was drained off, and the pot was filled up with clarified butter. The brawn would keep thus for two or three months. Potted beef was prepared in like fashion, and neats' tongues, rolled into a circular shape, were also candidates for potting.

Early in the eighteenth century it was found that the meat could be made to keep better if it was first finely minced and beaten with butter, and then pressed down very firmly to exclude as much air as possible. Thereafter beef, ham, tongue and many other meats were potted in this way. Two different meats could be combined together. Beaten to a paste, they were inserted in the pot usually in lumps or layers to create a marbled effect when cut. The veal and tongue mixture was known as marble veal.[62]

Of the byproducts of slaughtertime, blood went into black puddings, suet into forcemeats and the increasingly popular sweet puddings, marrow into pies. The pie of fleshmeat and dried fruits remained in favour until well into the eighteenth century. A sweet veal pie of that period contained steaks of veal with a layer of marrow or beef suet both above and below, raisins, currants, candied orange and citron, sweet mountain wine flavoured with cinnamon, and finally a glass of French brandy or shrub, added when the pie came out of the oven.[63]

But already savoury pies were gaining ascendancy over sweetened meat pies, even as speciality dishes. By contrast, mince pies had begun to lose their meat, although they still retained their suet; while the traditional meaty plum pottage of Christmas yielded in the next decades to the meatless plum pudding.

Jelly, too, underwent a division into sweet and savoury forms. An established feasting dish of medieval times, it was carried forward into the Tudor and Stuart banquet. The banquet emerged during the sixteenth century as a third and final course to the formal dinner, a development of the earlier dessert of spiced cakes and apples, hippocras and wafers. The participants withdrew to another room, or in summer to an outside arbour or summerhouse (the gentry built banqueting houses in their parks for the purpose), and regaled themselves on sweet wines, fruit tarts, marmalades, preserves, suckets, marchpane and jelly, which had recently become a sweetmeat.

In a jelly recipe of 1584 a pottle (half a gallon) of calves' foot liquor was added to a bottle of claret wine, two pounds of sugar, several spices, 'isinglass being fair washed and laid in water a day before, turnsole being aired by the fire and dusted [i.e. powdered]', and all were boiled together. To clarify the jelly at the end, the liquid was run through a jelly-bag along with the whites of two eggs, an early example of a practice that was to continue for many years to come.

Shavings of hartshorn now also came into use to stiffen jelly, though the traditional neats' foot or calves' foot jelly still continued to be made. Seventeenth-century jelly was sweetened with sugar, and often seasoned with rosewater and spices. Lemon juice was sometimes added too, and later came to replace rosewater as the regular flavouring. It was also common for a pint or so of rhenish or sweet white wine to be added to the liquor to give the jelly a pale amber colour.

Robert May tried to introduce the idea of fruit jellies, based on grape verjuice, or the juice of grapes, lemons, bitter oranges, woodsorrel or quinces. But it was slow to win acceptance, and in early Georgian times the emphasis was still on colour rather than flavour. For a ribbon-jelly of that era, run in stripes into narrow high glasses, 'you must colour red with cochineal, green with spinach, yellow with saffron, blue with syrup of violets, white with thick cream; and sometimes the jelly by itself'. It was only in the later part of the century that the juice of Seville oranges was adopted as an alternative to that of lemons for flavouring jellies.

Jelly was much in vogue at that period for decorative dishes at the second course. It provided the background water for 'floating island' or 'rocky island' tableaux; and was made into the sky in which a flummery moon and stars, previously produced in special moulds, were arranged, or a pond in which flummery fish were set to swim. Recipes were devised for 'transparent pudding' in which layers of sliced almonds, raisins, citron and candied lemon shone forth through the jelly. Sometimes a handsome still life of fruit – 'three fine ripe peaches and a bunch of grapes with the stalks up, put a few vine leaves over them' – was sealed in a bowlful of jelly, to be turned out next day for a set-piece.[64]

The old medieval meat jellies survived in seventeenth-century recipes for soused meat pieces, or hogs' feet, ears or snouts stewed in a broth of white wine vinegar and water which was then allowed to set. Robert May also recommended ox tongue boiled tender, 'larded' with candied fruits and run over with jelly.

Georgian meat jellies were seasoned with salt and peppercorns, and the earlier cinnamon and ginger flavourings were dropped. A final development was the introduction of aspic jelly from France, where it took its name from a sauce made with vinegar and bitter herbs and noted for its asp-like bite. English aspic jelly in the 1770s was produced from veal, ham and vegetable broth, jellified with isinglass and sharpened with tarragon vinegar. It covered cooked fowls, or baked fillet of veal cut into fancy shapes. It was still recognizable as a descendant of the fourteenth-century jelly of flesh.[65]

Game animals continued to contribute to Britain's diet. Of those formerly pursued, wild boars soon became extinct; while red deer gradually disappeared from the south-eastern half of the country, and by the eighteenth century survived in few places other than Exmoor and the Scottish highlands.

In Tudor and Stuart England, game could be taken by all, apart from the coveted deer whose meat, in theory, could neither be bought nor sold. But the hunters' freedom was curtailed by an act of 1671 which prohibited the killing of game, even on one's own land, to all except a very limited group of 'qualified persons'. The act contained loopholes, and for many years to come poached venison and game birds were sold openly in the season by London poulterers, and at taverns and coffee houses. They were obtained illicitly, either from 'qualified persons' or from middlemen who had connections with poachers.

From 1700 onwards several further acts were directed against poachers of small game, including the notorious Black Act of 1723, which allowed an armed or masked poacher to be punished by death if he was taken. Even hares were now legally out of reach of the ordinary man and his family.

Rabbits were in a different category. From Tudor times onwards coneys multiplied 'to the benefit of good housekeeping and the poor's maintenance'. The number of warrens was actually increased in the later seventeenth and eighteenth centuries, when dry, sandy, hilly land was thought to be more profitable under rabbits than if used for sheep-walks alone, or manured to bear crops. It is true that poachers were active here, too; but rabbit meat was widely sold by the warreners, and it was not expensive. The animals were bred for their fur as well as their meat, and when the furriers had been provided for, the carcases were sold off in the neighbourhood and sometimes far beyond. Those from the many rabbit warrens of the East Riding of Yorkshire were sent to Hull and York, and in later years to the new industrial towns of the West Riding, where they were one of the cheapest forms of fleshmeat.[66]

Rabbits were sometimes enjoyed by the gentry and those of ample means, but what they really liked was venison. Venison dinners given and attended by the wealthier citizens were a regular feature of the social life of seventeenth-century York. Pepys' *Diary* records many venison meals which he consumed both at home and at friends' houses, usually with great pleasure. The venison was roasted, put into pies, or occasionally stewed. The roast venison of Tudor and Stuart England was well larded if lean, and stuck with cloves or sprigs of rosemary. The Elizabethans ate with it a sauce of vinegar, sugar, cinnamon and butter boiled together so as not to be too tart. A sugared and spiced wine and vinegar sauce thickened with breadcrumbs was common in the seventeenth century. In Georgian times the sweet sauce theme was continued, with a syrup of wine or vinegar and sugar; but a new alternative now was redcurrant jelly.[67]

Venison pasty, highly seasoned and made to eat hot, or filled up with butter for a cold bakemeat, remained almost unchanged from medieval days. For longer preservation the venison was spiced and potted under a protective layer of butter.

When red deer was to be put into a pasty, the meat was first marinated overnight 'in a meare sauce made of vinegar, small drink and salt. . . . And if to your meare sauce', wrote Gervase Markham, 'you add a little turnsole, and therein steep beef, or ram-mutton, you may also in the same manner take the first for red deer venison, and the latter for fallow, and a very good judgement shall not be able to say otherwise, than that it is of itself perfect venison, both in taste, colour, and the manner of cutting.'

The fact that venison was so much a food of the gentry and their associates brought a social cachet to anyone able to offer it to guests. Failing the genuine article, counterfeit venison could be produced by following Markham's instructions or one of several other such recipes published during the next two centuries. It probably had most success with those who seldom tasted true venison. Cognoscenti were not so easily taken in. Samuel Pepys and his wife went out to dinner on 6 January 1660, 'which was good, only the venison pasty was palpable beef, which was not handsome'.[68]

Twelve hours' immersion in meare sauce would also disguise the flavour of tainted venison, so that it could be baked in a pasty. Robert May still advocated the medieval treatment of overnight burial underground for such venison. In the earlier eighteenth century four hours' steeping in cold brine was recommended, followed by four hours in hot; while Hannah Glasse advised washing the flesh in tepid water and fresh milk, and then rubbing it all over with beaten ginger. The same method could be applied to a hare.[69]

'A hare is ever good, but best from October to Lent', according to the author of *A Proper Newe Booke of Cokerye*, *c.* 1570. A roasted hare was given a pudding in his belly, a forcemeat of grated bread, suet, and herbs or spices. In the seventeenth century he was sometimes roasted with his skin on, flayed when almost cooked, and covered with finely grated manchet, flour and cinnamon, with a few cloves stuck over him.

Hares were also hashed in broth and wine, with herbs and onions; and indeed the medieval hare in civey returned again from France, where it still existed under the name *lièvre en civette*. In a recipe of 1682, the hare was cut into six or seven pieces, and stewed in white wine, water and a little vinegar with seasonings that included cloves and an onion, thyme and parsley, bayleaves and orange peel. Jugged hare came into English printed recipe books in the 1720s. The animal was cut up, laid in an earthenware pot or jug within a larger kettle of boiling water, and left to simmer for three hours. Seasonings were similar to those for *lièvre en civette*, but there was no additional liquid, and the hare cooked in its own blood.[70]

Rabbits, like hares, were stuffed and roasted, stewed whole or otherwise, or baked in pies. Sixteenth- and seventeenth-century recipes for either creature often demanded that his head and ears should be left on, so that he appeared lifelike when served. Piecrusts were also shaped to the animal's body and head, and sometimes its ears were left on the outside. Another type of hare pie, with the meat very well minced, beaten with marrow or suet and closely packed in the crust, could be sealed with butter when it 'will keep much longer than any other pie'. Potted hare was prepared in the same fashion.[71]

Robert May's recipe for baked leg of wild boar was borrowed from La Varenne's *Cuisinier françois*, for by the later seventeenth century English wild boars were a thing of the past. But May's next entry reads: 'To bake your wild boar that comes out of France'. The flesh was evidently salted for the journey, for it had to be soaked for two days, parboiled, and then seasoned with pepper, nutmeg, cloves and ginger and baked in a pie to be filled up with butter.[72]

La Varenne and other French cookery writers were also the inspiration for several recipes for snails which now appeared in English books. In France this animal delicacy had remained in favour since Roman times, but it had been lost to most of Britain. Now English instructions were published for snail pottage, well flavoured with onions and herbs, followed by others for stewed, fried and hashed snails and for snail pie. Snail water, distilled from snails, herbs, spices and wine, with a pint of earthworms for good measure, or boiled from similar ingredients in water, was recommended about the same time as a cure for consumptions.

Recipes for cooked snail dishes were still appearing in English household books in the early eighteenth century, but by then were probably regarded mainly as a curiosity; and after two or three decades they disappeared. Nevertheless there was, and is, a folk tradition of snail eating in a few places in Britain. One such is the Bristol region. There, in the proximity of the many Roman villa sites of Somerset and Gloucestershire, one would like to believe that snails have been a continuous part of the local diet for nearly two thousand years.[73]

Chapter 4

Wild fowl, tame fowl and eggs

a. WILD FOWL AND TAME FOWL

Prehistoric period

Wild fowl as well as fish and quadrupeds were a source of protein food in prehistoric Britain. Large seabirds on the coasts and large waterfowl around inland lakes and marshes were well worth catching, and in some places were the mainstay of their captors' diet. The little birds of the forests and clearings were a different matter, except when there was a dearth of other meats. Nets big and strong enough to take them did not begin to be made until Roman times; and for the small prehistoric population they can rarely have been an essential source of food.

In the mesolithic era the larger birds were clubbed or grabbed on the nest at the breeding season, trapped in nooses and snares, and perhaps shot with arrows having blunt wooden heads such as were in contemporary use in Denmark. Most of these methods continued throughout the prehistoric period. At Glastonbury lake village about the beginning of the first century AD slings and clay pellets were the favourite missiles whereby waterfowl were caught in large numbers for food.

The seafowl most commonly eaten included the great auk, razorbill, gannet, cormorant and various gulls. Among the inland waterbirds were wild duck, teal, whooper swan, heron, crane, bittern, grebe, pelican and several more.

As with other flesh foods, the common modes of cookery would have been roasting, and after the advent of pottery, stewing. The unplucked birds may often have been baked in the embers, their feathers perhaps smeared over with clay. The practice survived into the eighteenth century on some Scottish islands. Seabirds are rich in fat. On St Kilda in 1698 the 'great and beloved catholicon' of the inhabitants was the flesh and suet of solan geese or gannets, cut up together and cooked in the gut and known under the name of 'giben'. This type of cookery, too, is of prehistoric origin.

Bird catching is seasonal, inasmuch as it is easier to surprise the larger fowl when they are moulting or broody. Birds taken in quantity at such times may have been wind or smoke dried to preserve them; and for waterfowl with very oily flesh such treatment may have been successful. The St Kildans were still air drying their solan geese when Martin Martin visited them in 1698. And it was only in the case of geese that the tradition of bird drying survived into historic times in other parts of Britain.[1]

Wild ducks and geese were plentiful in prehistoric Britain. But the idea of taming them only arose among the Celts in the late pre-Roman Iron Age, and they probably learnt it from their kinsmen in Gaul. The same contacts brought them the bird which was destined to be most important of all as a supplier of food – the domestic fowl. The red jungle fowl of north-west India was the original ancestor of the cocks and hens of Britain. Travelling westwards it was domesticated first in Persia and later in Greece; it subsequently reached Rome, and then the Roman provinces and the countries that traded with them. It had arrived in Britain by the middle of the first century BC; but was still rather rare there. Caesar observed that the inhabitants of Britain kept geese and hens for pleasure, but that there was a taboo on eating them. The taboo may only have been in force among those tribes where the birds had been adopted as totem animals, and other groups may not necessarily have shared the objection. At all events a small number of the bones of hens and cocks have been found on pre-Roman Belgic sites in southern and eastern Britain.[2]

Roman period

After the Roman occupation domestic fowl became more plentiful. Their remains are often found in poor cave dwellings of the period, as well as on the richer villa farms. The Romans in Italy sometimes fattened hens and capons (raised from castrated male chicks) by battery methods, though it is not known how far this was done in Britain. But another Roman practice, the intensive rearing of more delicate birds in special enclosures, is likely to have been adopted when the pheasant, peacock and guinea-fowl were first introduced into the country. Partridges may have been kept in captivity too, as they were in contemporary Italy.

Wild pigeons were encouraged to roost in man-made pigeon-houses, the Roman *columbaria*, built in the form of high towers with layers of niches inside where the birds could nest and breed. Only a few *columbaria* have been found on Romano-British villa sites. But some town dwellers may have had smaller earthenware dovecotes built on to the roof tiles of their houses, as was commonly done in Mediterranean towns.

The geese which the Celts had kept for pleasure were probably of the grey lag variety which has remained the principal domestic goose of Britain. Pliny described another goose, the *cheneros*, as the most sumptuous dish known to the Britains, and this was probably the barnacle goose which could also be tamed. The mallard or common wild duck was domesticated too, although great numbers of these ducks still remained wild, and were taken from time to time by fowlers along with other waterfowl. Small birds such as thrushes may have been caught in nets, as they were in other Roman provinces.[3]

Boiled or roasted birds were served with well-spiced sauces, which were either produced separately or made by thickening the seasoned cooking liquor from the bird. Sometimes forcemeat was inserted beforehand. A typical Roman stuffing for a chicken incorporated pepper, lovage, ginger, chopped meat, boiled spelt-grits, a shredded brain, eggs, *liquamen*, oil, peppercorns and pine kernels. Small birds like thrushes were added to dishes of many ingredients, along with sausages, pieces of liver and brain from larger creatures, vegetables, pulses and herbs.

The larger wild fowl were hung for some days to tenderize them, and there was a special sauce for those that were high. Not surprisingly it was strongly flavoured and contained pepper, lovage, thyme, dried mint, filbert nut, Jericho date, honey, vinegar, wine, *liquamen*, oil, wine-must and mustard.

Peacock was so tough that Apicius' only suggestion for cooking it was in rissoles. But it was sometimes served whole at Roman banquets. According to Anthimus elderly peacocks had to be killed five or six days before needed, young tender birds only two days. They were stewed in broth to which a little honey and pepper was added after they were cooked.

Roman cooks knew how to deal with the problems of sinews in larger birds. 'When you cook a crane, see to it that the head does not touch the water but is outside it. When the crane is cooked, wrap it in a warm cloth and pull its head: it will come off with the sinews, so that only the meat and the bones remain. This is necessary because one cannot eat it with the sinews.' And crane or duck cooked and served in sauce with separately boiled turnips was a Roman dish for which parallels can be found both in the French *canard aux navets* and in the Elizabethan English recipe 'To boil a duck with turnips'.[4]

Early medieval period

Such elaborate cuisine was lost to Britain in the invasions and migrations of the fifth century AD. The more exotic birds died out, for they were too delicate to survive without special care. The guinea-fowl disappeared; it was to be more than a thousand years before it returned to Britain again. The peacock vanished for a while, but was reintroduced from the continent in later Saxon times. The remains of at least one, which perhaps ended its days as the adornment of some splendid feast, were found in the excavations of the Anglo-Danish town of Thetford.[5]

Peacock flesh was condemned by the Anglo-Saxon leechdoms, on the grounds that it was hard and not easily digested. But so handsome was the bird when served in the full array of its skin and feathers that it continued to be a centrepiece at great feasts all through the Middle Ages.

The common domestic fowl made a big contribution to everyday diet, and to monastic diet too. The rule of Benedict demanded abstinence from the flesh of all quadrupeds, but quite early it was decided that the ordinance did not include the meat of fowls. Annual donations of hens and geese bequeathed to monasteries are recorded in a number of Anglo-Saxon wills, and the monks reaped a double benefit from their eggs and their flesh.[6]

In Wales both geese and hens were important, and were the subject of several laws. A contrast is drawn between the turbulent goose which could be summarily executed if found damaging standing corn or corn in barns, and the gentler hen which, if discovered in a flax-garden or barn, was to be restored to its owner on payment of no more than an egg.[7]

The mountain and moor fowl of the upland north and west, the waterfowl of the marshes (a huge area of the East Anglia fens was now waterlogged again, following a fall in the land level in the fourth or fifth century AD), and the small birds of the woodland and the open spaces helped to supplement the food of Britain throughout the Middle Ages. For prodigious quantities of fowl were eaten, especially in winter when animal meat was in short supply.

The fowler had an accepted position in the Anglo-Saxon community, and he hunted his quarry with nets, snares, birdlime, traps, whistle-lures, and with hawks. The birdlime, a legacy from

Roman practices, was smeared on to twigs along with bait, and birds which landed on it stuck fast and could not get away. Large nets, another Roman heritage, were operated in conjunction with decoy birds; and smaller ones were dropped over little birds at night as they roosted in flocks in low bushes. Both methods continued into the Victorian era.[8]

Falconry came to Britain from the continent, probably about the middle of the ninth century AD. It had been an ancient skill in Egypt and the Middle East, but was slow to spread to western Europe, where it arrived in the last years of the Roman Empire, or perhaps even later. It was soon adopted among the upper orders of western European society not merely as a means of procuring food (which the well-to-do could obtain from other sources), but as a favourite sport. It was linked with the medieval system of chivalry, and in England falcons of different species were alloted to men according to their social rank: the king's bird was a jerfalcon, an earl's a peregrine falcon, a yeoman's a goshawk, a priest's a sparrow-hawk, while a lady had the small merlin.

The various hawks bred most readily in the mountainous north and west of Britain, and falconry soon spread to Wales. The king's falconer was one of the principal officers at the Welsh court, and he received frequent gifts from the king; but he was allowed 'to drink three times only in the hall lest there be neglect of the birds through his drunkenness'.

Much time and patience went into the training of hawks and they were rewarded with the head and neck of the birds they took. The bigger hawks were flown at the larger fowl – the peregrine falcon at such birds as the heron, bittern, curlew; the goshawk at cranes, geese, pheasants and partridges. The kestrel, one of the hawks permitted to the ordinary people, would take small birds and young partridges; while the hobby (a small falcon) was used in the 'daring of larks', petrifying them with fear on the ground, where the fowler took them easily in nets.[9]

Hawking for heronsewe (another name for the common heron, and especially for young heron) was very usual, and gave rise to the proverbial ignorance of one who did not 'know a hawk from a heronsewe'. Later the name was corrupted to 'handsaw', so that the proverb seemed to be nonsense.

Later medieval period

After the Norman Conquest, falconry became more popular than ever among the gentry; while commoners still took their wild fowl and small birds by the old methods, with slings, snares and nets. Bustards, which fed in flocks in the open country of the south and east, from Dorset to the Yorkshire wolds, were run down with greyhounds. They were the largest British landfowl, weighing on average twenty-five pounds each, and because of their bulk they took to the air with difficulty, though they were very fast runners on the ground.[10] In the marshes waterfowl were driven by beaters into nets.

Some larger households had connections with one or more bird catchers who supplied them with wild fowl. In others the steward or a trusted servant went out and bargained where he could for the best and freshest birds. At the Yorkshire establishments of Henry Algernon Percy, fifth Earl of Northumberland, a 'catour' was appointed so that 'all manner of wild fowl be bought at the first hand where they be gotten', on the grounds that the 'poulters' in the neighbouring villages had been taking 'great advantage of my lord yearly'.

The poulterers themselves depended much upon the catchers of wild fowl for their own stock-in-trade. For they dealt in such birds no less than in domestic poultry. Poultry dealing was recognized early as a separate trade, and in London the Company of Poulters was active from the end of the thirteenth century. Their shops were in the area of the city still known as The Poultry, though later they also traded at Leadenhall and Smithfield markets.

From their tariffs over the years between 1274 and 1634 we learn that swan was always the most expensive bird. But its flesh was tough and hard to digest, and from 1575 onwards only the younger birds were sold, under the name of cygnets, though they were still the costliest of all the fowl. Crane, heron and bustard were fairly dear too, and so at times was pheasant, but its price dropped when supplies were plentiful. Stork first appeared on the price lists in 1507 when it cost two shillings (swan at this time was three shillings and fourpence, and crane and bustard two and eightpence each). Quails also began to be sold by the city poulterers. They had been condemned by the Romans, who thought they fed on hemlock and suchlike poisonous plants. But eventually northern quails were found to be quite safe, and recipes appeared for roasted quail served with camelyn sauce.[11]

Of the small birds blackbirds were the most expensive, followed by larks. Sparrows only once received a separate mention in the price lists of the city poulterers, but at other times were probably concealed under the heading of 'small birds'. Finches, greenbirds (perhaps greenfinches), stockdoves (wood pigeons) and thrushes were priced separately, as were such larger birds as bittern, brewe (a kind of snipe), egret, gull, lapwing, mallard, partridge, plover, ruff, shoveller, snipe. Elsewhere in the country the range of wild fowl eaten was equally wide, and was often supplemented by local moor, freshwater or seabirds which did not reach the London market.

Outside the towns most families kept hens, which could scratch up a living around the hut doors of even the poorest; and where conditions were suitable, many also raised geese or ducks. Hens were the favourites, since they had a long life as egg producers before they were consigned to the pot. In the towns the poulterers sold them cheaply, and for many years they cost no more than a penny ha'penny or twopence each.

The manorial fowl were kept in the courtyard or some other enclosed space, where their welfare was often the responsibility of the dairymaid. Sometimes the poultry and geese were put up in coops and crammed on pastes made of cereals and milk, so that they should be succulent and 'in good grease' for the table. And once more peacocks, pheasants and partridges were reared and cherished. Dame Alice de Bryene fed her capons, hen pheasants and partridges on coral-wheat, according to her steward's account for 1418–19. But her care was ill rewarded. She lost 'in murrain at divers times this year, sixty-three' of the seventy-six partridges acquired during the period, and the household had the pleasure of eating no more than thirteen.[12]

Some had been received as presents, for both wild and tame fowl were favourite gifts at New Year, Twelfth Night (Christmas presents were given during the twelve days of Christmas rather than on the day of the nativity itself) or for a celebration. They were also brought in by tenants, either as part of a rent or again as a gift. Fowl were always eaten fresh, and the fowl enclosure attached to the house provided a temporary home for new acquisitions until they were wanted for the table.

Dovecotes were built on most manors in lowland Britain, while in Scotland and Wales they were part of the medieval castle. The manorial pigeons were not popular with the villagers, since they liked to feed on the standing corn in the open fields.

Swans were kept on rivers up and down the country, but their ownership was restricted to the larger freeholders of land. The Thames swans made a great impression on a Venetian visitor to England about the year 1500. He wrote: 'It is truly a beautiful thing to behold one or two thousand tame swans upon the river Thames . . . which are eaten by the English like ducks and geese.' The last remark indicates the scale on which he must have been entertained, for swans appeared usually only at feasts among the well-to-do.[13]

Birds had a two-fold appeal in Britain's diet, firstly as suppliers of fresh meat, especially in winter when much salted flesh was eaten, and secondly because of their varied species. The dinners of the nobility and gentry, who kept large households and entertained guests, were served in two main courses (at the greatest feasts sometimes in three) each made up very largely of meat dishes, unless it was a fasting day. The menus that have survived show that it was rare for the meat of any type of animal to appear more than once in a course, or indeed in a meal. By serving birds in all their diversity, it was possible to avoid any hint of repetition.

Even at everyday meals in a household of moderate size, fowl were usually a part of the fare. A typical entry from the day book of Dame Alice de Bryene, for 11 May 1413, gives: 'one quarter of bacon, one capon, two chickens, twenty pigeons'. At her house pigeons appeared on the menu on almost every meat day during the summer, as they did at all manors which had their own dovecotes.

For peasants and labourers wild birds were a special treat. They provided almost the only fresh meat such people ever enjoyed, except on the rare occasions when they killed a pig or a domestic fowl. And even those who were a little better off and could afford butcher's meat welcomed birds for a change. 'I have no delight in beef and mutton and such daily meats. I would only have a partridge set before us, or some other such, and in especial little small birds that I love passingly well', was a schoolboy sentiment in the fifteenth century.[14]

Fowls had their own seasons when they were 'in good grease' or plump so that they made satisfactory eating.

> Hens be good at all times, but best from November to Lent. Fat capons be ever in season. Peacocks be ever good, but when they be young and of a good stature, they be as good as pheasants, and so be young grouses. Cygnets be best between All Halloween day and Lent. A mallard is good after a frost, till Candlemas, so is a teal and other wild fowl that swimmeth. A woodcock is best from October to Lent; and so be all other birds as ousels and throstles, robins and such other. Herons, curlews, crane, bittern, bustard, be at all times good; but best in winter. Pheasants, partridge and rail be ever good, but best when they be taken with a hawk. Quail and larks be ever in season . . . chickens be ever good, and so be pigeons if they be young.

Goose was in season twice in its life, young goose in early summer, and the fattened bird at Michaelmas.[15]

How were the birds cooked? For wild fowl roasting was the favourite method. 'Cranes and herons shall be enarmed with lards of swine [i.e. larded] and roasted, and eaten with ginger.' In cookery books of the fifteenth century the recipes for roasting swan, crane, pheasant, heron, bittern, curlew, egret, brewe and several more all began with instructions for slaying the birds. With waterfowl the blood was sometimes reserved to colour the sauce.

'Crane roasted. Let a crane bleed in the mouth as thou didst a swan; fold up his legs, cut off his wings at the joint next the body, draw him, wind the neck about the spit; put the bill in his breast: his sauce is to be minced with powder of ginger, vinegar and mustard.'

Large fowls were roasted on the usual meat spit, but there were special little bird-spits for small birds which were tied on to the full-sized ones. Larks were the favourite small birds, and were most commended by the physicians. Blackbirds and thrushes were the next most digestible; but sparrows were 'hard to digest, and are very hot, and stirreth up Venus, and specially the brains of them'.[16]

Roasted birds in medieval times had their own special sauces. Alexander Neckam in the twelfth century gave us the earliest English examples of seasonings and sauces for poultry that we know: cumin was appropriate to a boiled hen, and a simple sauce, without garlic, to one that was larded and roasted. He thought that a domestic goose (he must have meant a stubble goose) required a strong garlic sauce, made with wine or verjuice of grapes or crab apples. Garlic sauce was still recommended in Elizabethan times when Thomas Moufet wrote: 'If any goose be eaten above four months old, it is badly digested without garlic sauce, exercise and strong drink.'[17]

Two other sauces peculiar to medieval goose were 'sauce madame' and 'gauncil'. To make the former the goose was first stuffed with herbs, quinces and pears, garlic and grapes. The hole was sewn up and the bird roasted. When it was done, it was cut apart and the forcemeat removed and combined with wine and spices to form a sauce that was poured over the pieces of goose. 'Gauncil' was a thick flour-based sauce.

Black sauces, confected from the offal, accompanied roasted hens, capons and mallards; and chawdron was made for swans. A white sauce of ground almonds, verjuice and ginger was put to boiled hens to produce one of the white dishes so much admired in medieval times. Ginger sauce went with partridge and pheasant; camelyn was recommended for heronsewe, egret, crane, bittern, shoveller, plover, and bustard; while small birds were served with salt and cinnamon.

Domestic fowls were often stuffed before roasting. Pigeons were forced with peeled garlic and herbs, and were stewed in broth in an earthenware pot.[18]

The carver in a large medieval household was kept very busy by the various fowls, every one of which had to be carved in its own particular way. The terminology attached to their carving was picturesque: rear that goose; lift that swan; sauce that capon; spoil that hen; unbrace that mallard; dismember that heron; display that crane; disfigure that peacock; wing that partridge; thigh that pigeon; thigh all manner of small bird.

But the actual work of dismembering them was tedious, and could be hard work: ('The crane is a fowl that strong is with to fare.') With some large roasted birds the legs were first removed and then the wings; with others the wings were first cut off; and others again had to have their necks broken before carving could proceed.[19] Then the flesh had to be shredded, and served in the appropriate sauce.

In smaller households the fowls must have been carved up with less ceremony. Citizens of London could buy birds ready roasted at the cookshops. They were sold at prices controlled by regulations of the mayor and aldermen. In 1378 best roast heron cost eighteen pence, twopence more than the uncooked bird bought direct from the poulterers. Medium-sized fowl, such as goose or hen, cost an extra penny for their roasting, and the smaller ones a ha'penny, while ten roast finches could be had for a penny as against twelve uncooked ones.[20]

As an alternative to roasting, birds were stewed in well-seasoned pottages. Goose in hotch-potch was a favourite recipe. 'Take a goose, and make her clean and hack her to gobbets, and put in a pot and water too, and seeth together; then take pepper and burned bread, or blood boiled, and grind fair ginger and galingale and cumin and temper up with ale, and put it thereto; and mince onions, and fry them in fresh grease, and do thereto a portion of wine.' Stewed partridge had ginger and other spices and also 'hard yolks of eggs minced' in the broth; and hard-boiled egg yolks very commonly appeared in recipes for fowl, whether in pottage, sauce or stuffing.

Sometimes the bird stew had onions and raisins in it, and it is from pottage of that type that the Scottish cock-a-leekie is descended; the onions were replaced by locally grown leeks. Fynes Moryson, who was in Scotland in 1598, ate what seems to have been this dish at a knight's house there. 'But the upper mess', he reported, 'instead of porridge, had a pullet with some prunes in the broth.' The recipe stemmed, in all probability, not from England but from France, as one minor result of the auld alliance.[21]

The smaller birds, too, were often boiled in spicy broth. Otherwise they might be put into open or closed tarts, surrounded with creamy egg custard, gobbets of bone marrow, dried fruit and spices. For feasts great pies were made, which contained capons, hens and mallards together with woodcocks, teals and other wild fowl. The birds were parboiled and laid inside a pastry coffin enveloped in a mixture of minced beef and suet, marrow, egg yolks, dried fruit, spices and perhaps wine. When chickens were baked, they were first yellowed with saffron, and then couched in their coffin with spices, verjuice, and diced lard of pork. Few birds, other than those of the goose family, were fatty enough to be baked without additional larding. Rook pies, well baked, were 'good meat for poor folks'; and the same people could capture, or buy cheaply from fowler or poulterer, sparrows and other little birds to stew or bake.[22]

Apart from the wild and tame fowl for everyday consumption, there were a few which were outstanding as celebratory birds for feasts and festivals. These were the larger fowl, and in the Middle Ages the favourites were swans and peacocks among the rich, and herons and bustards for those less well off.

The peacock made a fine show on a festive occasion when served up in its hackle, that is, in the full glory of its skin and feathers.

> Take a peacock, break his neck and cut his throat, and flay him, the skin and the feathers together, and the head still to the skin of the neck, and keep the skin and the feathers whole together; draw him as an hen, and keep the bone to the neck whole, and roast him. And set the bone of the neck above the broach, as he was wont to sit alive, and bow the legs to the body, as he was wont to sit alive; and when he is roasted enough, take him off, and let him cool; and then wind the skin with the feathers and the tail about the body, and serve him forth as he were alive.

An earlier recipe mentions the gilding of his comb as an added adornment. Peahens, though less spectacular, were still worth producing for important guests, and the tender peachicks were also enjoyed.[23]

More usual than peacocks at the feasts of the nobility were swans. The Percy family ate them on the principal festivals of the church at the rate of five for Christmas Day, four for Twelfth Night, three for New Year's Day, and two each for St Stephen's day, St John's day, Childermass day and St Thomas' day. The family consumed an enormous range of both moor and waterfowl during the year, but the swans were appointed for those special days.

Swan was roasted like goose, and served with chawdron sauce; but it was not made into a spectacle as a peacock was. Instead its neck was cut off, and was sometimes stuffed and served separately as 'pudding de swan neck'.[24]

Those who were not in the swan-eating class had goose or chicken, and sometimes all three were in evidence. When Dame Alice de Bryene gave a great dinner to a hundred people on New Year's Day 1413, the meats of the feast were: two pigs, two swans, twelve geese, two joints of mutton, twenty-four capons, seventeen coneys. Further down the social scale the yeoman farmer of late medieval times had goose and capon on his Christmas table, and even the ploughman was given a goose at harvest home.[25]

The domestic fowls supplied two other distinctive dishes for the entertainments of the nobility. One was the mythical animal known as 'cokagrys' (the second part of its name taken from the gris or sucking pig which made up half the animal), or 'cokatryce'. A capon and a young pig were neatly divided. Then, 'take a needle and a thread, and sew the fore party of the capon to the after party of the pig; and the fore party of the pig to the hinder party of the capon, and then stuff him as thou stuffest a pig; put him on a spit and roast him'.[26]

The other was two capons made of one. The original fowl was carefully skinned and the skin stuffed with forcemeat of hen's flesh and egg yolks, and then parboiled and roasted. In the meantime the actual body of the capon was also roasted and dressed in a covering of batter. Then the two 'birds' were served together.

Early modern period

The medieval dependence upon birds for food waned as fresh animal meat became more plentiful, better in quality and above all, a regular item of diet through the winter months. Domestic fowls were as important as ever, but the less palatable of the wild birds were gradually abandoned.

The choicer wild fowl were still pursued by fowlers with an eye to markets in the expanding towns, and by the gentry in the way of sport. 'Neither do I marvel', wrote Thomas Cogan, 'considering the goodness of the flesh, that gentlemen be at such cost to keep hawks, and take such toil to kill partridges and pheasants.'

But already the winds of change were blowing. Sir William Petre's household accounts as early as 1555 and 1559 mention payments made to men for gunpowder with which 'to shoot at crows about the house', and 'to kill fowl'. In the next century the sport of falconry was eclipsed by the more serious pursuits of the civil war; and when sportsmen again had leisure to hunt birds, they used guns instead of hawks.[27]

Fowlers continued to operate with the aid of nets and decoy birds. By Elizabethan times decoys were in use to capture waterfowl in the fens of East Anglia and around Glastonbury, and in the following years the decoy systems became very elaborate. The fowl were enticed or driven along series of narrow channels or 'pipes', following in the wake of a decoy duck, until at the end they found themselves trapped under nets. There was a growing trade in waterfowl, especially in the eighteenth century when better roads and faster transport made it possible to send them some distance to the large towns.

Other local specialities now became more widely known. Wheatears (migrant birds of the thrush family) taken in autumn with horsehair snares by shepherds on the downs near Eastbourne, were half-roasted or potted with butter and sent for sale to London. Dottrells caught in open country in the midlands were another delicacy for the capital.

But the ruffs of Lincolnshire and east Yorkshire were rarely sent long distances. They were trapped alive in nets, crammed for ten days or so on bread and milk until each was 'a lump of fat', when they were beheaded with scissors and roasted.[28]

Such birds were eaten as luxuries. By contrast, seafowl still supplied the main summertime food in the remoter Scottish islands, where the inhabitants, at some peril to life and limb, scaled the rocks to seek both the birds and their eggs. But solan geese from the Bass Rock or Ailsa Craig were smoked to provide a fashionable appetizer or relish in Edinburgh and elsewhere in Scotland during the seventeenth and eighteenth centuries.[29]

In England seabirds and some freshwater birds were losing their appeal. By the eighteenth century gulls, cranes and herons were greatly neglected: their flavour was too fishy for the taste of the age. The range of land birds accepted for human consumption was narrowing too. Bustards, 'much prized' in the 1690s (they were stuck with cloves and roasted or baked like turkeys) had become 'this curious fowl' in the fourteenth edition of the *Compleat Housewife*, 1750. Twenty-five years later they were still to be found in open country in the south and east: they were particularly partial to the turnip fields of Wiltshire, where they congregated in flocks of fifty or more. But they were 'very scarce' in the markets by 1788, and within a few decades became extinct. Cookery books still recommended that a bustard be prepared in the manner of a turkey; Richard Briggs even thought that it was 'the real wild turkey'.[30]

Fewer of the small wild birds were now accepted as a regular part of the diet. Larks were enjoyed, and sparrow dumplings were not unknown, but blackbirds, thrushes and finches were losing their appeal. In the 1770s song birds were taken alive on the outskirts of London, with the aid of nets and tame decoys, to be sold not as food but as cage-birds. The females, however, could not sing, so they were killed off and disposed of at threepence or fourpence a dozen. 'These small birds are so good', wrote Thomas Pennant, 'that we are surprised the luxury of the age neglects so delicate an acquisition to the table'.[31]

Pigeons were still eaten in great numbers, though not perhaps on quite the same scale as in the medieval manorial household. Dovecote pigeons came to be less well regarded by landowners when they no longer fed upon the peasants' standing corn in the common fields but upon the farmer's own crops. Many people still bred them nevertheless; they were valued for their dung, a rich fertilizer, as well as for their meat. But others were keen to shoot pigeons for the damage they did.

In Scotland too, pigeons were a regular part of the diet until late in the eighteenth century, for fresh meat was more scarce there in winter than it was in England. Pigeons were reared not only in the dovecotes of the gentry, but also in the little wooden pigeon-houses which ordinary folk had fixed to the gable-ends of their cottages.[32]

Partridges and pheasants were sometimes preserved in enclosures, for greater convenience. Sir William Petre's estate at Ingatestone boasted one in the mid-sixteenth century, made of thin wooden lattice and running along the inner side of his orchard wall. 'In this frame both partridges, pheasants, guinea-hens, turkey hens, and such like do yearly breed and are severally fed and brought up, so as they become tame as other chickens.'[33]

Guinea-fowl had recently been rediscovered by the Portuguese on the coast of west Africa, brought back to Europe and thence reintroduced to Britain. The turkey had already been domesticated

Hawking

From *Luttrell Psalter*

Feeding chickens

Carving and serving a medieval meal
From *Luttrell Psalter*

in Mexico and central America when the early explorers brought it back to Europe about 1523 or 1524. It may have owed its northern European names (Turkey bird; *coq d'Inde*, hence *dindon*; *Calecutische Hahn*) to the fact that it was brought on the last lap of its journey from southern Europe to the countries of the north by agents of the East India spice trade. In New England wild turkeys were still plentiful when the Pilgrim Fathers caught some for their first Thanksgiving dinner in 1621.

By that date turkeys had already won their way as domestic birds in old England. The earliest written record of their existence there was supplied by Archbishop Cranmer in 1541 when, seeking to curb the gluttony of the higher clergy, he defined the 'greater fowls', of which but one was permitted in a dish. Along with crane and swan he listed turkey-cock. Fourteen years later enough turkeys were being sold in the London market to warrant their price being legally fixed along with those of other poultry. Turkey-cocks at that time cost six shillings, while turkey chicks were two shillings and eightpence. By 1572 turkey-cocks had dropped to three and fourpence, and the hens, which always fetched a much lower price, to one and eightpence.

Turkeys grew in popularity, and eventually replaced the old celebratory birds of the Middle Ages, the peacocks and swans of the rich, the bustards and herons of the poor, in the nation's diet. The peacock was abandoned in the seventeenth century. It had always been a problem on account of its toughness, even after as much as fifteen days' hanging. The young birds were still occasionally eaten as a curiosity: those who tried them were recommended to put them up for three or four weeks before they were killed, and to fatten them on corn.[34]

Swans appeared at seventeenth-century feasts, and on the tables of the gentry, but thereafter were 'commonly kept for their stateliness and beauty'. The young cygnets could be 'extra-ordinary good meat, if fatted with oats', whereby they lost their fishy taste. A recipe for potted swan, first published in 1727, had the flesh beaten in a mortar with fat bacon 'till it is like dough', and then well seasoned with salt, pepper and other spices before it was baked.[35]

But turkeys became farmyard fowls. Soon they were a usual part of the husbandman's Christmas cheer. During the seventeenth and eighteenth centuries great numbers of turkeys, and also geese, were brought to the London market from as far away as Cambridgeshire, Suffolk and Norfolk. They were driven to the city on foot, beginning their journey in August at the end of the harvest, and taking three months on the way.

Geese travelled in the same manner from Lincolnshire. They were plucked regularly five times a year to supply quills and the down for goosefeather beds, and among the birds marched off to London were 'all the superannuated geese and ganders (called here cagmags) which, by a long course of plucking, prove uncommonly tough and dry'.[36]

By the eighteenth century a constant stream of domestic fowls from east Berkshire and ducks from the Aylesbury district was reaching London's markets. But fowls were also raised in most other country areas; and making capons was one of the arts of the country housewife, although it was now practised less than in former days.

Shortly before coming to market or table, hens, capons and chickens were often crammed on pellets of wheatmeal or barleymeal mixed with milk, and geese upon oatmeal, barleymeal or ground malt. Sir Kenelm Digby wrote of chickens fed on a soft paste of crushed raisins, white breadcrumbs and milk, and claimed that 'the delight of this meat will make them eat continually; and they will be so fat (when they are but the bigness of a black-bird) that they will not be able to stand, but lie down upon their bellies to eat'.[37]

In late spring professional crammers sometimes collared the market, buying up young chicks to sell fat after three weeks' feeding, so that there were few left to grow 'until they are fit to spend lean at seven or eight weeks'. Scottish fowls fared less well. Captain Burt reported that the hens were 'so lean they are good for little' and that 'one of them might almost be cut up with the breast of another'.[38]

In England the price of poultry fluctuated greatly at different periods. The hen had been the poor man's bird in medieval times. In early sixteenth-century London it still cost only three or fourpence. By the end of the century the price had risen to nine or tenpence, making it a luxury food, for the wages of labourers and artisans had by no means kept pace. By 1634 a hen sold in London for as much as one shilling and fourpence. Later the price fell again, and in the reign of Queen Anne hens were once more within reach of the purses of ordinary folk.[39]

It paid the purchaser of poultry, as of most other articles, to be alert, in order to distinguish young from old, fresh from stale birds. At the end of the seventeenth century 'directions for marketing' began to appear in printed recipe books, which offered guidance on the subject.[40] An additional hazard arose from a cruel custom current among some breeders, of sewing up the birds' vents a few days before they were slaughtered. This treatment was believed to fatten them more quickly; but in fact it often meant that the fowls were diseased by the time they came to market.

Birds that were sound could be cooked in one of several ways. Roasting was still much in favour. Large fowls with black flesh, such as swan, crane and bustard, were to be 'brown roasted' a long time before a slow fire, according to Gervase Markham. The birds with white flesh 'which must be pale and white roasted (yet thoroughly roasted)' were to have 'a quick and sharp fire without scorching'.

Little birds had to be well basted with butter (they were served on sops of bread or toast to absorb both butter and gravy, a custom which has continued in the case of woodcocks and some others). Large fowls were basted with butter, or larded with pork fat, or covered with strips of fat bacon to prevent them drying too much as they roasted. The Christmas turkeys of late Tudor and Stuart days were 'sticked full of cloves in the roasting'.[41]

Waterbirds were served with galantine sauces made from their own blood with breadcrumbs or stewed prunes and spices. The Tudor and Stuart galantines were in effect an amalgam of the fifteenth-century sauce galantine with the black sauces of the same era.

By Elizabeth's reign new sauces were being added to those

which had been handed down from earlier days. Some were quite simple, like the thinly sliced boiled onions, with pepper and the bird's gravy, that were a sauce for capons or turkey-fowls. Others were complex, rich and strange. Such was the sauce for a capon containing claret wine, rosewater, sliced oranges, cinnamon and ginger. In the next century oranges, lemons, anchovies and oysters were all well to the fore in the sauces made to be eaten with fowl.

The fashionable sauces of the Georgian period were garnered from the culinary successes of previous generations. Thus a spiced bread sauce with onions to accompany roast turkey recalled the bread-based sauces of medieval times; while Hannah Glasse's 'pretty little sauce' made from the liver of a fowl was close to the black sauce of the same era. Of more recent ancestry were sauces containing oysters or celery or lemons; while a simple egg sauce proper for roasted chickens, consisting of finely chopped hard-boiled eggs and plenty of butter, was very much a sauce of the eighteenth century itself.

The Elizabethan accompaniment to a green goose had been sorrel sauce; to a stubble goose, mustard and vinegar. A green sauce (made with green wheat and gooseberries and melted butter, faintly echoing 'sauce madame') was retained for the green goose; but the Michaelmas bird was now served with apple sauce.[42]

It was still customary to stuff birds, especially domestic fowls. Some of the forcemeats of the seventeenth century were very exotic, and along with breadcrumbs, minced meat, herbs and spices, included dried fruit and crystallized oranges. They were coloured yellow with saffron, or green with spinach juice. In the eighteenth century oyster stuffing became fashionable; and so also did chestnut stuffing, made with minced bacon and the bird's own liver. Stuffings had now lost their dried fruits and the sweet element, and were flavoured only with herbs, nutmeg and perhaps a little fine-cut lemon peel.

Separate forcemeat balls were sometimes made. And in the eighteenth century, by an inversion of the usual process, small birds sometimes appeared from inside the stuffing. Such was the way to dress larks pear fashion. . . . Wrap up every lark in force-meat, and shape them like a pear, stick one leg in the top like the stalk of a pear.'

Not all birds were given elaborate stuffings. Sir Kenelm Digby's suggestion for forcing wild ducks with sage and a little onion wrought into a lump with butter before they were roasted was soon adopted also for tame ducks and for stubble geese.[43]

Bird pottages were common. Elizabethan sparrows were stewed in ale with herbs, and served upon sippets of bread. Larks were cooked in wine with bone marrow, raisins, a little sugar and cinnamon. Alternatively either larks or sparrows could be boiled in 'the best of mutton broth' with 'a little whole mace, whole pepper, claret wine, marigold leaves, barberries, rosewater, verjuice, sugar and marrow, or else sweet butter'. 'Stockdoves, or teals, pheasant, partridge or such other wild fowls' were simmered in good beefstock with plenty of coleworts.[44]

Other bird stews were flavoured with fresh barberries or gooseberries; and capons and hens were sometimes boiled with bitter oranges or lemons. These fruity stews continued into the Stuart period, often in the form of hashes with mushrooms, chestnuts, anchovies or oysters as extra ingredients. During the eighteenth century, however, the fruit element tended to be discarded.

Rich stewed broth was sometimes made with the meat of a cock, instead of the more usual beef or mutton. 'Take a red cock that is not old, and beat him to death, and when he is dead: flay him and quarter him in small pieces, and bruise the bones every one of them', begins a recipe of 1584. Flesh and bones were to be simmered twelve hours in an earthen pipkin with many different herbs, some spices, dried fruits and licorice. 'If you put in a piece of gold, it will be the better, and half a pound of prunes, and lay a cover upon it and stop it with dough.'

Cock broth was drunk to cure consumptions, and the recipe persisted in various forms until well into the eighteenth century. The cock was always done to death in some cruel manner in order to release the greatest amount of his virtue for the benefit of the sick person. The gold coin (sometimes gold-leaf was substituted) was intended to transfer its imperishable quality to the drinker.[45]

Other broths of hen or capon were made in a more conventional manner. The flesh of these fowls was highly regarded and was often added to stews containing beef, mutton or other flesh. Some people enjoyed chicken broth alone. Queen Henrietta Maria had concentrated chicken-stock made from a whole hen and boiled down to less than a pint for her 'ordinary *bouillon de santé* in a morning'.[46]

The Elizabethan recipe 'To boil a duck with turnips' deserves mention, if only for its affinity with a much earlier Roman recipe. It runs: 'Take her first, and put her into a pot with stewed broth, then take parsley and sweet herbs, and chop them, and parboil the roots very well in another pot, then put unto them sweet butter, cinnamon, ginger, gross pepper and whole mace, and so season it with salt, and serve it upon sops.'

Duck with turnips achieved no great success in English cookery. But duck with green peas 'in the French fashion' was foreshadowed in a recipe of the 1660s, and within the next hundred years became an accepted combination.[47]

Pigeons were always popular and appeared in many different guises. By the eighteenth century they could be braised, fricasseed, jugged, boiled with bacon, in a hole (i.e. in a batter pudding, like toad-in-the-hole), and transmogrified, which meant that each bird was tucked inside a large hollowed cucumber, with its head and legs sticking out at each end, and a bunch of barberries in its bill by way of decoration.

More simply, pigeons and sparrows too, were rolled up in paste and boiled as dumplings. Pigeon dumplings were a well-loved dish in Scotland.[48]

When potting became fashionable in the mid-seventeenth century, pigeons were among the first birds to be chosen for the new treatment. Sir Kenelm Digby's recipe, 'To bake pigeons (which are thus excellent, and will keep a quarter of a year) or teals, or wild-ducks', has them baked in a pot for eight or ten hours in claret wine and butter; and then butter-sealed in their pot.

Soon moor-game, woodcocks, all kinds of small birds, and even swans and geese were being potted in similar fashion; and recipes proliferated. Hannah Glasse sounded an ominous note in her directions 'to save potted birds, that begin to be bad'. The remedy was to throw the birds into boiling water for half a minute and whip them out again, dry them thoroughly, season them with mace, salt and pepper and then seal them again under fresh clarified butter.[49]

Perhaps pickling was a safer way to preserve fowls. But it was only suitable for large and fatty birds, for geese or fat turkeys. Capons needed to be well larded before they were put into the sousing drink. Pickles of a different kind were made from sparrows, squab-pigeons or larks. According to a recipe of 1727, they were boiled and then put up in a strong liquor of Rhenish wine and white wine vinegar, well seasoned with herbs, spices and plenty of salt: 'once in a month new boil the pickle, and when the bones are dissolved, they are fit to eat; put them in china-saucers, and mix with your pickles'.

Fowls were baked in pies to be eaten both hot and cold. The hot pies, most often of chickens or pigeons, followed in the medieval tradition, and the birds were well spiced, moistened with butter or marrow, and accompanied by fruits. For a time dried fruits and sugar were still not unusual in such pies. But from the Elizabethan era onwards fresh or pickled gooseberries, grapes, red currants and barberries were increasingly popular; and a caudle of melted butter and verjuice was added just before the pie was served. The seventeenth century saw a widening in the range of additions in the form of such delicacies as oysters, morels, artichoke bottoms. But thereafter the dividing line between sweet and savoury became firmer; and by the Georgian period chicken pies had separated out into sweet chicken pies (with sweet potatoes, chestnuts, etc. to accompany the birds, and a sugar and white wine caudle added at the last), and savoury ones, in which the additional ingredients were of a non-sweet nature and the caudle was replaced by good gravy.[50]

Pheasants, partridges and other birds were for a long time baked in rich pies of a comparable kind. A partridge tart in a recipe of 1655 was made with the flesh of the birds minced small with its own weight of beef marrow, orange and lemon candied peel, spices, rosewater and orange juice. The next century saw a swing towards plainer pies: and Hannah Glasse's duck pie of 1747 has the fowls seasoned with nothing more than pepper and salt. Rook pie, now elevated to the cookery books, could be made from six young rooks with the same simple seasoning.[51]

When birds were baked to be eaten cold they were given a double dose of spices, and plenty of butter, and the cooked pie, on cooling, was filled up with clarified butter. Turkeys quickly became popular as bakemeats, whether hot or cold. Several Elizabethan recipes exist for turkey pie, which was a useful dish to have on hand for the entertainments of the twelve days of Christmas. A simple pie was made thus: 'To bake turkey fowl. Cleave your turkey fowl on the back and bruise all the bones. Season it with pepper gross beaten and salt, and put into it good store of butter. He must have five hours baking.'

According to the cookery books of the seventeenth century, pigeons, doves, quails, rails, bustards, peacocks, cranes, swans and all manner of moor-fowl and waterfowl were baked in much the same fashion, well spiced with nutmegs, cloves, pepper and salt, and sealed in butter within the cold pie, which could then be kept for several days. But with the advent of potting, pies of this type became less common. One notable exception, however, reached the apogee of its fame in the eighteenth century. This was the celebrated Yorkshire Christmas pie, a descendant of the great bird pies of the Middle Ages.

> First make a good standing crust, let the wall and bottom be very thick: bone a turkey, a goose, a fowl, a partridge and a pigeon. Season them all very well. . . . Open the fowls all down the back, and bone them; first the pigeon, then the partridge, cover them; then the fowl, then the goose, and then the turkey, which must be large; season them all well first, and lay them in the crust (one inside the other), so as it will look only like a whole turkey; then have a hare ready cased,

> and wiped with a clean cloth. Cut it to pieces . . . and lay it as close as you can on one side; on the other side woodcocks, moor game, and what sort of wildfowl you can get. Season them well and lay them close; put at least four pounds of butter into the pie, then lay on your lid, which must be a very thick one, and let it be well baked. . . . These pies are often sent to *London* in a box as presents; therefore the walls must be well built.[52]

Other versions have the goose as the outermost bird, which presupposes a smallish turkey within. In this form the pie was famed as a 'Yorkshire goose pie'.

b. EGGS

Prehistoric period

Wild birds' eggs contained an accessible form of nourishment that appealed to the primitive food-collector. They were especially useful because they could be gathered in spring and early summer, a bleak season in the food year before the crops had ripened or the meat animals had had time to fatten themselves on the new leaves and grasses. At that time a few birds' eggs would have enriched a pottage of herbs and dried cereal, and if thoroughly mixed into the liquor as it cooked, they would also have thickened its texture. The eggs of the larger fowl may have been roasted in their shells in the ashes at the edge of the fire. But it is possible that birds' eggs were most often sucked raw out of their shells, for, if the eater was really hungry, that was the quickest and easiest way to consume them.

Perhaps by later prehistoric times eggs were preserved for long periods. Deep ash deposits that could have been employed for food conservation have been discovered in store-chambers built into the thickness of the walls of aisled round-houses in places in eastern Scotland, the Hebrides and the northern Scottish islands. Similar ash deposits have been found in underground chambers in Cornwall and in Ireland. In all cases the ash could have been used to store sea birds' eggs, a procedure that was still common in the western Scottish islands at the end of the seventeenth century.[53]

Roman period

But eggs took on a much greater importance in Roman times, when domestic fowl first became common. Though the laying habits of these birds were to some extent seasonal, they produced far more eggs than did any of the wild fowl. The medieval hen was expected to yield one hundred and fifty-five eggs a year, and the Romano-British hen, provided it was reasonably well fed, could have done the same. But it must be remembered that the eggs of both would have been much smaller than those of most of our hens today.

With eggs for the first time available on such a scale, it was now possible to consider them seriously in cookery. The Romans already did this. From Apicius' cookery book we learn that they sometimes boiled their eggs and served them with simple sauces; or else fried them in oil and put a dressing of wine and *garum* over them.

But they also exploited eggs as a thickening or binding agent for other foods. They borrowed from the Greeks the idea of combining eggs with milk to form a custard mixture, which was either cooked very slowly in an earthenware pot, or fried in oil, as in the following recipe: 'Egg sponge with milk. Mix together 4 eggs, ½ pint of milk, 1 oz. oil; pour a little oil into a thin frying-pan, bring to sizzling point, and add the prepared mixture. When it is cooked on one side turn out on to a round dish, pour honey over, sprinkle with pepper, and serve.'

Another kind of egg confection was made of fruit or vegetables, or fish or shredded meat, bound with eggs and lightly cooked in the open dish called a *patina*. This was placed over a brazier or in the ashes at the edge of the kitchen fire. There were many different versions. For 'everyday *patina*', boiled brains were pounded up in a mortar with seasonings, milk and eggs, and the dish was cooked over a slow fire or in a water heater of the type of a *bain-marie*. More exotic was *patina* of roses. But *patina* of pears was nearer to modern tastes. 'Boil and core pears, pound with pepper, cumin, honey, wine-must, *liquamen*, and a little oil. Add eggs to make a *patina*-mixture, sprinkle with pepper and serve.'[54]

The Romans used beaten eggs to bind their rissoles, sausages and stuffings; and chopped, hard-boiled or hard-fried eggs were an additional item in some of their *patinae* and other dishes of mixed ingredients. Although gourmets ate the eggs of geese, partridges and pheasants, hens' eggs were now usual in everyday diet, and Roman cookery was based upon them.

Early medieval period

During the post-Roman era in Britain we lose touch, for several centuries, with the details of egg cookery. But hens were kept and eggs were eaten wherever farming was carried on; while even the poorer peasants usually owned a few fowls. As town life revived again eggs were brought into the town markets from the surrounding countryside. Those that came by boat to London were eventually made to pay duty; 'and from one hamper of eggs, five eggs [are given] as toll, if they come to the market', according to Aethelred's law of 927.[55]

Eggs appear to have been simply cooked at this period, and were probably either roasted in their shells in the embers, or fried in butter or lard. The Anglo-Saxon vocabularies give no indication that any more subtle egg dishes were known.

Later medieval period

Medieval hens on the manor farm had their production quota of a hundred and fifty-five eggs each, plus seven chicks, three of which were to be made capons. Poor folk's hens may not have done quite so well, lacking the feeding that was given to the manorial birds. But most people could count upon the occasional egg as a source of extra nourishment. Chaucer's poor widow in the *Nonnes Preestes Tale*, with her diet of milk, brown bread, smoked bacon, 'and sometimes an egg or two', was probably quite typical.

In the towns eggs were plentiful and cheap to buy. Their price in London from 1320 to 1416 fluctuated between sixteen and ten for a penny. In London, eggs were vended by the poulterers; but 'foreigners', that is country people from outside the city, were permitted to come in and sell their eggs and other produce in some London markets. Cooked eggs were an item on the price lists of the city cookshops in the fourteenth century.[56]

Eggs could be eaten on ordinary fasting days, but not in Lent. According to the medieval recipe books they could not even be used in cookery at that time. Dame Alice de Bryene's household, for which frequent purchases of eggs were made during the rest of the year, had none in the year 1413 from Ash Wednesday until Easter Sunday when fifteen pence was spent upon them, representing probably at least two hundred eggs. Some guests were present to share the Easter feast, at which boiled eggs with green sauce, traditional fare for Easter Day, would almost certainly have been eaten.

People with clever cooks could serve 'eggs' even in Lent. They were made by blowing hens' eggs and inserting into the shells (we are not told how) first some thick white milk of almonds, mixed with sugar, and a little ginger and cinnamon, then a portion of the same mixture coloured yellow with saffron to represent the yolk, and lastly some more of the white to fill up the remaining space. The shells with their new contents were then roasted in the ashes in the manner of real eggs.[57]

It is probable that many families were not too scrupulous in their observation of the Lenten fast: Lent, after all, coincided with the hens' spring-laying season. In London the sale of eggs during Lent was never specifically banned, except for a few years during the reign of Elizabeth I.

On fast days outside Lent eggs were eaten; but they could not be sold openly in London on Fridays until as late as the middle of the seventeenth century. At a much earlier date Saturday had ceased to be so stringently observed. By 1512 the members of the Percy family had the choice of a piece of salt fish or a dish of buttered eggs for their breakfasts on Saturdays out of Lent. Forty years later the Petre household at Ingatestone Hall in Essex ate meals that included eggs as well as fish on both Fridays and Saturdays.[58]

The simple, long-established methods of preparing eggs by roasting them in their shells, or frying them in butter or lard, were still followed. But the complex egg recipes of the Middle Ages, like so many of the dishes of Norman French and hence Anglo-Norman cookery, were descended and developed from those of the Roman empire.

The Roman concept of egg and milk custard was revived in such pottages as 'Cream boiled. Take cream of cow milk, and yolks of eggs, and beat them well together, and do it in a pot, and let it boil til it be standing, and do thereto sugar, and colour it with saffron, and dress it forth in leaches [slices], and plant therein flowers of borage, or of violet.' Another unsweetened custard of eggs and milk was reinforced with finely ground pork meat and sage. Others again were thickened with flour, or flavoured with sugar and spices; while a runny custard of milk and egg yolks was poured over sops of pandemain to form a more liquid pottage. Another sweet thin custard flavoured with ginger and saffron was sometimes added to poached eggs; but these were often eaten in the water or broth in which they had been poached as 'potage de egges'.

Several other pottages were thickened with strained eggs. Typical was 'jusshell', based upon meat broth, eggs, breadcrumbs and seasonings which included saffron. The contemporary attitude to eggs is illustrated by one recipe which advocates yolks only when the pottage is prepared for a lord, but whole eggs, whites and all, when it is for mere commoners.

Wine or ale mixed with egg yolks and gently heated made caudles, which were heartening drinks at breakfast or bedtime. They were often sugared and spiced, and were sometimes rendered very thick by the addition of breadcrumbs. 'Caudel ferry', a favourite medieval dish, was made in this manner, being brought to the consistency of mortrews according to one recipe, or until it could be cut into slices according to another.

It could be reinforced with pulped pork or chicken meat, and appeared at feasts 'departed' with a blancmange, its golden colour providing a contrast with the white of the latter.

'Chardewardon' recalls the Roman *patinae* of fruit and eggs. It comprised warden pears, boiled and sieved, flavoured with sugar, honey and cinnamon and thickened with egg yolks. Similar dishes were based on quinces, bullace plums and apples.[59]

The 'flathons' (flans), 'crustards' and other open tarts of medieval cookery again recall the old *patinae*, with the shallow open dish of the Romans replaced by an open pastry crust, and the filling once more mixed and bound with eggs. Strained eggs went into closed pies too, especially those which contained a mixture of meat and dried fruits, like the fifteenth-century 'pies of Paris'. Sometimes the yolks of hard-boiled eggs were included, to give extra bulk to the filling.

The precursor of the omelette in Britain was known as a herbolace and in the late fourteenth century was a mixture of eggs and shredded herbs, baked in a buttered dish. A contemporary French recipe under the same name is much more detailed, and gives instructions for heating oil, butter or fat thoroughly in a frying pan before pouring in eight well-beaten eggs (of medieval size) mixed with brayed herbs and ginger. The French version was finished off with grated cheese on top, and appears to have been quite close to the modern concept of an omelette. But the English herbolace, even in the fifteenth century, was still only a form of scrambled eggs, enriched with cheese and milk as well as with herbs.

An English alternative was the tansy, flavoured with the leaves of that plant. They were often mingled with other herbs in the mortar, and the juice was pressed out and put to raw strained eggs. The mixture was fried in fair fresh grease, being turned and gathered together in the pan as it cooked with the edge of a dish or saucer.[60]

Pancakes were made from flour and egg batter, but were not grand enough to win a place in the recipe books except in the case of the pale ones called crisps (from the Norman French *crespes*) made from the whites of eggs only, and served along with fritters. They were sprinkled first with sugar.

Egg-batter fritters containing meat, fish or fruit were fried in lard or oil. Apple fritters, strewn with sugar when it was available, were perhaps the best loved, but fritters of skirrets or parsnips were well liked too, because of their natural sweetness. The physicians condemned fritters as indigestible, but they remained irresistible to the layman, and appeared regularly in medieval menus, usually as part of the last course. John Russell observed that 'apple fritter is good hot, but the cold ye [should] not touch'. Herb fritters, the batter aerated with a little yeast, and 'fritters of milk' made from curds and egg whites were two other popular versions.

The uses of eggs in the field of bakery in enriched breads and cakes are mentioned in Chapter 7. One interesting fact that emerges from a study of medieval cookery books is how late in time it was before the raising power of beaten egg whites, or rather of the air enmeshed by them, was fully appreciated. Egg yolks were considered highly nutritious, and very often the yolks alone were put into tarts, pies, forcemeats and other confections. But 'the white of an egg is viscous and cold, and slack of digestion and doth not engender good blood', according to contemporary opinion. In the Middle Ages egg whites had only one useful function: they could supply the basis for, or at least bind together, one of the dishes of white food which were a fashionable feature in the table arrangements of the time.[61]

Early modern period

Eggs retained and even increased their popularity, and in due course the prejudice against their whites died away. Hens were encouraged to lay by special feeding on such delicacies as hempseed, horsebeans, buckwheat or 'toast taken out of ale with barley boiled'.

Both duck eggs and goose eggs were an occasional springtime food in lowland Britain. On the rocky coasts of the north and west, seabirds' eggs were taken regularly at that season. The islanders of St Kilda, at the end of the seventeenth century, not only ate seafowl eggs in spring, but also preserved them for six, seven or eight months, buried in the ashes of burnt turf; 'and then they become appetising and loosening, especially those that begin to turn'.

In southern Britain many people preserved hens' eggs in bran, meal or sand. Others advocated packing eggs in wickerwork hampers with the broad end downwards; while the common higglers turned their eggs upwards or downwards alternately once a week.

The marketing of eggs was still primarily the concern of the country housewife, who often earned her pin-money by her labours. In the eighteenth century careful housewives scrubbed the shells clean with warm water and sand before sending their eggs for sale in London.[62]

The most usual ways of dressing eggs at the end of the Middle Ages were to roast them in the embers, to poach them in hot water or broth, or to fry them in lard. Andrew Boorde approved of new laid eggs rare-roasted and eaten in the mornings with a little salt and sugar. But it was difficult to rare-roast eggs successfully, for they soon dried and hardened in the hot ash, and this method of preparation gradually went out of favour.

By the later sixteenth century the boiling of eggs in their shells in water had become a common practice. Prepared thus they were more digestible than roasted eggs; but less so than poached eggs, which always earned the highest praise from the medical men.

Fried eggs were the least wholesome of all; 'yet it is less unwholesome if the eggs be not fried hard'. In fact, fried eggs got such a bad name that 'the best collops and eggs' in some seventeenth-century recipes were made with eggs poached separately in water 'in a fair scoured skillet white and fine, dish them on a dish and plate, and lay on the collops [slices of bacon toasted crisp before the fire], some upon them, and some round the dish'.

Eggs served with butter were familiar fasting-day food in Tudor times. Buttered eggs, later to be known as scrambled eggs, came into the cookery books in the seventeenth century. They were laid upon buttered rounds of toasted manchet, and the dish was garnished with pepper and salt. For those who enjoyed the scented foods fashionable at that period, musk and ambergris could replace the pepper. Buttered eggs were also eaten with bitter orange juice, sugar and spices.[63]

The medieval tansy and herbolace were superseded by the omelette, derived from France where it had already existed under the same or a similar name for two or three hundred years. In English recipe books it was for long referred to as an 'amulet'; and in the mid-seventeenth century there was still some divergence of opinion as to whether it should be fried 'only on one side or bottom', or turned over and cooked on both sides like a pancake. Eventually the former version prevailed, though a hot salamander was sometimes held over the top of the omelette for half a minute 'to take off the raw look of the eggs'.

The tansy still existed, but it gradually changed its nature. Puddings were becoming increasingly popular, and beaten eggs often went into their composition. Early in the seventeenth century the old herb-flavoured tansy was reinforced with a few crumbs of bread, some spices and a little cream, and was served with sugar strewn over it. Then, with the addition of more breadcrumbs or grated Naples biscuits and some sugar, the tansy was turned into a sweet pudding, no longer fried, but baked or boiled in a pudding-cloth. A sprig or two of tansy-herb was still chopped into it, but its green colour was now supplied mainly by spinach juice.[64]

Pancake batter was made with flour, eggs, powdered spices and either milk or water. 'There be some', said Gervase Markham, 'which mix pancakes with new milk or cream, but that makes them tough, cloying, and not crisp, pleasant and savoury as running water.' The controversy over the respective merits of pancake batters mixed with milk or water continued, but by the eighteenth century milk was generally used. Hannah Glasse also had some extra rich recipes, such as one which included half a pint of cream, half a pint of sack and the yolks of eighteen eggs beat fine. Even her ordinary pancake batter, which was mixed with milk, was reinforced with a glass of brandy. *Crepes suzettes*, with the brandy added afterwards and flamed, were still a thing of the future, for they were not invented until the end of the nineteenth century. Pancakes of another kind admired during the eighteenth century were those known as 'a quire of paper'. The batter was run as thin as possible over the pan and was cooked on one side only; and the completed pancakes were laid evenly one upon another with sifted sugar strewn over each.

Skirret fritters and herb fritters survived from medieval times. In the mid-seventeenth century there were recipes for fritters made from the pulped leaves of spinach, or beets, or clary, bugloss or lettuce. During the next hundred years these fritters underwent a further development into the elegant pancakes of vine leaves or clary leaves, for which each individual leaf was dipped in batter and fried, or else laid on top of a small spoonful of batter in the frying pan.[65]

The medieval egg-thickened caudles of wine or ale continued as substantial breakfast or supper drinks until well into the eighteenth century. An innovation was the tea caudle derived, perhaps, from the recipe of the Jesuit who came from China in 1664.[66] The ingredients were a quart of strong green tea, a pint of white wine and the yolks of four eggs, all heated together with sugar, and a grated nutmeg. Another use for a caudle of wine or verjuice with egg yolks and sugar was to fill up a sweet lamb, chicken, potato or other pie before it was brought to table.

Elizabethan 'tartstuff', a thick pulp of boiled fruit, was often drawn up with eggs in the manner of the earlier 'chardewardon'. So were some of the later fruit 'creams', for which not only cream but also beaten eggs were mingled and boiled with the fruit purée. Eggs and thick cream made a filling for custard tarts. From the later seventeenth century custard was frequently separated from its pastry case and was baked and served by itself, at first in a deep dish and afterwards in special custard cups.[67]

Hard-boiled chopped eggs were still put into some pies of

mixed ingredients. In 'Lent minced pies' they replaced the shredded meat of the usual 'minced pie'.

But the greatest innovation was the discovery of eggs as a raising agent in cookery. Whites of eggs produced the Elizabethan 'dishful of snow', a spectacular centrepiece for the banquet course following a festal meal. They were beaten with thick cream, rosewater and sugar until the froth rose, and the latter was gathered in a colander, and then built up over an apple and 'a thick bush of rosemary' on a platter. In some versions the snow was gilded as a final touch.

The beating of egg whites was not altogether easy before the fork came into common use late in the seventeenth century. At the beginning of that century Sir Hugh Platt described some methods of his own day. 'How to break whites of eggs speedily. A fig or two shred in pieces and then beaten amongst the whites of eggs will bring them into an oil speedily: some break them with a stubbed rod, and some by wringing them often through a sponge.' A 1655 recipe for 'cream with snow' suggested a cleft stick, or 'a bundle of reeds tied together, and roll between your hands standing upright in your cream'.

For the dishful of snow was still being made under the name of 'cream with snow' (it had lost the rosemary and the gilt), and as 'snow cream' or 'blanched cream' it continued into the eighteenth century. A variant form with the addition of apple pulp came to be known as 'apple snow'. The same recipe was made up with other fruits in season. Syllabubs were also produced on occasion from cream reinforced by white of egg to enhance their light, frothy texture.[68]

In the field of bakery well-beaten eggs served to raise early forms of sponge cake, and eventually, used in quantity, they succeeded in holding up even heavily fruited cakes. Frothed egg whites were prominent in some of the recipes for fancy cakes and biscuits which stemmed from France and Italy. Macaroons and similar almond cakes were raised and aerated with their help.

Italian biscuit, a confection of fine sugar, with a little aniseed and musk, and beaten egg white, was baked in a warm oven until it rose 'somewhat high and white'. Not dissimilar were the 'puffs' of the later seventeenth century, flavoured with grated lemon peel, chocolate or ground almonds.

Then at the turn of the century a still lighter creation was introduced from France, in which the proportion of frothed egg white to sugar was greatly increased. The new arrival was quickly added to the sweetmeats of Britain, among which it is still to be found. Its French name remains unaltered. It was the *meringue*.[69]

Chapter 5

Milk, cheese and butter

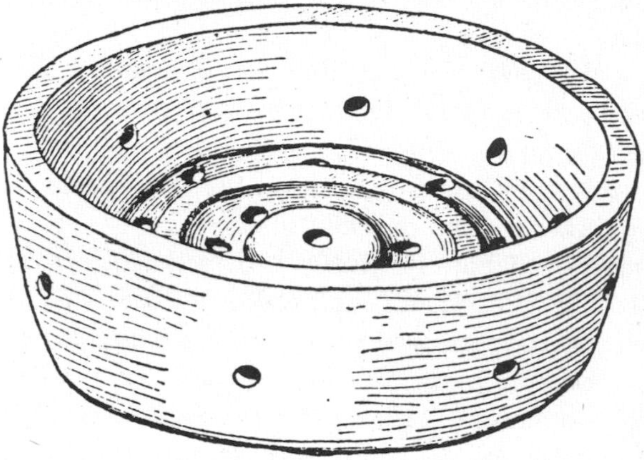

Prehistoric period

Milk played a part in the diet of the people of Britain from the time when the first neolithic farmers brought their domestic cows, sheep and goats into the country. At that period cow milk was the kind most often drunk; for cows, which could live off the leaves of the forest that covered almost the whole country, far outnumbered the grazing animals. Over several hundreds of years some parts of the woodland were gradually cleared, and by Bronze Age times there was more open terrain in which sheep and goats could be kept. Ewes, like cows, were milked; so also were she-goats.

The animals were milked into containers of leather, porous pottery or perhaps wood. It would have been difficult to clean vessels of any of those materials satisfactorily and the new milk must often have soured quickly, especially in the hot dry summers which Britain enjoyed from the mid-third to the mid-first millennium B.C. Much of it would therefore have been drunk – or eaten – sour, in the form of curds and whey.

Large beakers were the typical pottery of the various groups of Bronze Age immigrants who settled in Britain from 2000 B.C. onwards. These receptacles were very suitable in shape and size for holding milk or whey, and both must often have been drunk from them.

During the next centuries the idea of making cheese from sour milk was evolved. The remains of perforated colanders have been found on a few Bronze Age sites in Britain, and it is thought that they could have been used as cheese-wrings, to drain off the whey from the milk solids.

The making of butter is likely to have been introduced into Britain by the Celts during the pre-Roman Iron Age. The Celts were noted as coopers, skilled makers of stave-built buckets and churns. Within such vessels milk was agitated until the cream solidified into butter. As the Celts also produced salt, and used it to preserve meat and fish, they no doubt soon learned the advantages of salting their butter: for butter salted, packed into jars and stored in a cool place could be kept for long periods without going rancid.

Pliny described butter making among the barbarians (by whom he almost certainly meant the Celts, both within and without the Roman empire). He said that they considered butter their choicest food, 'the one that distinguishes the wealthy from the lower orders', and that they usually made it from cows' milk (hence its name *boutyron* or cow cheese), but ewes' milk produced the richest butter, and goats' milk was also sometimes used for the purpose. The milk, warmed in winter, was shaken rapidly in a tall vessel stopped at the mouth except for one small hole to admit the air. 'The part that curdles most, floating on the top, is butter, a fatty substance.' The rest of his account is rather jumbled, because he had become confused between the making of butter and the making of sour milk, known to the Greeks and Romans as *oxygala*.

Milk soured by lactic acid fermentation was widely consumed in ancient Europe. In Mediterranean countries it was commoner than butter, probably because the climate induced souring so quickly. Sour milk in its simplest form was made by merely leaving milk to stand for a period of time until the fermenting process had brought it to a semi-solid state. No art was needed to achieve this result. Tacitus described the primitive German tribes, for instance, as living off wild fruits, newly killed game and 'solid milk' (*lac concretum*); and 'solid milk' must have been consumed in Britain all through the prehistoric period.

The Romans took their name for sour milk from the Greeks, and from them they may also have learned their practice of adding certain herbs to the milk to encourage the process of souring. Herbs came to be used for the same purpose in Britain, though whether this was done under Roman influence, or discovered independently much earlier, we do not know.[1]

At first cheese was made simply by drawing the whey from the curds of soured milk. The curds might be squeezed and pressed by hand to facilitate the escape of the liquid, and when they had become solid enough they were shaped into cakes and left to dry. Pottery colanders or cheese-wrings might be used to help with the drainage: but otherwise baskets of rushes or twigs were employed. Such soft curd cheeses had to be eaten fresh, for they would not ripen and merely grew moulds if they were kept for too long.

A big advance in cheese making took place when rennet came into use, at an early and unrecorded time. Rennet is the digestive juice secreted in the stomach bag, or vell, of several mammals. The idea of using it to make cheese probably arose from the discovery of milk curd inside the stomachs of young milk-fed animals such as calves and lambs when they were slaughtered for meat.[2] The curd itself was no doubt taken out and eaten in prehistoric times: and then, as a next step, people tried using the juice from the stomach, or part of the maw itself, to coagulate other milk. The importance of rennet was that it produced a different kind of fermentation from the ordinary souring caused by contact with the air and its bacteria, and it was a source of enzymes which continued to work on the cheese over a long period, and so to ripen it. Hard cheese with good keeping properties could now be made in summer, and kept against the lean times of winter.

Roman period

The earliest descriptions we have of cheese making with rennet in western Europe come from Roman authors. Columella recommended that cheese be made from very fresh milk, unmixed with water, and normally curdled with lamb's or kid's rennet. But sometimes the juice of wild thistle or other plant coagulants were used instead. A little rennet was added to each pail of milk, which was then left in a warm place to thicken. When sufficiently solid it was drained in wicker baskets or moulds, with weights above it to press out the whey. Thereafter the cheese was taken out of the moulds, salted and compressed. It was allowed to dry, with further salting to draw out the moisture, in a shady place out of doors for nine days; and finally the individual cheeses were stored on shelves indoors and left to mature. 'This kind of cheese', said Columella, 'can even be exported overseas.'

But cheese was also produced locally in most of the Roman provinces. Pottery cheese-strainers have been found on many Romano-British sites; and as the Britons still kept large herds and flocks of milk-producing animals, especially in the highland zone, we may believe that a good deal of cheese was eaten.

Cream cheeses may also have been made in the shallow pottery bowls known as *mortaria*, which were widely used in Roman Britain. Milk could have been left in such bowls to curdle, when the whey would have been poured off through the spout on the rim. The grits on the inner surface of the pottery would have retained the curd-forming bacteria from one cheese-making day to the next, thus obviating the need for rennet, herbs or old whey to set the milk working. Cream cheese is made in similar bowls in parts of France to this day.[3]

Curd cheeses were often flavoured with herbs. Columella mentions also cheese which was hardened in brine and coloured with the smoke of apple-tree wood; and the Celts, who already had a reputation for their smoked meat and fish products, may have made smoked cheese at this time.

Much of the cheese must have been eaten simply by itself or with bread. But the Romans sometimes incorporated cheese in their cookery. Hard cheeses were sliced into salads. The softer curd cheeses were put into the more complex *patina* dishes, along with several other meat or fish ingredients, hard boiled eggs, nuts and seasoning. Cheese of this kind was also used in cake and pastry making in Mediterranean lands, but those confections were already being made with butter in some Roman provinces, and Britain may well have been among them.[4]

In Roman times butter and lard are likely to have been the principal cooking fats of Britain. Imported olive oil was more costly than either, and was for the cuisine of the richer and more Romanized inhabitants only.

Early medieval period

During the centuries following the end of Roman rule very little olive oil reached Britain at all, and butter became more important than ever. 'Boil in butter' is an instruction that often recurs in the Anglo-Saxon leech books. Everyday foods, as well as medicaments, were prepared in this way; while melted butter served as a sauce for vegetables and pulses.[5]

In eastern England much of the butter and cheese of this period was made from ewes' milk, for the Anglo-Saxons kept many sheep. It was the duty of the Anglo-Saxon shepherd, according to the *Rectitudines Singularum Personarum*, a late tenth-century document, not only to milk his charges twice a day, but also to make the butter and cheese from the milk. He received certain perquisites, which included a bowl of whey or buttermilk every night during summer. The butter itself went to the lord of the manor. So also did the cheese. But the shepherd had the right to the milk of the whole flock for seven nights after the spring equinox, during which time he could make cheese and butter for his own use during the ensuing year. Butter was usually salted, as was cheese. 'You would lose all your butter and cheese, were I not at hand to protect it for you', claimed the salter in Aelfric's *Colloquy*.

In Wales too, salt was used in the preparation of cheese, which was allowed to rest for a time in a brine solution. This is apparent from a section in the early Welsh divorce law wherein a couple on parting make division of their common property. 'The provisions are thus to be shared: to the wife belong the meat in the brine, and the cheese in the brine; and after they are hung up they belong to the husband; to the wife belong the vessels of butter in cut, the meat in cut and the cheese in cut. . . .'[6]

Butter and cheese of cows' milk were more usual among the Celtic peoples of Wales and northern England, for cattle were still the chief wealth of the Celts. The production of cheese and butter was closely linked with the system of transhumance: the cattle were wintered in the stubble and fallow fields around the village or farm, and taken up into the high summer hill pastures (the Welsh *hafod*) when it was time to sow the grain in spring, and it was there that the butter and cheese were made. The beginnings of this seasonal alternation in Britain may go back very far, perhaps to a time well before the Roman conquest. In parts of Wales, Ireland and Scotland it continued late, to the end of the eighteenth century and longer.

Later medieval period

Both ewes and cows were milked to supply the manor dairy. Goats too yielded milk, and although their numbers dwindled in eastern England during the later Middle Ages, they remained plentiful in the south-west, the border country and Wales. Large stocks of sheep and goats were recorded on Mendip in the *Exon Domesday* of 1080, and their milk provided the material for early forms of Cheddar cheese. As late as the sixteenth century it is probable that 'the Cheddar cheese-maker milked whatever milch cow came to his hand, as did his Cheshire colleague; for the secret of his cheese lay in his soil formations, not his stock'.

In the Yorkshire dales, where grazed the great flocks of sheep owned by the monastic houses, local cheeses were based upon ewes' milk. In other parts of northern England cows were common. Rents of a milch cow were often paid on the bishopric estates of County Durham; and during the late thirteenth century there were vaccaries along the Pennine edges in Yorkshire and Lancashire where both milch cows and working oxen were bred and raised. Even in the south the peasant's milch animal was often a cow; and by the end of the medieval period the cow was already ousting both sheep and goats as the usual supplier of milk.[7]

In cheese-making country the yield of two cows or twenty ewes in the fourteenth century was set at a wey of cheese and half a gallon of whey butter a week. (In this context, a wey is probably a copyist's error for a stone.) Cows were milked at all times of year, but those that had spring calves went dry in autumn; while those that bore autumn calves produced only a small yield in winter, when their milk fetched three times its summer price. It was inadvisable to milk ewes later than August, lest they should be too much weakened to survive the winter. Cheese making was therefore confined to the summer months.

The milking of ewes was abandoned altogether by some farmers in the sixteenth century on the grounds that it took too much of the animals' strength. But others maintained that good pasture could make up the loss. Ewes' milk was given up reluctantly, for it was thought, at least by some people, to be 'fulsome, sweet and such in taste as no man will gladly yield to live and feed withal'. It was also claimed that cows' milk to which a lesser proportion of ewes' milk was added, produced a cheese that 'doth the longer abide moist, and eateth more brickle and mellow than otherwise it would'.[8]

Milk and milk products were useful adjuncts to the cuisine of the gentry, and enriched certain of their dishes; but fleshmeat and spices were the true mark of the rich man's diet. White meats (the collective name given to milk, milk products and eggs) were the food of the poor. The peasant's cow was his 'commonwealth', providing him and his family with 'butter, cheese, whey, curds, cream, sod [boiled] milk, raw-milk, sour-milk, sweet-milk, and butter-milk'.

The well-to-do rarely consumed milk in its raw state, for it was known to curdle in the stomach, and was thought to engender wind there.

> Cows' milk and ewes' milk, so be it the beasts be young and do go in good pasture, the milk is nutritive . . . but it is not good for them the which have gurgulations in the belly, nor is it not all the best for sanguine men, but it is very good for melancholy men, and for old men and children, specially if it be sodden [boiled], adding to it a little sugar.[9]

Among the varieties of fresh milk that of women and that of asses were regarded as the two most digestible kinds, and as the two most suitable for children and convalescents. Women acted as wet nurses to adult invalids as well as to babies. The high rate of mortality among infants meant that it was not difficult to find a recently bereaved mother who was able and willing to be employed in such a capacity. 'To increase milk in women's breasts. Rice sodden in cow milk with crumbs of white bread, fennel seed in powder and a little sugar, is exceeding good', according to a recipe of 1585. It was intended that sympathetic magic should transform the white ingredients into white milk.

Other types of milk were often boiled with honey or sugar for drinking purposes; or they were seethed with chopped pork, or herbs or cereals to produce pottages; or were combined with eggs to form sweet or savoury custard mixtures. A thick milk and egg custard, yellowed with saffron, was the basis of a medieval recipe for roasted milk. It was strained and pressed firm on a board, and when cold was larded, stuck upon skewers, and roasted on a gridiron. This dish survived long in slightly variant forms, some of which are to be found in cookery books of the eighteenth century.[10]

The amount of milk drunk fresh or used in cookery was however, small compared with that which was processed to form the other white meats. In the first place the cream could be skimmed off, some to be churned into butter of the best quality, and some to be eaten in its raw state. Alexander Neckam described how cream and curds from the twelfth-century manorial diary were brought in on large round platters for consumption by the lord and his fellow diners. Even the peasant with his single cow could enjoy cream during the summer months, though according to the physicians he did so at some risk. 'Raw cream undecocted, eaten with strawberries or hurts [bilberries], is a rural man's banquet. I have known such banquets hath put men in jeopardy of their lives.'[11] Medical opinion was not well disposed either to the mixture of fresh and clotted cream, another popular delicacy.

But cream could also be substituted for milk to enrich made dishes. It was a regular purchase in the household of Dame Alice de Bryene on Wednesday fish days in summer. We may guess that some of it was turned into 'creme boylede' (a thick bland custard of cream, egg yolks, sugar and breadcrumbs) or rich custard tarts of the kind which appear among fifteenth-century recipes.

When cream was made into butter, the resultant skimmed milk was turned into cheese; while the residue of the butter making was available in the form of buttermilk. Alternatively full milk was renneted for cheese, and yielded a rich whey; and this was then skimmed to produce whey-butter. Both buttermilk and whey were very plentiful in dairying districts, and the surplus from large households was bestowed upon the poor.

Whey and buttermilk were both the source of curds. Whey and buttermilk gently heated together, or buttermilk mixed with some hot, fresh milk and left to stand made better curds than either whey or buttermilk alone. The curds were eaten with honey, cream, ale, wine or the whey itself, according to the circumstances of the eater. The final thin curded whey, also known as whig, was a refreshing summer beverage for country people.

Hot posset drinks were made from milk curdled with ale. And a sweet lechemeat for the second course was produced by mixing drained posset curds with dairy curds and honey, and pressing them into a solid mass that could be cut into slices.[12]

Another use for curds in cookery was in tarts such as the elegant sambocade, or in 'darioles', for which one form of filling comprised curds, egg yolks and marrow. Curd fritters were also made. When whey or buttermilk curds were not to hand, fresh milk was renneted to produce curds for cookery.

But the principal use of rennet was, of course, to curd new milk for cheese. Through most of the medieval period rennet was probably secured from which ever young suckling animal, whether lamb, kid or calf, could best be spared for slaughter. Towards its close, as cows' milk replaced that of ewes and goats, more calves were bred, and the calf supplanted the other young creatures as the provider of rennet for the dairy.

The calf's vell was taken out, and the curd within it removed and cleaned. Then the vell was washed and salted and put up in a pot with the cleaned curd inside it (and sometimes spices, herbs, cream and eggs as well), with the idea that this meal would feed the vell and increase the flow of rennet. If the salted vell was kept long, its own brine turned to rennet; or fresh brine could be added later, which likewise took on the nature of rennet. Herbs and spices put in the brine helped to conceal ill flavours if the vell deteriorated.[13]

But vells stored thus, or alternatively hung up in the kitchen chimney to dry, must often have produced rennet of a curious quality; and it is hardly surprising that cheeses did not always turn out well. Other unpredictable factors, such as the content of the milk, the temperature and humidity of the air, and airborne microbes which came into contact with milk or curd, also affected the maturing of the cheese.

Some of the faults that could result were recognized in several little poems that were in circulation by late medieval times. Thomas Tusser adapted one or more of them when he listed the ten unwanted guests in the English cheese-dairy as:

> Ghezie, Lots wife, and Argus his eyes,
> Tom piper, poor cobbler, and Lazarus' thighs:
> Rough Esau, with Maudlin, and Gentiles that scrall,
> With Bishop that burneth, thus know ye them all.[14]

His first line describes cheese that was white and dry, or too salty, or full of eyes; his second, cheese that was hoven (i.e. swollen with its own internal gas), tough or spotted; his third, cheese that was full of hairs (said to have been a particular fault of Welsh and Scottish cheeses), of whey, or of maggots; and his last refers to the flavour imparted when the milk had burned on the pan while being heated before renneting.

Surplus cheese was sold locally, or at one of the great regional fairs. Cheeses from Suffolk and Essex were sent as far as London, but cheese did not usually travel any great distance from its place of origin.

Medieval cheeses were classified according to their texture, not their district. There were three main types: hard cheese, made of skimmed milk and rendered still harder by long keeping; soft cheese of whole or at least only semi-skimmed milk, matured for a time but still retaining enough moisture to keep it from being really hard; and new or 'green' cheese, which was curd cheese and had to be eaten quickly, for it was too damp to mature properly. There were also herb-flavoured cheeses, which usually belonged to the last group.

Most of the full-cream milk cheese was destined for the table of the lord of the manor, while the skimmed or semi-skimmed kinds went to the servants, farm workers and peasants. There were no doubt many variations in the richness and texture of such cheeses, according to how much cream was left on the milk, but it was well known that the worst and hardest cheeses came from butter-making counties. Suffolk and Essex cheeses were notorious, and a rude little rhyme about Suffolk cheese ran:

> Those that made me were uncivil:
> They made me harder than the devil.
> Knives won't cut me, fire won't sweat me,
> Dogs bark at me, but can't eat me.

Neverthless hard cheese was a staple of the peasant's diet. Bread and cheese formed a large portion of the provisions sent out to boon workers in the manorial fields, and special purchases of cheese were made for the purpose against harvest time on manors which did not produce a big enough surplus at home.[15] It was an important item in monastic diet; and it was bought in quantity to help victual the armies of the Middle Ages, and to supply ships bound on long voyages.

Hard cheese, although admitted to be a suitable food for labouring men, was not approved by the physicians, and the well-to-do avoided it altogether, or ate a little only at the end of a meal to close the stomach.

Soft cheese, with its greater content of cream and richer flavour, was less harmful. When cheese was identified in the cookery books of the nobility, usually in recipes for cheese tarts, it was described as 'good fat cheese', and occasionally the favourite kind of all, known as 'Rewain' or 'Irwene' was called for. The Anglo-Norman cheese tart was titled 'Tart de Bry', and this suggests that brie had already acquired some fame in France, even though in England the recipe might be made up with Rewain or other rich cheese. But medieval brie may not have resembled today's brie very closely, for types of cheese did not become fixed in their modern cast until much later.

Another soft cheese was eddish or after-math cheese, made from the milk of cows that had grazed the damp autumn grasses of the second growth after the hay had been harvested. In some accounts this cheese is equated with Rewain, and in one, of the late thirteenth century, the milking of cows after Michaelmas in order to make Rewain cheese is interdicted on the grounds that it weakened the cows too much. Eddish cheese had a different quality from high summer cheese because in colder weather the milk was slow to acidify, the curds would not drain properly, and the cheese 'will be soft always'.[16]

Green cheese was fresh moist curd cheese. 'Green cheese is not called green by the reason of colour, but for the newness of it, for the whey is not half pressed out of it.' It was often drained on a mat of nettle leaves and stalks, and came to be known as nettle cheese.

A special form of green cheese was junket. It too had its origins in Norman France, where the cheeses were drained in

Milking sheep
From *Luttrell Psalter*

Milking a cow
From *English rural life in the middle ages*

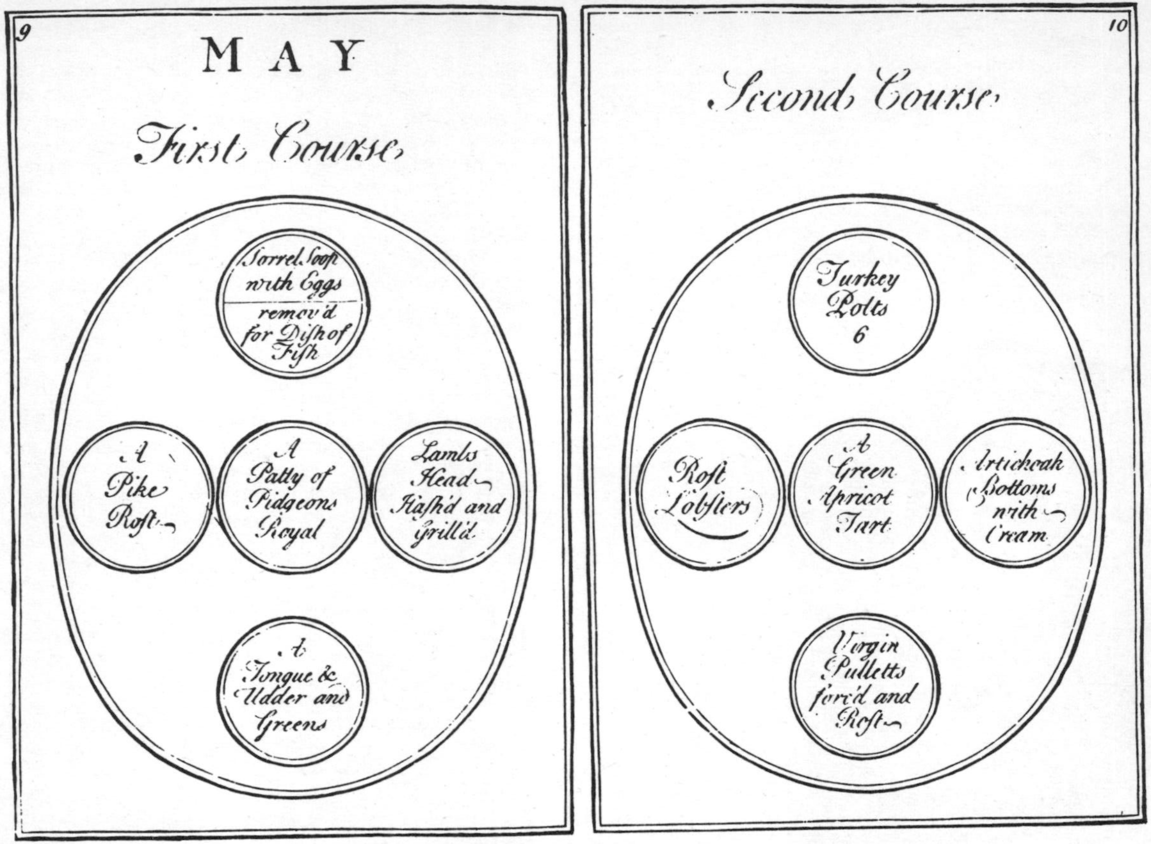

18th century menu for May
From *The whole duty of a woman*, 1737

little rush baskets (*jonquets*) used in the same manner as the mats of nettles in England. Junket was a very rich confection (too rich to be eaten with impunity late in the evening), comprising pure cream curdled with rennet. In course of time it became customary to mingle sugar and rosewater with the curd, and the junket was eaten as a sweetmeat at the end of a meal.

'Spermyse' was the name given to curd cheese to which chopped herbs or their juices were added. Many different herbs were 'jumbled' in spermyse, for every country housewife had her own private recipe for it. The making of herb-flavoured cheeses was a continuous tradition that went back to Roman times, and probably to far earlier days.

Also traditional was the employment of certain herbs to induce the curdling of milk. In fact herb coagulants are weaker than rennet and tend to produce bitter flavours in the cheese. But they remained in use in some parts of Britain until the nineteenth century.[17]

In cookery cheese went sometimes into wafers, and often into the tarts which the gentry enjoyed. The Countess of Leicester's household accounts, for instance, show that on 16 May 1265 she spent ninepence on 'cheese for tarts', while on the 22nd of the same month three cheeses from the manor dairy were supplied to her for further tarts. Rich, tender cheese was used for the purpose. It was not grated, but had to be reduced in the mortar before being mixed with egg yolks, ginger, cinnamon and sugar to make the tart filling. In one fifteenth-century recipe it was even tempered with milk to the consistency of raw cream. Other tarts contained green cheese, which was naturally soft, and was sometimes mingled with meat and dried fruit.

Harder cheese was grated to be eaten with 'macrows', the prototype of macaroni, or was brayed in the mortar with pork and spices to make a tasty meat loaf that was roasted and batter-basted; while cheese of an unidentified type was boiled with milk and butter to be added to eggs and herbs for a fifteenth-century 'herbolace'. Toasted cheese was very popular in Wales, where it was something of a national dish in Tudor times.[18]

Butter was the other principal milk product. The manner of

making it had changed little since Pliny's day. The chief innovation, adopted early in the Middle Ages, was the wooden plunger which passed through a hole in the lid of the tall churn and was worked up and down by hand, thus bringing the cream within to a solid state more quickly than the simple shaking of the churn itself.

Even the churn was not in universal use. As late as the eighteenth century butter was made in Devon and other parts of the west country from scalded cream which was placed in large open bowls or tubs and churned solely with the naked hands of the milkmaid.[19]

When butter was made in the churn, the milk was first left to stand for some time in wide shallow bowls for the cream to rise. The first skimming produced the finest butter; and the cream of the second rising was skimmed some hours later for butter of an inferior quality. The worst butter of all was the whey butter made from the curds that rose on the whey after full-cream milk had been renneted and drained for cheese.

The cream was strained into the churn through a clean, strong cloth, and was agitated with swift strokes until the sound of the beating began to change as the butter formed. It was then gathered together into a single lump and lifted from the buttermilk.

The next stage depended upon the projected use of the butter. Sweet butter for immediate consumption was beaten in fresh water until it was free of buttermilk and then slightly salted. Salt butter for long keeping was made by working out the buttermilk by hand alone (water caused the butter to go reesty) and then beating salt or strong brine into it. It was packed into well-glazed earthenware pots or wooden casks with more salt strewn over it. Because butter easily became rancid, especially if any buttermilk remained in it, it was salted very heavily in medieval times. According to a record of 1305 one pound of salt was required for every ten pounds of butter or cheese produced in the dairy at Overton Manor, on the estates of the Bishop of Winchester. But it was customary to wash out most of the salt in water before the butter was used.[20]

Butter intended for cooking purposes was clarified. It was melted and strained and then put up into pots and kept for use.

In early summer May butter was prepared for the benefit of children. Thomas Cogan described how it was made by setting new, unsalted butter on open platters out in the sun for twelve to fourteen days. This bleached out the colour and much of the vitamin A, and made the butter very rancid. But it acquired extra vitamin D from exposure to the sun's rays, and thus had some curative power for children with rickets or pains in the joints.[21]

Ordinary butter was thought to be good for growing children and for old men in their decline, but 'very unwholesome betwixt those two ages'. Children were given 'bread smeared with butter in the Flemish fashion', as a Venetian visitor to England noted shortly before 1500.

The poor ate much butter with bread and also with herbs. The well-to-do viewed it more cautiously, in the belief that it lingered at the top of the stomach 'as the fatness doth swim above in a boiling pot'. Proverbially, butter was gold in the morning, silver at noon and lead at night, so that breakfast was the most suitable meal at which to eat it.

It was however taken as an aperitif before dinner along with such fruits as plums, damsons, grapes and cherries. And despite the warnings of the physicians it was eaten extensively upon fish days.[22]

Its oiliness also gave it some value as a laxative. 'Some which have been wonted to a fine diet, and to eat no bread but manchet, by eating of brown bread and butter in a morning fasting (which is a country man's breakfast) have been made as soluble as if they had taken some purgation.' In producing this effect, the branny brown bread must have been quite as active as the butter.

The pattern of butter consumption among the well-to-do is not clearly defined by the household accounts of the later medieval period, for the butter of the gentry was usually produced on the manor, and was only noted when a special additional purchase was made. But it appears that although children ate butter in Lent, adults who kept the fast strictly avoided it then.

Olive oil was bought for fish frying; while almond butter could be served at table in place of the more usual kind. Fasting days at other times of year were not so stringently observed; and by the mid-sixteenth century the eating of butter and buttered eggs had become acceptable in Lent too.[23]

On ordinary fast days the fish could be fried in clarified butter, while sweet butter supplied a sauce for salt fish, stockfish, whiting and mackerel. Alternatively bread and one or more dishes of butter were laid upon the table to be eaten with the fasting-day fish.

In other branches of cookery butter was an enricher, the accompaniment of cheese in herbolaces or with macaroni; of eggs, milk and sugar in the filling for a flathon; of plain or fancy breads in *pain perdu* or rastons. For short pastry and cakes, it was at first an alternative to fresh cream, but eventually superseded it, for butter had a more highly concentrated fat content, and was more easily stored. It served too to baste roasting meat, and to seal the contents of a cold pie for long keeping.

Nevertheless butter appeared in a relatively small proportion of the dishes in medieval recipe books, which were written mainly for and by the cooks of the nobility. It was only in Tudor times that an emerging middle class, which did not despise butter as the food of the poor, began to use it liberally in every possible sphere of cookery, setting a trend that was to last for some two hundred years.

Early modern period

The changeover to the cow as the universal milch animal of Britain had begun by the sixteenth century, but was by no means completed then. The huge, hard, sharp-flavoured cheeses that reached Elizabethan London from south-east Essex were produced from skimmed ewes' milk; and in some mountainous parts of Wales, northern England and Scotland both goats and ewes were suppliers of milk at a much later date. In the eighteenth century the more backward sheepmasters of Northumberland were still milking their ewes; fat ewes' milk was mixed with skimmed cows' milk to make cheese in the vale of Glamorgan; while the milkmen of the Scottish highlands carried down the milk of any or all of the three milch animals in goat-skins slung over their shoulder, from which they sold it in the nearest village or town.[24]

In lowland Britain cows' milk virtually superseded all other kinds during the seventeenth century. But it was no longer the stay and support of ordinary country folk. During the late Tudor period the price of victuals rose steeply, and wages did not keep pace. Moreover landlords enclosed substantial parts of what had formerly been the common grazing land, so that fewer labourers could afford to keep a cow.

In the next century enclosure continued, and as a result there were now more milch cows in the country than ever before; but increasingly they were kept in the fields belonging to farms or large estates. Their owners found it more profitable to convert their milk straight into cheese and butter, and sell it at local markets or send it to the larger towns. Some of the whey and buttermilk was also sold in the towns: both were popular drinks until the end of the eighteenth century. Most of the rest was utilized as pig food, and little of it now reached the country labourer in southern or midland England. By the eighteenth century his share of white meats was almost confined to butter and cheese, and not much of either of those in years of dearth and high prices. People in northern England, Scotland and Wales fared better, for more open grazing land was to be had, and milch animals were more often kept by small farmers who would sell milk directly to the local people.

From Tudor times onwards the towns of Britain were constantly expanding and as they grew the problems of urban milk supply had to be met. During the Middle Ages cows had usually grazed not far beyond the town walls. Their milk was sold in the markets along with other dairy produce; and the townspeople themselves often walked out to the neighbouring farms when they wished to purchase fresh milk.

By the later seventeenth century milk was being purveyed in a more regular fashion. There were town dairy shops in Restoration

London; and milkmaids walked the streets bearing pails slung from yolks across their shoulders, and sold milk from door to door. Some may have worked for the dairy shops, but in smaller towns the milkmaids themselves brought the milk in from the surrounding countryside. Those of eighteenth-century Edinburgh rode in on horseback with buttermilk (called 'sour-dook') in barrels strapped to their saddles, as well as supplies of fresh milk, though the latter was also carried round more conventionally in pails.

The establishment of dairy shops was closely connected with the new practice of keeping cows within the towns. In some places farms formerly on the outskirts were engulfed by streets and buildings. Elsewhere town dairies were deliberately set up to meet the increasing demand for milk within the larger conurbations such as London and Liverpool. There the animals were both housed and fed, for it was no longer possible to graze them in the open country. Some of the big dairies of London were well kept, but all too often the cows lived in insanitary sheds and basements and ate the rankest fodder. Brewers' grains, cabbage leaves and bean shells were used by the cowkeepers of Moorfields early in the eighteenth century, and during the bean season the milk, according to a contemporary writer, carried a strong flavour of beanpods.

Town milk was often diluted with water by the milkmen; and furthermore, since it was carried through the streets in open pails, was liable to have all sorts of filth either blown or thrown into it. Such milk was in any case of poor quality, owing to the unsuitable way in which the cows were fed and cared for; and whether it was watered or not, it was well skimmed of all its cream before it was sold. The 'blue milk' mentioned occasionally in eighteenth-century recipe books must have been town milk.[25]

The safest way to buy milk was straight from the cow, and sometimes the animals were driven through the streets and milked at house doors, so that the customers could enjoy their output while it was still new and warm. Alternatively cows could be found grazing in certain open spaces, such as St James's park in London, where their milk was sold, and often drunk, on the spot.

Not only cows but also asses were driven through the streets to be milked on demand. Asses' milk retained its reputation as invalid food, and it was often bought on behalf of sick people or young children.

Country cattle on the larger estates now fared better than before. From the mid-seventeenth century onwards progressive farmers took an interest in stockbreeding and in the growing of new fodder crops, which resulted in a rise in both quality and quantity of milk produced.

In southern and midland England less and less was sold off fresh for drinking; and beer became the countryman's usual beverage, later supplemented by tea. It was only in the northern counties that, even at the end of the eighteenth century, 'the general drink of the labouring classes is whey or milk; or rather milk and water'. Much fresh milk was still drunk by all classes in Scotland. In southern Britain that which was consumed by the well-to-do and by people of the middling sort more often went into cooked dishes or made drinks; though sometimes the ladies of the gentry turned their dairies into elegant rooms, adorned with pieces of fine china, and took their friends there to drink syllabubs and milk warm from the cow.[26]

In cookery milk continued to be heated with bread or flour to make pap for children and invalids, and with wheat or other cereal for frumenty and similar milk porridges. As puddings increasingly took the place of the earlier thick pottages, milk was often the liquid in which the breadcrumbs, rice, sago, oatmeal or other basic ingredient was softened.

Milk was already in use in possets, and it came to be of importance for the new beverages of the seventeenth century. Chocolate was at first mixed with wine, but it was not long before milk became an acceptable alternative. Tea and coffee were sweetened but otherwise taken neat for some decades. Then milk began to be added to tea, perhaps in order to diminish its supposed pernicious side effects. A similar addition was later made to coffee.

The almond milk of medieval times did not survive into an age that was more relaxed in its observation of the Lenten fast. In a few confections animal milk took its place. One such was a lechemeat based upon calves' foot broth and milk of almonds, sometimes left in its natural colour and sometimes coloured red. It was allowed to cool and set, and was cut into leaches (slices) and eaten with a wine sauce. The pale form became known as white leach.

It was then developed with dairy milk or cream, flavoured with spices and rosewater and mixed with a portion of beaten almonds, in place of the original almond milk, while isinglass was substituted for calves' foot jelly. By the mid-seventeenth century the almonds were often omitted altogether. White leach (and sometimes coloured leach made from similar recipes) was a favourite dish for the Tudor and Stuart banquet and it retained its popularity into the eighteenth century.[27]

But already in some households it had acquired a new name: flummery (the earlier, traditional flummery was distinguished in later cookery books as 'oatmeal flummery'). It usually consisted of spiced cream set with calves' foot, isinglass or hartshorn jelly, though in some recipes ground almonds were used in place of cream. It could be coloured in the same manner as clear jellies. Flummery was eaten in the second course with cream or wine poured over it. For special occasions it was made up in moulds to produce set-piece dishes, such as flummery fish in a jelly pond, or flummery eggs in a hen's nest of shredded lemon peel in jelly.[28]

Cream was still consumed at all levels of society in Tudor times. During the next centuries it ceased to be 'a rural man's banquet'; but among the more well-to-do it was added increasingly to made dishes and sauces. Whereas the most sumptuous medieval fare had been marked by its content of spices, sugar, dried fruits and wine, that of the eighteenth century was rich with butter and cream.

Among the creamy dishes of the Tudor and Stuart period were trifles, fools and white pots. An Elizabethan trifle was made thus: 'Take a pint of thick cream, and season it with sugar and ginger, and rosewater, so stir it as you would then have it, and make it luke warm in a dish on a chafingdish and coals, and after put it into a silver piece or bowl, and so serve it to the board.'

In later recipes the cream was boiled and lightly renneted to make it thicker and 'when you serve it in, strew on some French comfits'. By 1751 trifle was being made with broken Naples biscuits, macaroons and ratafia cakes wetted with sack at the bottom of the bowl, good boiled custard in the middle, and 'then put a syllabub over that'. Subsequent recipes replaced the syllabub with whipped cream, milled in a chocolate mill; and the modern trifle was established.[29]

Norfolk fool was seasoned cream thickened with eggs and boiled; and whitepot, sometimes called Devonshire whitepot, contained the same ingredients together with currants, and was baked in a pot or pan. Both were popular during the seventeenth century. Fresh or boiled cream, sweetened and mingled with fruit pulp, beaten almonds or sack, stirred in carefully to prevent curdling, was a confection for the second course or supper during the seventeenth and eighteenth centuries. Sage cream, a quart of boiled cream seasoned with the juice of red sage, rosewater and sugar, was another variant, said to be an excellent dish.[30]

Clotted cream was prepared by leaving new milk in shallow bowls over a low fire for several hours, making sure that it never came to the boil. It could be rendered still richer with additional fresh cream. By the 1650s the clotted cream of the west country had become more widely known, and the Countess of Kent's recipe for such cream is titled 'How to scald milk after the western fashion'.

Clotted cream was eaten alone with sugar, or with fresh cream. It could be formed into 'cabbage cream' if the skins of cream were lifted carefully from the bowls with a skimmer, and were built up in a dish 'round and high like a cabbage'. Sugar and rosewater were sprinkled between the layers.[31]

Ice cream began to be made in the eighteenth century (one result of the development of ice-houses on country estates). At first it was prepared in tin icing pots with close-fitting lids which were buried in pails full of ice; and the contents could be 'any sorts of cream you please, either plain or sweetened'. But after a few years proper ice cream recipes were evolved, in which finely sieved apricots or other fruits were worked together with sugar and scalded cream. In some, the use of raspberry or peach jam in place of fresh fruit was advocated. Sets of pewter basins, an inner, smaller one to contain the cream and an outer larger one to hold ice all round it, were produced by the pewterers for makers of ice cream. It was also discovered that the cream set more evenly if it was removed periodically from the ice and beaten to prevent the formation of large ice crystals in its texture. The brown bread ice (half a pint of brown breadcrumbs, one and a half pints of cream and some sugar) was introduced later in the century, but never acquired the popularity of the fruit and cream ices.[32]

Cream was whipped with egg whites to make the dish known as 'snow'. Cream beaten frothy with whisks or rods was eaten with raw cream and sugar in a recipe of the 1660s. Three or four decades later chocolate mills came into general use, and it was found that cream could be made still frothier if it was worked through such a mill. The whipped cream was eaten by itself in glasses, or spread over tarts; and later it became a covering for trifles.

The syllabub of Tudor and Stuart times was a confection of white wine, cider or fruit juice, well sweetened with sugar and flavoured with lemon or nutmeg, to which cream or milk was added with considerable force. Instructions of 1655 advised spooning cream in 'as hard as you can, as though you milk it in'. Other recipes recommended milking the cow directly on to the liquor in the syllabub pot; and by 1696 it was possible to 'squirt your milk and cream into the pot with a wooden cow sold at the turners'. The object was to produce a frothy head to the drink, with a clear liquid below. The latter was drunk from the spout of the syllabub pot, while the creamy foam was eaten as spoonmeat.

Non-alcoholic syllabubs were made on a base of orange or

lemon whey (the thin liquid that resulted when milk and fruit juice were mixed, and the curd removed): and these may have been the fruit syllabubs sold at the little cake-houses in the Kings Mead at Bath 'to entertain the company that walk there' when Celia Fiennes visited the town in the 1680s.

In Georgian times the cow, wooden or otherwise, was abandoned in favour of the hand-held whisk with which cream and wine, mingled usually with a little lemon juice and grated lemon peel, were frothed together. Whipped-cream syllabubs were a well-loved dessert dish all through the eighteenth century. They were served in special syllabub glasses, so that the effect of the creamy whip above contrasting with the clear liquid below could be fully appreciated.

The same period saw the apogee of cream cookery. Butter had long been an important cooking medium, but now cream was added liberally to braises, fricassees, cakes, puddings and sauces. Even boiled spinach had to have half a pint of cream and a quarter of a pound of butter beaten into it before it was sufficiently 'dressed' to appear 'for a supper or a side-dish at a second course in the homes of the well-to-do.[33]

In dairying districts where skim milk was sold off locally whey or whig was still a summer drink for country people. It went up in the world in the middle years of the seventeenth century when whey-houses were opened in London where the fashionable could go to drink it. Whey was also sold in the town streets, as was buttermilk.

Whey was particularly approved as a springtime drink, when its purgative properties were believed to cleanse the blood. To this end herb juices were sometimes added to it. In the eighteenth century whey was made at home by curdling blue milk with cream of tartar; or with scurvy-grass juice and old verjuice, when it was 'very good to drink in the spring for the scurvy'.[34]

Both sour milk and buttermilk remained important in the diet of the highland zone. Buttermilk from south Wales was sent over in barrels to Bristol, where large quantities were sold in the eighteenth century. It was plentiful in Scotland too, and 'sour-dook' was a regular summer drink in Edinburgh. In some parts of the country whey or buttermilk was boiled with oatmeal to make porridge. Buttermilk was used to mix scones and other girdle cakes. The Shetlanders, who lacked malt-liquors, made 'bland' by fermenting the whey drained from their buttermilk in oaken casks for a few months. When sweetened, it was claimed to be indistinguishable from the best mountain wine.

In Skye a drink called 'oon', 'which in English signifies froth', was made by boiling goats' or other milk or whey, and then working it up with a long wooden stick with a cross at the lower end until it frothed at the mouth of the pot; 'and being thus made, it is supped with spoons. It is made up five or six times in the same manner, and the last is always reckoned the best.'[35]

The 'wild Irish' in the early seventeenth century still fed mostly upon white meats, delighting in milk warmed with pot-boiler stones. Fynes Moryson reported that they 'esteem for a great dainty sour curds, vulgarly called by them Bonaclabbe'. The reputation of bonny-clabber spread to England. Instructions of 1653 advised leaving renneted milk to stand for two days when 'it will be all in a curd, then season it with some sugar, cinnamon and cream, then serve it, this is best in the hottest of the summer'.

In the same book was a recipe, not dissimilar, for junket in modern style which differed from medieval junket in that the curd was not broken and drained. 'Take ewes or goats milk, if you have neither of these then take cows milk, and put it over the fire to warm, then put in a little rennet to it, then pour it out into a dish, and let it cool, then strew on cinnamon and sugar.' It was eaten with clotted cream and more sugar.

The earlier form of junket continued as a dish for the banquet, but by Elizabeth's reign it had acquired the new name of fresh cheese (perhaps a corruption of French cheese). The creamy curd was flavoured at first with cinnamon, later with nutmeg, and with rosewater and sugar, and the fresh cheese was always eaten with fresh cream. It went out of fashion in the eighteenth century, in favour of the numerous unrenneted creams of the day.[36]

Curds were still incorporated in certain cooked dishes which had survived from medieval times. The spiced cheese tarts of that period were continued in tarts of curds which were still known as cheesecakes in the seventeenth century (as they are today). Fresh curds formed the basis of the filling, supported by eggs, spices and sometimes currants. By the middle of the century some cheesecake recipes contained neither cheese nor curds, but instead a rich custardy mixture of eggs, butter, flour and unrenneted cream, duly sweetened and spiced.

A further development a few decades later was the lemon cheesecake. Its filling consisted of pounded lemon peel, egg yolks, sugar and butter: in fact, it was what we now call lemon-cheese, or lemon-curd. Orange cheesecakes were made in similar fashion, from the skins of Seville oranges which were first boiled in two or three waters to take off their bitterness.[37]

The traditional curd fritters were still enjoyed, as were spiced curd-enriched loaves which were eaten hot with sugar and butter as buttered loaves. Curds were tried out in boiled puddings, but were more successful in baked ones for which they were mingled with eggs, cream or butter and dried or crystallized fruits. All required cheese-curds from the dairy, and when these were not available milk had to be deliberately set, renneted and strained to make them.

Posset drinks in which milk was curdled by amalgamation with an acid liquid were still acceptable beverages. A mid-seventeenth-century 'posset simple' was made thus: 'Boil your milk in a clean scoured skillet, and when it boils take it off, and warm in the pot, bowl or basin, some sack, claret, beer, ale or juice of orange; pour it into the drink, but let not your milk be too hot, for it will make the curd hard, then sugar it.'

Ordinary eating posset was produced by adding breadcrumbs to ale or beer posset. Rich eating posset for the gentry was made with cream and sack (later, sherry) or brandy reinforced with eggs, grated Naples biscuits or beaten almonds.[38]

Curds were becoming less prominent in the nation's diet, but cheese waxed in importance. A sucking-calf's stomach-bag was now the usual source of rennet. The bags might be salted, dried and hung in the chimney to keep, as they were in Lancashire and elsewhere: a small piece cut off and boiled in water then produced the rennet. Alternatively they were salted and potted up in their own brine. The practice of putting back the curd to 'feed' the bag in the brine was eventually abandoned.

But even in the eighteenth century it was thought necessary to add herbs and spices to the rennet to counteract any strong disagreeable flavour it might have acquired, and these in turn seasoned the cheese. 'As for the famous Stilton cheese', wrote Richard Bradley in 1736, 'we are to make the rennet strong of mace, by boiling the mace in the salt and water, for without that is done, the cheese will not have the true relish that the first famous Stilton cheeses had'.[39]

Skim milk, whole milk and cream cheeses were still made, the methods of manufacture varying in different parts of the country. The richest cheeses assumed a golden hue as they matured. As a result the practice arose of colouring other cheeses artifically. Saffron was one dye used, but it was expensive and marigold petals were found to be a satisfactory substitute. Towards the end of the eighteenth century 'Spanish' annatto from the West Indies was employed as a colorant for the cheaper grades of Cheshire and north Wales cheese, and its use then spread to other parts of the country. A finishing touch was put to the best cheeses by scrubbing their outsides with a brush and then rubbing them over with whey butter to give them 'a fine saleable yellow-colour'd coat'.[40]

On large farms it was easy to make large cheeses from each milking. But in the west and north-west farms were often small, and individuals continued to own single cows; and here cheese was sometimes produced on a co-operative basis. In Cheshire villages, as at Cheddar, it was 'the custom of the country to join their milking together of a whole village and so make their great cheeses and so it goes round'.[41]

Local cheeses now became more widely known than in medieval times. By the seventeenth century there were noted cheese fairs at Weyhill in Wiltshire, Burford in Oxfordshire, St Giles' Hill in Hampshire, Atherstone-on-Stour in Warwickshire and several other places, besides the more general fairs, like the famous one at Stourbridge, where dairy produce was always on sale. There cheese was purchased for family consumption.

Now merchants, factors and pedlars appeared at the same markets and fairs, and bought up cheeses to resell at a distance. Fine-flavoured ones were selected for sale to rich clients; and poor, hard ones for those who wanted cheap, serviceable cheese to feed to servants and labourers. Towards the end of the century the cheesemongers of London formed themselves into an unofficial guild, and their factors travelled all through the cheese-making counties procuring cheeses in great numbers. These were shipped by sea, river and later by canal, or were sent by land-carriage to London, where the cheesemongers were able to make their own prices.

The ill-famed skim-milk cheese from Essex and Suffolk was still badly thought of in 1661 when Pepys' wife was 'vexed at her people for grumbling to eat Suffolk cheese'; and in 1724 when Defoe wrote of High Suffolk that it was 'famous for the best butter, and perhaps the worst cheese in England'.[42] It was nevertheless bought up in large quantities to feed labourers and the London poor.

Banbury and Cheshire cheeses had a better reputation. Thomas Cogan commended both, but deemed Banbury the best, 'for therein you shall neither taste the rennet nor salt, which be two special properties of good cheese'.

Some of his contemporaries preferred foreign cheeses to any native product. Barnaby Googe's view in 1577 was that Parmesan was the finest of all, Dutch (an early version of Edam) next best, Normandy third and English last. Parmesan was greatly admired at this time, 'by age waxing mellower and softer and more pleasant of taste, digesting whatsoever went before it, yet itself not heavy of digestion'.

During the seventeenth century Cheddar cheese acquired considerable fame. It was rich, and at first was 'seldom seen but at noblemen's tables, or rich vintners' cellars'. A recipe for home-made Cheddar cheese, published in 1727, shows that it was produced by working three pounds of butter into curd from milk already augmented by extra cream, which explains why it was more expensive than other cheeses.[43]

At the village of Cheddar Defoe witnessed co-operative cheese making during his travels in the 1720s. He described how everyone in the village grazed one or more cows on the village green, how the villagers pooled their milk, every man's quantity being noted down carefully after each milking, and how 'every meal's milk makes one cheese, and no more; so that the cheese is bigger, or less, as the cows yield more, or less, milk. By this method, the goodness of the cheese is preserved, and without all dispute, it is the best cheese that *England* affords, if not, that the whole world affords.' The cheeses were at their best between two and five years old, and individual ones weighed from thirty to a hundred pounds.[44]

Cheshire cheese, also made on a co-operative basis, was not considered to have reached its best until it was at least a year old. The cheeses had to be turned very often and rubbed with a dry cloth (as had all long-keeping cheeses) while they were coming to maturity. Imitation Cheshire cheeses made at home could be improved if, after a year, a hole was bored in the middle, filled with a quarter pint of sack and then stopped up. Six months later the cheese would have mellowed, and the sack and hole have disappeared.[45]

Stilton came to the fore early in the eighteenth century. Defoe called it the English Parmesan, and wrote that it was 'brought to table with the mites or maggots round it so thick that they bring a spoon with them for you to eat the mites with as you do the cheese.'[46]

At about the same time writers began to sing the praises of the cheeses produced in the vale of Gloucester and in adjoining parts of north Wiltshire. Single Gloucester cheeses were thin, and were made between April and November, sometimes, but not always, from semi-skimmed milk; double Gloucester were thick, and were made when the milk was at its richest and most plentiful in early summer.

Skimmed-milk cheeses were very common. But the only one that had a tolerable reputation was the Blue Vinney of Dorset, pressed from sour skimmed milk collected from several days' milkings, which yielded a very acid curd. Part of this cheese developed streaks of blue mould.[47]

Some of the rich, fatty Yorkshire dale cheeses also acquired internal blue moulds after a time, caused by dampness in a wet loose-textured curd. The moulds supplied a special tang that appealed to connoisseurs of food flavours. But before and during the eighteenth century such cheeses as Wensleydale, Nidderdale, Coverdale and Swaledale were still marketed locally and rarely reached other parts of Britain.

Welsh cheese, described in 1662 as 'very tender and palatable', was not all for home consumption. The dairy farmers of the vale of Glamorgan supplied Bristol and the Somerset ports. Those of north Wales found a more distant market when the demand for Cheshire cheese increased, and large amounts were shipped from Chester and Liverpool to London and the south-east. Soon 'Cheshire' cheese was produced in north Welsh dairies too, and was despatched from Chester along with the cheeses actually made in the county. During the eighteenth century 'thick strong Cheshire cheese' was the favourite cooking cheese in many parts of the south-east, and was regarded as a frugal eating cheese, for a little went a long way.[48]

Scottish cheese was only sold locally. It was cheap, but of poor quality, for Scottish dairy farmers preferred to turn their milk into butter. Ayrshire eventually produced a slightly better cheese, based on full instead of skimmed milk, but even in 1826 this was still described as 'not a very delicate cheese for the table'.[49] It was later to achieve fame under the name of Dunlop.

In all dairy districts soft curd cheeses continued to be made in the summer months. Slipcoat cheese, also known as water cheese, was popular in the seventeenth and eighteenth centuries. A recipe of the 1650s gave five pints of new milk, one quart of water and one spoonful of rennet as appropriate quantities; but in some other recipes the proportions of milk and water were varied. The curd was taken up without breaking and was drained in the vat, at first by itself and then under weights. After a few hours the cheese was removed and salted. 'Then let him lie a day or a night, then put nettles under and upon him, and change them once a day: the cheese will come to his eating in eight or nine days.' Some advocated a richer cheese, based upon 'stroakings' (the last and creamiest milk coaxed from the cow at the end of milking).[50] Slipcoat and other nettle cheeses were usually made little more than an inch thick, so that they could dry and ripen quickly.

The richest curd cheeses were those for which the cream from the previous milking was put to the new milk or stroakings. The Normandy Angelot was of this type, much admired in Tudor and Stuart England and copied there for the tables of the gentry. Later some of the locally made cream cheeses gained a wider reputation, and recipes such as that for making 'the thick square cream-cheese as at Newport' were published in cookery books.[51]

Country housewives may still have made a variety of herb-flavoured cheeses in the tradition of spermyse, but in polite circles cheeses were now often coloured and flavoured with the juice of marigolds, spinach or sage. They were served at the banquet course of Tudor and Stuart times. 'So soon as the meat [i.e. food] is quite taken away, have in readiness your cream cheeses of several sorts and of several colours upon a salver, then some fresh cheese with wine and sugar, another dish of clotted cream, and another with cabbage cream of several colours like a cabbage; then all sorts of fruits in season. . . .'[52]

Sage cheese held its popularity through the eighteenth century. It was green cheese within the narrower meaning of the term; and if it was not green enough, 'spinach juice is added to it to make it more bright to the sight; it also serves to take off the bitterness of the sage'.

At this time 'sage cheese in figures' was admired. A sage cheese and a plain cheese were prepared, and pressed for half an hour. Then equivalent pieces or figures were cut from each by means of tinplate shapes made for the purpose. They were most effective if the cheeses were no more that two inches thick. The pieces were exchanged, and after further pressing the cheeses emerged one green with white figures in it and the other white with green. They were ripened for eight months before eating. A variant was 'marigold and sage cheese in chequer work'.[53]

For most people cream or herb cheeses were no more than an

extra summer treat. Mature cheese was for everyday eating, and it was still consumed, as in medieval times, at the end of a meal. In the mid-eighteenth century among those who were comfortably off and who dined upon meat with vegetables, and a pudding, 'cheese nearly always concludes the meal. Commonly, there is set on the table, whole, a large and strong cheese, and each person cuts what he likes from it.'[54]

Cheese usage in cookery also remained close to medieval practice. The fifteenth-century herbolace was succeeded by the cheese omelette. Robert May's recipe has quite a modern ring: 'Slice cheese very thin, beat it with the eggs, and a little salt, then melt some butter in the pan, and fry it.' He also advocated grated cheese with buttered (scrambled) eggs; and thought it gave a good relish to poached eggs if scattered over them in the dish.

Toasted cheese, castigated in Elizabeth's day by Dr Thomas Cogan, who said that 'roasted cheese is more meet to bait a trap, to catch a mouse or rat, than to be received into the body', continued to be eaten with enjoyment; and as time went on, more complex versions were devised. Sir Kenelm Digby had a tasty one, the cheese being melted with butter and chopped asparagus, gammon, onions, cibols or anchovies. Other recipes combined grated cheese with breadcrumbs, egg yolks and butter, and browned the mixture on slices of toast. Simple toasted cheese appeared as 'Welsh rabbit' in Hannah Glasse's *The Art of Cookery*, along with Scotch and English rabbits. For the English version, the toast was soaked in wine, and in other cookery books the cheese was sometimes stewed in wine too.

Wine also enhanced the flavour of potted cheese. Following the success of potting in other fields, strong mature Cheshire cheese was potted too, though in a rather different way. One and a half pounds of cheese shaved thin, half a pound of fresh butter, a quarter of an ounce of mace and a glass of sack were beaten and incorporated together. 'Then put it in a pot, what thickness you please, and cut it out in slices for cream cheese, and serve it with the dessert.'[55]

Cheese tarts made in medieval style survived into the

Elizabethan era. One recipe of that time shows that hard cheese had to be sliced and laid in water or milk for three hours before being broken up in the mortar, strained with egg yolks, seasoned with sugar and butter and baked. Thereafter fresh curd tarts, the latter-day cheesecakes, became more usual.

Continental influence extended the use of cheese in cookery from the mid-seventeenth century onwards. The French had a long tradition of adding cheese to pottage. Recipes for the Jacobins' pottage (named from the French Jacobins or Dominican friars) were now to be found in several English cookery books. An early version, of 1655, began: 'Take the flesh of a washed capon or turkey cold, mince it so small as you can, then grate or scrape among the flesh two or three ounces of Parmesan, or old Holland cheese, season it with beaten cloves, nutmeg, mace and salt.' The pottage was really a form of hash.[56]

In the course of the next decade or two, grated cheese was included in other recipes for hashed meat, in forcemeat for fowls, and in 'little pasties, called in Italian tortelleti'. In the last the cheese was mingled in a filling of minced meat, herbs, spices and egg yolks, 'and serve them with sugar, cinnamon and grated cheese in a fine clean dish'. These dishes of foreign inspiration were eaten by only a small section of the population, but they pointed the way to a greater use of cheese in later English cookery.

In the eighteenth century the concept of toasted cheese and that of grated cheese sprinkled over cooked food were amalgamated with the introduction of a cheese topping for some vegetables. Cardoons, Mediterranean plants of the artichoke family, were among the first to receive such treatment in the French-inspired *chardoons à la fromage*. Stewed in gravy which was afterwards thickened, they were covered with grated Parmesan or Cheshire cheese which was browned with a hot cheese-iron. The recipe was soon adapted for cauliflowers. Macaroni, boiled, drained and tossed in cream, was also treated to a cheese covering. A hot salamander (a utensil developed for the purpose), held over the top, could brown the cheese; failing that, a heated fire shovel was recommended.[57]

Cheese was incorporated in a relatively small proportion of cooked dishes. But butter, oilier, more malleable and less strongly tasted, was in constant use, both in the cooking processes and as a sauce. For many years it was still produced in the traditional upright churn. Only in the later eighteenth century did the barrel churn, hung horizontally and with paddles turned by two handles to agitate the cream within, become the usual butter-making vessel. For long keeping, butter was put up in earthware pots or wooden tubs, well packed with salt above and below and topped up with heavy brine. If one day's churning was not enough to fill the pot, the butter was laid in layers, each sealed with salt; and the resultant potfuls must have varied greatly in their degree of saltiness.

The best summer butter, made when the cows had browsed the fresh young grass, was rich and golden. It therefore became customary to colour paler butters, such as after-butter, whey-butter or the butter of wintertime, with juice expressed from marigold petals or even carrots, so that they would sell more readily. Market places always had an area devoted to dairy produce, and many of the stone-built butter-markets erected during the seventeenth and eighteenth centuries to protect the perishable butter and cream can still be seen today. Butter could also be purchased at chandlers' shops.

Some was sent for sale far beyond the local market town. London demanded great amounts. Epping butter was the favourite among Londoners. But higglers bought up sweet butter from dairies within a radius of forty miles of the city, so as to resell it there. Much of London's butter came from Suffolk (where the butter was as good as the cheese was bad), and more from Yorkshire, and these butters were salted in pots or barrels and conveyed by sea. In other parts of the country, butter made shorter journeys to market, usually by road or inland waterway, though Glamorganshire butter was sent across the channel to Bristol.[58]

At market the best and sweetest butter sold at a higher figure than whey-butter or the butter of the second skimming called also after-butter. The latter two were paler in colour, were apt to be somewhat rank in flavour, and soon became rancid. It was as well for customers to be circumspect: unscrupulous sellers sometimes put a piece of fresh sweet butter in the middle of the whey- or after-butter, and offered it as a tasting morsel to prospective buyers.

The poor still ate butter, as they had always done, as a relish with their bread. Bread and butter with herbs were a country breakfast.[59] And as long as fasting days were kept, butter was eaten frequently with salt fish. With an increasing population, growing towns and a gradual decline in the supply of fresh liquid milk, poorer people became more dependent on butter. It was a recognized part of their diet. Army rations in Elizabeth I's reign included a quarter of a pound of butter as well as half a pound of cheese a day; and butter appears regularly in institutional diets for hospitals, workhouses and the like from that time onwards.

Among the rich the consumption of butter rose dramatically, for the seventeenth and eighteenth centuries were the golden age of butter in English cookery. Not only was it employed, as hitherto, in cake and pastry making, in fish frying and meat basting, in cereal pottages and buttered ales; but it was now added as well to virtually all forms of boiled food, being put to them as they cooked, or else melted and 'run over' them afterwards in the serving dish. Boiled salads, herbs and roots, meat in stews, hashes and fricassees, and fish in *court bouillon* were all liberally buttered.

The drawn or beaten butter used to 'run over' dishes before they were brought to table was specially prepared. 'To draw butter', according to a recipe of 1653, 'take your butter and cut it into thin slices, put it into a dish, then put it upon the coals where it may melt leisurely, stir it often, and when it is melted put in two or three spoonfuls of water, or vinegar, which you will, then stir and beat it until it be thick.'

No wonder M. Misson, visiting England from France in the 1690s, viewed with amazement the meals of English people of the middling sort.

> Another time they will have a piece of boiled beef, and then they salt it some days beforehand, and besiege it with five or six heaps of cabbage, carrots, turnips or some other herbs or roots, well peppered and salted, and swimming in butter: a leg of roast or boiled mutton, dished up with the same dainties, fowls, pigs, oxtripes and tongues, rabbits, pigeons, all well moistened with butter, without larding.[60]

For roast meat too, was given a buttery sauce, formed from the basting butter mingled with its own gravy, which was taken up from the dripping pan and duly seasoned. As puddings came more and more to the fore, butter went into the pudding mixture for baked varieties, while boiled suet puddings were eaten with melted butter. Hot pies were filled up with a caudle of wine or verjuice, egg yolks and butter. Cold pies were sealed, as in earlier years, with butter; and when their preservative function was usurped by potting, the fish or meat, having first been baked in butter, was once more defended from the air by a butter seal.

Butter was everywhere, and the garnishes of sliced lemons, barberries and other sharp fruits, and the lemon juice or vinegar sometimes beaten into the melted butter, must have brought only slight relief to the palate of the eater faced with the rich, oleaginous dishes. Towards the end of the seventeenth century the butter added to meat stews was somewhat tempered by being incorporated with a little flour; and separate sauces were thickened in a similar manner. And after a few more decades vegetables were no longer sent to table swimming in butter. They were boiled simply in salted water, drained and served. The butter, however, was still at hand, and was offered separately in a cup or basin to accompany most vegetables, and many fish dishes too. With the latter it was sometimes sharpened by the addition of a little mustard. Melted butter, with a dusting of flour in it, was perhaps the commonest sauce on the tables of the well-to-do throughout the eighteenth century; while white flour sauce, with little or no butter in it, was the equivalent among the poor and the thrifty.

Sliced bread was spread with butter. A middle-class breakfast in the 1740s consisted of tea and 'one or more slices of wheat-bread, which they had first toasted at the fire, and when it was very hot, had spread butter on it, and then placed it a little way from the fire on the hearth, so that the butter might melt well into the bread. In the summer they do not toast the bread, but only spread the butter on it before they eat it.' For afternoon tea, later in the century, there were poppy-thin slices of bread and butter, as well as buttered toast.[61]

The herb and butter combinations which had been recommended, with bread, by the physicians of the Tudor period had been further developed by the early sixteenth century. Sir Hugh Platt described how to make 'sundry sorts of most dainty butter having a lively taste of sage, cinnamon, nutmegs, maces, etc. This is done by mixing a few drops of the extracted oil of sage, cinnamon, nutmegs, mace etc. in the making up of your butter: for oil and butter will incorporate and agree very kindly and naturally together.' A recipe published in 1696 'to make parsley, sage, savoury, thyme or lemon thyme butter' by mixing the 'chemical' (i.e. distilled) oils with newly made butter, stated specifically: 'this will excuse you from eating the plants therewith'.[62]

A very different butter confection, which also had medieval antecedents, was a pound of butter roasted. Among the roast meats of the Middle Ages were the balls and other shapes of minced pork or beef which were spitted and dredged with spiced flour batter as they roasted. From the dredging and consolidating of fatty meat-balls it was only a short step to the application of similar treatment to butter. In a recipe of 1615:

> To roast a pound of butter curiously and well, you shall take a pound of sweet butter and beat it stiff with sugar and the yolks of eggs, then clap it roundwise about a spit, and lay it before a soft fire, and presently dredge it with the dredging before appointed for the pig [fine breadcrumbs, currants, sugar and salt mixed together]: then as it warmeth or melteth, so apply it with dredging till the butter be overcome and no

more will melt to fall from it, then roast it brown, and so draw it, and serve it out, the dish being as nearly trimmed with sugar as may be.

Variations of this recipe are found in cookery books over the next two centuries. In Hannah Glasse's version the butter was allowed to drip over a pint of oysters previously stewed in their own juice, and the roasted butter was served on top of them. The concoction was known in Ireland too, and during the eighteenth century butter, salted and dredged with fine oatmeal, was roasted as a Christmas food there. 'A certain Irish woman told me this eats very nicely, insomuch that she has done on a Christmas Eve twenty-seven different pounds so, at a farmer's house in her country, where it has been kept all the holidays, to accommodate a friend with a slice or two, as we do cakes or minced pies here.'[63]

Chapter 6

Cereals, potherbs and pottage

Prehistoric period

The neolithic farmers who introduced domesticated animals to Britain were also the first people to plant and harvest cereals there. They grew their corn in forest clearings, reaping it in autumn and keeping the greater part to serve as food in the ensuing year. But some was always held back to be sown in the following spring.

Emmer wheat formed a large part of their seed corn, mingled with a little einkorn. They also had hulled and naked barleys. All these cereals had been brought into cultivation much earlier, in areas of Asia Minor and the land between the Black Sea and the Caspian Sea where the plants were indigenous in their wild form. Subsequently they spread into Europe as food crops, and as they were taken westwards, so they gradually adapted themselves to differences of climate and soil.

Down the years new types of wheat emerged in Europe as mutants of earlier varieties, and by the time of the early Celtic Iron Age, spelt and club wheat were coming to the fore. Barley too existed in more than one form, and during the Bronze Age it became the predominant cereal of Britain.

The first farmers harvested their crops with the aid of flint reaping knives. It was not easy to thresh the early wheats, for emmer and einkorn, like the spelt of later days, have their grains tightly clamped inside stiff, close-fitting glumes which are almost impossible to remove unless they have first been parched. At a later stage of prehistoric farming cob-ovens of clay were devised to heat and dry the heads of grain; and when the Romans arrived they introduced their characteristic T-shaped corn-drying ovens for the parching of spelt.[1]

Of the drying arrangements of the earliest farmers we know little. They may have practised the primitive technique known as *graddan*, which survived in the western islands of Scotland almost to within living memory. Its name goes back to the Celtic period (the word is akin to the Irish *grad*, meaning quick); but the method itself could have been developed at a far earlier time.

Martin Martin wrote an eye-witness account of *graddan* as practised at the end of the seventeenth century.

> A woman sitting down takes a handful of corn, holding it by the stalks in her left hand, and then sets fire to the ears, which are presently in a flame. She has a stick in her right hand, which she manages very dexterously, beating off the grain at the very instant when the husk is quite burnt; for if she miss of that she must use the kiln, but experience has taught them this art of perfection. The corn may be so dressed, winnowed, ground, and baked within an hour after reaping from the ground.[2]

When the farmers of the prehistoric period had learnt how to scorch their grain they would also have discovered that it could, as a result, be stored safely through the winter without sprouting. Only the seed corn had to be left unparched.

To grind the corn they and their families used saucer querns in which a stone rubber was moved round and round on a circular course. The saddle querns, which were adopted fairly generally in later prehistoric times, made grinding somewhat easier in that the user propelled a rubbing stone backwards and forwards across a flat stone base, and could thus exert greater pressure and grind more grain at a time. After grinding, the corn may have been sieved, but there is no evidence for such sieving before the Celtic Iron Age.

The rough, branny grain could be made into a coarse, rather unpalatable bread to be baked on the hearthstone. But the first farmers already had an alternative way to prepare their cereals. Some of them, at least, came equipped with pottery cooking vessels, and with the knowledge of a technique for making and firing such pots.

They moulded them from soft clay with fingers and thumb, producing round-bottomed, rather baggy-looking vessels, the deeper ones in appearance not unlike the leather containers already in use among them. The pots were given a long, slow firing at a lowish temperature in a smoky fire. The shallow bowls may have been used mainly as drinking cups; but the deeper ones were cooking pots, and in them the first British pottages were stewed.

Later came the technique of building up flat-bottomed vessels, the sides formed from rings of clay pressed together. Beakers were made in this fashion. Still later, but only with the arrival of the most sophisticated Celts who had already been in contact with Roman influence, came the potter's wheel. But the round-bottomed cooking pots recurred constantly all through the prehistoric period, and when metal cauldrons began to be made, they too were given a circular shape with a curved base which closely resembled that of the pottery vessels.

Behind the first cooked pottages lay a long tradition of food processing of a more primitive kind. At the most rudimentary level was the soaking of roots, leaves, seeds, nuts and berries in cold water for several hours in order to soften them and make them easier to chew and to digest. Next the potboiler method was devised for cooking meat in water within a vessel, with the same object of making the tougher parts more digestible and more satisfying. The contribution of pottery containers was that they allowed many varied foodstuffs to be combined and cooked together over external heat. Thus was made possible the development of an art of cookery, whereby different ingredients, each with its own particular taste and consistency, could be combined and simmered together until they produced food of an attractive and hitherto unknown flavour.

In a primitive farming community there must usually be a lean period between the killing off of one food animal and the next. In the interim the group has to live on whatever is available in the way of cereals, seeds, leaves and roots, with perhaps some fish or a piece of dried meat left over from the last beast to be slaughtered, or a small trapped animal or bird. In pottage all could be united to the best advantage.

But even when the pottage was made almost entirely from cereals, it had neither the smoothness nor the flavour of similar confections in more recent years. The weeds which grew among the corn were reaped and harvested in prehistoric times along with the grain. The large weed seeds, roughly ground, had a food content comparable to that of the ears of corn. The weeds were hardier than the cereals, and their presence was an insurance, for they were more likely to survive in a bad season when the true crop failed.

In addition, both weed seeds and wild green plants supplied natural salts which to some extent compensated for the shortage of common salt in the diet of the early farmers. Hunters could satisfy their salt needs from the meat and fish they caught. But farmers lived for long periods mainly upon vegetable foods. It was many centuries before the means of winning true salt were discovered. Until then primitive man, lacking this condiment, may have found that weed seeds with their strong and bitter flavours, did something to ease his craving for salt.

Families settled near the rocky coasts of northern and western Britain could also have added seaweeds to their pottages. Laver, dulse and carrageen, with their pungent flavours due to their high content of potassium iodide, are known to have been eaten far back in the historic period (the monks of the early Celtic church gathered dulse, according to the *Hymn of Columba*); and seaweeds, like land weeds, were almost certainly a part of prehistoric diet.[3]

A particular quality of cereal-based pottage is its consistency. The starch in ears of corn is in the form of minute grains which are not dissolved in cold water, although they can absorb a certain amount of it when soaked. As the cereal is heated in water, the granules take in more moisture and finally burst altogether, releasing their starch which combines with the liquor and causes it suddenly to thicken. Cereal cooked in this way is at once more digestible and more nutritious than in its raw form. A stew containing some portion of wheat, barley or other corn might be anything from a thinnish soup to a thick porridge, according to the amount of starch released.

A richer pottage resulted when fat or oil was added to the pot, to be taken up by the starch as it thickened. Animal fat, when available, or oil-bearing seeds previously crushed on a quernstone, would have produced this effect. Plants with seeds which had a high oil-content were important in the diet of the early farming communities of Britain. Some which are likely to have been incorporated in their pottage are linseed (found at Windmill Hill neolithic settlement, where flax is assumed to have been a food-plant in the absence of any equipment for spinning or weaving: like the cereals, it had been brought in by immigrants from continental Europe); and the seeds of wild cabbage, charlock (*sinapis arvensis*), white goosefoot, knotgrass (*polygonum*), and some other native herbs now regarded as weeds.[4]

The green leaves of these wild plants were also eaten. Cooked in pottage they became both more platable and more digestible. Thus nettles, plantain (a weed which closely follows human settlement), mallows, docks, and indeed a very large number of native green plants must have gone into the stewpot, and many of them continued in use as potherbs until at least the seventeenth century. Other herbs with striking aromatic properties are likely to have been sought out from the earliest days of pottage. Such were the native plants of the onion family – ramsons, field garlic, wild leeks and chives – and the various mints. During winter, in the absence of green leaves, the roots of wild carrots, parsnips or turnips may have been added to the pot, but it must be remembered that in their undeveloped state such roots were thin, wiry and tough, and were much less desirable than the root vegetables of later times.

Fruits and nuts in their season, though often eaten raw, must also have enhanced many primitive pottages. And in the ruins of the neolithic village of Skara Brae, on Orkney, a vessel was found containing a mass of minute fragments of fishbones which had apparently been pounded to make a kind of meal. It may have supplied a substitute for cereal grains or weed seeds in pottage. As late as the nineteenth century meal of ground-up fishbones was eaten in the Orkneys to eke out grain supplies in time of need.

Tangible evidence of neolithic or Bronze Age pottage in Britain has not yet appeared. But on several occasions pots have been found on the sites of the contemporary Swiss lake villages with desiccated remains of food clinging to them. They show the very mixed nature of these early meals. One summer stew, for instance, comprised several soft fruits such as wild raspberry, strawberry and elderberry, flax, wheat, rush, nuts and fish.[5]

Winter pottages were quite different, for they contained great quantities of seeds. Again we have no examples as yet from Britain, but parallels may be sought, of a rather later date, in Denmark. The bodies of a number of people, preserved almost intact for some two thousand years, have been discovered in bogs there. In some cases it has been possible to take out the viscera and analyse the contents in order to learn the exact nature of the last meal consumed by the dead person. It was found that the stomach of the corpse known as Tollund man had contained a gruel prepared from barley, linseed, gold-of-pleasure (*camelina sativa*), a very large number of seeds of knot-grass, and many other weed seeds. Grabaulle man had eaten a last meal made up of fifty-three different varieties of grain and weed seeds. Although these may have been meals of a ritual nature (for it is thought that most of the bog corpses were people who had been killed either sacrificially or in punishment for transgressing the laws of their tribe), the cereal and weed seed gruel must have been very typical of the food of the peasant farmer, both in Denmark and Britain, from neolithic times onwards.

The seeds of flax, black bindweed (*polygonum convolvulus*), pale persicaria (a species of knotgrass) and white goosefoot were almost certainly gathered deliberately in Britain during the later part of the Bronze Age. They may even have been grown as crops at that time, and so may corn spurrey and gold-of-pleasure (an oily-seeded plant which grew as a weed with flax). Both were food-plants of the early Iron Age in Denmark.[6]

Our first record of an imported flavouring herb of Mediterranean origin, coriander, goes back to the late Bronze Age. Barley appears to have been the predominant cereal of Britain then, and perhaps the sophisticated newcomers who brought in the coriander were accustomed to gruel made on a southern European pattern. (Several centuries later Greek peasants were still flavouring their barley pottage with a generous admixture of linseed and coriander seed, duly roasted and pounded.)[7] But most British pottages of the day continued to depend for their savour on native aromatic plants.

During the pre-Roman Iron Age two entirely new cereals reached Britain. Oats and rye had originated as weeds of cultivation which sprang up among wheat and barley and were harvested, in the usual prehistoric fashion, along with the parent crop. They probably arrived in Britain mixed in other seedcorn brought by new immigrants, and at first were rather rare. Of several oat varieties introduced, the most common was the wild oat.

The pulses followed not long afterwards. The Celtic bean was the earliest arrival. Known elsewhere in Europe from neolithic times, it now came to south-west England where the lake-village dwellers of Glastonbury and Meare were among the first

Potherbs
From J. A. Comenius:
Visible world, 1664

Pot-herbs *grow in Gardens,*
as, Lettice, 1.
Colewort, 2.
Onions, 3.

In hortis nascuntur
Olera.
ut, *Lactuca,* 1.
Brassica, 2.
Cepa, 3.

C 3 Gar

An Elizabethan kitchen

A handquern in use about 1902 at Foula, Shetland
From O. G. S. Crawford: *Archaeology in the field*

Early 17th century diners (note squared trencher-bread)
From *Roxburghe Ballads*, vol. 1

people to add it to their food-plants. The Celtic bean is a very small variety, and the finds at Glastonbury were at first mistaken for peas. But true peas arrived somewhat later direct from the Roman world. There the pulses were grown as field crops, and the bines ploughed back to enrich the soil.[8]

They were a great addition to Britain's food. Not only could they be eaten green (young peas were especially attractive because of their high sugar content), but they could also be dried and stored to yield both protein and starch for the winter months. They could then be ground to meal and added to bread grains, but they were preferred as pottage legumes; for when they had simmered in liquid they burst open and took up the broth and any fat present to become a palatable purée.

Vegetable pottages became much tastier after the discovery of techniques for winning free salt. Once salt had begun to circulate widely through trade, the peasant farmer could add a piquancy to his cereal, herb or pulse pottages which had hitherto existed only in meaty broths.

The adoption of metal cauldrons also had implications for cookery. It was now possible to distinguish between those foods which responded to rapid boiling over the flames, and those, such as thick pottages of cereals or pulses, or confections of flour, milk and eggs, which needed slow cooking at the edge of the fire. For foods in the latter class, pottery was still the preferred vehicle. Pottery remained cheaper than metal, even if its life expectation was shorter, and earthenware was still the material of the poor man's cooking pot.

Roman period

The Romanization of lowland Britain brought not only new crops to the region, but also new culinary ideas and practices. Among the latter was the separation of the techniques of grinding and pounding. The rotary quern had already arrived in the country during the first century BC, but its use only became widespread under the Romans. For many centuries the saddle quern (which had replaced the saucer quern of the first neolithic settlers) had been the sole implement for pulverizing all cereals, weed seeds and herbs, whether intended for bread making or for the pot.

Now the quern was confined to the grinding of cereals. For pounding operations the Romans introduced the mortar and pestle, already well established in the kitchens of Italy. The mortar of imperial times was a shallow pottery bowl with a lip at one side, and a sprinkling of gritty stone particles baked into the fabric. Against these, herbs, cereal grains (often simply hulled for pottage making) and other foodstuffs were worked with a wooden or pottery pestle.

The traditional barley pottage could now be made in Greco-Roman fashion, under the name *tisana*. The recipe ran:

> Soak chick-peas, lentils and peas. Crush barley and boil with the dried vegetables. When it has boiled long enough, add sufficient oil and chop the following greens: leeks, coriander, dill, fennel, beet, mallow, and tender cabbage. Put all these finely chopped greens into the saucepan. Boil cabbage shoots, pound (in the mortar a generous quantity of fennel-seed, origan, asafoetida, lovage, and after pounding blend with *liquamen*. Pour this mixture over the dried vegetables and barley and stir. Put chopped cabbage leaves on top.

For a hot savoury stew of kid or lamb, the following method was recommended: 'Put the pieces of meat into a pan. Finely chop an onion and coriander, pound (in the mortar) pepper, lovage, cumin, *liquamen*, oil, and wine. Cook, turn out into a shallow pan, thicken with *amulum*.'[9]

These Roman recipes represented a more sophisticated approach to cookery than anything hitherto known in Britain. They called for imported spices and condiments such as pepper, asafoetida and *liquamen*, for a wider range of cooking vessels, and for new methods of food preparation.

The *amulum* mentioned in the second recipe was one of the standbys of Roman cookery. It was a wheat-starch thickener invented by the Greeks and taking its name from a Greek word meaning 'unmilled'. The Romans used it in stews and sauces as an equivalent to the modern cornflour.

Cato's recipe of the mid-second century BC shows that *amulum* was prepared from hard wheat soaked in changes of water for ten days, and then squeezed through a new linen cloth. The resultant creamy substance was dried in the sun. It was now ready to be cooked with milk to make a bland, smooth pottage.[10] At the time when Britain was taken into the Roman empire, *amulum* had become the standard thickener for sauces, which were either made separately (for the best results they had to be heated in small saucepans over charcoal braziers), or produced by thickening the stock in which meat or fish had already cooked. They were poured over the solid food before the dish was served.

Roman-style cookery also called for a number of herbs and roots of Mediterranean origin. To supply the needs of Roman settlers in Britain, several were now introduced as garden plants. Among the aromatics were alexanders, borage, chervil, coriander (a second introduction), dill, fennel, garden mint and thyme, garlic, garden leek, onion and shallot, hyssop, parsley, rosemary, rue, sage, savory and sweet marjoram. Although initially they would have been raised in carefully tended plots on villa estates, some, including alexanders, coriander and fennel, soon escaped beyond the confines of gardens and naturalized themselves in the country round about. They are still to be found here and there as wild plants, especially in southern Britain.

Other new Roman arrivals were the garden varieties of a number of green vegetables, among them cabbage, beet, mallows, orache (atriplex), lettuce and endive. Not all were entirely new. Wild cabbage is thought, on the grounds of linguistic evidence, to have been a food-plant among the Iron Age Celts along the Atlantic seaboard of Europe before they ever reached Britain. Roman cabbage included several headed varieties, some which were raised for the sake of the succulent sprouts that grew under their leaves, and an open-headed kail which was closely akin to wild cabbage. It was the last type which was most readily adopted among the British Celts of the Roman period. For centuries thereafter it remained the commonest cabbage of Britain, and it became the cole-plant of the medieval peasant.

Wild varieties of mallow and goosefoot (related to orache) were already in use as food-plants in prehistoric Britain, so the Roman introductions were easily accepted. The Romans grew beet, mallow and orache for the sake of their green leaves, which were boiled in pottages like the *tisana* described above. As an alternative, beet leaves, lettuce leaves, alexanders, smallage, tender cabbage shoots and other greens could be purèed and eaten with a dressing of oil, wine or vinegar and aromatic herbs.[11]

Garden carrots, parsnips, turnips, radishes and probably also skirrets were brought to Britain at this time. Pliny observed that both radishes (the large-rooted varieties favoured by the Romans) and skirrets did best in the colder climate of northern Europe. Turnips and rapes may have been grown as field crops in southern England, and used not only as fodder for cattle, but also among the peasants as pottage roots. More elegantly, root vegetables were fried or boiled, and served inevitably with a sauce. Cumin sauce, made up on a base of honey, vinegar, *liquamen*, wine-must and oil, was popular with turnips and carrots. This sauce could be adapted to taste by the addition of extra herbs.[12]

Oats were not a pottage cereal in Italy, where they were still regarded as weeds in Pliny's day. But the German tribes raised them to eat in the form of porridge, and they became an economic crop in Britain too, especially in the cold, wet, upland parts of the country where no other cereal would survive. They were doubly useful, furnishing pottages for humans and fodder for the horses of the Roman cavalry which was active in the same areas.

Examples of ribwort plantain, sheep's sorrel and corn spurry have been found on Romano-British sites in contexts which suggest that the seeds may have been deliberately gathered for use as food; and among the poorer and less Romanized Britons the pottage plants of prehistoric times were no doubt still often eaten. They, together with other native herbs, had an important role too in traditional folk medicine.

Another compelling reason for clinging to the food-plants of earlier days was the ever-present fear of famine. The need years of Roman Britain are unchronicled, but there must have been many seasons when the grain supply was inadequate, despite attempts to save unripe corn by parching it in corn-drying ovens. Records of a later period show that between AD 679 and 1320 nearly one year in ten was a famine year with several periods of minor shortage in between, and there is no reason to doubt that the economic situation in Iron Age and Roman Britain was equally precarious. Wild food-plants, hardier than cultivated varieties, were the last resort against starvation.[13]

Early medieval period

Cereal pottage already bulked large in the diet of the Anglo-Saxon and other Germanic invaders when they reached Britain. Not only oatmeal, but also hulled barley (on the slender evidence available, their most common cereal: it supplied malt for brewing as well as bread and pottage) and rye-meal went into their porridges. The cultivation of rye on the sandy lands of eastern England may have begun among the Anglo-Saxon farmers; that area was a great producer of rye all through the later Middle Ages.

Green-leaved vegetables grown for pottage included beet, orache and the inevitable cabbage, no less a favourite among the Anglo-Saxons than it was with the Celts in western Britain. Peas and beans were raised, and when after a few centuries systems of crop rotation were developed on manorial estates, the pulses took their place as field crops, alternating with the cereals.

The root vegetables of the Anglo-Saxon were those already known in Roman Britain: radishes, skirrets, parsnips, turnips and rapes. Six members of the onion family were distinguished under the names *cropleac* (perhaps everlasting onion or chives), *garleac* (garlic), *porleac* (garden leek), *ynioleac* (onion), *hol-leac* and *brade-leac*. In Wales garden leeks were the commonest onion type: leeks and cabbages are the only two cultivated vegetables named in the laws of Hywel Dda.[14]

Most of the other aromatic seasoning herbs grown in Roman times were re-established in lowland Britain, brought in from the wilds if they still flourished there, or reintroduced from continental Europe. They were augmented in cookery by many native wild plants, still valued both as food and as medicine.

Extant Anglo-Saxon pottage recipes are not very typical of everyday diet, for the only ones we have are those of the leechdoms, the collections of remedies, mainly herbal, with which the Anglo-Saxons tried to fight off numerous unpleasant and dangerous diseases. Garlic simmered in 'hen broth' cured constipation; a pottage of cropleek, radish and helenium (an unidentified herb) shredded small and stewed in butter with barley-meal and plenty of white salt was helpful for lung complaints.[15] The pottages of ordinary diet are likely to have been meat broths with potherbs and rye- or barley-meal; or vegetable and cereal stews often enriched with butter, a favourite cooking fat of the period.

Spices were rare until the last centuries before the Norman Conquest. When they became more plentiful, the nobility and the higher clergy could enjoy spicy pottages with new sophisticated flavours.

How they were made can be guessed from the cuisine of contemporary France. Here the traditions of Roman cookery had survived both Gothic and Frankish invasions. A link between imperial Roman and later medieval recipes can be traced in the earliest western European account of a beef stew. It comes from a long letter about food and dietetics written in the sixth century AD by Anthimus, a much-travelled Greek physician, for Theoderic, King of the Franks.

Beef had not played a big part in Roman cookery in the Mediterranean lands, which lacked rich pastures for fattening cattle. But in north-western Europe, in France no less than in Britain, cattle were much more important to the economy: hence the relevance of Anthimus' recipe in the Frankish domains.

He recommended that the beef be washed, and boiled in clean water until almost done. Then sharp vinegar, heads of leeks, a little pennyroyal and roots of smallage or fennel were to be added, together with honey (to the quantity of half the vinegar, or according to taste). The stew was simmered over a slow fire for a further hour, the pot being frequently shaken by hand. In the meantime a seasoning was prepared in the mortar from a very little ground pepper, costmary, spikenard and cloves dissolved in wine; and this was blended in to give its aroma to the whole pottage. Anthimus' final word of advice was that an earthenware cooking pot would produce a better flavour than a metal one.

His beef pottage has two features which supply a link between Roman cookery and that of the later Middle Ages. One is the use of leek or onion to flavour a meat stew; the other is the sweet-sour combination of honey and vinegar.[16]

Later medieval period

In Britain pottage remained in favour at every level of society. Bread, pottage and ale were the three great staples of diet, and as late as 1542 Andrew Boorde, who had travelled through several European countries, wrote: 'Pottage is not so much used in all Christendom as it is used in England. Pottage is made of the liquor in the which flesh is sodden in, with putting-to chopped herbs, and oatmeal and salt.'[17]

The materials of pottage were, in fact, many and varied. The only object was to produce a semi-liquid spoonmeat, often of very thick consistency. There were several forms of cereal pottage based upon the breadcorn of the region, which in medieval times might be wheat, rye, maslin (a combination of the first two), barley, oats or dredge-corn (a mixture of the two last). For a long time such cereals were often ground at home, either with a hand quern (the use of which later became illegal, since it was held to defraud the manorial mill of its dues), or in a mortar. The result was a rough, branny grain, which needed some kind of winnowing before use.

Early recipes for frumenty describe the process. 'Take clean wheat, and beat it small in a mortar, and fan out clean the dust; then wash it clean, and boil it till it be tender and brown.' In other recipes wheat was boiled in water till the grains burst, then cooled and mixed with cows' milk or milk of almonds;

and well beaten egg yolks were often stirred in too. If the eggs did not colour it enough, it was yellowed with saffron.

At the meals of great families wheaten frumenty was the accompaniment of venison or porpoise. But the frumenty of poorer folk was a breakfast or supper dish in itself, and it was usually made of maslin or barley, mixed with milk when that was to be had, or with water alone, or with a little cream or butter.[18]

The cereal pottage of Scotland was *brochan*, the old Gaelic word for oatmeal porridge or gruel. It was eaten with milk, or in the lowlands sometimes with kail. 'Muslin kail', also a lowland dish, was a pottage of maslin (often in Scotland a spring-sown mixture of oats and barley) containing kail and perhaps onions too.

In the north of England the Pennine dalesmen ate oatmeal porridge similar to that of Scotland; and in Wales either oats or barley went into the pottage. Even in southern England oatmeal became a favourite thickener for meat and herb pottages, and purchases of groats or oatmeal appear often in medieval household accounts, such as those of Eleanor, Countess of Leicester, or the two priests who lived at Munden's Chantry, near Bridport.

The simplest form of pottage was gruel made from oatmeal boiled in water. Chopped meat and herbs could be added to taste. 'Drawn gruel' was a variant for which lean beef was boiled and pulled to draw out the gravy, to which were added oatmeal, parsley, sage and salt. In 'forced gruel' the oatmeal pottage was reinforced with pork worked to a pulp in the mortar.

Other thickeners for pottage were breadcrumbs, and, for the well-to-do, 'amidon'. The latter was wheat starch, a kind of cornflour, still made by a recipe which hardly differed from Cato's *amulum* of some sixteen hundred years before.

Occasionally eggs were beaten up and stirred into a pottage to consolidate its texture; but they were regarded as rather an extravagance. 'Thick it with grated bread', says a recipe for cabbages cooked in broth of beef, 'but for a lord it shall be thicked with yolks of eggs beaten.'[19]

The new cereal of the period was rice, imported from southern Europe and an acquisition for the pottages of the wealthy. Dried rice from India had occasionally reached Italy by the spice routes in Roman times, but it did not become important in contemporary cuisine. The trade with the west still survived in Anthimus' day, and he recommended rice pottage for those suffering from stomach upsets. His recipe had the rice grains first boiled in water, and then mixed with goats' milk and cooked over a slow fire until they coagulated.

But rice was hardly known in Britain until the Arabs had begun to cultivate it, along with other oriental food-plants, in the lands bordering the Mediterranean. The new crop spread into Sicily, lower Aragon in Spain, and eventually to the Lombardy plain of Italy, whence stemmed the medieval recipes for 'rys Lumbarde', dressed with spices and the yolks of hard-boiled eggs. Rice was exported to England on the spice ships, and it was for many years an item on the spice account, watched over and locked up along with the true spices. The Countess of Leicester and her family used a hundred and ten pounds of rice in the four months between Christmas and April 1265 (it was an ingredient of many Lenten dishes), and she paid about a penny ha'penny a pound for it. But in the smaller household of Dame Alice de Bryene only three pounds, costing a penny a pound, was consumed in the whole year from September 1418 to September 1419.

The simplest rice pottages were made on the following lines: 'Take rice and wash them clean, and do them in earthen pot with good broth, and let them seeth well. Afterwards, take almond milk, and do thereto, and colour it with saffron and mess forth.' Rice for fish days was tempered with almond milk only, and was usually sweetened with sugar. Rice flour, made from dried rice grains pounded in the mortar was used in much the same way as amidon.[20]

Peas and beans, now cultivated as field crops in due rotation, were in constant demand for pottage, especially among the peasantry and in religious houses. At least three kinds of peas were grown: greens and whites, both small varieties, and grey peas which were larger and were often used as fodder, or were eaten by the poorest people. Dame Alice de Bryene used nine bushels (504 pounds) of green peas in pottage for herself and her household servants during the year 1418–19; but even larger quantities of grey peas went to feed her horses and her pigeons over the same period.[21]

Beans were somewhat bigger than the Celtic beans of prehistoric times, but they were still of the broad bean family (*vicia faba*). The coarsest variety was the horse-bean, usually fed to animals, but eaten by humans in time of dearth. Chick-peas and lentils were raised in a few places, lentils sometimes forming part of a mixed crop with spring-sown cereals. Vetches, grown principally as fodder, became human food under pressure of famine.

The pulses had the great advantage that they could be dried and kept through the year. Pottage vegetables named by Alexander Neckam included lentils, peas, beans with pods, beans without pods, groats, onions and frizzled beans. The last named were beans which had been boiled in their pods, shelled and frizzled in a heated metal spoon; and under the name of *fèves frasées*, they were a French preparation well known in Paris (where Neckam had lived for a time). The English equivalent was 'canebyns'. To make them beans were steeped for two days and nights in several changes of water, were hardened in the oven and hulled with a handmill. Then, 'cleave the beans in two or three or four at the most and fry them, and ye may keep them as long as ye will'. Either form of treatment was a precaution against the beans sprouting if they became at all damp while in store.

Young green peas were cooked in good beef broth flavoured with parsley, sage, savory and hyssop; while old dried peas were boiled in bacon stock and eaten afterwards with the bacon meat. Dried beans and canebyns were likewise cooked in stock and served with bacon. For the gentry, canebyns and bacon went together like frumenty and venison.

The labourer's family often had to make do with a miniscule lump of bacon, or perhaps none at all, in which case the pottage was thickened with oatmeal, flour or breadcrumbs to give it more substance. This thick pease pottage remained a basic country dish for several hundred years.

For Lenten pottages, white peas were recommended. They were usually flavoured with minced onions and sugar or honey, and often coloured with saffron. Canebyns could be cooked with almond milk and sugar for Lent, or cows' milk and honey at other times, to make a sweet dish.[22]

Thick vegetable pottages were supplied by some of the many garden herbs. 'Worts we most have/Both to master and to knave', wrote Mayster Ion Gardener about 1440. Sown at intervals through the year, the open-leaved cole could be brought to maturity at any season; and Mayster Ion supplied full instructions for sowing, transplanting and harvesting the young coleworts after six weeks' growth. Both red and white varieties were grown. Headed cabbage took longer to mature. Sprouts were a vegetable of the Low Countries, especially of the region about Brussels, but their cultivation in Britain began only in the seventeenth century.

Medieval English cookery books recommended that coleworts and cabbages should be parboiled, cut up and added to a marrowbone stew, preferably one which already contained a piece of beef or a hare or a goose. The dish was called 'long worts de char', or 'hare [or other animal] in worts'. Leeks, onions and other flavouring herbs were sometimes chopped up with the cabbage leaves, and the pottage might be coloured with saffron. The 'buttered worts' of the late fifteenth century, boiled in water with plenty of clarified butter and eaten with the buttery broth, foreshadowed the more general boiling and buttering of vegetables in years to come.[23]

Onions were in constant use for pottages. Although they were often grown in gardens, supply could not keep up with demand, and both onions and onion seed had to be imported from the Netherlands and even from Spain. Garlic too was brought in regularly from the continent, and was peddled through the streets in London.

Leeks were raised for Lent,

Now leeks are in season, for pottage full good,
and spareth the milchcow, and purgeth the blood:
These having with peason, for pottage in Lent,
thou sparest both oatmeal and bread to be spent.

The gentry ate them in white porray. 'Take the white of the leeks, and seeth them in a pot, and press them up, and hack them small on a board. And take good almond milk, and a little rice, and do all these together, and seeth and stir it well, and do thereto sugar or honey, and dress it in.'[24] On fasting days it was accompanied by salted eels, parboiled, grilled and sliced. At other times white porray was based on meat broth or ham stock, and was reinforced with pieces of bacon or even small birds.

The name porray stemmed from the Latin *porrum* (leek), but, perhaps on account of its likeness to the word purée, came to be applied to thick pottages of greenstuff in general. They were eaten by rich and poor alike, and were a great standby of peasant families. Beet leaves were the favourite green porray, but many other large-leaved green plants were employed in this pottage, including orache, clary, mallows, patience dock, borage and bugloss; while seasoning was provided by the aromatic potherbs such as parsley, sage, thyme, mints and fennel.

Parsley was perhaps the best loved of all medieval flavouring herbs. It was eaten mainly in the leaf; but the roots, which carry the flavour of the plant no less strongly (Thomas Cogan maintained that 'the chief virtue of parsley is in the root'), were on occasion sliced for pottage. Mayster Ion Gardener gave a long disquisition on how to grow parsley, and said that the leaves could be cut thrice in a season to make green porray and meat stews.

The green porray most usually described in the recipe books was called 'joutes'. It was simple to make. 'Take borage, colewort, bugloss, parsley, beets, orache, avens, violet, savory and fennel, and when they are sodden [boiled], press them well small, cast them in good broth, and seeth them, and serve them forth.' Some joutes were thickened with breadcrumbs. For fish days the herbs were boiled in 'broth of fresh salmon or of conger, and cast thereto powder of canell [cinnamon]. . . . Also there be joutes made with sweet almond milk, and cast thereto a little sugar for Lent, but put thereto no bread.'[25]

For such pottages the medieval housewife grew a very wide range of plants in her garden plot. An early fifteenth-century classified list (MS. Sloane 1201) gives no fewer than forty-eight herbs for pottage, including all those already mentioned, together with dandelion, marigold, daisy, red nettle, lettuce, chives, leeks and garlic, several aromatics, and one or two roots, such as rape and radish, of which the leaves were eaten while young. Many of the plants had to be brought in from the wilds; and indeed could be gathered there by those who had not stocked up their gardens. But a joutes recipe in the *Liber Cure Cocorum*, a poem written in the dialect of north-western Lancashire in the early fifteenth century, is unique in admitting plum-tree leaves, which suggests that the plum tree was then still a novelty in gardens in the region.

It may be thought that the frequent consumption of green herb pottages should have helped to stave off the scurvy that appears to have been so common in medieval times. But all pottages at that period were very thoroughly cooked by modern standards, and indeed long boiling would have been necessary to reduce some of the plants to an edible consistency. In the course of such boiling, all trace of vitamin C would have been destroyed.[26]

Root vegetables were not yet raised as field crops. Parsnip, carrot, radish, turnip, the longer-rooted navew, and rape were grown in gardens. The seeds of the last named were the source of a cooking oil now much in use among the less affluent. But before the Tudor period, when Dutch immigrants began large-scale rape cultivation in south-east England, most of the oil was still imported from Flanders.

The earliest English recipe devoted to a root vegetable is for 'Rapes in pottage. Take rapes and make them clean and wash them clean. Quarter them, parboil them; take them up, cast them in a good broth and seeth them. Mince onions and cast thereto saffron and salt, and mess it forth with powder douce. In the likewise make of parsnips and skirrets.'[27]

The pottages of Scotland and Wales appear to have been based on a much narrower range of vegetables than those of England. The Scottish highlanders scorned garden plants and plucked nettles for their pottage. The lowlanders grew a few pottage vegetables in their kailyards, comprising a little bere (six-rowed barley), oats, peas, beans and the inevitable cole or kail. It was not until the eighteenth century that a wider variety of vegetables was introduced among the poorer families. In Wales the leek was still the common pottage plant.[28]

While the ordinary people of lowland Britain ate their pease pottage or their green porray or their stewed roots, the nobility and gentry enjoyed some of the rich spicy meat and fish pottages introduced from Norman France. The great Anglo-Norman pottages – 'civey', 'gravey', 'charlet', 'bukkenade', 'mortrews', 'blancmange' and others – took their character not from the meat or fish they contained, but from the sauce in which those ingredients were cooked.

'Civey' might include gobbets of hare, coney or mallard on a meat day, or tench, sole or oysters on a fasting day, but its principal feature was the use of onions to flavour the stock in which the gobbets stewed. The pottage was thickened with bread and pointed with pepper or mixed spices.

'Gravey' was an amalgam of ground almonds and good broth, seasoned with sugar, ginger and sometimes other spices. It could be the vehicle for chunks of coney or chicken meat, eels or oysters. The same sauce with the addition of yolks of boiled eggs and pieces of fat cheese was called 'gravey enforced'.

'Charlet' was boiled shredded pork well mixed with eggs, cows' milk and saffron. For special occasions it was augmented with powdered ginger and sugar, and served in dishes with sweet spice powder floating on the top. 'Charlet counterfeited of fish' was made from cooked and flaked codling, haddock or thornback seethed in almond milk.[29]

'Bukkenade' was another meat pottage for veal, kid, hen or coney. It was seasoned with herbs and spices, thickened with egg yolks, and sometimes sharpened with a little verjuice or vinegar. An alternative version has currants, sugar and spices added to the meat, and the broth tempered with ground almonds and thickened with amidon. Again the dishes were 'flourished' with drage or mixed spice powders. The second form closely resembled 'brewet of Almaynne', another Anglo-Norman pottage.

'Egerdouce' was a sweet-sour pottage in which kid or coney or sliced brawn was cooked. The sour element was supplied by young red wine or vinegar, the sweet by sugar or honey and dried fruits. More simply, coneys and hens could be produced in 'clear broth', which meant that the stock was strained, mixed with wine and reheated with the meat, now chopped in pieces.[30]

These were running pottages, in which the chunks of meat or fish lay at the bottom of the bowl with the broth or 'sewe' above, the surface scattered with a garnish of spice powder. Thicker and more solid were the standing pottages, such as 'mortrews', 'mawmeny', 'blancmange' and 'blanc dessore'. Ordinary 'mortrews' was made of pork or chicken meat, cooked and ground to pulp in the mortar (whence the pottage took its name). It was mixed with breadcrumbs and egg yolks, was well spiced and was coloured golden with saffron, '. . . and look that it be standing and flourish it with powder ginger'. For 'white mortrews' the same meats were combined with ground almonds, milk and rice flour.[31]

'Blanc dessore' was very close in conception to white mortrews, and was eaten sometimes with a contrasting syrup of red wine combined with vinegar, sugar, saffron and ginger. Everyday 'mawmeny' resembled white mortrews; but the richer 'mawmeny royal' comprised 'teased brawn [flesh] of pheasant, partridge or capon, a good quantity', mingled with pinenuts and many spices and tempered with almond milk made of 'mighty wine'. Currants and chardequince might be included, and for special occasions a wine sauce reinforced with *aqua vitae* was poured over the pottage in dishes, set alight with a wax candle and served flaming.[32]

'Blancmange' was another standing pottage, chiefly notable for the absence of strong spices in its composition. The ingredients were capon flesh, teased small with a pin, whole boiled rice, almond milk and plenty of sugar. It was decorated with a surface scattering of red and white aniseed comfits or blanched almonds. At a feast, blancmange was sometimes 'departed' or divided into two parts, one of which was coloured red or yellow as a contrast to the other which was left white; or it was departed with a different pottage, such as the yellow 'caudel ferry'.

Needless to say 'mortrews of fish' and 'blancmange of fish' were eaten on fasting days. Fish roes and livers were recommended for the former; and perch or lobster or dried haddock for the fish day blancmange.[33]

The essence of pottage cookery was the sauce, whether created by or around the fleshmeat or fish as it cooked. But a further sophistication of pottage, the development of the separate sauce, had already taken place hundreds of years earlier in the food preparation of the Greeks and Romans. Not surprisingly this too was carried forward into medieval cookery.

'Egerdouce' was not only a pottage, but also a spicy sauce for fish. 'Take luces [pikes] or tenches, and hack them small in gobbets and fry them in olive oil; and then take vinegar and the third part of sugar and minced onions small, and boil all together; and cast therein cloves, maces, and cubebs, and serve it forth.'[34] Also eaten with fried fish was 'rapeye', a thick, sweet pottage of dried fruit pounded in the mortar and combined with breadcrumbs or rice flour. On other occasions it could be enjoyed by itself, as a dish in its own right.

For roast meat or boiled fish, sauces were often made entirely separately and were served in saucers which were placed near the trencher plates of the diners. Sauces, no less than standing pottages, relied upon mortar and pestle for their manufacture. Their liquid element was most often vinegar, but could also be ale, or wine or milk.

The range of sauces was not as wide as it had been in Roman imperial cuisine, as represented in Apicius' cookery book; but each one had a well-defined character and was constantly associated with its own particular food or group of foods. It was one of the duties of the server in a noble household to know that mustard went with brawn, beef or salt mutton; chawdron was appropriate for swan; ginger sauce for lamb, kid, sucking-pig or fawn; camelyn for the larger wild fowl, such as heronsewe, egret, crane, bustard; and so forth. For fasting days he had to be *au fait* with a similar distribution of sauces among the various species of fish.[35]

The cooks of the wealthy had likewise to be skilled judges of quantities, and able at chopping, stamping and grinding the ingredients. 'Woe was his cook, but if his sauces were/Poignant and sharp', wrote Chaucer of his Franklin. Lesser folk who were disinclined to go to so much trouble could sometimes, if they lived in town, fall back on the products of a professional saucemaker.

Sauces, unlike pottages, were often eaten uncooked. The bread which thickened camelyn, galantine, ginger sauce or 'sauce alepevere' (garlic sauce for roast beef) was sometimes toasted before being strained with seasonings, wine and vinegar; but the sauces themselves were not heated or boiled. All were strongly flavoured. 'And look that it stand well by cloves and by sugar' is the instruction given in one recipe for camelyn sauce. Green sauce must have been truly poignant, since it comprised not only parsley, mint, garlic, wild thyme and sage, ground small with the usual bread and vinegar, but sometimes four or five different spices as well. It was eaten with green fish, which probably needed a strong appetizer to help it down.[36]

Boiled sauces fell into two main categories: those which contained animal blood and entrails; and those thickened with flour. Of the first kind was 'chawdron' for swan, confected from the bird's own guts, cut small and boiled in broth with its blood and vinegar and strong spices. Similar dark-coloured sauces were made to eat with roasted wild duck, hen or capon. That for capon contained the bird's liver only, and was spiced with aniseed, ginger and cinnamon.

Of the second type was 'gauncil' for goose, or occasionally hen. 'Take flour and cow milk, saffron well ground, garlic, and put into a fair little pot; and seeth it over the fire, and serve it forth.' Another boiled sauce was 'peverade' or pepper sauce for veal and venison: its ingredients were fried bread, broth, vinegar, salt and plenty of pepper.[37]

Thick sauces prepared by culinary art were not deemed suitable for every kind of meat and fish; and even in great households vinegar or verjuice accompanied some dishes. Vinegar alone was eaten with salted sturgeon and porpoise, and vinegar laced with powdered cinnamon and ginger was for roasted eels, lampreys, freshwater crayfish and seabream. Verjuice was for roach, dace, bream, sole or mullet on fish days, and for boiled capon, veal, chicken or bacon at other times.

Later the juice of citrus fruits was adopted as a sauce. At first it was used by itself, most often with hen or capon; but during the sixteenth century it was added to seasoned vinegar or wine to produce a new range of thin spiced sauces; and whole oranges and lemons were also put into pottages with mutton or poultry.[38]

Early modern period

Meat pottages underwent changes both in flavour and texture in the years between the Tudor period and the end of the eighteenth century. Cereal pottages remained more static, perhaps because they were so often eaten by humble folk, who could afford little high-protein food, and found the soft, warm cereal confections a comforting substitute. Such people were hardly affected by the introduction of new foodstuffs or foreign culinary ideas at other levels of society. Even the potato, though it quickly became a staple food in Ireland, took some two centuries to gain acceptance in all parts of Britain.

Cereal pottages tended to be breakfast or supper dishes. Pottage for breakfast was common in all classes until late in the seventeenth century (though among the gentry it was often meat based). Thereafter the well-to-do adopted a lighter breakfast of spice-bread or cake with coffee or chocolate. Country people still continued for some decades to enjoy cereal pottages at breakfast, and the custom survived in northern Britain long after it had been dropped in the south.

For, by the end of the eighteenth century, 'in the south of England the poorest labourers are habituated to the unvarying meal of dry bread and cheese from week's end to week's end. . . . The aversion to broths and soups composed of barley-meal or oatmeal is in many parts of the south almost insuperable.' Milk pottage and water gruel lingered on longest in the workhouses (a further reason for them to be despised outside). The cost of fuel did not loom so large for an institution as it did for the individual poor family, and once firing was available, broths and gruels could be prepared quite cheaply to feed numbers of people.[39]

Cereal pottages were based on the local breadcorn. Wheat was turned into frumenty, still made in the traditional manner. It was often sugared and spiced, and could be enriched with egg yolks and dried fruit. In barley areas frumenty was made with pearl barley.

A thinner pottage was barley broth or gruel, for which the cereal was boiled long in water, together with dried raisins, currants or prunes. A version of this, seasoned with white wine, rosewater, butter and sugar was said to be a great favourite with Oliver Cromwell.[40]

Thinner still was barley water. It had a long history as an invalid beverage. In the sixth century AD Anthimus had recommended a thin drink made of barley with pure warm water as beneficial for fever patients. The later medieval version in France had the name tisane, was sweetened with sugar and seasoned with licorice and sometimes also figs. Adapted for English use it more often comprised barley boiled in water with licorice, herbs and raisins. It was still a licorice-flavoured drink in the first part of the seventeenth century, but soon afterwards was brought up to date by the substitution of lemon juice for licorice.[41]

Another variant of barley water in France, called *orgemonde*, was flavoured with ground almonds. This too reached England during the seventeenth century, its name softening to 'orgeat' or 'ozyat'. Subsequently the barley dropped out, and English ozyat was made from ground almonds and sugar with orange-flower water or the juice of citrus fruits boiled with spring water. It was a cold drink similar to lemonade. Milk ozyat was boiled, spiced milk, cooled and mixed with ground almonds; and special ozyat glasses with handles were designed to serve it in.[42]

Buttered cereals came to the fore in late Tudor times, the beginning of the great era of buttering of all sorts of animal and vegetable foods. They were homely dishes. Gervase Markham described with enthusiasm the oat-based form eaten by seafarers: 'nay, if a man be at sea in any long travel, he cannot eat a more wholesome and pleasant meat than these whole groats boiled in water till they burst, and then mixed with butter, and so eaten with spoons; which although seamen call simply by the name of loblolly, yet there is not any meat how significant soever the name be, that is more toothsome or wholesome'.

Hulled wheat, barley and rice could all be buttered in like fashion. In the mid-eighteenth century there were street vendors in London who went their rounds crying, 'Buy a bowl of wheat', and selling buttered wheat or barley by the dishful. The cereal was previously boiled in water to a soft jelly, and then stored in a pitcher. When a customer appeared, a little was taken out and reheated in a skillet with some sugar, spice and butter.[43]

Even softer and mushier was the pap on which babies were weaned. To make it, bread or flour was boiled in milk to a glutinous consistency. For the infants of the poor, the milk was all too often replaced by water, when the pap gave quite inadequate nourishment. Richer paps, which could serve as a light repast for adults, were sweetened and thickened with egg yolks as well as flour. With the addition of rosewater, such paps were even used to fill tarts.[44]

Bread dough was the basis of dumplings, pot-balls that were boiled and eaten with butter. Their place of origin was Norfolk, and from Elizabethan times Norfolk dumplings were a byword far beyond that county. The earliest dumplings may well have been boiled in broth in the stewpot (as puddings often were in the seventeenth century). But by the time they reached the printed cookery books they had become items to boil and butter. To make dumplings in 1653: 'Season your flour with pepper, salt and yeast, let your water be more than warm, then make them up like manchets, but let them be somewhat little, then put them into your water when it boileth, and let them boil an hour, then butter them.'

Nearly a hundred years later Hannah Glasse described Norfolk dumplings made from thick pancake batter, boiled in water, drained and eaten hot with butter. She also gave a recipe for hard dumplings of flour and water paste which 'are best boiled with a good piece of beef. You may add for change, a few currants.'[45]

Oatmeal went into milk porridge and water gruel. The latter at its simplest contained no more than oatmeal and water, but it was often flavoured with shredded onions or leeks, and enriched with butter or dripping. Smallage gruel, tasting 'strong of the herb and very green', was eaten to purify the blood. Other herbal gruels were made from a variety of curative plants, for the old beliefs in herbal medicines were still widespread in the eighteenth century.

Late in that century 'hasty pudding', 'crowdie' and 'boiled milk', all oatmeal pottages, became more and more confined to northern and western Britain. In the north hasty pudding was a constant part of the diet. Thirteen ounces of oatmeal and a quart of water, boiled together with salt, was said to be 'sufficient for a meal for two labourers. It is eaten with a little milk or beer poured upon it, or with a little cold butter put into the middle, or with a little treacle.' Crowdie was made by pouring boiling water on to oatmeal and stirring it: a piece of fat taken from meat broth was put to it as seasoning. It was 'a very common dish in the north among labourers of all descriptions, particularly miners'. In Scotland the finest ground oatmeal and cold spring water or fresh buttermilk were combined to make crowdie.[46]

Another oatmeal dish was the Welsh *llymru*, which spread into Cheshire and Lancashire with its name anglicized to 'flummery'. It was also known in the west country as 'wash brew'. It comprised fine oatmeal steeped a long time in water, strained, and boiled with continuous stirring until it was of an almost solid consistency, like that of the modern blancmange. Country people often made it with the soaked husks and leavings from oats that had been ground, skimming off the upper layer as the basis for their flummery. Gervase Markham praised flummery for its 'wholesomeness and rare goodness'; and explained that 'some eat it with honey, which is reputed the best sauce; some with wine, either sack, claret or white; some with strong beer or strong ale, and some with milk'. In the later seventeenth century the name was extended to a form of sweet jelly flavoured with cream or ground almonds, a successor to the earlier white leach, which became a popular dessert dish for entertainments.[47]

Two new forms of cereal were introduced into the diet of the gentry during the years following the Restoration. Vermicelli, which had already spread from Italy into the cuisine of France, now came to England where it was put into the new, thinner meat soups. Sago arrived from more distant regions through the East India trade: it was made from the pith of certain varieties of palm tree native to Malaya. Like vermicelli it became a fashionable adjunct to fine pottages, and in particular to clear chicken broth. Lady Grisell Baillie still thought it rather special when she wrote down her Christmas Day menu for 1715. The first course included 'plum pottage with sago and a few fruit', as well as 'plum pudding'.[48]

An ounce of sago mixed into a pint of water and seasoned with sack or white wine and lemon juice made an invalid drink, held to be efficacious against consumption. Another starch-based drink which was in great favour in the later seventeenth century was salop. It too probably owed its rise in the world to the East India traffic. In most countries of the east drinks were prepared from the dried and powdered roots of various species of orchids, and were widely consumed because they were regarded as aphrodisiacs. English merchants would have encountered a sugar-sweetened version in the East Indies. A similar drink was already known in parts of England, produced from 'dogstones', the roots of the native early purple orchis, which country folk dried, ground to powder and made into a thin gruel. But salop now became a beverage of fashionable townspeople; and English druggists began to sell imported Turkish orchid roots with which to make a superior form.

Salop powder was stirred into water until it thickened, when the liquid was sweetened and seasoned with rosewater, orange-flower water or in a similar fashion to the thin sago drink. The powder could also be made up with milk. 'Drink it in China cups as chocolate; it is a great sweetener of the blood', advised one recipe. The aphrodisiac side was played down – at least in the cookery books. At the height of its popularity salop was served in the coffee houses as an alternative to coffee or chocolate; and salop-vendors peddled the drink in the streets, or sold it from booths.[49]

Pottages of green vegetables diminished in importance after the adoption of boiling and buttering as an alternative mode of preparation for herbs and roots. Potherbs were still stewed with meat and fish; but several new vegetables now became popular, among them cauliflowers, celery, asparagus and artichokes, and in comparison the flavours of some traditional native potherbs lost their appeal. Daisies and pellitory are not heard of in that context after the fifteenth century. The avens (herb bennet), betony, liverwort, mallows, mercury, primroses and violets, which the Elizabethans grew to put into their pottages, lingered on for several more decades, but eventually they too were abandoned.

Gervase Markham recommended herbs 'which have no bitter or hard taste' for boiling with mallard, hare or coney, and listed in that category lettuce, strawberry leaves, violet leaves, vine leaves, spinach, endive, succory. When Sir Kenelm Digby transcribed into his notebook a French friend's recipe for *potage de santé* containing sorrel, borage, bugloss, lettuce, purslane, chervil and green beet leaves, he added his own opinion: 'The beets have no very good taste, peradventure it were best leave them out'.

Coleworts and cabbages, the supreme pottage plants of the Middle Ages, proved more acceptable when boiled and buttered than when stewed in meat broth, and they appeared in the latter far less often than before. Only in lowland Scotland did kail pottages made in medieval style survive virtually unchanged until late in the eighteenth century.

In England the range of acceptable greenstuff had narrowed

further by that date; although some herbs still remained in use that are rarely heard of in cookery today, such as hyssop, chervil, purslane (a salad as well as a cooking herb) and marigold flowers. But the large-leaved green beets, mallows (discarded because of their slimy texture), orache, mercury, bugloss and others were abandoned in favour of spinach; pennyroyal and other native mints yielded, in course of time, to spearmint; smallage was replaced by celery, green or blanched. And only country folk still sought out young turnip tops or nettles and other wild herbs in springtime to add to their broths.[50]

Among the aromatics preference was given to those of Mediterranean origin, in particular those described in seventeenth-century French cookery books as 'sweet' or occasionally 'fine' herbs. French cuisine had considerable influence on contemporary English cookery, especially after the Restoration. It was then that the 'faggot of sweet herbs' (the modern *bouquet garni*) was adopted into English usage.

Pulse pottages changed less. It is true that bean pottage was no longer as common as in medieval days; though the early colonists in America cooked it, and it returned to us after many years in the guise of Boston baked beans. But the traditional, pease porridge was a national dish of Tudor and Stuart England, referred to in French recipe books as 'pottage in the English style'. It was eaten at most levels of society, but more particularly among labourers' families, when it was often made very thick with flour or breadcrumbs and was called pease porridge. With the advent of the pudding boiled in a cloth, peas were given similar treatment, being packed into a pudding-cloth or bag, simmered in water or broth, and turned out as a solid mass that was sliced and eaten with bacon or pickled pork.

But in the course of the eighteenth century pease pottage lost much of its importance. Per Kalm reported that people of the middling sort, although they ate green peas avidly in the summer season, had little use for dried peas or beans. Later pease soup, like all other soups, ceased to be labourers' fare in the south; and even in the pottage-eating north of England it was not very popular. It remained an occasional item of diet in most parts of the country, but it could no longer claim to be one of England's national dishes.[51]

The medieval roots such as carrots and turnips, were still well liked in meat pottages and broths, especially in winter. But skirrets were now often stewed separately with marrow, spice and wine, as was the oyster-flavoured scorzonera or Spanish salsify, introduced during the seventeenth century. Beetroots arrived earlier, but failed to become pottage roots in Britain. William Rabisha's recipe for a spicy red beetroot and venison pottage published in 1673 was a rare exception that seems to have had no successors in English cookery.[52]

The new root destined to make the greatest impact on British eating habits was, of course, the potato (*solanum tuberosum*). The plants are indigenous to Chile and the Andes, and in Europe were first grown in Spain where they were introduced about 1570. Sir Francis Drake brought some roots to England, having apparently obtained them at Cartagena in Columbia. But on his homeward journey he touched the Virginian coast in order to pick up some English settlers; and this led to a misunderstanding about the provenance of the first English potatoes. For many years afterwards they were called 'Virginia' potatoes to distinguish them from the sweet or 'Spanish' variety. Their introduction to Ireland, ascribed variously to Sir Walter Raleigh and to the looting of ship's stores from a wrecked Armada vessel, took place probably no later than 1588.

It was a long time before Virginia potatoes became at all common in England. Through most of the seventeenth century it is clear from recipes that they were regarded as a speciality food, whether baked in pies or used to garnish rich boiled meats, such as beef olives, turkeys, capons, chickens and game birds. In most cases sweet or Virginia potatoes could be used interchangeably, and probably were, since sweet potatoes continued to be as well or even better liked than the Virginia ones. It was late in the century before the starch potential of the latter was recognized, and boiled, mashed potatoes came into occasional use as a foundation for puddings, in place of bread or cereal flour.

In Ireland, however, the native population was quick to

appreciate the virtues of the new roots. Not only were they easier to grow than oats and barley, they were also safer. It was an era of turbulence and uprisings, with the military practising a scorched earth policy; and an underground crop of potatoes was far less easy to find and destroy than a visible one of standing corn. Before 1657 soldiers who returned to England gave reports of whole fields in Ireland over-run by potatoes. The Irish peasant boiled the roots in his three-legged cauldron over his turf fire, skinned and mashed them, and ate them with a little butter or milk when either was available.

Irish influence no doubt accounted for the cultivation of potatoes in Lancashire. Here, as in Ireland, oats were the common cereal, and potatoes were received more readily by oatbread eaters than they were in wheaten bread areas. Potatoes were raised on the plots of the Lancashire smallholders, and by the end of the seventeenth century 'lobscouse', the famous local potato pottage, had been invented. A hundred years later, when it was already the traditional dish of the region, it was described as being made of potatoes 'peeled or rather scraped raw, chopped and boiled together with a small quantity of meat cut into very small pieces. The whole of this mixture is then formed into a hash with pepper, salt, onions, etc.' Another potato dish of northern England comprised the roots 'first boiled, then mashed, and the pulp boiled again in milk, in which they stir some flour, and eat it like hasty-pudding'.[53]

In the first part of the eighteenth century potatoes spread more widely through England, Wales and lowland Scotland; and thereafter they even reached the Scottish highlands. They were cultivated increasingly in the second half of the century, for each time there was a poor cereal harvest potatoes advanced in popularity. At first they were grown only in gardens, but later they were developed as a field crop.

They were used in a wider variety of ways than were other roots.

Some people when they are boiled have a sauce ready to put over them, made with butter, salt, and pepper; others use gravy sauces, others ketchup, and some eat them boiled with only pepper and salt; some cut the large ones in slices and fry them with onions, others stew them with salt, pepper, ale or water. It is a common way also to boil them first, and then peel them, and lay them in the dripping-pan under roasting meat. Another way, very much used in Wales, is to bake them with herrings, mixed with layers of pepper, vinegar, salt, sweet herbs and water. Also they cut mutton in slices, and lay them in a pan, and on them potatoes and spices, then another layer of all the same with half a pint of water; this they stew, covering all with cloths round the stew-pan, and account it excellent.

The Irish have several ways of eating them: the poorer sort eat them with salt only, after they are boiled; others with butter and salt, but most with milk and sugar. Also, when they can get a piece of pork, bacon, or salt beef, they account it excellent with boiled potatoes.

Adam's Luxury and Eve's Cookery, 1744, from which the last paragraphs are quoted, goes on to give recipes for bacon or pork broth thickened with mashed potatoes, potato stuffings, sausages, cakes, puddings and fritters. Fried potatoes are mentioned; only chips are lacking, but these were a much later invention which arrived from France as recently as 1870. But by the middle of the eighteenth century the common way to eat potatoes was with boiled or roasted meat.[54]

Potatoes had an interesting career before they settled down into their modern food-style. Had they been discovered sooner they would probably have become a universal pottage vegetable, supplying a thick brew analogous to pease pottage. As it was, their early years saw them as a delicacy and almost a sweetmeat, while they emulated the sweet potato; and later they moved into the tradition of 'roots to boil and butter' or to fry, rather than that of pottage roots.

Meat pottage flavoured with herbs and thickened with oatmeal, the successor of the medieval 'long worts de char', continued through Tudor and Stuart times as the everyday vehicle for pieces of boiled beef or mutton. It was 'of use in every good man's house', according to Gervase Markham, who described it as 'ordinary pottage'. It too acquired the status of a national dish, being recorded in French recipe books as 'pottage after the English fashion'. It could be seasoned with onions alone, or with the juice of herbs expressed in the mortar, instead of the whole leaves.

Skink was the Scottish version, made with a leg of beef chopped in pieces, and seasoned with saffron and herbs. Those in northern Britain who could not afford beef made barley broth instead, with a singed sheep's head stewed in it which sat triumphantly in the middle of the bowl when it was served at Scottish tables. In the eighteenth century the recipe was adapted for middle-class families in the south, but they could not face the head in its entirely and had it chopped to pieces for their broth, or replaced by a chicken.[55]

But there were also new alternative methods of preparing stewed meats. For the gentry, from Elizabethan times onwards, fricassees, hashes, ragoos and other made dishes comprising meat cooked and served in a flavoured sauce, took the place of the richer standing pottages of medieval days. Bisks and similar French-inspired confections of fish simmered in *court bouillon* succeeded the earlier thick fish pottages. The sauce was an important part of all such dishes, and under French influence sauces now took on a new consistency. For French cooks had begun to thicken their ragoos with a liaison of flour and lard fried together and then combined with a little broth.

Sir Kenelm Digby learned a slightly different version from the French cook of Queen Henrietta Maria, widow of Charles I. It was part of his recipe for 'the Queen Mother's hotchpot of mutton'.

> About a quarter of an hour before you serve it up, melt a good lump of butter (about as much as a great egg) till it grow red; then take it from the fire, and put to it a little fine flour to thicken it (about a couple of spoonfuls) like thick pap. Stir them very well together; then set them on the fire again till it grow red, stirring it all the while; then put to it a

ladleful of the liquor of the pot, and let them stew a while together to incorporate, stirring it always.

The result was then amalgamated with the rest of the liquor.[56]

In the next decades the flour and butter liaison (called at first 'fried flour') came into universal use as a thickener, not only for stews and made dishes but for sauces that were prepared separately to accompany meat, fish or vegetables. Hitherto thick sauces had been based upon breadcrumbs or beaten egg yolks, for the medieval amidon had gone out of fashion.

The seventeenth century also saw a proliferation of thinner sauces comprising gravy, wine, verjuice or orange or lemon juice or some combination of those liquids with capers, herbs, dried or garden fruits and spices in a great number of permutations. Four out of no fewer than fourteen sauces for roast mutton commended by Robert May were: '5. Onions, oyster-liquor, claret, capers, or broom-buds, gravy, nutmeg, and salt boiled together. . . . 10. Salt, pepper, and juice of oranges. 11. Strained prunes, wine and sugar. 12. White wine, gravy, large mace, and butter thickened with two or three yolks of eggs.'

Fewer sauces appeared in the recipe books of the eighteenth century. But some of them were very complex and included such items as mushroom pickle, lemon pickle or ketchup (each of which already contained an agglomeration of different ingredients), as well as anchovies, lemon juice, wine and often a proportion of prepared cullis or gravy. At the same time, however, a small number of simpler sauces came to the fore, and in many households these superseded the richer and more highly flavoured types. For egg sauce, fennel sauce, onion sauce and mushroom sauce, only a little seasoning and some melted butter (with or without flour thickening) were added to the main constituent.

Simpler still was the sauce that contained no more than flour and butter thickening; and by the second part of the eighteenth century this had become all too common in many English homes and in inns and taverns. Carl Moritz, a Swiss visitor, reported on the average dinner which he ate on his travels through England in 1782. 'To persons in my situation [it] generally consists of a piece of half-boiled or half-roasted meat; and a few cabbage-leaves boiled in plain water; on which they pour a sauce made of flour and butter, the usual method of dressing vegetables in England.'

Fresh uncooked sauces became comparatively rare in the eighteenth century for they were replaced by the preserved pickles, sauces and ketchups which were eaten with cold meats. But a simpler successor to the complex green sauce of medieval times existed in mint sauce, notable for the brevity of its recipe: 'Chop some mint, put to it vinegar and sugar'.[57]

The sauces that surrounded the hashes, ragoos and other made dishes, were often based upon prepared broth, for the medieval practice of extracting stock from knuckles, scrag-ends and tough cuts of meat was still current. The meat and bone pieces were boiled in water with sweet herbs and mace or cloves until a highly-concentrated broth was produced, which was strained and kept for use.

During the eighteenth century strong broth was gradually ousted by the rather similar gravy and cullis. The word gravy, which signified a sweet spicy sauce in medieval times, had taken on its modern connotation by Elizabeth's reign. During the seventeenth century gravy was drawn from half-roasted meat, which was slashed and then pressed to release the liquid blood. Presses with screws existed for the purpose of crushing the meat to extract every last drop. It was then seasoned very highly with wine, anchovies, nutmeg and herbs. Later it was found easier to cut up the meat and stew it very slowly in a little liquid to draw blood, and then to boil it long with flavourings that included wine, spices and ketchup. Gravy for brown sauces was made by browning coarse beef in fat before stewing it; gravy for white sauces from knuckle or neck of veal; and fish gravy from tench or eels. There was also poor man's gravy: 'a glass of small beer, a glass of water, an onion cut small, some pepper and salt, a little lemon peel grated, a clove or two, a spoonful of mushroom liquor, or pickled walnut liquor'.

At the other end of the scale were the extravagant gravies and sauces produced for rich men by their French chefs. Hannah Glasse poured scorn upon them. 'Your fine cooks always, if they can, chop a partridge or two and put into gravies.' She prided herself on the fact that her own gravy recipes were far more economical, and just as good. But, 'so much is the blind folly of this age, that they would rather be imposed on by a French booby, than give encouragement to a good English cook!'[58]

Cullis likewise was a prepared broth. In Anglo-Norman cookery it has been an amalgam of chicken liquor with the flesh of the chicken after it had been pulped in the mortar. Later any meat, or even fish or roots could supply the basis; and these were well seasoned, stewed and incorporated with their broth. Eventually the pounding in the mortar was dropped, and the cullis was strained off its solids. The pre-made cullis or gravy was added regularly to made dishes, soups and sauces during the eighteenth century to enhance their flavour.

Simple broths and running pottages had also been part of medieval diet. They usually contained the pieces of meat which had been stewed in the cooking process, and like all pottages were served over sops of bread or toast. In the course of time the name of the latter was transferred to the liquid which in France became known as *soupe*; and in the later seventeenth century thin pottage became a fashionable dish among the English gentry under this new title. Cooked broth was strained clear and then reinforced with vermicelli or sago and finely sliced soup herbs such as celery, endive or lettuce. Sometimes it was dished up with a fowl, duck, knuckle of veal or other piece of meat in it; but it could contain nothing more substantial than a French roll. Occasionally both meat delicacies and bread rolls appeared together, as in Hannah Glasse's elegant chestnut soup, served with a crisp fried roll in the middle and a stewed pigeon on either side of it.

Soup soon acquired a different status from pottage in relation to other dishes, for early in the eighteenth century it began to take on the role of an appetizer. Menus and table plans of the period show that soup, although laid in the first course, was always set at the top of the table and 'removed', with another dish, often of fish, put in its place. Thus the way was paved for the division of the meal into four separate courses of soup, fish, entrée, and sweets together with savouries. But another hundred years elapsed before this arrangement of the courses became the established pattern.[59]

The separation of pottage or soup from the meat which had cooked in it soon spread down the social scale. François Misson in the 1690s and Per Kalm in the 1740s drew attention to the fact that in England, unlike other parts of Europe, boiled meat was eaten by people of the middling sort with vegetables, and not in pottage. In this development the general adoption of the fork, late in the seventeenth century, played an important part, for it was no longer necessary to eat the soft boiled flesh chopped up as a spoonmeat. The broth might be consumed separately, but it was usually a thinnish liquid. The carbohydrate element of the meal came now not from cereal-thickened pottage, but from pudding, and later also from potatoes eaten with the meat.[60]

With the vogue for thin soup based on chicken or veal broth came a new invention. Its earliest name was 'veal glue', and it was the forerunner of the bouillon cube. Strong veal stock was slowly stewed for many hours, strained and simmered again, allowed to set, scraped free of sediment, and then gently cooked until

> the jelly grow of a gluish substance. . . . Put it into little sweetmeat pots till it is quite cold; then you may take it out and wrap it in flannel and afterward in paper and it will keep many years. A piece the bigness of a nutmeg will make half a pint of broth. The whole leg of veal, unless very large, will not make a piece of glue bigger than your hand. It is made into broth by pouring hot water on it.[61]

It was a great deal of work for such a small output. But veal glue, its name later changed to 'pocket' or 'portable' soup, continued in demand all through the eighteenth century. Ham or beef or sweet herbs were now often boiled with the veal, to give a tastier flavour.

Bees flying into hives

Table laid for banquet course
From F. Massialot: *New instructions for confectioners*, 1702

Soups could be based on fish as well as meat. Eel soup and oyster soup were two eighteenth-century favourites; and mussels, crayfish, and bony fish such as skate or thornback boiled until their bones dissolved, were the foundation of others. Vegetable soups were made from herbs or roots first stewed in butter and then boiled in water. Pease pottage reappeared as a thinner pease soup.

An innovation of the middle years of the eighteenth century was turtle soup. At that time it was discovered that West Indian green turtles, said to be far superior to the other local varieties in wholesomeness and rareness of taste, could survive the ship-board journey to England if kept in tanks of fresh water. With them came recipes for cooking them 'in West India fashion', to furnish the feasts of the wealthy. A turtle of sixty or a hundred pounds was large enough to provide a whole first course in itself. Its belly and back were boiled and baked respectively, and laid out at the top and bottom of the table, the fins and guts were stewed in rich sauces to provide corner dishes, while a tureen of turtle soup, made from the head and lights, had the place of honour in the centre.

Only a few people could aspire to turtle dinners; but mock-turtle made its appearance in the cookery books almost as soon as the genuine article. The fourth edition of Hannah Glasse's *The Art of Cookery* tells how to dress a turtle the West India way; mock turtle (a calf's head, well seasoned and stewed in strong mutton or veal gravy and a quart of Madeira, and served in its soup in an empty turtle shell, if one could be procured) is in the sixth edition.[62] The emphasis was on the soup; and thereafter mock-turtle made regular appearances among the other soups in the cookery books.

Prominent among the festal foods of medieval times had been the pottages made from meat with sweet dried fruits, almonds, sugar and spices. Of the thick ones blancmange was the principal survivor; and it gradually changed its nature. Elizabethan blancmange, like its predecessor, was based usually upon teased or carded capon meat, and ground almonds were still a frequent flavouring, though they were often supplemented and sometimes supplanted by rosewater. 'And when it is as thick as pap', said a contemporary recipe, 'take it from the fire, and put it in a fair platter, and when it is cold, lay three slices in a dish, and cast a little sugar on it, and so serve it in.' But an alternative version now existed as well, a meatless blancmange made with cream, sugar and rosewater, thickened with egg yolks or with beaten egg whites.

Blancmange, which had been a first course dish in medieval times, now tended to appear in the second course, sometimes offered along with leach. During the seventeenth century both the capon flesh and meatless types coexisted, the latter now sometimes thickened with wheat or rice flour; and Robert May still offered recipes for fish blancmange too. Then, late in the century, a new concept of the dish arrived from France. It began with a hen, but this hen was boiled with calves' feet, and the resultant jelly was thickened with ground almonds, flavoured with rosewater and allowed to set. In another recipe the hen was omitted altogether, and a hartshorn jelly made, which was strained with ground almonds and milk. Such blancmange closely resembled white leach. It also foreshadowed the English blancmange of the eighteenth century, which was always a kind of jelly, stiffened with isinglass or hartshorn, coloured with milk, cream or beaten egg whites, but still flavoured with the almonds which had so long been associated with the confection of that name.

The final transformation came from the new world. In the West Indies, as in the East Indies, arrowroot was cultivated as a source of starch. Perhaps the early settlers recognized its potential as a thickener for meatless blancmange. By the early 1820s arrowroot was being exported to Britain, and soon afterwards recipes were published there for American or West Indian blancmange. Boiling milk, sweetened and seasoned with a little cinnamon and lemon peel, was poured upon a solution of arrowroot and stirred briskly the while, since it thickened instantly. It was put into a mould and turned out the next day. Here at last was the true precursor of the modern cornflour blancmange.[63]

The medieval running pottages of meat and dried fruits also

continued through the sixteenth and seventeenth centuries, though they lost ground to the newer stews and made-up dishes of meat or fish to which were added sharp fresh fruits or recently introduced vegetables. Nevertheless capons and hens were on occasion boiled in white broth with ground almonds, currants, raisins, dates, prunes, sugar, spice and sack; or a lamb's head was stewed with sweet herbs, strained oatmeal and cream, and currants. But by Georgian times such compositions had lost their appeal and were rarely eaten.

There were one or two notable exceptions. Cock-a-leekie still survived in Scotland. Lady Grisill Baillie in 1743 wrote a special instruction to her housekeeper to use a measured six ounces of prunes in its making. Mrs Margaret Dods affirmed in 1826 that 'the soup must be very thick of leeks'; but she omitted the prunes.[64]

Another traditional pottage of meat and dried fruit was the English stewed broth. We first hear of it in the early fifteenth century under the title 'stewet beef to potage'. It then comprised gobbets of beef boiled in a little water and much wine with minced onions and fine herbs. Bread was the thickener, powder of cloves, cinnamon and mace were the seasonings, a red colour was supplied by sanders, and currants were put in to complete the pottage.

The recipe recurs in various guises over the next four hundred years. The Elizabethan version was called 'how to make stewed broth with either veal, mutton or cock'. 'Take it and set in a fair pipkin of water, and when it is sodden and fair skimmed, take a handful of good herbs and put in it, and grated bread, prunes, raisins and currants, nutmeg, pepper and salt, and let them boil all together.' The prunes were an Elizabethan touch, for the imported dried plums which had already become an ingredient of meat pies were now added also to stewed fleshmeat. They created such an impression that they subsequently became a token of the other dried fruits; so that plum cake and plum porridge were confections containing some dried fruits, but not necessarily prunes.

By Gervase Markham's time the herbs in stewed broth had

been dropped; but the other ingredients were all there, together with turnsole or sanders to give the pottage a rich wintertime colour. Markham called his recipe 'ordinary stewed broth'. But if we consult the bills of fare laid out at the beginning of Robert May's *The Accomplisht Cook*, we find it was not so ordinary after all. Stewed broth appears there as a festive dish in the first course on All Saints' Day, Christmas Day and New Year's Day. A few years later, in 1673, William Rabisha pinpointed it as a special Christmas food ('a dish of stewed broth, if at Christmas' was an item on his menu for the Christmas quarter). Not long afterwards stewed broth became known as Christmas broth or pottage, or as plum pottage or porridge. The last name emphasizes the thick texture of the broth.

The association of plum pudding with the same festival is recorded early in the eighteenth century. But until late in the century plum puddings, although well fruited and spiced, rarely had any alcoholic addition. Plum porridge, like the Christmas puddings of more recent times, was usually laced with liquor such as claret and sack, and it could be made in good time and stored away in earthenware pots to keep until the festal days. One of the latest recipes for meaty plum porridge was that given in 1826 by Mrs Margaret Dods among her national dishes, and it perhaps lingered longer in Scotland than in other parts of Britain. Elsewhere the meatless plum pudding had already prevailed.[65]

Chapter 7

Bread, cakes and pastry

Prehistoric period

Bread, which was destined to become the staff of life and the mainstay of the working Briton, had not yet acquired that vital role in neolithic times. The earliest bread would have been made from emmer wheat or naked barley (the two commonest cereals of the time), well mixed with weed seeds, all ground together in a saucer quern to produce a rough kind of meal full of husks and chaff. Even if put several times through the quern it would, when mixed with water, have yielded an extremely coarse dough and a crumbly and unpalatable bread. It may well have been necessary to add honey or fat to hold it together in flat cakes that could be cooked on hot stones on the edge of the fire. And the breadcakes would have had to be eaten hot, for when cold they would have been so rough and hard that they would have cut and hurt the eaters' mouths. It is therefore likely that through most of the prehistoric period cereals were consumed more often in pottage than in bread.

The earliest surviving examples of hearthcakes are those found at the first-century BC lake village of Glastonbury. They are in the form of very hard little buns, one of which proved on analysis to be composed of fragments and whole grains of wheat, hulled barley, wild oat, chess and a seed of common orache. They showed no sign of having been leavened.[1]

The first step towards oven-baked bread was taken when an inverted pot or large potsherd was put over the flat cakes as they baked. The warmth from the baking-stone was thus kept circulating around the dough so that some of the steam was retained inside the small bun, causing it to rise a little and producing bread of a lighter and less dense consistency. Bakery of this type is common among primitive peoples (Cato described it in second-century BC Italy).[2] Once established in Britain it continued among the peasantry into medieval times and beyond.

The development of the clay oven dome took place in the early Iron Age. Celtic settlers who reached Britain at that time used clay domes to parch their corn and perhaps also to bake their bread. They introduced spelt as their wheat, and began growing hulled barley in place of the naked variety. Both had good resistance to cool, damp weather conditions. Nevertheless they must at times have had to be harvested before they were fully ripened; and spelt, which has its grains very tightly clamped inside their glumes, would have needed parching in any case to release the seed.

A well-organized early Iron Age farm was therefore equipped with racks where unripe corn could be hung to dry (similar to those still used in alpine regions of Europe), and places where it could be parched, probably on primitive cob-ovens. Parching made the chaff more brittle and easy to shed, and also prevented the germination of the corn, especially necessary since it was stored in containers in underground pits. Seed corn was housed separately in granaries above ground.[3]

Grain was parched on top of clay domes, and bread may likewise have been baked at first over, rather than inside, such domes (a practice known to have been common in the Middle East). Eventually it was realized that the dome could be employed more profitably if food was cooked in the hot air inside it. In the final stage of development it was given a floor on which fuel could be burnt to create the initial heat, thus producing an oven of the type of the Roman and medieval baker's oven.

Another technological improvement which affected bread making was the introduction of rotary hand querns, probably derived from the Celts in Spain. These were reaching Britain early in the first century BC, and they enabled corn to be ground with far less expenditure of labour than the old saddle querns. The Celts in Gaul had an improved form of horsehair sieve which was no doubt known at least in south-eastern Britain, and which secured a finer separation of flour from chaff.

But perhaps the most important new discovery, and one that may even have preceded the Iron Age in Britain, was the use of beer barm as leaven. Leavened bread probably first occurred accidentally at some time when uncooked bread dough was left lying about in hot weather until it began to ferment. The multiplication of organisms inside it and the consequent release of carbon dioxide would have caused the texture to change, and the resultant bread, when cooked, would have been lighter and more spongy than usual. The Celts of Gaul and Spain deliberately encouraged fermentation by adding beer barm to their dough, so that they had a lighter bread than the Greeks and Romans; and we may believe that the Celts in Britain did the same.[4]

Roman period

With the Roman settlers came further innovations. Some new or hitherto little-known cereals were now raised in Britain. Club wheat was introduced, and was sometimes grown together with spelt. Oats and rye became more common. Rye was occasionally sown and reaped alone, but often still formed part of a mixed crop. Alone it produced an extremely dense dark bread, with a greyish tinge, but it could be combined with wheat and barley in varying proportions to make brown breads.

Barley was, however, the predominant cereal crop of Roman Britain, used both for bread making and beer brewing.[5]

Grain was needed in greater quantities than ever before to provision the army of occupation. Large areas of the East Anglian fens were drained and turned over to farming, and a canal system was created by which both corn and livestock could be waterborne via Lincoln as far as the vale of York. Elsewhere cereal growing was intensified to feed the local population and to fill the granaries, capable of holding two years' supply, which existed in every permanent fort.

Corn-drying ovens were improved; and the characteristic T-shaped kilns, where a fire was lit in a lower chamber provided with a long flue and the corn was laid out and parched on a floor above, became common on Romano-British villa farms. Threshing floors were constructed where the parched cereal could be 'beaten with flails and winnowed with fans', or else battered by a threshing sledge with iron or flint teeth.

Rotary querns came into more general use, and as time went on were made with flatter and thinner stones so that they were more easily portable. Their diffusion to even the remotest parts of northern and western Britain was helped by the fact that they were part of the regulation equipment of the armed forces: one was carried by each group of ten men.

Hand querns met the needs of the smaller household. In the towns professional bakers had larger rotary mills turned by donkey, horse or human slave treading a circular course, and doughmixers, similarly powered, to knead their dough. Water-mills with undershot wheels, which harnessed the river's current by means of axle and gear-wheels to turn the upper of a pair of millstones, were in use by the fourth century AD. Examples have been found at three places on Hadrian's Wall, and at Silchester and Great Chesterford in the lowland zone. Mills of this type were described by Vitruvius in the first century AD, but not put into practical operation for some three hundred years.[6]

The Romans also introduced their bread ovens into Britain. The usual kind was the fixed oven with a domed roof of rubble and tiles, and a flue in front. Wood or charcoal was burnt inside for a time and then raked out so that bread and cakes could be baked in the heated chamber. The *clibanus* or portable oven also served to bake bread and cakes.

The Romans in Italy preferred bread made from soft white wheats. Leavened wheaten bread is lighter than that of any other cereal, for it contains a superior quality and quantity of the gluten which holds the carbon dioxide gas within the bread dough while it bakes. Bread of the finest and whitest flour, sifted after the first grinding of the wheat, was most favoured. What remained in the sieve was passed again through the mill, and the resultant flour made 'secondary bread' or 'military bread', a coarser, darker product containing a higher proportion of bran. This was of course the food of the poorer people, whether soldiers or civilians.

The Romans admired whiteness in bread, and even adulterated their flour with chalk to enhance its appearance. 'To know the colour of one's bread' was their expression for knowing one's place, and the lowlier the place, the darker the bread.[7]

The distinction between white and brown breads must have been even more pronounced in Britain. Because of the climate less wheat was grown there than in the Mediterranean region, and more rye or barley must have been added to the cheaper grades of bread, as well as a greater proportion of bran. Barley bannocks were the bread of some areas where land and climate would not support wheat, while in the upper, wetter reaches of the highland zone oaten hearthcakes were probably already coming into use as the local bread.

The Roman wheaten loaves of the first century AD, were made in a form which resembled the modern teacake. Those found at Pompeii, carbonized but otherwise perfect, were round and low, about eight inches in diameter, marked into eight wedge-shaped sections. But the Romans made several other kinds of bread, too, including loaves baked with anise or cumin placed beneath the bottom crust for flavouring, loaves baked in tins on top of the hearth, and enriched breads in which eggs, milk or butter were added to the dough. Not all were made at Rome: some were specialities of particular places in the provinces. It is easy to believe that in Britain milk-bread and honey-bread were produced, for milk and honey were both important foodstuffs of the country.

Roman bread was not only eaten by itself, but was also put into the made dishes of cookery, especially those that were sweetened. One Apician recipe runs: 'Remove the crust from wheaten loaves and break up into largish morsels. Steep in milk, fry in oil, pour honey over, and serve.'

The evidence for early forms of cake in Britain is elusive. In any case the boundary between primitive bread and primitive cake was tenuous, honey- and milk-breads being made when the extra ingredients were available. If fat was also added, to be taken up as the starch granules of the flour swelled and burst during cooking, the result might be a kind of cake. Sheep or goat cheese supplied the fat content of early cakes made in Roman Italy, such as the *libum* (two pounds of cheese, one pound of wheat flour or half a pound of fine flour, and one egg well mixed, patted out into a loaf and baked on the hearth under a crock). Small fried cakes of similar ingredients and a rudimentary cheesecake were other Roman products.[8]

Cakes made along these lines must have been familiar in Roman Britain. There were professional pastry cooks in Romano-British towns who produced, among other things, sweetmeats in moulds. A pottery pastry-mould found at Silchester carries a representation of four figures standing around a tripod which has been interpreted as the emperor Septimius Severus, his wife and two sons celebrating a Roman victory over the Caledonians.[9] It is well known that Roman coin faces were designed to carry political propaganda and news of Roman military successes to the far corners of the empire and beyond: but it now appears that the honey-bun or cheesecake of the Romano-Briton served the same purpose.

In Roman times too an early kind of biscuit was made, in concept not unlike a cracknel. 'Take best wheat flour and cook it in hot water so that it forms a very hard paste, then spread it on a plate. When cold cut it up for sweets, and fry in best oil. Lift out, pour honey over, sprinkle with pepper, and serve. You could make it better if you used milk in place of water.' The idea behind this recipe survived in western European cookery in the simnels and cracknels of the Middle Ages and later centuries.

The Romans sometimes wrapped fowls or fleshmeat in an oil and flour paste to seal in the juices during cooking, as is done by means of aluminium foil today. And at feasts they served eggs, small birds and other delicacies inside a rich pastry covering. But they do not seem to have developed the pies and pasties which were to become such an important feature of the medieval cuisine of western Europe.[10]

Early medieval period

Elaborate forms of cookery were abandoned in the fifth century with the decay of the towns and the disappearance of the former civilized villa life; and the cakes of the Germanic settlers were probably simple, homely confections. Loaves of bread occasionally formed part of food rents, but never cakes.

The cereals of the early medieval period were those already known in Britain. It is possible that the Saxons grew proportionately less wheat than their predecessors in Roman times had done, and more of the barley which they had formerly raised in their continental homelands. They certainly favoured the mixed crop of wheat and rye that was later called maslin (from *miscelin*, its name in the Merovingian and Carolingian domains in France; the Saxon term for it was later corrupted to mancorn or monkcorn). The mixed crop was well regarded, as it had been in prehistoric times, for it acted as an insurance against the failure of wheat on its own in a bad season. But wheat was grown where soil and climate would bear it; and the ninth century saw not only Viking invasions, but also more peaceful trading expeditions from Norway, when the Norsemen came to England to purchase surplus wheat.

Kiln-drying of corn was usual in England, as it was also in Wales. For a long time grinding was carried out solely on a rotary hand quern, or even occasionally on a saddle quern. But during the fifth century the Vitruvian watermill with its undershot wheel was developed on the continent and improved by the substitution of an overshot wheel which could harness a greater force of water. Mills of this type reached Britain before AD 762 (when one in Kent was mentioned in a charter), and thereafter watermills increased in number so that 5,624 were recorded in Domesday, most of them in the lowland zone.[11]

The mill was closely linked with the manorial system, since it was always the property of the landlord. But even at the time of the Norman Conquest there were regions such as Yorkshire where mills were distinctly sparse; and elsewhere there were many individual manors (two-thirds of those named in Domesday) without a single one.[12] So in spite of attempts made by Norman lords of the manor to force their Saxon tenants to bring their grain to be ground at the communal mill, paying some part of it as a toll for the privilege, a high proportion of the country's breadcorn must have been ground at home until quite late in the medieval period.

The bread oven was another fixture that took its place in the feudal scheme of things, for such ovens were to be found in the manor or the monastery, but seldom in the home of the peasant. The latter was encouraged to take his dough to be baked in the manorial ovens, but again he had to give a proportion of it in payment. Bread baked in the poor man's home often took the form of unleavened hearthcakes called therf-bread. But small raised loaves could be cooked in a makeshift oven formed by inverting the deep Anglo-Saxon cauldron or *cytel* and heating it from without with slow burning fuel or hot ashes. The three-legged cauldron buried in burning peats was the peasant's oven in the highland zone. In the towns professional bakers once more appeared, producing leavened bread and cakes for sale to the townspeople.

Wheaten bread was made in at least two qualities: 'clean' bread from flour finely sifted after milling; and ordinary wholemeal bread which was either from more coarsely sieved whole grain, or else from reground husks, as in the Roman *panis secundarius*. A very fine grade of flour called *smedma* was produced, from which bread might be made and also cakes, including perhaps the crumpets and honey-dumplings mentioned in the Anglo-Saxon vocabularies.[13] Professional bakers and the bakers of large households were men; but hearth-baked bread was made by the woman of the house. This is reflected in the etymology of the word 'lady', which derives from *hlaefdige*, kneader of the bread; while 'lord' was formerly *hlafward*, keeper of the bread.

In the highland zone the hardier cereals fitted into the farming year, for oats and barley were spring sown, after the cattle had been taken up to the summer pastures. Wheat was also grown here and there in Wales, especially in low-lying fertile areas such as the island of Anglesey and the vale of Glamorgan. 'Twenty-six loaves of the best bread that shall grow on the land; if it be wheat bread, six of them of fine flour' were part of a food rent paid by the king's bondmen under the Welsh laws. Wheat was highly valued; and even the cat which guarded the king's barn from mice had its blood-price: the pile of wheat which would cover it completely if it was held head downwards and tail upwards on a clean level floor.[14]

Oats and barley ground on rotary hand querns supplied the everyday breadcorn in Wales, which was baked in flat cakes on an iron griddle. If oatcakes formed part of the bondman's food rent, they had to be 'as broad as from the elbow to the wrist, and so thick as not to bend in holding them by the edges'. Oats and barley (a six-rowed variety known as bere) were likewise the main breadcorn of lowland Scotland; but only oats could withstand the harsh climate of the Scottish highland valleys.

Later medieval period

The coming of the Normans meant that an already existing feudal system was more strictly enforced. The rich, English and Norman alike, could enjoy a sophisticated cuisine based on that of Norman France, which had been inherited from the Roman era and modified through the centuries under Gothic and Frankish influence. But the pease pottage and hearth-bread of the serf remained unchanged. It is true that he quite soon began to demand the same white bread that his social superiors were eating, but it was to be several more centuries before such bread became common to all.

In the Middle Ages white wheaten bread of the finest quality only appeared on the tables of the well-to-do. The best soil in the country was given over to wheat, which fetched a higher price than any of the other cereals. But before there could be enough fine white bread for everyone, much land which would not in its natural state bear wheat had to be worked and enriched and persuaded to do so.

The lord of the manor could render his own land more fertile by having it marled and dunged. But it was not worth the labour of the small peasant to dig, cart and spread the clayey marl on his strips in the open field, when these would shortly be reallotted to neighbours. So they remained unimproved, and the villagers grew maslin, rye or barley on land that might, with attention, have been made to produce wheat.

Even maslin soon degenerated, after a few poor seasons, into something approaching pure rye. 'All wheat on damp soil is changed after the third sowing into *siligo*', Columella had written in the first century AD. He was referring to a phenomenon that occurred when hard and soft wheats were grown as a mixed crop and *siligo* (a soft white wheat) fared better in moist conditions. But owing to a confusion of words *siligo* was later taken to mean 'rye', and the medieval farmer believed, in accordance with his experience of maslin, that wheat and rye were different manifestations of the same cereal; though he noticed that the change took place in one direction only, and was irreversible.[15]

So maslin was raised as a breadcorn akin to wheat, though its proportions must have varied from season to season and from village to village. It was grown in the first place as a safeguard, lest pure wheat should fail, and in the second place because it was a heavier producer than wheat alone. For these reasons it still had a high reputation as late as the seventeenth century.

Clean rye was also grown, and was mixed with wheat at the mill in whatever proportions were desired to produce maslin meal.

> Some mixeth to miller, the rye with the wheat,
> Temsed [sieved] loaf on his table to have for to eat:
> But sow it not mixed, to grow so on land,
> Lest rye tarry wheat, till it shed as it stand.

These verses by Thomas Tusser explain the great drawback of maslin: the rye ripened anything up to a fortnight earlier than the wheat, and if it was left to stand, began to shed its grain. The compromise solution, when both were sown together, was to cut the maslin in the middle week, after the pure rye harvest, but before that of wheat; and such was still the practice in the seventeenth century.[16]

Barley was grown universally because it was the brewing corn, and in some western regions it supplied breadcorn too. Oats were raised as a pottage cereal in lowland Britain, but in the coldest and wettest upland regions of both north and west they were still the only cereal able to survive and were therefore the sole breadcorn.

In most parts the age-old practice of reaping weed seeds along with cereal grains continued. Among the weeds permitted to grow in cornfields were cockle

> that may well be suffered in a breadcorn but not in seed [corn], for therein is much flour. Drake is like unto rye, till it begin to seed, and it hath many seeds like fennel-seeds, and hangeth downward, and it may well be suffered in bread, for there is much flour in the seed. . . . Darnel groweth up straight like an high grass . . . and there is much flour in that seed, and groweth much among barley. . . .[17]

All were an insurance against the bad season and the wasted cereal crop.

In the remoter parts of the north and west, people continued to grind their corn at home on hand querns. These were still in common use throughout the highlands and islands of Scotland even in the late nineteenth century.

In lowland Britain, however, increasing numbers of mechanically powered mills came into operation in the course of the Middle Ages. More watermills were built. And windmills, already known elsewhere in north-west Europe (the principle by which they operated appears to have been discovered originally in Persia), were introduced into England in the thirteenth century. The earliest were postmills, in which the entire structure was pivoted on a post so that it could be turned for the sails to catch the prevailing wind. They were later succeeded by towermills, on which the cap and its attached sails only were swivelled round. In time windmills became as common as watermills, and the lord of the manor had the same rights over them, so that he could compel his tenants to bring their corn to the manorial mill. Within the mill the grain was still ground in the traditional manner between two stones: and the corn of Britain continued to be stone-ground in windmills or watermills until the first rollermill in the country was opened in Glasgow in 1872.[18]

In the towns bread was produced by professional bakers, who made up the flour themselves, but would also bake their customers' own dough. But over most of the country bread was made at home. And for several centuries home baking still meant hearth baking for the majority of people. At first only the largest houses had their own bread ovens, and they were part of the kitchen which, because of fire risks, was often a separate building in the early medieval residence. Later the kitchen became incorporated into the rest of the house, but the bakehouse remained separate. Smaller homes took longer to acquire ovens, partly because the houses of peasants and labourers were often of such flimsy construction. When the central hearth was moved on to a side wall, an arrangement introduced in the twelfth century, but not universally adopted until the sixteenth, cottages began to be built more sturdily:

and a stone or tile oven could be inserted, either on an inside wall near the fireplace, or sometimes in the thickness of an outside wall. Like the baker's oven it was preheated by burning wood or furze within it, which was removed before the dough was set inside to bake.

The techniques of bread making long remained unrecorded. They formed a secret lore, learned by the housewife from her mother and by the baker from the master craftsmen who were his seniors in the 'mistery'. The *White Book* of the city of London laid down 'that bakers shall instruct their servants twice a year how to bolt and how to knead their dough'.

The best white wheaten bread, made of the finest flour which had been two or three times sieved through woollen and linen bolting cloths, was in the Middle Ages called wastel bread (from the Norman French *gastel* or cake) or pandemain (probably originally from *panis domini*, the sacramental bread, because that was made of the most delicate flour obtainable: the bakers often stamped their pandemain loaves with the figure of Christ). Cocket, another fine white bread, but a slightly less expensive one, was produced until about the beginning of the sixteenth century. But before that time the name manchet had begun to be applied to white bread of the finest quality. Manchets were made up as rather small loaves: in Elizabeth I's reign they were supposed to weigh 'eight ounces into the oven, and six ounces out', and forty were to be made out of the flour bolted from one bushel of corn. Bread described as being 'of whole wheat' was of wheat flour more coarsely sieved than that used for wastel or cocket; while a still coarser and more branny wheat bread was made under the name of 'bis' or 'treet'.

All these different grades of bread were taken into account in the Assize of Bread, which was in operation from 1267 (the date of the first full version that we have) until 1815. It is indeed thought to go back still earlier, to the reign of King John. By this statute the weight of the farthing loaf and later, when all prices had risen, of the penny loaf, of bread of each grade was fixed on a sliding scale according to the prevailing price per quarter of wheat. It was not easy to implement, partly because fluctuations in the price of wheat meant that the weight of the loaf was constantly changing from season to season. And even in large towns there were variations in the regulations to cover locally made and locally named breads. The assaying of the bread of individual bakers seems often to have been done in an irregular and erratic fashion, especially in small country towns, and it must have been almost impossible to enforce the Assize properly. Nevertheless bakers were from time to time convicted of selling underweight loaves, and paid appropriate penalties.

> Item, if default shall be found in bread, the first time, let the baker be drawn [through the streets on a hurdle], and the loaf about his neck; the second time, let him be drawn and set upon the pillory; and the third time, let him be drawn, and his oven pulled down, and let him foreswear the trade within the city.[19]

In London the white bakers and the brown or *tourte* bakers for a long time had separate guilds. The *White Book* of the city of London laid down 'that a tourte baker shall not have a bolter nor make white bread'. His brown bread was to include all the husks and bran in the meal, just as it came from the mill. But he was permitted to bake the dough which people brought to him ready made up, and to make horse-bread of peas and beans. In Ipswich, on the other hand, the bakers who baked the fine white loaves, such as wastel and cocket, were also allowed to make treet bread from the leavings, after they had sieved their meal and removed the whitest and finest flour.[20]

The brown bakers also baked the *panis de omni blado*, 'bread of every grain' (later through a mistranslation called 'bread of common wheat') which was the cheapest of all the breads in the Assize of Bread. It was made wholly or partly of cereals other than wheat, and was dark in colour.

By the ruling of the Assize the medieval brown or treet loaf sold for a farthing weighed twice as much as the finest white wastel loaf at the same price; the farthing wholewheat loaf weighed one and a half times as much as cocket, which was the second grade of white bread; and the loaf of other cereals twice as much as cocket.

The gentry ate fine bread with their meat or fish, but they had bread of the second quality for their trenchers. In the Middle Ages the firmer lechemeats were eaten directly off thick slices of bread into which any surplus gravy or sauce could be absorbed. At the end of the meal, the diner might eat his trencher-bread if he felt so inclined, and in a humble home he probably did so. Among the rich, the trenchers were collected in baskets and given as alms to the poor. Trencher-bread was supposed, ideally, to be used when it was four days old, and the trenchers were cut from large loaves of wholemeal or similar quality flour. The regulations in the *Northumberland Household Book* enjoined 'that the trencher-bread be made of the meal as it cometh from the mill'; and menus for breakfasts for my lord and lady throughout the year began, 'First a loaf of bread in trenchers'. In households exalted enough to employ a carver, his was the task of cutting the trencher loaves and squaring and smoothing the slices. He also had to pare the outsides of the rolls or manchets of fine bread to make them ready for eating, which was evidently done in the interests of hygiene. 'Touch never the loaf after he is so trimmed', ran the instruction.[21]

Among the well-to-do the practice arose of putting a platter of gold or silver plate or pewter under the trencher-bread, while poorer people used treen (wooden) platters. By the end of the sixteenth century the slices of trencher-bread had lost their original use and only survived in the form of sops of bread that were placed in the dish under boiled or stewed meats before they were brought to table.

In the country, where baking was done at home and the Assize of Bread did not run, there was less standardization of both white and dark breads. Dame Alice de Bryene, early in the fifteenth century, appears to have had white wheat bread of one quality only at her table. As two hundred and twenty white loaves and about thirty 'black' loaves, made from the residue, were baked regularly out of one quarter of wheat every five or six days at her house at Acton in Suffolk, her white bread was probably less fine than pandemain or manchet. On the other hand the number of 'black' loaves was so small compared with the white that even the least of her servants must often have received white bread as well as 'black' in their ration.

Dame Alice's servants probably fared better than those in many households. A Venetian visitor to England about the year 1500 commented that: '. . . the English being great epicures and very avaricious by nature, indulge in the most delicate fare themselves and give their household the coarsest bread, and beer and cold meat baked on Sunday for the week, which, however, they allow them in great abundance'.[22]

The rougher breads of servants and labourers and their families were made up of maslin or the local grain: rye in Norfolk, barley in north-west England, lowland Scotland, parts of Wales and Cornwall, oats in upland Wales and the Pennines and the Scottish highlands. In Wales much of the bread was still flat-bread baked daily upon a griddle, 'bread made of oats and of barley, broad, round and thin . . . that people doth eat seldom wheat that is baken in an oven'.

The Scottish knights and esquires in the same century aroused the admiration of Sir John Froissart during the wars of Edward III because each carried a metal bakestone and a bag of oatmeal behind his saddle with which, over the fire, they 'make a thin cake like a cracknel or biscuit, which they eat to warm their stomachs; it is therefore no wonder that they perform a longer day's march than other soldiers'.[23]

One other kind of bread was made in manors and monasteries and even by some of the town bakers, and that was horse-bread. Peas and beans were the official ingredients. The same pulses made peasant bread, too, in times of dearth. Havercake (oatcake) and two loaves of beans and bran were the bread of Piers Plowman and his children in the lean weeks before the harvest.[24]

Peas made an ill-tasting bread, and beans one still worse. Nevertheless townspeople as well as peasants had to accept pulses in their bread flour after a poor season. In Elizabeth I's reign there were years when the common bakers were ordered to make their bread of rye, barley, peas and beans.[25]

William Harrison's description of Britain's bread at that period shows how precarious was the supply of cereal flour:

> The bread throughout the land is made of such grain as the soil yieldeth; nevertheless the gentility commonly provide themselves sufficiently of wheat for their own tables, whilst their household and poor neighbours in some shires are forced to content themselves with rye, or barley, yea, and in time of dearth, many with bread made either of beans, peas, or oats, or of all together and some acorns among, of which scourge the poorest do soonest taste.

He went on to complain of the high price of corn which he attributed to profiteers, and which was such 'that the artificer and poor labouring man is not able to reach unto it, but is driven to content himself with horse corn – I mean beans, peas, oats, tares, and lentils: and therefore it is a true proverb, and never so well verified as now, that "Hunger setteth his first foot into the horse-manger" '.[26]

In times of great shortage wheat and rye were imported, when they could be obtained elsewhere in Europe, to be sold at a price to those who could afford them. And by the later Middle Ages special provision was being made for the London poor: from 1438 there are records of cereals being brought in on their behalf. Not long afterwards the city companies were made financially responsible for importing grain for Londoners when home supplies failed.

But although many country people in Britain ate bread of branny wheat, maslin or inferior grains until late in the eighteenth century, a movement in favour of white bread for all had begun several hundred years earlier. The poet Gower complained about 1375 that farm workers were now demanding wages and food above their station in life: 'Labourers of old were not wont to eat of wheaten bread; their meat was of beans or coarser corn, and their drink of water alone. . . . Then was the world ordered aright for folk of this sort'; while Langland in *Piers Plowman* was also unsympathetic to beggars who claimed the right to bread of 'cocket or clere matin [wheat bread of the second sifting] or else of clean wheat'.[27]

The fact was that even the poorest people could not fail to be aware of the bread of their social superiors, because on various occasions it came their way too. The alms-bread given out at a monastery gate on a special festival; the bread which fell to the servants and their friends and relations after a great medieval feast; part at least of the bread issued to boon workers at harvest time, when the quality of the food was apt to be rather good in order to encourage the tenant-workers to greater efforts – all these were white wheaten bread. And apart from the fact that wheat bread was generally, though not always, believed to have a better flavour than the bread of other cereals, it was a symbol of status.

London and the large towns were the places where the movement towards whiter bread made most headway. By 1574 there were sixty-two white bakers in London and thirty-six brown bakers, a very different proportion from the thirty-two brown and twenty-one white of 1304; and in the seventeenth century the separate guild of the brown bakers disappeared altogether.[28]

Bread of one kind or another was eaten at all levels of society, either alone or more usually with cheese, fish, meat or pottage. But bread was also a valued ingredient of cookery, which acted as a thickening and consolidating agent for a wide variety of dishes.

Finely grated dried breadcrumbs were kept locked away along with the spices, according to Alexander Neckam, and were brought out to be used as a coating for fish that was to be fried. Fresh bread was crumbled into many of the pottages and sauces of the day. For poor people's pottage branny brown breadcrumbs were an alternative to oatmeal as a thickener. For the well-to-do white breadcrumbs bulked out the mortrews and other light-coloured pottages which were thickened until they were 'standing'.

Breadcrumbs were helpful in sauce making, too, not only as a stiffener, but also because they could be brayed in the mortar after the spices and other seasonings, and could take up 'that which remaineth from the spices'. Brown breadcrumbs went into the dark-coloured sauces, such as chawdron and galantine, and white into the paler ones.

Breadcrumbs were equally useful in recipes containing much fat or fatty meat. They were an alternative to oatmeal in haggis, and were often preferred to ground cereals for sausages and stuffings.

Drinks crumbed with bread were popular. Ale caudles were often made with breadcrumbs as well as eggs. White bread in hot milk, known as 'milk sops', was a supper for a Saturday night.[29]

Compacted breadcrumbs were the basis of gingerbread, a favourite medieval sweetmeat for those who could afford it. At first the spices in its composition made it expensive. It was, however, imported in some quantity in the thirteenth century, probably from the Netherlands, for it paid a small customs duty at London. The Countess of Leicester gave twelve shillings for four pounds sold loose, and two and fourpence for a box which must, *pro rata*, have contained less than a pound. This was a high price in 1265; imported almonds, for instance, bought at the same time, cost no more than twopence ha'penny a pound.

Homemade gingerbread could be prepared by mixing breadcrumbs to a stiff paste with honey, pepper, saffron and cinnamon (ginger is omitted from the earliest recipe we have, but this may be due to an accidental slip on the part of the scribe). Then it was shaped into a square, sliced, and decorated with box leaves impaled on cloves. 'And if thou wilt have it red, colour with sanders [sandalwood] enough.'[30]

Thin pottages were often poured over 'brewes' or sops – pieces of bread or toast laid at the bottom of the dish. These were the counterpart of the trenchers of bread upon which lechemeats were usually served. One such pottage, 'sops dorry', was made thus: 'Take onions and mince them small and fry them in olive oil. Take wine, and boil it with the onions; toast white bread, and do it in dishes, and good almond milk also, and do thereabove and serve it forth.'[31]

In this dish the sops were toasted, for toast had already entered the national diet. It has been suggested that toast was an English invention for freshening up stale bread. But in fact trencher-bread was preferred at least four days old, when it was easier to slice and square, and was drier and more absorbent. And although Andrew Boorde claimed that bread 'is not good when it is past four or five days old', he also added, 'except the loaves be great'. Sops in pottage were another outlet for stale bread, and it was often left untoasted for that purpose.

The origin of toast may well lie in the medieval enriched toasts. Pieces of white bread were browned on the gridiron, soaked in wine, reheated and crisped, and then served with almond milk. There were also semi-solid versions, the most notable being 'toste rialle'. This comprised a thick paste of sugar, spice, sweet wine, quinces, raisins and nuts, with rice flour added 'for to make it binding and standing', spread hot over toasted trenchers of white bread and decorated with sugar plate cut in lozenges and gilded at the tips. 'And lay, for a lord, in a dish, four trenchers; and serve it forth.' Similar, though simpler, was 'pokerounce'.[32]

These richly spiced toasts declined into the seventeenth-century toasts covered with 'fine beaten cinnamon mixed with sugar and some claret'. Cinnamon toast recipes were taken by the early settlers to America, where the confection became a traditional foodstuff. On a more austere note, a 'saltyd toste' was the recognized diet for a seasick pilgrim on shipboard bound for Rome, according to a fifteenth-century ballad.[33]

Another well-known bread dish of the Middle Ages was *pain perdu*. It follows the principle of an Apician recipe, and may have survived in the cookery of France from Roman times. Anglo-Norman *pain perdu* was made by dipping slices of pandemain or manchet bread into beaten yolk of egg, frying them in butter and then sprinkling them liberally with sugar.

'Wastels yfarced' were white loaves with the crumb removed, mixed with eggs, mutton fat, currants, spice powder, saffron and salt, and then pressed back into the loaf as a stuffing. By the fifteenth century the idea had been developed into 'rastons'. For these a special bread dough enriched with eggs and sugar was made up into a loaf. When baked its top was cut off 'round above in the manner of a crown'; and the crumb was removed, shredded, mixed with butter and filled again into the shell. The top was put back and the loaf returned briefly to the oven; 'and serve it forth all hot'.

A further change was made in the 'buttered loaves' of the sixteenth century. Still richer bread was produced with sugar, butter, egg yolks and many spices mixed into the dough. It was made up in small loaves, 'and when they are baked through: set a good dole of sweet butter upon a chafingdish and coals, then cut your loaf in three pieces and butter it, then strew sugar betwixt every piece and serve it out'. Buttered loaves continued in the recipe books for some time longer, and finally disappeared during the later eighteenth century.[34]

Enriched bread was a form of food that went back at least to the Roman period. In earlier medieval times the art of making such breads was more highly developed in France than in England. But from the later thirteenth century English bakers too were making what they called French bread or puff. It appears to have been a kind of milk bread confected with butter and eggs. At Southampton it was the most expensive bread that could be bought; in London it sold for the same price as wastel. Like wastel or manchet it was often made up in the form of small individual cakes. When a regulation of 1440 laid down that the white bakers of London 'shall bake all manner of bread that they can make of wheat . . . white loaf bread, wastel, buns and all manner of white bread that hath been used of old time', the buns were almost certainly bread-cakes of enriched bread.[35]

'Buns made with eggs and spices' were a treat for the Elizabethans, and buns with the addition of currants and raisins were a particular Lenten food.[36] The special association of hot cross buns with Good Friday began only after the Reformation. Before that time it was customary to mark all loaves with a cross before they went into the oven, to ward off evil spirits that might prevent the bread rising. The practice was abandoned as popish in the seventeenth century, and was retained only for that day in the church's year when the symbol of the cross had its greatest significance.

The line between enriched breads and cake was not in medieval times very easily drawn. The Anglo-Saxons had the term 'cake' in their vocabulary, and the Saxon version appears to have been made up in a small size, from the fact that the word is glossed with the Latin *pastillus* (little cake) in one of the later word lists.

As oven baking became more widespread a new kind of cake made its appearance, distinguished by its very large size. The miller in the Reeve's Tale in Chaucer's *Canterbury Tales*:

> He half a bushel of his flour hath take
> And bade his wife go knead it in a cake.

If the miller's bushel was fifty-six pounds Chaucer may have been exaggerating a little. Nevertheless, when recipes for baking a cake began to appear in household books (which did not happen much before the seventeenth century), the quantities used were very generous by modern standards. Half a peck (seven pounds) of flour was quite usual, along with four or five pounds of currants, and butter, cream, eggs, sugar and spices proportionately. To prevent it being sad, the cake had to be raised with a considerable amount of ale-barm.

Such huge cakes were made only for special occasions, and in medieval and Tudor times little cakes were still far more usual. Small spiced cakes were served as an alternative to wafers to accompany the wine, bragot or mead that ended the fifteenth-century feast. The ingredients for some cakes for a church feast at St Ewen's Church, Bristol, in 1478 were stated in the accounts of that year:

A bushel of meal for cakes . . .
Item for saffron for the same cakes
Item for milk and cream
Item for eggs to the same.

A recipe 'To make fine cakes' of more than a century later indicates how they would have been mixed. For greater fineness the flour was first baked in the oven in an earthen pot and then sieved;

> then take clotted cream or sweet butter, but cream is best, then take sugar, cloves, mace, saffron, and yolks of eggs, so much as will seem to season your flour, then put these things into the cream, temper all together, then put thereto your flour so make your cakes, the paste will be very short, therefore make them very little, lay paper under them.[37]

The medieval baker made not only plain and enriched breads, but also the light biscuity confections called simnels and cracknels, which had to be boiled before they were baked. Something of the kind had been known in Roman times and had since been further developed. During the Middle Ages simnels were given an official place in the tables of the Assize of Bread: since it was boiled as well as baked, a farthing simnel was permitted to be lighter in weight than a farthing wastel.

On occasion the bakers of the Middle Ages produced biscuit too, which was at first ship's biscuit. It was literally rusks of twice-cooked bread (*panis biscoctus*) which bakers put into their ovens to dry out after their loaves of bread had been drawn. In Italy it was produced on a commercial scale, to provision whole fleets and armies on the move.

By Tudor times biscuits of finer quality were being made in England as a sweetmeat for the banquet. Here they supplied an alternative to the earlier wafers or spiced cakes to accompany hippocras or mead at the end of the meal. Wafers were in great demand in medieval times. They were not the province of the baker, but were made on special wafer irons by the wafer-maker, or at home by the cook. In towns the waferer was one of the street traders, selling his wares to passersby; and an official waferer was attached to the royal court.

Wafers had been introduced by the Normans from France, whence also came their name (*gaufres*). We learn from the *Goodman of Paris* of the well-developed wafer trade in Paris, and of the types of wafers that could be made at home. Some required a rich batter of flour, eggs, salt and wine; others a plainer batter without eggs; while for cheese wafers slices of cheese were sandwiched inside the batter. The mixture was run between two greased wafer irons which were then heated.

English wafers were evidently complex too. In the earliest recipe that we have the paste is made of flour, white of egg, sugar and ginger, and the filling of tender cheese ground up with the womb of a luce (pike), 'and look that thine iron be hot, and lay thereon of thine paste, and then make thine wafers, and serve in'.[38]

One other medieval confection of flour paste which did not survive even into Tudor cookery was lozenges. 'Fried lozenges. Take flour, water, saffron, sugar, and salt, and make fine paste thereof, and fair thin cakes; and cut them like lozenges, and fry them in fine oil, and serve them forth hot in a dish in Lenten time.' Fried lozenges were either eaten on their own, as in this recipe; or in a runny syrup of wine, dried fruit and spices strained together and boiled.

But we can establish the venerableness of the dish we call macaroni cheese from the following recipe which must have been introduced from Italy, where macaroni had recently been invented, into the court cookery of Richard II. 'Macrows. Take and make a thin foil of dough, and carve it in pieces, and cast them on boiling water, and seeth it well. Take cheese, and grate it, and butter, cast beneath, and above as for lozenges, and serve forth.' It was not apparently made in England during the next few hundred years, but it returned from Italy in the eighteenth century, when Elizabeth Raffald published a very good recipe entitled 'To dress macaroni with Parmesan cheese'.[39]

The pie was a development of the Roman idea of sealing meat inside a flour and oil paste as it cooked. In northern Europe, where butter and lard were the common cooking fats, pastry began to be made which was strong and plastic enough to be moulded into a free-standing container; and thus, at an unknown date and place, the pie was invented. Even its name is a mystery, unless it was derived from the pie or magpie, known as a collector of miscellaneous objects. For the true pie often combined a mixture of ingredients; whereas the bakemeat and the pasty were more usually confined to a single form of meat or fish, with seasonings.

Pies were well established in the life of medieval Britain. In the towns the piemaker took his place along with the baker and the waferer. In 1378 a special ordinance of Richard II controlled the prices charged by cooks and pie bakers in London for their roasted and baked meats. The best capon baked in a pasty cost eight pence, the best hen baked in a pasty five pence. If the customer provided his own bird, the charge 'for the paste, fire, and trouble upon a capon' was a penny ha'penny, and for the same upon a goose, twopence.[40]

That some piemakers took advantage of the peppery and spicy recipes of the time to make up their pies from tainted meat is clear, for several regulations were issued during the fourteenth and fifteenth centuries to try to prevent such malpractices. Concerning the quality of their pastry less is known: but a standing pie to contain one of the larger birds had to be made of a strong, firm dough, so the use of the cheaper rye or coarse wheaten flour for the paste would have been accounted no bad thing.

Pastry making was one of the crafts which the medieval cook or housewife had to learn by hearsay, and there are no instructions in contemporary cookery books on how to make the pastry for a meat pie. There is just one mention of 'strong dough', used for a very large pie containing several layers of meat filling coloured variously white, yellow, black and green to create an interesting striped effect when it was cut.

For open pies or tarts the shell was baked blind. 'Then take and make fair coffins and let them hard in the oven', or 'then take harded coffins', say the recipes. They were usually filled with a mixture comprising strained egg yolks with various dried fruits and spices, and occasionally extra titbits such as small birds. Cheese tarts were also enjoyed.

To make a bakemeat for a special occasion two or more coffins could be united, as in the handsome 'chastletes' or little castles. For this, four coffins were made of 'good paste' and arranged on four sides to form a fifth one at the centre. The tops were carved to look like battlements. They were baked blind and then filled with separately coloured mixtures, yellow for the middle, and white, red, brown and green for the four sides. The edifice was baked again and served forth.

When closed pies were made of meat or fish, the contents were well seasoned with spices and wine or vinegar, and often dried fruits were added. A problem of their production was to prevent the lid sinking inwards as the pie baked. The following solution was suggested in the case of a lamprey pie:

> then cover him [the lamprey] fair with a lid, save a little hole in the middle, and at that hole, blow in the coffin with thine mouth a good blast of wind. And suddenly stop the hole, that the wind abide within, to raise up the coffin, that he fall not down; and when that he is a little harded in the oven, prick the coffin with a pin stuck on a rod's end for [fear of] breaking of the coffin, and then let bake, and serve forth cold.[41]

Many different small tarts and pasties were made. There were 'chewettes', with a filling of pork and chicken on a meat day, and turbot, haddock, codling and hake on a fish day; and 'darioles' which contained egg yolks and cream, mixed with wine, spices, minced dates 'and strawberries, if it be in time of year'. From the former developed the pies known as 'shred' or 'minced' pies, from the shredded meat in them, and these by Elizabethan times had become part of traditional Christmas fare.

Sometimes little pasties were fried in lard instead of being baked in the bread oven. The 'pety pernollys' or 'pety pernauntes' of medieval times were usually fried. The paste was made of 'fair flour, saffron, sugar and salt', and the filling was pieces of bone marrow, egg yolks, dried fruit and spices. In the later fifteenth century little fried pasties of similar type, but with pulped pork or veal added to the filling were made in the form, and given the name, of hats. Hats for fishdays had almond milk in the pastry and fish liver with saffron for the filling.

A few decades later hats were succeeded by peascods, a change of shape and also of filling, for now the marrow, raisins, dates, sugar and spices were often reinforced with chopped veal kidney. Special moulds in the form or peascods or dolphins were available in the early part of the seventeenth century, in which the little pies were made up before being turned out and fried.

Also of enriched short pastry was the medieval 'payn puff', apparently another small pie. The paste had to be like that of 'pety pernauntes', but more tender. The bottom of the crust was pared away and the top cut off before the puff was eaten.[42]

Early modern period

The bread, cakes and pastry of medieval times were only gradually modified during the Tudor and Stuart era. The movement in favour of white wheaten bread for all had made headway in London and some other towns; but in the country such bread was for a long time to be seen solely on the tables of the gentry.

In the sixteenth and seventeenth centuries the finest white bread was still manchet, sometimes baked without leaven which gave it a very close texture. But recipes show that it was often raised with best ale-barm and was thoroughly kneaded, either manually through a kneading machine called a 'brake', or else by foot power, when the dough was wrapped in a cloth and trodden 'a good space together'. It was then put to prove for an hour, and moulded into 'manchets round and flat, scotch them about the waist to give it leave to rise, and prick it with your knife in the top, and so put it into the oven and bake it with a gentle heat'.

Superior forms of manchet, eaten by some of the gentry, were enriched with butter, eggs or milk as the earlier French bread had been. Wheaten milk bread was still often called French bread, and after a time the individual manchets came to be known as French rolls.[43]

Cheat bread was the sixteenth- and seventeenth-century successor of the medieval 'bread of whole wheat'. For this the flour was more coarsely bolted than for manchet. The dough was moulded into 'reasonable big loaves' which were baked at a fairly strong heat. Cheat bread came in more than one grade, ravelled cheat being an inferior and more branny kind made in country households. It would have been at least as dark as modern brown bread; while even the finest manchet would have been creamy in colour compared with modern white bread, owing to the yellow pigment in the wheat-germ which was mostly retained by stone-milling.

The name brown bread was now applied to the coarsest and most branny wheat bread of all, the 'bis' or 'treet' of medieval times. Many other country breads, made of local grains other than wheat, were also eaten.

Rye bread was still universal in Norfolk and parts of Suffolk and other areas of eastern England. Where wheat would also grow maslin bread was made, baked in the same manner as wheaten cheat bread, and raised with the help of a piece of sour leaven 'saved from a former batch, and well filled with salt, and so laid up to sour'.[44]

In parts of northern and western Britain there was a strong barley bread tradition, and wheaten bread was little known, except among the gentry, even at the end of the eighteenth century. Upland areas of Northumberland and Durham had bread of barley or barley and peas, although rye and maslin breads were more common in places near the east coast, because the grains for making them could be imported from southern England or from the Baltic.

The bread of Cumberland was of pure barley, sometimes baked in unleavened cakes a foot broad and half an inch thick, 'but more commonly leavened and made into loaves of about 12 lb. each. This bread will keep good four or five weeks in winter, and two or three in summer, and is almost the only bread used by the peasantry of that county'. It was dark in colour and 'somewhat sour' in flavour.

In the south-west, Cornwall was another barley bread area. But by mixing the flour with scalded skim milk and more than the usual amount of yeast or barm, bread could be produced that was 'little inferior to the second sort of wheat bread'. It was baked on the hearth under a large inverted iron cauldron with a covering of hot ashes over it; and in some Cornish households, pies, puddings and the best wheaten bread were all baked by the same method.[45]

The same practice was common in Wales, also a barley bread region. Although ovens were known in the vale of Glamorgan at least from Tudor times, in more remote places the pot oven or 'cetal' (kettle), a metal vessel heated with burning peats piled around it and on top of its lid was retained until late in the nineteenth century. Sometimes the dough was placed not on the hearth, but on the griddle, with the metal container inverted over it.

These techniques allowed raised bread to be made even in parts traditionally devoted to flat-bread. Wheaten bread was becoming more common in Wales by the end of the eighteenth century, but there were still areas, such as Cardiganshire, where it was hardly known.

In the Scottish lowlands barley bannocks were much eaten, as well as maslin bannocks of mixed barley, peas, oats and rye. Wheaten bread was little used there, and even in the eighteenth century could only be bought from bakers in Edinburgh and a few other towns. The barley bannocks were about an inch and a half thick, unleavened and very hard; so that most people found them less appetizing than oatcakes.[46]

In the upland oatgrowing regions of Wales, northern England and Scotland, large flat circular oatcakes baked on the griddle were the common fare. There were several local variations, and the thickness of the cake was no longer considered such a virtue as it had been under the laws of Hywel Dda.

The clapbread of Lancashire and Westmorland was beaten out to wafer fineness by means of a special round board, slightly hollow at the centre. On this a ball of soft flour and water dough was cast:

> and so they clap it round and drive it to the edge in a due proportion till drove as thin as a paper, and still they clap it and drive it round, and then they have a plate of iron same size with their clap board and so shove off the cake on it and so set it on coals and bake it; when enough on one side they slide it off and put the other side; if their iron plate is smooth and they take care their coals or embers are not too hot but just to make it look yellow, it will bake and be as crisp and pleasant to eat as any thing you can imagine.

In Cumberland clapbread was also made of barley meal.[47]

Several other kinds of oatcake were baked in the north of England, such as kitcheness bread, 'thin oatcakes made of thin batter'; and riddle cakes, which were thick and were leavened with ale-barm or sour leaven. The bakestones were usually of iron, unless there was a suitable local stone to be had, as in Nidderdale where 'a very fine bedded soft micaceous flaggy sandstone' from Bakstone Gill was pressed into use.

In Scotland barley and maslin bannocks and also oatcakes were baked on an iron griddle with a semi-circular handle. The oatcakes, when they came off the griddle, were rubbed with meal and finished by being toasted before the fire on a toasting stone: the quern sometimes served this purpose. They kept well, and were often stored in the meal-kist.[48]

Although some wheat was grown in north-western England, it was often sold in the south. 'And so attached are many of their people to the eating of oatcake or brown bread', reported William Ellis in 1750, 'that when they come up with their waggons of wheat and cheese to Hempstead Market, they bring their own coarse heavy bread to prevent their being forced to eat our Hertfordshire wheaten bread, saying – They do not like such a corky, bitter sort'.

Coarse breads of which peas and beans formed a part were not unusual during the seventeenth century, but were becoming less common in the eighteenth. Early in the period Gervase Markham wrote: 'For your brown bread, or bread for your hind-servants, which is the coarsest bread for man's use, you shall take of barley two bushels, of pease two pecks, or wheat or rye a peck, a peck of malt; these you shall grind together and dress it through a meal sieve'. The dough was leavened overnight in a sour trough, and extra sour leaven was added in hot water if needed. The dough had to be mixed with boiling water: 'for you must understand, that the hotter your liquor is, the less will the smell or rankness of the pease be received'.

The sour trough was maintained to help leaven the heaviest breads. It was still in use in the eighteenth century in parts of Yorkshire where rye bread was made. 'Here they employ leaven in common to make their bread, and as their kneading-tub has always part of this leavened dough sticking to it, it contributes towards leavening and fermenting the next dough.'[49]

The brown bread eaten by Henry Best's farm labourers at Elmswell in east Yorkshire was baked from a meal of equal parts of rye, barley and peas, mixed and ground together at the mill, according to his *Farming Book* of 1641. 'Poor folks put usually a peck of peas to a bushel of rye; and some again two pecks of peas to a fundell of maslin', he wrote.

Still less palatable was bread of bean-meal, the rankest of all breads made in England, which could not be formed into loaves

> because it will crack and be brittle, therefore it is commonly made into cakes in some parts of the north; its meal is of a yellowish colour, and so is its bread. Pea bread is much sweeter; yet in some parts of the north they grind beans and make bread of them, and sometimes they mix bean flour with barley meal for bread.

These unattractive breads were still made in the mid-eighteenth century. William Ellis, who described them, also claimed that 'coarse hearty bread' could be made from lentils (usually grown for fodder) provided that they were ground and mixed with fine oatmeal. But although pulses contributed to some of the roughest breads known in his day, the deliberate cultivation of weeds among the corn for the sake of the flour in the weed seeds had nearly died out. The corn was weeded late in May, and any weeds that survived did so accidentally.

Weed seed bread lingered on only in the remotest places, as for instance among the Orkney islanders who, at the end of the eighteenth century, 'ate at breakfast bannocks made of barley which had been ground in their hand-querns; mingled with the barley were seeds of all manner of weeds which had been carefully retained'. At the same date labourers' families in Kent, though their diet was a meagre one of tea, bread, potatoes and cheese, were refusing to eat any but white wheaten bread of the finest sifted flour.[50]

The movement in favour of white bread, already noticeable in London in late medieval times, had grown and spread. By Elizabeth's reign the wheat for Londoners' bread was coming not only from the home counties, but by sea from as far away as Norfolk, Lincolnshire and Yorkshire. The city companies had the responsibility of importing corn from Europe when supplies at home were scarce; and in 1616 the Grocers' Company reported that 'the poor would not buy barley or rye, either alone or even if mixed with two-thirds wheat'. The blend had to be nearly four-fifths wheat before it could be sold for breadcorn.

The appeal of white wheaten bread lay not only in its pleasing pale colour (foods that carried the colour white had been held in special esteem during the Middle Ages) and its agreeable flavour; but also in its greater digestibility. Many of the gentry ate it from necessity as much as from preference, for their lives were less physically demanding than those of manual labourers, and they were unable to digest branny or bitter breads. Thus Celia Fiennes complained that when she ate bread containing rye in the course of her travels about England, even if she failed to recognize it by taste, yet 'it so disagrees with me as always to make me sick'.

The lower orders liked to think they had digestions of equal delicacy, and undoubtedly some did. People who worked in sedentary or cramped conditions may well have found coarse bread too heavy. This could be the reason why white wheaten bread was at first in greater demand among the artisans of London than it was in country areas.

But by the last decade of the eighteenth century Sir Frederick Eden reported that the poor in most parts of Kent 'buy the finest wheaten bread and declare (what may be much doubted) that brown bread disorders their bowels. . . . Twenty years ago scarcely any other than brown bread was used.'

Rye bread was already equally unpopular in the midlands. The days were past when English husbandmen preferred barley and rye brown bread 'as abiding longer in the stomach, and not so soon digested with their labour'. By 1796 the labourers of Nottinghamshire had 'lost their *rye teeth* as they express it', and would have nothing but bread of wheat.[51]

The movement in favour of white wheaten bread gained great impetus, in southern and midland England at least, during the years from 1715 to 1755. In those decades agricultural methods were improved, wheat was increasingly grown, and a series of good harvests made wheaten bread plentiful and cheap. In the second half of the century, when there were several bad seasons, wheat again became scarce and dear. But by that time the wheaten bread habit had become so firmly established that it could not be checked, and indeed continued to spread.

To meet the demand grain had to be imported from abroad, and even so bakers had to supplement their wheat flour with other cereals and with bean-, pease- and potato-meal. This inferior bread was not well received. Neither was the government-sponsored 'standard' loaf, a darker wheat loaf containing more bran, which was baked and sold at a lower price than white bread during the worst times of shortage. Those who had once eaten white wheaten bread refused to be satisfied with anything less.

Moreover, wheat alone was not enough. It had to be the whitest, brightest wheat obtainable. Before the middle of the seventeenth century Henry Best in east Yorkshire found that the bakers of Beverley would not buy his dodd red wheat, which produced a flour of a bluish flinty colour, except for the purpose of mixing it with rye to make brown bread. It was not white enough to please their wheaten bread customers.

During the next century the number of common bakers grew rapidly in the southern part of the country, though in the north they were still rare and only to be found in the larger towns. To meet the demand for whiter bread, professional bakers began to use artificial colorants. They did so with the utmost secrecy and the bread was always offered for sale as finest quality white wheaten bread, at the appropriate price.

William Ellis discovered the methods used by two country bakers. One added alum dissolved in hot water to his leaven. At the other's bakery, alum was burned in a fire shovel, beaten to powder inside a leather bag, and strewn among the flour in place of salt 'for making the bread white, light and relishing'. Ellis's informant, the baker's daughter, added that the alum also made the bread 'quickly stale, crumbling, harsh, and hungry, therefore it does not satisfy like home-made bread'. But she observed that she had never in many years bought common bakers' bread that did not contain alum.[52]

This, then, was the 'corky, bitter sort' of bread which the oatcake-eaters of Manchester spurned when they came south. But it was undeniably white.

Even alum was not such a health hazard as some of the substances said to be used as adulterants of bread. According to several pamphlets published in the 1750s there were bakers who incorporated not only alum, but also chalk, lime, ground bones from the charnel-house, and even the highly toxic white lead as bleaching agents. Such charges were indignantly denied. But in time it came to be generally recognized that 'stuff' (the name given to alum mixed with salt) was employed in bread making, and it was many more years before anything was done to prevent the practice.

In Frederick Accum's day (he wrote *A Treatise on Adulterations of Food, and Culinary Poisons* in 1820) the worst kinds of damaged foreign wheat, with grains of other cereals, peas and beans still often went into the artificially whitened bread flour of London.[53] And it was 1872 before the use of alum in bread, along with that of many other food adulterants, was finally proscribed by law. But the principle of white wheaten bread for all, even the lowest in the land, was publicly recognized in 1795, when the Speenhamland system of poor relief was based upon the price of the gallon loaf of such bread.

The role of bread as a thickener for cooked dishes, well established in medieval times, continued for many years thereafter. As long as thick pottages, possets, 'ale crumbed with bread' and such confections were made, it retained its importance in this field.

But with the coming of the flour and butter roux in the later seventeenth century, breadcrumbs were gradually ousted from soups and many sauces in favour of the new thickener. By the mid-eighteenth century the bread sauces of the Middle Ages survived in only a few instances, notably as an accompaniment for a roasted fowl (usually a hen or capon), turkey or sucking pig.

Breadcrumbs were, however, still the foundation of sausages and stuffings. When puddings were developed independently, shredded bread was again used, not only in the 'pudding in haste' (which did not require much cooking), but also as the basis of a number of other puddings. Bread and butter pudding was in the recipe books by the 1720s. It is interesting to note that it was then made of freshly sliced and buttered bread, with currants, beaten eggs and nutmeg, and only later became a means of putting stale bread to good use.

The old Anglo-Norman *pain perdu* was adapted to contemporary tastes. By the early seventeenth century the beaten eggs in which the bread was dipped were well seasoned with sugar and spices. A few decades later it had become usual to submerge the bread slices in cream as well as liquid egg before they were fried, the dish being known as 'poor knights', 'cream toasts' or 'fried toasts'. Recipes from the 1730s onwards reverted to the French name of *pain perdu*.[54]

Red gingerbread, beloved in medieval times, continued in favour until the seventeenth century. It was then made with 'the grated crumb of stale manchet', flavoured with cinnamon, aniseed and ginger, and darkened with licorice and red wine. It was still an uncooked sweetmeat, for the mixture was stirred together, rolled thin, 'printed' with moulds, and the resultant cakes put to dry in a cool oven. White gingerbread had also become fashionable. But that was a confection of marzipan flavoured with ginger, and was therefore gilded (as was customary in the case of a marchpane); hence the proverbial gilt on the gingerbread.

In the same period cake baking was on the increase, and soon gingerbread changed its nature and lost its breadcrumbs. Before the end of the century it was being composed of flour, sugar, butter, eggs and black treacle, with ginger, cinnamon and chopped preserved fruits for flavourings, made up stiffly into cakes and baked in the oven. Eighteenth-century gingerbread followed the same pattern.[55]

Thinner pottages containing meat were still served upon the traditional sops during the seventeenth century. Very often the bread was dried hard first, so that it could suck up the juice of the pottage more thoroughly. A pottage of beef palates in a recipe of 1655 was dished up over the bottoms and tops of two or three cheat loaves dried. But other contemporary recipes recommended split manchets or rolls for the purpose; and when later in the century clear soups began to be fashionable, a dried French roll usually made its appearance at the bottom of the soup bowl. The French roll continued as an addition for several more decades. Later it was fried rather than dried, and so did not always sink beneath the soup. 'You may fry a French roll, and let it swim in the dish', wrote Hannah Glasse of her soup of green peas.

Thicker stews and hashes were likewise dished over sops or

sippets of bread through the seventeenth century, though the custom was dying out by early Georgian times. Thereafter sippets appeared with only a few particular preparations, laid around the edge of the bowl when minced meats, such as pig's liver, goose giblets or hashed veal, were brought to table.[56]

A new device which linked bread with meat was the sandwich, said to have been invented about 1760 by John Montagu, fourth Earl of Sandwich, so that he could eat meals without having to lose time away from the gaming board. An early recipe for sandwiches ran: 'Put some very thin slices of beef between thin slices of bread and butter; cut the ends off neatly, lay them in a dish. Veal and ham cut thin may be served in the same manner.'[57]

The spread toasts of Elizabethan times had a covering of finely chopped veal kidney mixed with egg yolks, cinnamon, ginger, sugar and a little rosewater. Veal toasts remained popular through much of the seventeenth century, but towards its end toasts with a savoury relish came to be preferred. Among the items put on toast were buttered (scrambled) eggs; poached eggs, which until Elizabethan times had been cooked in broth and served upon sops like other pottages; ham; bacon; anchovies; and well-seasoned melted or toasted cheese. The wine-soaked toast which formed part of the eighteenth-century 'English rabbit' recalls the enriched toasts beloved in medieval times.[58]

'Toast and water' was a simple drink comprising water in which a well-browned slice of toast had been infused for a considerable time. It enjoyed some vogue at the end of the eighteenth century. More attractive was the earlier 'panada for a sick or weak stomach', made from the crumb of a penny loaf boiled in a quart of water with a blade of mace, to which was added 'a bit of lemon-peel, the juice of a lemon, a glass of sack, and sugar to your taste. This is very nourishing, and never offends the stomach.'[59]

Enriched breads retained their popularity, whether made up as single large cakes or as small buns. In the later seventeenth century spice bread became usual breakfast fare among the gentry. The old heavy meal of ale, bread and meat or fish pottage was given up after the introduction of coffee and chocolate, and instead a lighter repast was taken, at a later hour and accompanied by one of the new drinks. A recipe of 1727 for a well-fruited spice bread describes it as 'an ordinary cake . . . good to eat with butter for breakfasts'.

Wigs were also now eaten at breakfast. They were small cakes of lightly spiced and sweetened bread dough, sometimes containing caraway seeds; and had been known under that name since late medieval times. Like currant buns they became associated with Lent, and wigs and ale were a Lenten supper in Pepys' day. There are many eighteenth-century recipes for them in varying degrees of richness. Economical wigs, with neither eggs nor butter in the paste, accompanied the harvest workers' four o'clock beaver (drink) of ale, or were dipped in a bowl of ale for his supper.

Buns sometimes contained currants, but were often flavoured instead with caraway comfits. Bath cakes contained caraway comfits, and a few were kept back to be sprinkled over their tops. 'Lun's cake', baked from enriched bread dough to be sliced, buttered and eaten hot for breakfasts, may also have stemmed from Bath, as one of the wares of the famous Sally Lunn.[60]

In Wales spiced and fruited cakes of fine wheatmeal were baked on the griddle, as was 'pitchy bread' (*bara pyglyd*), breadcakes formed from a leavened batter of flour and milk. The latter became well known in the west midlands, where their name was corrupted to 'pikelets'.

Muffins, leavened and cooked much as pikelets, originated in northern England, while in other parts of the country the old Saxon word 'crumpet' was revived and applied to bread of this type. Muffins, for which Hannah Glasse gave a recipe in her *Art of Cookery*, 1747, reached the zenith of their popularity in the nineteenth century, when muffin men traversed the town streets at teatime, ringing their bells.[61]

In northern England and in Scotland fine wheaten bakestone bread was produced from seasoned flour mixed with buttermilk. Scotland in particular became famous for the variety of its sour milk and buttermilk scones.

Griddle cakes of all sorts, like spice bread, were eaten fresh and even hot from baking. In contrast were the sixteenth- and seventeenth-century cakebreads, diet breads or biscuit breads which were made as sweetmeats for the banquet, or to offer with wine to the afternoon visitor; for these were intended to be boxed and kept until occasion arose for them. The principal ingredients were finely sieved wheat flour, plenty of sugar, spices and seeds (anise, coriander or caraway), two or three egg yolks, and sometimes butter or cream. Little or no yeast was used, and the paste was made up in small cakes to be baked in the oven on metal plates, in tin biscuit-pans or even in well-buttered mussel shells, when the confection was known as shell bread. Flat cakes were often preferred for easier storage; and if the mixture showed signs of rising too much in the baking, the cakes were to be turned over when nearly cooked, and 'thrust down close' by hand.

Sometimes biscuit bread was leavened and made up in long rolls, to be sliced after it was baked. The slices were then sugared and dried out again like rusks. This type was also known as French biscuit. Italian biscuit, Naples biscuit and prince biscuit were other biscuits of Tudor and Stuart times. 'Comfit-makers' biscuit' is to be found in some contemporary recipe books, for biscuits were no longer the province of the baker, but were made up by the comfit maker to be sold alongside his sugared fruits and spices. Not all biscuits were as elegant as this. The sailors' biscuit was still made in the form of rusks which would keep through long voyages.

But whether biscuits were prepared as biscuit bread, or were baked in individual 'little long coffins' of tin plate, they were always returned to the oven when cooked so that they could be thoroughly dried out; and they were then packed between layers of white paper in tightly lidded metal boxes; 'and set them in a temperate place where they may not give with every change of weather'. The secondary drying process, which recalls the origin of biscuit as 'twice-cooked bread', was only abandoned in the eighteenth century. New forms were then developed, such as sponge biscuit 'baked in little long pans buttered'; drop biscuit, mixed to batter consistency and dropped on to sheets of tin; long biscuit; round biscuit; lemon biscuit, and several more.[62]

Simnels and cracknels kept their traditional character for some time. The medieval simnel died out in the later seventeenth century, and its name was transferred to a rich fruit cake baked for mid-Lent. Cakes of the latter kind were taken home by daughters out in service as a gift to their mothers on what came to be known as 'Mothering Sunday'. Cracknels were still made medieval fashion in the early eighteenth century, being started off in a kettle of boiling water ('when they swim, take them out with a skimmer'); but later recipes show them baked directly upon tin plates, without the preliminary swim in the kettle.[63]

Wafers became less varied than in former times, and they were now always sweet. Flour, cream, rosewater, two egg yolks and a little searced cinnamon and sugar were the ingredients in a recipe of 1605. The practice grew up of rolling them off the hot irons on a small stick, so that they were in a curled form when put to cool, which helped to make them crisper. Brandy snaps are modern descendants of the rolled wafer. Wafers were eaten at the banquet in the sixteenth and seventeenth centuries, and in the eighteenth were offered among the dessert sweetmeats to accompany jellies. They also began to appear at the tea table. Flat wafers served as bases for almond paste confections, such as the marchpane while it still had a separate existence, 'French macaroons', and almond cakes.[64]

Other items for the banquet were small, sweet, flattish cakes of short paste. One Elizabethan recipe warns 'take . . . a little Godsgood [barm] about a spoonful, if you put in too much they shall arise, cut them in squares like unto trenchers, and prick them well'. Elizabethan short cakes were flavoured with saffron, cloves and mace. Further variants gained favour in the following decades, including Shrewsbury cakes, made with minced ginger in a 1655 recipe, but with cinnamon in the

1670s. Other small thin cakes were iced. Jumbals, their name derived from a gemmel or twin finger-ring, were fashioned as interlaced rings, knots and other such devices. Their texture varied, the paste for them sometimes resembling biscuit bread and at other times short cakes.[65]

Small cakes and biscuits were often baked in the bread oven as it cooled after the loaves had been drawn. But an additional oven was available once wall fireplaces and coal fires had come into general use. It became customary to construct a cupboard fitted with an iron door in the kitchen wall, near enough to the fire to take some of its heat. Food could be put inside to keep warm, and if the fire was well stoked up, small cakes, biscuits and even pies could be baked there.

Finally in 1780 a kitchen range was invented by Thomas Robinson. Thereafter an oven became an integral part of the fireplace of either kitchen or living room (according to the circumstances of the householder); and the separate bakehouse survived only in large establishments.

Large cakes were for long baked in the bread oven, for they retained much of their medieval character of enriched bread. By the middle of the seventeenth century they were still often enormous, and contained prodigious amounts of dried fruit; hence their name of 'plum cakes'. A typical recipe gives as ingredients fourteen pounds of flour, three of butter, one and a half of sugar and some spices. When these had been worked together for a matter of two hours, one quart of ale yeast, two quarts of cream, half a pint each of sack and rosewater and sixteen eggs were kneaded in and the cake was put to prove. Finally, just before it went into the oven ('a little hotter than for manchet') six pounds of currants and two of stoned raisins were combined with the paste. After three hours' baking the cake was frosted over with white of egg beaten with rosewater, was strewn with sugar; 'and then set it in the oven again that it may ice'.

Cakes were made up round, or sometimes oval, and were laid in the oven upon buttered papers. Before the end of the century the tin hoop had come into use as a means of holding the cake in shape and helping it to rise evenly. The size of the cake was also diminished; seven or five pounds of flour were now thought enough, with other ingredients in proportion. But even in the eighteenth century a 'little plum cake' called for two pounds of flour and one of currants.[66]

For some cakes a pound or so of caraway comfits was worked into the dough in lieu of dried fruits. Caraway cakes, like plum cakes, were always raised with ale-barm or yeast.

But an alternative agent was already in use to lighten the texture of biscuit bread. Four eggs 'beaten together for two hours' went into 'fine biscuit bread' in a cookery book of 1596, and it was baked in buttered moulds filled only half full to allow it to rise. There were several variants of this recipe. Gervase Markham's 'fine bread' of a quarter of a pound of fine sugar, and the same of sifted flour, aniseeds and two eggs, beaten well together and baked in a single buttered mould ('and so serve it whole or in slices at your pleasure'), could have been a prototype sponge cake, provided it was not overcooked.

Several more decades elapsed before eggs were used to raise larger cakes, and the earliest to be thus treated were seed cakes, since seeds, no longer added in the form of caraway comfits, were lighter to support than dried fruits. One early recipe says: 'you must keep beating your cake till it goes into the hoop which must be just as the oven is ready', while another carries the warning: 'it must not stand to rise'. Housewives had to learn the new technique of handling cake mixture when it was not yeasted.[67]

Seed cakes were very popular during the eighteenth century. Economical ones were still raised with yeast, but richer ones were held up by eggs alone, and often included chopped candied fruits as well as seeds, and a generous helping of sack or brandy.

Before the middle of the century eggs became the sole raising agent for many plum cakes too. Elizabeth Raffald's very luscious 'bride cake' used eggs at the rate of eight to each pound of flour.

This wedding cake was notable for the manner in which it was iced. For many years cakes had been frosted with sugar, in ever-increasing quantities, and put back into the oven to 'ice' after they were baked. Not dissimilar had been the frosting of the Tudor and Stuart marchpane. But by the eighteenth century the earlier banquet had been replaced by dessert dishes, among which the marchpane no longer held its former position as centrepiece. It was then rescued from oblivion by being united with the rich plum cake. The 'bride cake' was doubly iced, first with an 'almond icing' and then with a covering layer of sugar icing.[68]

A Banbury cake appeared at some seventeenth-century wedding feasts. It was a single large cake, comprising two elements: currants and a very rich sweetened and spiced dough, part of which was broken up and mingled with the currants. With the other part the cake was covered 'very thin both underneath and aloft'.

The Scottish rich bun was a similar confection, always large, made on a sheet of enriched bread paste which was gathered up round the filling. The quantities for a bun were five pounds of flour, one of butter, two of raisins, one of currants, four ounces of caraway seed, four ounces of sugar and barm, according to the household book of Lady Grisell Baillie.[69]

True pies large and small, custards, pasties, patties and tarts were as popular as ever. The art of pastry making had not been well documented in medieval times, but from the mid-sixteenth century onwards there is no shortage of recipes. In some of the earliest ones the flour was mixed with a hot liquor of butter and water or ale boiled together in varying proportions, and was often yellowed with saffron or yolks of eggs. Beef or mutton broth went into some pastes, cream into others, while in Lent 'thick almond milk seething hot' was combined with 'salad oil fried and saffron'.

In 1615 Gervase Markham recommended that the crust for raised pies containing red deer venison, boar, gammons of bacon, swan and other meats to be sealed with butter and kept long, should be made from rye paste. Turkey, capon, pheasant, partridge, veal, peacock, lamb and waterfowl, 'which are to come to the table more than once, yet not many days', required a rather thick wheat-flour crust; while chickens, calves-feet, veal olives, potatoes, quinces, fallow deer and such like, to be eaten hot, needed a thin short crust of fine wheat flour which had been first dried in the oven.

Some twenty-five years later Farmer Best, in east Yorkshire, recorded that the piecrusts for his family's eating were made of best wheat flour (though their bread was only maslin); while his labourers were allowed maslin piecrust, 'because that paste that is made of barley meal cracketh and checketh. . . . In many places they grind the after-loggings of wheat for their servants' pies.'

The rye paste described by Markham was made up with hot water and a little butter or suet; wheat flour for a thick crust was also kneaded with hot water or mutton broth and with rather more butter. But the fine wheat crust for the hot pies was to contain as much butter as water and three or four eggs to make it 'reasonable lithe and gentle', and it was mixed cold.[70]

Elizabethan dish tarts were made with even shorter and richer paste. For the florentine, another Elizabethan favourite, the paste had to be driven out so thin 'that ye may blow it up from the table', laid in a shallow buttered platter, and filled with a mixture of chopped veal kidney, sometimes spinach, herbs, spices, dried fruits and sugar, which had to be heaped much higher in the middle than elsewhere. It was topped with another sheet of paste, which was iced with rosewater and sugar after baking.[71]

Really rich butter paste was eaten by itself. The flour was mixed with butter, seven or eight eggs, rosewater and spices. The paste was divided into two or three pieces, 'and drive out the piece with a rolling pin, and do with butter one piece by another, and then fold up your paste upon the butter and drive it out again, and so do five or six times together'. It was baked in separate sections, which were sugared before they were served.

In 1605 Sir Hugh Platt gave to this type of pastry the name

'puff paste', and commended its use for florentines and fruit tarts. It continued to be used for the latter, and later for jam tarts too. In the eighteenth century it also covered little sweet or savoury patties, successors of the Elizabethan peascods and precursors of our vol-au-vents, which were either fried or baked. They were served as a side dish for supper or as a garnish to a more substantial dish.

Crocant or crackling paste made of flour, sugar and egg whites had been introduced from France at the turn of the century. It was either baked as a round flat sheet and sent to table with fruit or preserves piled on it; or made up in small flat shapes and laid on top of fruit sweetmeats.[72]

Sweetened pies of meat and dried fruits began to go out of favour in the Georgian period. The sweet veal or sweet lamb or sweet chicken pies in contemporary cookery books are counterbalanced by recipes for savoury pies of the same meats (with such seasonings as hard-boiled egg yolks, mushrooms, sweetbreads, asparagus tips) for those who could no longer stomach the sweetened fleshmeats enjoyed by earlier generations.

For 'minced' pies the change was in the other direction. A typical Elizabethan recipe ran: 'Shred your meat (mutton or beef) and suet together fine. Season it with cloves, mace, pepper and some saffron, great raisins, currants and prunes. And so put it into your pies.' For many years afterwards the pie filling was based upon lean meat minced with an equal quantity of suet, and by the later seventeenth century neat's tongue was emerging as the preferred meat for the purpose. After a few more decades it was discovered that the suet, the spices and the fruity ingredients, which now included chopped apples as well as dried fruits, could be mixed with brandy or sack as much as four months in advance, and stored in stone jars, provided that the shredded meat was not added until just before the pies were made. From this it was only a short step to omitting the meat altogether, and 'minced pies without meat' now became a feature of the cookery books.[73]

Standing pies were less common after potting had been devised as an alternative means of preserving cooked meat or fish. But some were still made, notably from pork, egg and bacon, or goose, in which the natural fattiness of the meat served to keep it moist and succulent. And during the eighteenth century improved roads and quicker transport allowed the famous Yorkshire Christmas pie to reach consumers in other parts of the country.

One former bakemeat that failed to survive was the pie that appeared at revels, such as those for Twelfth Night, and was cut open to reveal a flock of live birds, or a troop of frogs, or even occasionally a small human being. Such pies were made 'of coarse paste filled with bran and yellowed over with saffron or yolks of eggs, gild them over in spots'. After baking, the bran was removed and the livestock introduced through holes in the bottom crust. They were then produced to 'cause much delight and pleasure to the whole company'. This particular mixture of bread and circuses was lost to Britain in the days of the Commonwealth, and was not thereafter restored to the entertainments of the nobility.[74]

Chapter 8

Spices, sweeteners, sausages and puddings

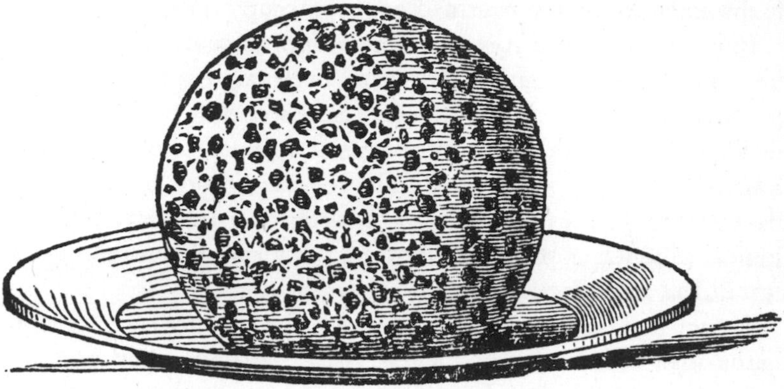

a. SPICES AND SWEETENERS

Prehistoric period

From neolithic times onwards Britain could supply all the elements of a well-balanced diet, and the means of combining those elements in cookery. Seasonings now took on a new importance, especially in the context of cereal pottages. And cereals also became more palatable if combined with sugars, whether derived from wild fruits, which ripened into sweetness in the sunny centuries between about 2500 and 500 BC, or from honey.

Honey became more plentiful as forests yielded to pasture land, where wild bees could profit from the flowers while herds and flocks cropped the grass (hence the proverbial 'land flowing with milk and honey'). At first the honey gatherers had to hunt down the bees' nests and rob the honey, an uncertain and hazardous business. But true beekeeping had probably begun by the later

Bronze Age. In the early stages the practitioners simply cut away a section of hollow tree trunk or branch where bees had swarmed, and bore it back to a 'bee-garden' close to their homes. Thereafter men learned to manufacture hives from tree bark or wickerwork, and by smearing them with honey and aromatic herbs to entice newly swarmed bees to occupy them.[1]

In the later Bronze Age the prime importance of bees was due less to their honey than to their wax, necessary for the *cire-perdue* process of bronze casting which was now being practised. But incidental to the wax came an increased output of honey. People learned to add it more plentifully to their food, to enjoy its flavour and to crave its sweetness, a craving that was psychological as much as physical, since the body can obtain the sugars it requires from the conversion of starch foods.

Honey served as a seasoning as well as a sweetener. Aromatic herbs also acted as condiments. Used sparingly they pointed other flavours; employed upon a larger scale they drowned them, an effect that may sometimes have been very desirable.

The coriander seeds found by archaeologists on the floor of a late Bronze Age hut at Minnis Bay near Birchington, Kent, represent our earliest record of a spice imported from the Mediterranean region.[2] They may have been brought in by immigrants who then established the plants around their settlement; but they could also have arrived through trade. Culinary herbs and spices retain much of their intensity of flavour when the leaves or seeds are dried, and they are then light in weight and relatively small in bulk, so that they form an ideal object of trade. Southern Europe is particularly rich in aromatic herbs, and it is likely that even before the Roman conquest they sometimes reached Britain, either as merchandise or gifts.

Roman period

The Romans were far from satisfied with the array of native flavouring herbs available in Britain, and soon established several of their own favourites as garden plants there. But even those were not enough. For exotic oriental spices now played a part in

Roman cuisine. Pepper, ginger, cinnamon, cassia, malabathrum and spikenard were carried to the ports of Asia Minor from the East by overland caravans, or were shipborne to the Red Sea coast and thence brought to Alexandria. From the first century AD the Romans themselves had trading stations as far away as the south-east coast of India, which acted as entrepôts for the spices of India, Malaysia and China.

The most popular of all was pepper, the fruit of a vine which grew wild in the hinterland of southern India. Pliny described three types, black, white and the superior, more pungent long pepper, which were in use in his day; and in AD 92 special pepper warehouses were built in Rome to receive these and other spices.[3] The custom of adding pepper to food spread through the Roman provinces and beyond (Alaric the Visigoth demanded three thousand pounds of it, along with much gold and silver, as his price for raising the blockade of Rome in AD 408). In distant Britain too, pepper and ginger must have reached the more Romanized homes, though the costly malabathrum (cinnamon leaf), cassia, asafoetida, sumach and spikenard may have been fairly rare. The hot spices were valued as medical drugs as well as seasonings. In food they performed a double function first stimulating the appetite and then aiding digestion.

Pepper with everything was the rule in Roman cookery. In the recipes of Apicius, pepper appears more often than does any other condiment, even the *liquamen* that was a Roman equivalent of salt. It was often sprinkled on to a cooked dish at the last moment before serving. Not only was it added to sauces and stuffings, to sausages and *patinae* of mixed ingredients; it was also scattered over confections of a purely sweet nature, such as a bland, thick custard of eggs, milk and honey, and the various mixtures of nuts, honey, wine and pastry or cereal which were eaten as sweetmeats. This was not illogical, for pepper is not in itself either sweet or savoury, but simply pungent.

Ginger was the next most popular of the oriental spices in Roman cuisine. It was put into several Apician sauces and stuffings, and also featured in aromatic salts to settle the stomach and move the bowels.

Saffron crocuses were raised in Mediterranean lands, though it is doubtful if the plants were established in Britain at this period. The dried stigmas were used to give colour and flavour to Roman sauces and spiced wines.[4]

Honey remained the universal sweetener. The sugar cane of India was not unknown. Pliny wrote of it: 'Sugar . . . is a kind of honey that collects in reeds, white like gum and brittle to the teeth; the longest pieces are the size of a filbert. It is only employed as a medicine.' The Romans apparently never admitted it into their cookery.

But beekeeping was practised throughout Italy and the Roman provinces. Columella, Varro and other writers gave advice on how to catch swarms, and how to house the bees in hives placed on raised platforms so that pests could not crawl into them. Earthenware hives enjoyed some vogue in lowland Britain, though they were not approved by the experts in Italy. They took the form of thick earthen jars with perforations in their sides or necks. Their mouths were sealed, and were only opened when it was time to collect the honey. Villa owners often employed a slave as beekeeper, an office which was to reappear on the establishment of the medieval manor.[5]

Under Roman rule the native British population followed age-old traditions of beekeeping. The Celts housed their bees in small conical wickerwork hives daubed with mud or dung (the 'baskets' of the ancient Irish laws); and they may have taken them to the heather in late summer, another practice known to be of great antiquity. It would have fitted in with the summer migrations of the tribesmen of the highland zone with their flocks and herds. Much of their honey was converted into mead.[6]

In Roman cookery honey was added to sweetmeats, pease pottage, and various dressings for root and salad vegetables. For salad dressings and sauces containing vinegar, the honey served to correct excessive sharpness. In addition honey could be used as a preservative for fresh fruit, vegetables and even meat, if they were submerged in it.

Also used for preserving purposes was mustard. Cultivated white mustard was an early Roman introduction into Britain (seeds have been identified at Silchester and elsewhere). The grains could be pounded, blanched with water and cooking soda and mixed with sharp white vinegar to make a pickle to conserve turnips. For table use it was in addition thickened with crushed almonds and pine kernels, producing a sauce of exquisite whiteness. Another recipe mixed honey, oil and vinegar with the powdered mustard.[7]

The Romans ate mustard with sausage, stuffed udder, boiled boar, and vegetables such as beet leaves or green beans. It was an ingredient too in several complex Apician sauces.

Early medieval period

The supply of pepper and other imported spices to Britain was interrupted in the fifth century AD. Anglo-Saxon piracy made the English channel precarious for shipping, and when it later abated, the more distant trade routes were blocked by Vandals and other Mediterranean pirates. Occasionally merchants succeeded in bringing spices overland from the Black Sea to the Baltic, or across central Europe; but such merchandise rarely travelled as far west as Britain, and when spices did arrive they probably came more often as gifts between kings or high dignitaries of the church than in the ordinary way of trade.

After the establishment of the Roman church in Britain, spices were one of the rare luxuries allowed to monks. The Venerable Bede counted pepper among his few small treasures which he distributed among his fellow-priests just before his death in AD 735.[8]

Late in the eighth century, when Arab dominion in north Africa and Spain had given some security to Mediterranean shipping, the seaborne spice trade between the orient and western Europe revived again. Overland trade also increased, and Mainz, at the end of one of its routes, became a centre of the spice trade in the west. Some merchandise from that area now reached Britain; and it is significant that Aethelred in 982 imposed an extra Christmas and Eastertide toll in the form of ten pounds of pepper on the subjects of the Emperor of Germany who came with their goods to London Bridge.

English merchants travelled too, to the great continental fairs and even, in the early eleventh century, as far as Pavia in north Italy, where they exchanged woollen and linen cloth and tin for the prized spices. Most of these were still destined for the cuisine of the great and wealthy. But pepper had become common again, and was cheap enough to be within reach of the small manorial landlord. A pepper-horn is mentioned as a necessary utensil for an English farmhouse in the eleventh century.[9]

Sugar, which had been something of a curiosity even to the Romans, was not among the oriental products that reached western Europe at this time. In Britain honey was still the sweetening agent for food and drink. The Anglo-Saxon farm estate employed its own beekeeper, and a honey-bin was another necessary receptacle in the farmhouse. Honey production was no less important in Wales and Ireland, where laws governed the ownership of bees and the price to be set upon swarms. In some places in the west of England at the time of the Norman Conquest wild honey was still being found in considerable amounts, if we accept the interpretation of the nine 'honeyers' (*mellitarii*) of Westbury in Wiltshire and the five of Lustleigh in Devon, who appear in Domesday as gatherers of wild honey in the woods.[10]

Later medieval period

The advent of Norman cookery in England led to a great upsurge in spice usage. Pepper alone was no longer enough. The rich and even the moderately well-to-do now had to season their made dishes also with cinnamon, ginger, saffron, cardamon, and several more. Nutmegs and mace, cloves, grains of paradise, zedoary, galingale and cubebs were among the new spices, unknown or hardly known in Roman times, which now reached Britain and were incorporated into both medicines and food.

Most of the spices came from southern China, the Moluccas, Malaya and India. They were carried by routes very similar to those used in Roman times to the ports of the eastern Mediterranean, whence they were shipped on Venetian or Genoese vessels to Italy. From there they were distributed through north-west Europe, to be sold at the great fairs of Champagne, southern Flanders and elsewhere. During the fourteenth century and until 1542 the Venetian galleys came out into the Atlantic and sailed as far as London and Southampton with their cargoes of spices.

The sad story is told of Robert Sturmy, who in 1458 tried to open up a direct spice trade between Bristol and the Levant, and who was rumoured to be bringing back pepper seed and other spices 'to have set and sown in England'. But the Genoese lay in wait for him off Malta, 'and spoiled his ship and other'.[11]

Spain was another source of spices during the later Middle Ages, for the Arabs had introduced there some of the economic plants of the Middle East. Among them were rice, sugar, saffron and licorice.

Sugar became accepted as a foodstuff. By the seventh century the crop had spread westwards from India into Persia, where the Arabs encountered it and carried it still further west in the wake of their conquests. It was rediscovered for western Europe at the end of the eleventh century by the first crusaders who 'beheld with astonishment and tasted with delight, as a thing unknown, the cane growing in the plains of Tripoli', where they had halted on their way to Jerusalem. They returned home full of enthusiasm for their discovery; and thereafter a small but ever-increasing sugar trade brought the new commodity into the countries of north-western Europe. When the galleys of Venice and other Italian cities bore oriental spices to Britain, they carried also sugar from Cyprus, Rhodes, Crete (known as Candia), Malta and Sicily.

The sugar was usually refined first in its country of origin. Sir Thomas Cogan spoke of sugar being 'made by art in boiling of the canes, much like as they make their white salt at the Witches in Cheshire'. In fact the canes were cut into short lengths which were pressed until they exuded their syrup. This was evaporated by boiling, and then poured into vessels of sugar-loaf shape to cool and harden. 'And when they want well refined sugar', wrote an eyewitness, 'they boil it three times, letting the imperfect liquor run out through a hole. . . .' The most highly refined sugar was, of course, the most expensive.[12]

Because of its initial rarity and costliness, sugar was highly valued. In medieval household books it always appeared on the spice account, and was treated accordingly.

London was the centre of both the sugar and spice trade in Britain, the place where rich cargoes came in and were distributed. Very early on the spice trade began to be organized by the Guild of Pepperers, later called Grocers (from *grossarii*, dealers in bulk or *en gros* transactions). The Pepperers were one of the oldest of the London guilds, and their existence was recorded in 1180. In 1316 the Pepperers of Soper Lane issued a set of regulations designed to control the quality of wares sold, and to protect the customer from being deceived into buying spices containing an admixture of old or inferior stuff.

> Also [the ordinance continued] that no one shall moisten any manner of merchandise, such as saffron, alum, ginger, cloves, and such manner of things as may admit of being moistened; that is to say, by steeping the ginger, or turning the saffron out of the sack and then anointing it, or bathing it in water; by reason whereof any manner of weight may be increased, or any deterioration arise to the merchandise.

Later in the same century they reorganized and rechristened their guild the 'Mistery of Grossers, Pepperers and Apothecaries' (for the druggists were still very much concerned with spices,) and not long afterwards they became the 'Compaygnie des Grossers'. Because spices so often arrived from foreign ports in an impure state mixed with rubbish to increase their weight and bulk, the Grocers also undertook the task of garbling or cleansing the bales. They appointed an official garbler, who had to inspect the newly arrived spices, and affix his stamp to them as a guarantee of their purity before they were weighed for sale. Members of the Company and sometimes of other companies too, then bought the goods and resold them to agents, chapmen and individual buyers.

Outside London spices could be obtained periodically at the great regional fairs; and the commoner and cheaper ones, such as pepper and ginger, were sold by itinerant chapmen. Prices at the fairs were sometimes keener than those of London. Dame Alice de Bryene in 1419 paid two shillings and a penny per pound for pepper in London, but only one and eleven a pound when it was bought at Stourbridge Fair.

But London could supply the rarer, more exotic varieties, and moreover they were available there throughout the year. So when a member of a household had to go to London on business, he was often commissioned to send or bring back several different spices.

The Grocers' Company encouraged this state of affairs, and for a time in the fifteenth century even tried to ban its members from selling spices at the fairs, lest trade should thus be diverted from London. In country towns the shopkeepers, who acted as agents for members of the Company, charged prices even higher than the London ones.[13]

A few landowners had another source of spices in rents, which were occasionally paid in agreed weights of pepper. A peppercorn rent was, of course, insignificant in this context, but a fixed rent of a larger quantity could supply a household for most of the year. The two priests living at Munden's Chantry in Bridport in the mid-fifteenth century received half a pound of pepper among their rents. Their household accounts show expenditure on cloves, ginger, cinnamon and saffron; but none on pepper, since their needs were already met.

The cost of spices fluctuated according to the supplies available, but in general cinnamon (often called canell), ginger and pepper were among the cheapest, cloves and mace were rather more expensive, while saffron was always very dear, retailing at fourteen or fifteen shillings a pound at various times in the thirteenth and fourteenth centuries. Saffron was a much-used spice of medieval times, at least in the homes of the well-to-do. But a little goes a long way, and Dame Alice de Bryene used only three-quarters of a pound in 1418–19, a year in which five pounds of pepper, two and a half of ginger, three of cinnamon, one and a quarter of cloves and one and a quarter of mace were expended in spicing the food for her household.[14]

At that time most of the saffron sold in England was still being imported, usually from Spain. But in some northern counties the Halifax autumn crocus (*c. nudiflorens*) may have supplied a form of saffron. The Knights of St John of Jerusalem are believed to have introduced this plant, and to have grown it on the farms belonging to their order. During the fifteenth century the more usual saffron crocus (*c. sativus*) was first raised in English herb gardens; instructions for growing it appeared in Mayster Ion Gardener's gardening treatise of about 1440. Somewhat later saffron growing became an important industry in Cambridgeshire and Essex, especially around Saffron Walden. But the spice remained expensive, for it was the labour involved in gathering the stigmas from a prodigious number of blooms rather than the cost of carriage from overseas which decided the final price.[15]

Less well-known oriental spices in use in medieval Britain included zedoary and galingale (both plants of the ginger family) and cubebs (peppery Javanese spice berries). Grains of paradise began to reach Europe from the Guinea coast of West Africa during the thirteenth century. They gained great popularity as a cooking spice, and were imported in such quantity that their place of origin became known as the 'grain coast'. By 1284 their price was no more than fourpence a pound.[16]

Not only individual spices but also mixed spices were often called for in recipes. The three commonest were 'blanch powder', 'powder fort', and 'powder douce'. Occasionally mixed spice was called 'powder marchant' because it was sold ready made up by the grocer or merchant. Blanch powder, as its name implies, was pale coloured from ingredients such as refined sugar and white ginger. 'Also with two ounces of sugar, a quarter of an ounce of ginger, and half a quarter of an ounce of cinnamon, all beaten small into powder, you may make a very good blanch powder, to strew upon roasted apples, quinces or wardens, or to sauce a hen', wrote Sir Thomas Cogan. In powder fort, hot spices such as ginger and pepper predominated; while powder douce contained some of the milder ones.

By the late thirteenth century a number of wealthy households had already gone some distance towards making the change from honey to sugar as the standard sweetener. Over a hundred pounds of sugar were obtained for Bishop Swinfield's establishment in the course of the winter of 1289 (at a cost of about sixpence a pound when bought in bulk in London; but eightpence when purchased a pound at a time from shopkeepers in Ross or Hereford). But thirty years later Dame Alice de Bryene's steward recorded that in her smaller and more conservative home one gallon and two and a half quarts of honey had been consumed in the course of the year, but only a single pound of white sugar.[17]

The accounts of both these households, in common with most surviving account-rolls of a similar kind, contain entries for large quantities of wax (a hundred or two hundred pounds is not unusual) for making candles and tapers. From this fact alone it is clear that bees were regularly kept and that honey, no less than wax, was plentiful. It was generally produced on the manor, and so its price was rarely recorded. In some areas rents for land were paid in wax or honey or both, thus further increasing the supplies of the recipient. The honey was in liquid form and was measured either by the gallon or by the large jarful (*lagena*). Half a gallon cost eightpence in the mid-fifteenth century.[18] It was then still much cheaper than sugar, and was the only sweetening agent known to poorer people.

In the homes of the gentry the spices were carefully looked after. Those for current use were put into the charge of the head cook, who stored them in a little chamber off the kitchen. Among the nobility the main supply was kept locked in the chests of the wardrobe, a small room or series of rooms which served as a storeplace for various articles of value; and the spices were issued to the cook as he needed them. An entry in the Countess of Leicester's household book states that on 30 April 1265 two pounds of cinnamon were released from the wardrobe for the purposes of sauce making.[19]

It has been said that the object of using so many spices was to conceal odours of tainting when fresh fish and meat were kept overlong, and to give interest to salted flesh. This must often have been the case. But for the gentry fresh meat, newly slaughtered on the manor farm, was in fact available through much of the year; while poultry was never killed until it was needed for table. Regular spicing, however, became a habit; and once palates were accustomed to strong, aromatic flavours, unspiced foods tasted insipid.

It is difficult to judge just how heavy the spicing was, for few recipies give any quantities. A rare exception is a small group devoted to special winter dishes. Here a very rich mawmeny for forty messes (to be shared by a hundred and sixty people, eating as messmates, two to a bowl) was seasoned with four ounces of minced ginger, half a pound of cinnamon powder, two ounces of cloves and two ounces of ginger powder. 'Viande Cyprus', also for a hundred and sixty people, included eight pounds of pinenuts, three of cooked dates, four of Cyprus sugar, rice flour and sweet wine, and was spiced with four ounces of powdered cinnamon.

The spicing seems on the heavy side, even allowing for the large number of servings. But spices must have been very variable in quality. Some would have lost their original intensity of flavour through exposure to heat, cold or dampness on their long journey to Britain, or by deliberate adulterations such as those that the Pepperers' Company tried to prevent. So although medieval food was undoubtedly well seasoned, the result may have been tasty rather than fiery.

But whatever the quality of the spices, they were in constant use, and there is hardly an area of cookery where they are not to be found. Pies and tarts of all descriptions, sweet fruit pottages and savoury meat stews, fine bread, and fasting-day fish dishes were all duly spiced. A typical recipe for stewed beef recommends the addition of cinnamon, cloves, maces, grains of paradise, cubebs, minced onions, parsley, sage and saffron. The stew was thickened with bread steeped in broth and vinegar, with extra salt and vinegar added at the last for good measure. The final instruction, 'and look that it be poignant enough', seems redundant. Fish dishes were spiced with similar abandon.

The complexity of a spiced fruit confection can be judged from the recipe for 'strawberry'.

Take strawberries and wash them in time of year in good red wine; then strain through a cloth, and do them in a pot with a good almond milk, allay it with amidon or with the flour of rice, and make it chargeaunt [thick] and let it boil, and do therein raisins of Corinth, saffron, pepper, sugar great plenty, powder ginger, canell, galingale; point it with vinegar, and a little white grease put thereto; colour it with alkanet, and drop it about, plant it with the grains of pomegranate, and then serve it forth.[20]

Spices were all important for sauces; and even vegetables did not escape. Powder douce and saffron were put with leeks and cabbages; and with rapes, parsnips and skirrets.

Saffron was added constantly to made dishes. Sometimes in winter, when red was the fashionable food shade, it was reinforced or replaced with sanders (sandalwood). 'And if thou will change the colour', says the early fifteenth-century recipe for 'Browet tuskey', 'take sanders and saffron, and make the pottage sanguine colour for winter season.'

Sanders came from India, while alkanet, another red food dye, was obtained from the roots of a south European borage. Indigo, which took its name from Pliny's *indicum*, was another Indian colorant which imparted a deep purple hue. Alternative purple dyes were turnsole and heliotrope. The remaining colours favoured in food were white (from ground almonds, rice, milk, etc.), green (from parsley juice) and black (from cooked blood); and parti-coloured confections were made for special occasions.

Some of the colour effects aimed at were very far from natural, but in other cases there was an attempt to enhance nature. Egg dishes were nearly always made more yellow with saffron. And when salmon had been boiled to make 'Vyand cypre of salmon', and then pounded and mixed with ground almonds, rice flour, spices and broth, its rosy colour was restored by the addition of alkanet.[21]

After cooking came the garnishing or flourishing of the dish at the dresser with a simple surface scattering of spice powder. More complex designs were achieved in the kitchen, like the white blancmange decorated with blanch powder and fried almonds, and served in with a second dishful coloured yellow or red which was strewn with powdered galingale, and stuck with cloves and maces. Cloves were considered appropriate to red food generally. Red or white aniseed comfits were sometimes laid over thick sweet pottages.

Feasts and the meals of the nobility were rounded off by a final course of fruits, spices, hippocras and wafers. At this stage the spices fulfilled a useful function as digestants. Typical combinations were hot apples and pears with minced ginger, or pippins with caraway comfits. Then if the occasion was a formal one, the company withdrew to another room where they took wine and more spices, a ceremony of French origin known as the *voidée*. The spices were offered on spice plates, which could be of gold or silver and very magnificent. Comfits were also handed around in special comfit boxes or drageoirs with separate compartments for the different sugar-coated seeds and spices.[22]

The imported oriental spices were inevitably more costly than aromatics produced at home. Medieval herb gardens were therefore planted with as many of them as could be persuaded to grow in Britain. Coriander, fennel, cumin, dill and peony were among the favourites. In due course aniseed, caraway, licorice and gromwell (a kind of borage) were introduced, though the first three, at least, could not be home-grown on a scale to satisfy the great demand, and they were still imported as well.[23]

Hot spices in use among the ordinary people were named by Beton the brewster in *Piers Plowman* as pepper, peony seed, garlic and fennel seed. The last was a particular condiment for fish dishes.

Probably the cheapest spice of all was native-grown mustard seed. It was purchased for less than a farthing a pound for the household of Dame Alice de Bryene in 1418–19; and in the course of a year eighty-four pounds were consumed. Mustard was eaten with fresh and salt meat, brawn, fresh fish and stockfish, and indeed was considered the best sauce for any dish. As in Roman times mustard seed was pounded in the mortar and moistened with vinegar. French mustard had powdered spices added to it, while Lombard mustard was made up thick with honey, wine and vinegar, and thinned for use with wine.[24]

Mustard for everyday use was made at home, but in towns it was also obtainable from professional sauce makers. The names of three such men were entered among the freemen of York in the reigns of Edward I and Edward II. For special occasions such as wedding feasts the townspeople could buy from them extra quantities of ready-made mustard, camelyn, verjuice and other sauces.[25]

Of all the items on the medieval spice account sugar was the one destined to have the greatest effect on Britain's eating habits. At first it had an additional value as a medicine. It will be recalled that the Romans had known it only as a medicine.

As well as plain sugars of several grades, sugar candy and rose- and violet-scented sugars were imported, and those who could afford them (they were more costly than even the finest ordinary sugar) consumed large quantities. The royal household in 1287 used 677 pounds of sugar, and also no less than 300 pounds of violet sugar and 1,900 pounds of rose sugar.

The fancy sugars, too, were viewed in part as prophylactics or remedies for colds and consumptions. This idea stemmed, like the sugar itself, from the Arab domains. In Britain little twisted sticks of sugar called *penidia*, resembling the later barley-sugar sticks, were a favourite form in which to take sugar against the common cold.

The draughtiness of most medieval dwellings and the consequent colds and chills suffered by their inhabitants were some of the reasons for the ever-growing market for sugar in Britain. Delicate children were encouraged to eat rose and violet sugars to keep them in health. One such little boy was Henry, the son of Edward I. Many purchases of rose and violet sugar and *penidia* were made on his behalf, all duly recorded in his household accounts: but they were not able to prevent his untimely death at the age of only six years.[26]

Sugar for kitchen use came in several grades, according to the degree of refining which it had undergone. The coarsest was sold in large loaves which could weigh several pounds apiece (three weighing between them fifty-three pounds are recorded in Bishop Swinfield's accounts). The sugar in these loaves was imperfectly refined and cured, so that the middle of the loaf might be made up of dark, impure crystals, brown or almost black in colour. Finer sugars were produced by a process known as claying.

Dark sugar, in which the molasses was still present, was sometimes called for in particular recipes, such as that for the brown-coloured camelyn sauce. It was then usually clarified before use.[27] When white sugar was specified it was often for a dish made up of white ingredients and intended to bear that colour when brought to table. But most recipes left the cook to decide which quality of sugar he would – or could – put into his preparations.

The addition of sugar to pottages of fruit, almonds or eggs was not strange, inasmuch as it simply replaced the honey of earlier years. But sugar frequently appears in medieval cookery in the company of meat or fish. When this happened the sugar seems often to have been used in the character of a spice rather than as a sweetening agent. In the recipes it was apt to be listed along with cinnamon, ginger, cloves and other spices, and we may suspect that it was used in very small amounts, comparable to the quantities of the other spices that were added. This theory is confirmed by one of the rare recipes in which measured quantities are actually given, that for 'chicken in sauge' (sage sauce) for forty people. The sauce was of broth and wine, thickened with pounded egg yolks and flavoured with parsley and sage: and further seasoning was provided in the form of one ounce of sugar, one ounce of cinnamon powder and a little saffron.

The exception to this way of using sugar was in the group of recipes for thick pale-coloured pottages such as blancmange, mawmeny and mortrews; for they included white meat or fish, pulped and well disguised by other ingredients, and fortified with 'sugar a good plenty'. 'Vyande Cypre' was another such pottage; and 'sauce Saracen' was blended from two parts of ground almonds tempered with red wine and almond milk, to one part of sugar. It was to be expected that the two last dishes would be well sweetened, for they took their names respectively from Cyprus and the Saracens, recalling the original introduction of sugar into Britain by the crusaders.

Sugar was also added in more than tiny amounts to sauces and pottages of the 'egerdouce' type. Here it tempered the sharpness of the vinegar, but not too much was used, for the sauce had to have enough of the vinegar's tang to make it 'somewhat biting'.[28]

Here and there in medieval cookery books it is possible to trace the changeover from honey to sugar. Honey appears in some recipes for 'appulmos', a popular pottage of apples and almond milk, but in others it has been replaced by sugar. Again, honey formed an element in the spiced fruit and vegetable preserve called 'compost' which was kept and eaten cold as a sort of winter salad. By the fifteenth century, however, a heavy sugar and wine syrup was employed instead.

But where honey contributed to the consistency of a dish, it was not replaced. 'Pokerounce' is an example. It comprised trenchers of white bread toasted and spread with a hot honey paste spiced with ginger, cinnamon and galingale. The honey was previously heated and skimmed clean. In other recipes it was clarified over the fire with whites of eggs and a little water.

When a ship called the *Mary Talbot of Lynne* was provisioned for a voyage of 1463, two hundred honeycombs were taken aboard to sweeten the crew's diet of salt meat, stockfish, oatcakes and beer. For honey remained the ordinary man's sweetener. Sugar was for the nobility and gentry, for whom the recipes in the medieval cookery books were composed. But even in Elizabeth's reign there were many common folk who had hardly tasted sugar.[29]

Early modern period

It was a long time before imported spices became cheap. Until the end of the fifteenth century the Venetians controlled the spice trade with the orient, and made their own prices when they sold to other European countries. When their monopoly was broken it was by the Portuguese, who were the first to round the Cape of Good Hope in 1488 and subsequently to reach India. They were thus able to bring back spices by a direct sea route. Portuguese spice ships were reported at Falmouth in February 1504,[30] and for another century Britain was still dependent on foreign traders for her spice supplies. Moreover, the Portuguese were soon charging prices even higher than those previously demanded by the Venetians.

The English made great efforts to discover a north-west or north-east passage to the orient, by which they could conduct their own spice trade; but they had no success. The Levant Company was formed by English merchants with a view to bringing back spices from an entrepôt at Aleppo. But spices which travelled overland, passing through the hands of Arab, Armenian and Greek middlemen, all of whom recouped themselves generously, had now become even more costly than the seaborne merchandise of the Portuguese. So the Levant Company was obliged to deal instead in currants and wines and oriental silks and cottons.

In the 1590s English seamen made exploratory voyages to the Far East, and in 1600 the East India Company was set up to try to secure a share in Portugal's trade. But the Dutch forestalled them. By 1651 Dutch merchants were 'monopolising three sorts of spices almost to the whole world, as cloves, nuts [nutmegs], mace, and lately much cinnamon'.[31] They had seized the Moluccas from the Portuguese and thus won the European market in nutmegs, native to the islands, and in maces (the inner coatings of the nutmeg fruits). Towards the end of the century the East India Company at last made some headway in spice trading; and it became still stronger in the eighteenth century as Dutch influence waned in the Far East.

There was a development of another kind in the spice trade when the trees and plants themselves were transferred to other tropical regions. In the later sixteenth century the Spaniards for a time held sovereignty over Portugal, and they succeeded in naturalizing ginger plants in their colonies in Mexico and Jamaica.

Much later, in 1769, the French introduced nutmeg trees into Mauritius, and the following year clove trees too. Subsequently they took the latter to Cayenne and also to Zanzibar. By the end of the eighteenth century the East India Company had established nutmeg trees in Penang on the Malay peninsula. Once the spice plants had been spread through the colonies of several European powers, monopolies in spices could no longer be maintained, and their market value fell accordingly.

A few new spices reached Britain after the end of the Middle Ages. The Spaniards brought back from central America several members of the capsicum family, which were naturalized in southern Europe. The larger fruits were imported thence into England under the name of Guinea pepper. The smallest, reddest and hottest of the American capsicums, when dried and powdered, produced cayenne pepper, the 'chyan' of English eighteenth-century recipe books. Allspice (*pimenta officinalis*) came to Britain from her West Indian colonies, where it was indigenous. It was also known as Jamaica pepper.

Vanilla, derived from the seed pods of a climbing orchid in the tropical forests of central America, had long been employed by the Aztecs to flavour chocolate. They gathered vanilla pods just before they ripened, and cured them in the sun to release their aroma. In the later seventeenth century vanilla came into use in Britain in the preparation of chocolate.

The careful housewife kept her spices in the small separate drawers of the wooden spice cupboards of the seventeenth century; or put them in round wooden boxes with radiating divisions inside, which could also be kept under lock and key. Her repertoire differed somewhat from that of her medieval predecessors. She had gained new cooking spices, but also lost a few, among them zedoary, galingale, cubebs and cardamom and the home-grown peony seed. All were still in use, however, for medical preparations. The pungent grains of paradise lingered on as a condiment for ale and beer.[32] Subsequently they gained a more sinister reputation as an adulterant of beer.

Sanders and alkanet were replaced by cochineal, derived from the dried bodies of a coccus insect found on a particular cactus in Mexico and the West Indies. Forty pounds of cochineal were among the imports of Bristol in 1613; but it was nearly another century before the earlier red food dyes were altogether abandoned.[33] Blue food became less common, and indigo was no longer in demand. Jellies were still coloured with turnsole in the seventeenth century, but in the eighteenth more often with syrup of violets.

Although saffron was now grown in England (in Essex a triple rotation of crops of saffron, coriander and teasels was carried on), it no longer served, even among the rich, to colour and season practically every dish. It made fewer appearances in the recipe books, and finally its chief role was in jellies and cakes, especially seed cakes.

Mixed spice powders were still made up. A recipe of 1682 prescribed two ounces of ginger and one ounce each of powdered pepper, cloves, nutmegs and cinnamon, mingled with a further pound of pepper. There were several versions of the mixture, which acquired the name of 'kitchen pepper'. By the 1780s even pre-mixed curry powder had found its way into the cookery books. Medieval blanch powder was replaced by clove or cinnamon sugar, made by laying pieces of sugar among the spices in a closed box.[34]

In some dishes whole nutmegs, cloves and cinnamon sticks were employed, and duly removed before serving. The flavouring device of an onion stuck with cloves was in use in England by the 1660s, borrowed, as Sir Kenelm Digby's recipe shows, from the cuisine of France.[35]

Mustard maintained its popularity. John Evelyn recommended 'the best Tewkesbury', or that which was 'composed of the soundest and weighiest Yorkshire seed'.[36] Pickled barberries were much in favour in the Tudor and Stuart era, as were capers, preserved in vinegar and imported by the barrelful from southern Europe. A homemade substitute was pickled broom buds, and many recipes existed for their preparation.

Pickled vegetables, herbs, mushrooms, walnuts and flowers were in constant use in Tudor and Stuart times. They supplied winter salads and garnishes for meat and fish, and also flavouring for stews and hashes. Occasionally some of the pickle was used too. That of mushrooms made a piquant seasoning, since it contained such spices as cloves, mace, ginger, nutmegs and pepper, and furthermore the juice from the mushrooms amalgamated itself with the vinegar or brine, giving it a rich, dark colour. In due course the pickling liquor came to be regarded as a condiment in its own right; and in some recipes the mushrooms were actually removed before the sauce was bottled up.

It was strong enough to resemble ketchup, which became known in Britain from samples brought back through the East India trade. The original ketchup of China and Malaya was a fish and brine pickle, though in England its true nature was not at first recognized: hence the application of its name to mushroom sauce. But anchovy ketchup, somewhat closer to the oriental prototype, soon began to be made. Walnut ketchup was another variant, containing walnut juice or pickle as well as anchovies. All were based upon a pre-made pickle liquor, well spiced and sometimes given added piquancy with garlic, lemon peel or grated horseradish.

Soy sauce was another oriental pickle which reached Britain in the second part of the seventeenth century, and was eventually imitated there. Jars of pickled mangoes also arrived then, and were copied with the aid of home-grown cucumbers or melons, and even onions or peaches.

A further introduction of the period was piccalilli. A recipe of 1694 with the title 'To pickle lila, an Indian pickle' describes a brine and vinegar sauce, flavoured with ginger, garlic, pepper and bruised mustard seed, and yellowed with powdered turmeric. In it were placed pieces of cabbage, cauliflower, celery and other vegetables. In the eighteenth century turmeric was also in demand among those who wished to make 'curry the Indian way'.[37]

The increasing use of spicy sauces had its effects also on cookery. In an early recipe, mushroom ketchup was described as 'ketchup to be put into any sauces'. Hitherto spices had been added direct to sauces and broths. But from the end of the seventeenth century there was a new trend. The spices were used initially to prepare a long-keeping liquid pickle, and the latter was employed to season made dishes.

New, strong-tasting ingredients were tried out. Lemons, formerly pickled whole with brine and spices for a winter salad, were now softened in spiced vinegar until they could be pressed through a hair-sieve and turned into a liquid pickle. Elizabeth Raffald 'found by experience that lemon pickle and browning answers both for beauty and taste (at a trifling expense) better than cullis, which is extravagant'.[38]

It was towards the end of the eighteenth century that bottled sauces were first produced on a commercial scale, thus saving the cook even the preliminary task of preparation. Two of the earliest recipes to achieve wide success were those supplied by Mrs Elizabeth Lazenby and her brother, an innkeeper named Peter Harvey. The sauces made from them were named respectively Lazenby's anchovy essence and Harvey's sauce; and they were retailed by Mr Lazenby, a London grocer.

Spices remained important in the pickling, preserving and potting of several kinds of meat and fish. In cookery there was a gradual scaling down in their usage. Robert May in the 1660s still offered recipes such as the following suggestion for a fillet of beef:

> Sprinkle it with rose-vinegar, claret-wine, elder-vinegar, beaten cloves, nutmeg, pepper, cinnamon, ginger, coriander-seed, fennel-seed, and salt; beat these things fine, and season the fillet with it, then roast it, and baste it with butter, save the gravy, and blow off the fat, serve it with juice of orange or lemon, and a little elder-vinegar.[39]

But even in his day simpler spicing was coming in, and in some dishes no more than one or two spices were thought sufficient. Cloves were often used for preparations of beef or ox tongue; nutmegs for mutton and fowls; and for a light seasoning, a mixture of salt, pepper and mace was favoured. The use of sharp fruits from Elizabethan times onwards to season cooked meat and fish helped to reduce dependence on spicing.

During the eighteenth century even the fresh sauces prepared in the kitchen were often based directly upon individual ingredients such as celery, onions or parsley, oysters or anchovies, chestnuts or eggs, and owed nothing to spices other than a little pepper. The spicy sauce which lingered on longest was the one for venison or hare made from red wine with sugar, cinnamon and breadcrumbs, a survival of the medieval galantine. But redcurrant jelly was now always suggested as an alternative; and in some cookery books it altogether replaced the spiced sauce.

The improvement in the quality and availability of meat animals in the course of the century meant that fresh meat no longer needed to have its flavour masked; and much less of it was heavily salted, requiring strong condiments to make it palatable. Better transport allowed fish to reach its destination more quickly and with less risk of tainting.

Reduced spicing in meat and fish dishes had repercussions in other parts of the diet, for palates became adjusted to a lower level of seasoning. The amount of spice put into cakes and puddings was gradually diminished during the eighteenth century. Both tended to contain more sugar than had their predecessors a hundred years before; but eventually flavouring came to be no more than 'a little fine spice', or the spicing was simply left to the cook's discretion. Musk and ambergris, which had some vogue in the seventeenth century, had been abandoned before the middle of the eighteenth. Only caraway seeds were still as well liked as ever, and were added regularly to seed cakes and biscuits.

One reason for the decline in spicing was the ever-increasing usage of sugar. Sugar made bland foods more appetizing, and sweetened bitter ones, so that eaters had less need of the stimulus of spices.

Sugar was an obvious choice as an economic crop for new colonies in the subtropical belt, and as the European colonists moved further south and west, so also did the sugar canes. In the 1420s they were established by the Portuguese in the Azores and at São Thomé. Thereafter they were carried to Brazil where the Portuguese set up refineries and processed the sugar before shipping it back to Europe. In the meantime the Spaniards transplanted the crop to the Canary islands, and then to their colonies in San Domingo, Cuba, Jamaica and Puerto Rico. The combined output of all these territories greatly increased the supply of sugar to Europe, and Britain won a large share. In the later part of Elizabeth's reign much of it arrived not through trade, but in the form of prize cargoes captured by English privateers. At that period sugars from Morocco and Barbary were also reaching Britain, and the Barbary Company was formed by a group of English merchants who imported the north African sugar.

By the 1640s Britain had new world sugar colonies of her own in Barbados and the Leeward Islands. Later she added Antigua and also Jamaica (seized from the Spaniards); while during the eighteenth century she acquired several more sugar-producing islands, including Grenada, Saint Vincent, Dominica, Tobago, Santa Lucia and Trinidad, as a result of political treaties with other European powers which had Caribbean possessions. The sugar colonies had varying fortunes at different periods, but production continued to increase, and sugar was shipped back to Europe in ever-growing quantities.

In medieval times sugar was despatched ready refined from its country of origin. But it was rarely white enough for European tastes, so refineries were set up in certain towns, notably Antwerp, where it could be reworked. By the 1540s London had its own refineries. There the coarse sugar was first boiled with a lye of ashes or lime, which drew impurities into a scum on the surface. The syrup was skimmed, clarified with white of egg, and then placed in cone-shaped moulds and covered with a layer of wet clay from which the water slowly dripped into the sugar, displacing any molasses that still clung to it. When the process was finished, the refined sugar loaf was knocked out of the cone and put to dry in a warm room. By the time they were ready for sale the loaves weighed from three to fourteen pounds.

Early in the seventeenth century England was again importing sugar that had been refined on the continent, this time at

Amsterdam. But within a few decades the number of refineries in London had grown to fifty, while others were being set up at such major seaports as Bristol, Chester, Liverpool, Lancaster, Whitehaven, Newcastle, Hull and Southampton; Glasgow and Leith; and Dublin. Among them they handled most of the raw sugar that came in from the English tropical colonies and elsewhere.[40]

Sugar was still refined to varying degrees of whiteness and purity; and the darker kitchen sugar seldom cost more than two-thirds as much as the finest white grade. It could be bought from grocers and general merchants in the towns, and at the periodic country fairs; while peddlars carried small quantities to sell to households in remote areas. The rich purchased it by the loaf; the poor had single pounds, or a few ounces scraped from a loaf and weighed out into a paper by the grocer or chapman.[41]

The price of sugar fluctuated according to the supplies available in any year, and the state of food prices at home. From 1651 it was subject to a specific import duty, low at first (on a scale from sixteen shillings and a penny a hundredweight for the best quality to one and fivepence a hundredweight for the coarsest). But it slowly and steadily climbed until by 1844 the highest grade cost £8. 16. 5d. a hundredweight in tax. Two years later, when the corn laws were repealed, the sugar tax was abolished. Scottish sugar, imported in Scottish hulks, escaped the imposition until 1723, but thereafter had to share it.

But taxation did nothing to check the growing demand for sugar in Britain. During Elizabeth's reign the amount eaten averaged no more than one pound per person each year, and in practice most of this went to the wealthy classes; for the cost of a pound was at least a shilling, which was a day's wage for an Elizabethan craftsman.

A century later sugar consumption was up to a yearly four pounds per head. This had doubled by 1720, and in the last quarter of the eighteenth century the figure crept up to eleven, twelve and then thirteen pounds a year, although the period was one of poor harvests and consequent high food prices. The cost of sugar rose too, of course; but by this time people felt quite unable to do without it, and even the very poor continued to buy a few ounces each week.[42]

In Tudor and Stuart times, ordinary folk still met their craving for sweetened food mainly with honey; dried fruits, then much cheaper than sugar; and other fruits and vegetables that were rich in natural sugars. Parsnips, carrots, skirrets and in due course sweet potatoes were very well liked, as were young peas and beans. But the wealthy indulged in sugar, even to excess. Paul Hentzner noted the blackness of Queen Elizabeth's teeth as 'a defect the English seem subject to, from their too great use of sugar'. Sugar loaves were given as presents to friends and as bribes to the influential, a practice which continued until well into the eighteenth century.

The medical reputation of sugar was still high. Seventeenth-century recipes recommended sugar candy or sugar mixed with powdered licorice, aniseeds and coriander seeds as cough cures; and pennet (the *penidia* of an earlier age) was made from the same ingredients, stiffened with gum tragacanth, formed into thin rolls and cut into pieces an inch long. Sugar dissolved with flower or herb juices made healing syrups. Syrup of violets was helpful in burning agues, and syrup of roses would purge choler and melancholy.[43]

Sugar also continued as a seasoning for meat and fish dishes. A showy way of making a little go a long way was to sprinkle it over the top of a cooked dish. A recipe book of the 1630s gives directions to 'scrape on fine sugar' over a dish of stewed trouts cooked with wine, herbs and mace; over balls of minced mutton, beef or lamb with suet and herbs, simmered in broth and served on sippets; and over a stuffed leg of lamb (the stuffing itself seasoned with a little white salt and a little sugar, together with cloves, mace, nutmeg, rosewater, caraway seeds and dried fruits).

Sugar was sprinkled conspicuously upon the pastry lids of pies and tarts, whether the contents were sweet, savoury, or both mixed together. For festive occasions the lids were iced: 'then take sweet butter and rosewater melted, and with it anoint the pie-lid all over, and then strew upon it store of sugar, and so set it into the oven again a little space, and then serve it up'. Large cakes were iced by a similar process.[44]

Fancy breads, cakes and puddings accounted for further sugar expenditure, and so did sauces. Sweet-sour dressings of the type of the medieval 'egerdouce' now became much more popular. 'I pray you, forget not my sugar', wrote Sabine Johnson to her merchant husband in the mid-sixteenth century, 'for if you do, you are like to have but sour sauce.'[45] Drinks likewise had to be sweetened. Dessert wines from southern Europe were in great demand, and when wine was too dry to appeal to the sweet tooth of Tudor and Stuart drinkers, sugar was put into it.

Sugar had long played a special part in the final course at the feasts of the well-to-do: in biscuits and comfits to accompany wine, scraped over cream cheese with sage leaves in summer, or eaten with roasted apples and spice in winter. But only in the sixteenth century did this final course expand into the full glory of the banquet, with its 'jellies of all colours . . . tarts of divers hues, and sundry denominations, conserves of old fruits, foreign and home-bred suckets, codinacs, marmalades, marchpane, sugar-bread, gingerbread, florentines . . . and sundry outlandish confections, altogether seasoned with sugar'.

Nor were feasts the only times for sweetmeats. Then, as now, they were offered as rewards or consolations on a number of occasions. Children were bribed with sugar-plate to learn their alphabet; while the wife with a loving husband could expect to receive 'a sugar-loaf against she lay in' (this partly to provide confectionery for the entertainment of visitors after the child's birth), as well as comfits, succade, dates, prunes and raisins to help her through the long months of pregnancy.[46]

It is hardly surprising, therefore, that the department of cookery which took up most sugar was that of preserving and candying. The arts of sugar working, invented in Italy and developed in France, were now practised widely in Britain. So also was the making of fruit jellies and preserves, which stemmed from Portugal, home of the celebrated quince marmalade. English cookery books began to offer recipes for banqueting fare; and soon separate handbooks appeared with titles such as *Delightes for Ladies* and *A Daily Exercise for Ladies and Gentlewomen.* For while other foodstuffs were the province of the cook and kitchen staff, it was the lady of the house, with her maids, who worked all through the summer months gathering and conserving the produce of her garden to provide delicacies for the rest of the year. Thanks to the preservative properties of sugar, these could be kept many months, if stored in tightly sealed boxes or jars where damp air could not reach them.

Some required great skill in their manufacture.

> To make shoes, slippers, keys, knives, gloves, etc. [runs one recipe]. All these and such like things, you may make of sugar plate paste [formed by beating together cold sugar, fruit juice and gum tragacanth], cut them with your knife, but fashion and finish them only with your hand and pincers, but if you want handiness, or have no leisure, then you must have moulds of tin, and having fitted your paste, cut it with the moulds, dry them leisurely, etc.

Comfit making demanded both leisure and special equipment: a ladle, a slice, a basin to heat the sugar suspended from cords over another bowl containing hot coals, and yet another basin in which the seeds, fruits or spices were treated. Molten sugar was ladled over them, and after each application they had to be dried and cooled. Several coats of sugar were needed. 'Caraways will be fair at twelve coats'; and even 'crisp and ragged comfits', for which the sugar was boiled to a greater height, required eight to ten coats.

Fortunately there were professional confectioners in the larger towns. So the gentlewoman unequal to the task of creating her own banqueting fare could purchase it herself, or commission kinsfolk or friends to bring back sweetmeats when they travelled on business.

Preserving, candying and comfit making used up much sugar, since its weight normally had to equal, if not exceed, that of the fruits, seeds or flower petals being treated. During the seventeenth century recipes referred to sugar boiled to 'candy height', the point at which it fizzled, thickened and candied. Sugar brought to this stage was employed in making sucket candy of whole fruits or of citrus fruit peels, pastes of fruit juice or pulp and sugar which were spread in spoonfuls on plates to form little cakes, and for a sweetmeat called 'manus Christi'. The last named comprised sugar candied with rosewater, mingled with gold leaf as it cooled, and cast into gobbets. It figures in a curious Elizabethan dietetic precept: 'To preserve nature, to eat a mornings. The yolk of an egg with Manus Christi.'[47]

French confectioners, however, observed more exact distinctions in sugar working which became more widely known in Britain towards the end of the seventeenth century through translations of two French cookery books, *The Perfect School of Instruction for the Officers of the Mouth* of 1682, and Massialot's *New Instructions for Confectioners* of 1702. According to these, the first stage in sugar boiling was the smooth, the second the pearled, the third the blown, the fourth the cracked, and the fifth the caramel boiling. Immediately beyond the last stage lay the danger-point at which the sugar stuck to the pan and burned. The caramel boiling was proper for barley sugar; the pearled for comfits. The terms were taken over into some English cookery books, but the achievement of the different degrees of heat was the province of the professional rather than the home confectioner, and the majority of recipes still demanded sugar that was candied or 'boiled to sugar again' in the old manner.[48]

Softer sweetmeats in the form of fruit conserves and jellies also took up much sugar. They were popular as a means of preserving the garden fruits of summer.

The early eighteenth century saw some basic changes in the pattern of sugar consumption. Imports rose, for a time the price of sugar fell, and its distribution became more widespread socially, with even the very poor buying a little of the coarser kinds from time to time.

The biggest single influence upon sugar usage was the introduction of coffee, chocolate and tea, each with a somewhat bitter natural flavour. Coffee was traditionally sweetened by the Turks, and so was chocolate made Spanish fashion. Both were expensive at first, but those who could afford them were already accustomed to sugaring their wine, and they readily transferred the habit not only to those two beverages, but also to tea which came initially from China as an unsweetened drink. Tea drinking spread through British society from top to bottom, and tea continued to be sugared. Even in the second part of the eighteenth century, when the poor of the south and midlands often lived on a miserably inadequate diet, a little money out of small budgets was set aside each week for tea and sugar.

Among the better off the banquet course with its many sweetmeats went out of fashion in the early eighteenth century. It was replaced by a similar dessert course, though it also became quite usual to serve the jellies and candied fruits as part of the second course instead, placing them on a dessert frame in the centre of the table. As more sugar was consumed in puddings, cakes, biscuits and beverages, so less proportionately went into the manufacture of candied fruits, nuts and spices. Sugared meat and fish dishes became rare, sweetened meat pies lost their appeal, and there was a decline in the use of sweet sauces with roasted and boiled meats.

Fruit pies, however, increased in popularity. In the later eighteenth century sugar consumption rose when apples were cheap, because apple pie was a favourite dish in the north of England. The apples were carried back from Kent and other southern counties as a return load on the coal barges from the north. At the same time extra sugar was needed in the apple growing counties themselves, especially in the west country and on the Welsh borders, for it went into the manufacture of cider.[49]

Sugar came in several grades. But when it had been refined, there always remained a thick, dark, viscous residue, very much less sweet than white sugar, but not without sweetening properties. Some of it was distilled to produce rough spirit, and eventually rum.

Molasses was rather slow in coming into general use as a sweetener, due perhaps to the influence of the apothecaries and treaclemongers. The name 'treacle' originated in the ancient world, for it came from the Greek *theriaca antidotos* (i.e. antidote for the bite of wild beasts). The Romans applied the term to a medical electuary said to have been invented by Nero's physician, Andromachus, which comprised a huge number of drugs and spices reduced and combined in a honey emulsion. It was considered a powerful specific for all poisons, and continued in use throughout the Middle Ages under the name *theriaca* or *triacle*.

The apothecaries made it up from their own secret recipes, which may or may not have approximated to that of Andromachus. For a long time Venice was the main centre of production, supplying most of western Europe. But in the fifteenth century Genoa treacle became better known in England, where Flanders treacle was also imported. Sugar syrup or molasses now often formed the base, and when sugar refineries were set up in London, the apothecaries were quick to take advantage of home-produced molasses and London treacle appeared on sale.

When the production of molasses in Britain's refineries outstripped the needs of both apothecaries and distillers, it was sold off in its natural unmedicated state as a cheap sweetener. Its name of molasses was taken by the early settlers to America. But in Britain in the later seventeenth century the alternative term 'common treacle' came into circulation, and thereafter it was known simply as treacle.

One of the first uses to which it was put was the making of gingerbread. Medieval gingerbread had been coloured red with sanders. In Tudor times dark gingerbread was made with powdered licorice. When the licorice was replaced by black treacle, it became possible to omit the honey which had sweetened the old gingerbread, and to add a much smaller amount of sugar instead. Treacle gingerbread, said to have been made for Charles II, had as ingredients three pounds of treacle, half a pound each of candied orange peel, candied lemon peel and green citron, two ounces of powdered coriander seed, and flour to make it into a paste. But ordinary folk made do with no more than two ounces candied peel and one ounce ginger and new spice to three pounds of flour and two of treacle.

By the later eighteenth century treacle consumption was much higher in northern England than in the south; for the diet of the poorer classes now differed considerably between the two regions. In the north a spoonful of treacle was often added to a bowl of oatmeal porridge, a dish almost unknown in the south. Fuel was more plentiful in the north, too, and home baking usual when it had been all but abandoned among the southern poor. Treacle went into parkin (the northern form of gingerbread, containing oatmeal), and into oatmeal biscuits of various kinds. It was still a thick, dark brown syrup. The refining methods which produce golden syrup were not invented until about 1880.[50]

The increasing use of sugar and treacle meant a gradual decline in beekeeping. But many country dwellers still maintained beehives, and several manuals were published in the seventeenth century, giving helpful advice to the keen apiarist. Wooden hives were introduced during this period, though it was many years before they finally replaced the traditional straw or wicker keps.

Honey was usually gathered at midsummer. The bees had to be killed, or preferably driven from their homes and rehoused. The honeycombs, warm from the hive, were crushed and wrung into bowls; and the emptied combs, wooden splints and any odd bees were tossed into a tub of clean water, 'for every hive's offal will serve to sweeten three gallons of water, and to make sufficient and good mead of the same'. The strained honey was quickly measured and put warm into a pot to throw up its own scum. Otherwise it had to be reheated gently and skimmed.

Connoisseurs preferred virgin honey, taken in autumn from bees that had swarmed the previous spring, and allowed to drain freely from the combs through a sieve. Honey from open country was preferred to heather honey; and best of all was that from 'dry countries, where there is much wild thyme, rosemary and flowers'.

Honey from Mediterranean lands was therefore well liked. Narbonne honey had been coming into Britain since medieval times, and Portuguese honey arrived at Bristol during the fifteenth century. Both kinds as well as Italian and Swiss honeys were on sale in London in the eighteenth century. The best

English honeys were said to come from Hampshire, from around Bicester, and from Norfolk.[51]

Many parts of upland Wales and Scotland were still as dependent on beekeeping as in former days, and there honey persisted long as the universal sweetener. In Scotland the old practice of taking the bees to the moorland heather in summer continued.

But in England honey was losing its place both in cookery and confectionery before the middle of the seventeenth century. In 1634 Charles Butler urged its use in making quince marmalade, marzipan, preserves, and rose and violet syrups, but admitted that many people 'unhappily neglect' honey in favour of sugar. Honey no longer featured in contemporary recipes for cakes and biscuits either, except in the occasional one for gingerbread.

Even honey-sops, an Elizabethan favourite, had by the 1660s become 'sugar or honey-sops'. The recipe ran: 'Boil beer or ale, scum it, and put it to slices of fine manchet, large mace, sugar, or honey, sometimes currants, and boil all well together'.[52]

The honey-based meads and metheglins underwent no such change. But they gradually dwindled in importance, yielding first to imported sweet wines, and by the eighteenth century to homemade ones too. More abiding was the remedial use of honey for chest complaints. It was praised for its efficacy against phlegm, and in curing hoarseness and asthma. One homely recipe of 1745 claimed that 'the juice or jelly of red cabbage, baked and mingled with honey is an excellent pectoral'.[53]

As a food, however, honey was now eaten most often in its raw state. Many a spoonful must have gone into bowls of frumenty or bread and milk, and many another have been spread upon bread or toast. 'The queen was in her parlour, eating bread and honey', says the rhyme. It is thought to have originated as a political lampoon on the occasion of the Rye House plot of 1683. By then honey was on its way to assuming the role which for most people in Britain it holds today – that of a delicious occasional treat rather than an everyday food.

b. SAUSAGES AND PUDDINGS

Roman period

Much of Roman cookery was highly spiced; and nowhere were spices more prominent than in the sausages and black puddings of the period. Made usually in the cleaned intestine or caul (*omentum*) of pig, sheep or goat, they were a sophisticated development of the more primitive haggis.

Some were produced for immediate eating, but others were smoked a long while above the hearth before they came to table. Lucanian sausages were of the latter type. The Apician recipe runs:

> Pound pepper, cumin, savory, rue, parsley, mixed herbs, laurel-berries, and *liquamen*, and mix with this well-beaten meat, pounding it again with the ground spice mixture. Work in *liquamen*, peppercorns, plenty of fat and pine-kernels, insert into an intestine, drawn out very thinly, and hang in the smoke.

Elsewhere smoked sausages of cooked and pounded pig's liver with pepper, rue and *liquamen* are described. Both smoking and the generous distribution of pepper through the mixture were deterrents to the growth of micro-organisms, and together with other herbs and spices helped to disguise off-flavours that developed as the meat grew old. The air-excluding fat also kept microbes at bay, as did the intestinal tube which contained the mixture. And when the time for eating finally arrived, spices and herbs had a role to play in making the fatty sausage-meat more palatable and easier to digest.

Other Roman sausages were prepared for immediate consumption. In these the meat was mingled with spelt grits or breadcrumbs, sometimes also with suet and often with eggs, and was duly seasoned before being forced into the intestine tube. They were either grilled or boiled, sometimes both. Black puddings called *botelli* were made and stuffed with chopped boiled egg yolks, pine kernels, onions, leeks, pepper and blood.

Apicius' sausages were for gourmets. But simpler versions provided a convenient and portable food for soldiers on the march; and it is possible that sausages were first introduced into the countries of north-western Europe by the conquering armies.

Once adopted into the national diet the sausage had many uses. If well spiced it could make fetid meats palatable; and it could disguise outlandish ones altogether. In this context it is interesting to learn that the bones of five aged horses were found lying together under the floor of a late third century AD building by the excavators of the Roman town of Verulamium (St Albans). 'From the interlocking of the bones of one animal with another, it was clear that they had been stripped of their meat before burial, and it is suggested that they are relics of a sausage factory.' This seems a likely interpretation when we remember that the eating of horse meat was not approved in the Roman world; and horseflesh could therefore be disposed of most profitably in the form of well-peppered and highly seasoned sausages.[54]

Early medieval period

The tradition of sausage making lingered on in northern Europe after the end of the western Roman empire. The Anglo-Saxons developed their own versions. Although their recipes have not survived Lucanian sausages appear in a Latin and Anglo-Saxon vocabulary as part of a list of pig products, together with the equivalent Saxon word.[55]

Later medieval period

The Norman Conquest brought the sausage varieties of Norman-French cookery into English cuisine. Three of them are named in Alexander Neckam's inventory of foodstuffs suitable for provisioning a castle under siege, their Latin names glossed with the Norman-English words 'aundulyes', 'saucistres', 'pudingis'. The words are from the French, and describe three products made at hog-killing time. Andouilles were the large guts stuffed with the chopped entrails and well seasoned. Sausages were made from the lean pork; and black puddings from the animal's blood.

The town cookshops often sold sausages and black puddings, and at least sometimes tainted meat was used in their manufacture. The best and also the safest were those made at home. For a full contemporary description of sausage making we have to go to a French source, the *Goodman of Paris, c.* 1393. Here we learn that the flesh of the pig's ribs and the best of the fat were minced together and seasoned with brayed fennel and spice powder; and the sausages were hung up in the smoke above the fire for four or five days. 'And when you would eat them, put them in hot water and boil them once and then put them on the grill.'

An English recipe of the same period suggests a more interesting way to cook a sausage of this type. It was carved into gobbets which were fried in fat and served in a sauce of butter, beaten eggs and shredded sage, with mild spice powder (powder douce) sprinkled on top.[56]

Black puddings were also made at pig-killing time and the favourite season for this was late autumn. The animal's blood was blended with minced onions and diced fat, spiced with ginger, cloves and a little pepper, and stuffed into lengths of intestine. The puddings could be kept for up to three days, and were boiled in water before being eaten.

In Britain puddings, rich with blood, fat and spices, became quite a delicacy, to be eaten on high days and holidays. The word pudding, moreover, soon took on a wider meaning than that of blood-sausage, and came to be associated with the idea of stuffing of any kind. In the mid-fifteenth century we read of pudding of porpoise, and pudding of capon's neck. The former was the old black pudding: 'Take the blood of him [the porpoise], and the grease of himself, and oatmeal and salt and pepper, and ginger, and mix these together well, and then put this in the gut of the porpoise, and then let it seeth easily, and not hard, a good while; and then take him up and broil him a little, and then serve forth.'

But the latter was forcemeat, stuffed into the capon's neck, which was sewn up, laid across the creature's back and roasted. And from the fifteenth to the eighteenth century the sucking pig with a forcemeat 'pudding in his belly' was a commonplace of the cookery books.

The pudding of porpoise was a dish for the nobility. The pig was the source of puddings for common folk. 'Take the blood of the swine, and swing it, then put thereto minced onions largely with salt, and the suet of the hog minced', begins an Elizabethan recipe. 'Brawn, pudding and souse, and good mustard withall' were the Christmas fare of the day; and the swine's puddings, no less than the brawn, must have required the sharpness of mustard to offset their richness.[57]

In contrast with black puddings were similar confections of other colours. The fourteenth- and fifteenth-century 'frawnchemyle' was made of breadcrumbs, pepper, sheep's suet diced and sometimes cream, all yellowed with saffron and boiled in a sheep's maw.

Elizabethan recipe books have white puddings of hog's liver: 'You must parboil the liver: and beat it in a mortar, and then strain it with cream: and put thereto six yolks of eggs and the white of two eggs, and grate half a halfpenny loaf of light bread, and put it thereto with small raisins, and dates: cloves: mace: sugar, saffron: and the suet of beef.' Similar puddings were made with shredded chitterlings.

Other kinds resembled the earlier 'frawnchemyle', except that they were given a sweeter, spicier flavour. 'How to make white puddings. Take grated bread, currants, yolks of eggs, nutmegs, cinnamon, and some sugar, salt and beef suet: and temper them with cream.' A Lenten pudding from the same cookery book had mainly similar ingredients, but omitted the suet so as to achieve the total absence of meat foods demanded on fasting days. Already much progress had been made towards the emergence of the kind of pudding which was to revolutionize the diet of the next generations of Englishmen.[58]

Early modern period

Both black blood-puddings and sausages continued to be made from the traditional ingredients. An innovation which had reached the recipe books by the 1630s was the dividing of sausages into links. The paste of lean and fat pork, duly pounded and seasoned, was made up.

> Then take the farmes [guts] made as long as possible, and not cut in pieces as for puddings, and first blow them well to make the meat slip, and then fill them: which done, with threads divide them into several links as you please, then hang them up in the corner of some chimney clean kept, where they may take air of the fire, and let them dry there at least four days before any be eaten; and when they are served up, let them be either fried or broiled on the gridiron, or else roasted about a capon.

Another recipe advised drying the links 'till the salt shine through them'. To help fill the gut compactly a funnel was used, or a special hollow implement, wide at the top and narrow at the bottom, called a tin fill-bowl. The links were usually twisted off at intervals of six inches or less.

Sausages were often broiled or grilled before eating, but they could also be stewed, and according to a mid-seventeenth-century recipe they were then eaten with a sweet sauce. 'To stew sausages. Boil them in fair water and salt a little, for sauce boil some currants alone, when they be almost tender, then pour out the water, and put in a little white wine, butter and sugar.'

The foundation of the sausages was usually a mixture of shredded lean pork with fat or suet, occasionally also grated bread and seasonings (chopped sage leaves and powdered cloves, mace, pepper and salt were the favourite ones). In the middle years of the seventeenth century experiments were made with more exotic fillings. 'I have made rich sausages of capons and rabbits', wrote William Rabisha, 'and could show a recipe for it;

but none so savoury as those of pork, by reason that sage and pepper is not so suitable to the nature of the other.'

Nevertheless one creation of the same period continued as a delicacy for more than a hundred years. This was the sausage enriched with oysters. Mutton was the preferred meat for the purpose, though pork was used in a few recipes. The mutton and oyster sausage was rather a specialized taste, but it appeared occasionally in cookery books even in the later eighteenth century. At that period pork was still the favourite everyday sausage-meat, though beef or veal or a mixture of veal and pork was sometimes recommended.

Pork sausages had now become rather less solid and more succulent than they had formerly been. This change was achieved by reducing the proportion of fat, which is very high in some early recipes, and mixing the meat instead with eggs, wine or water. The last was used to advantage by some professional sausage makers, who sold their wares by weight. Vendors also preserved their unsold stock by immersing it in salted water 'whereby the sausages may not lose anything of their weight'.[59]

The introduction of sausages in links was soon followed by the appearance of the skinless sausage. It was just at the time when potted meat and fish were coming into fashion. In like manner the seasoned sausage-meat was prepared and, instead of being pressed immediately into guts, was packed into pots where it would 'keep a fortnight upon occasion'. Thereafter the cook was recommended to 'roll out as many pieces as you please in the form of an ordinary sausage, and so fry them'. A later recipe specified more exactly: 'in rolling them up, make them the length of your finger, and as thick as two fingers; fry them in clarified suet, which must be boiling before you put them in. Keep them rolling about in the pan. . . .' To prevent them sticking they were previously coated in flour or beaten egg.

The skinless sausage was a great time-saver for the cook, who was thus spared the trouble of cleaning and filling guts. It became a useful standby in farmers' and country labourers' families; it was said that the paste, if seasoned highly enough, could be kept pressed down in a glazed earthen pot 'almost half a winter good'. The gentry also enjoyed sausage-meat made up into sausage shapes or into balls as a garnish for hashes, Scotch collops or thick soups.[60]

A popular smoked sausage of the seventeenth century was the Bologna or Polony sausage. Perhaps its distinctive colour contributed to its success. In one of the earliest English recipes its redness was achieved by chopping the fillets of a hog 'very small with a handful of red sage'. Later the colour was produced by adding saltpetre to chopped gammon of bacon or pork, so that it reddened upon being smoked. Cloves, mace, pepper, nutmegs and caraway seeds were seasonings, and sometimes thyme and sage too. Red wine or a little cochineal dissolved in sack supplied a further colorant. Beefers' guts, or a sheep's great gut were used as containers, and the sausages were smoked for three or four days, and then dried and kept for some months. 'And when you will use them', says William Rabisha's recipe, 'they must be cut out very thin round ways, and put them in your dish with oil and vinegar, and serve them for a salad for the second course, or for a collation before you drink.'

Nearly a hundred years later Hannah Glasse gave recipes not only for a modified form of Bologna sausage, but also for Hamburg sausages, made of beef and suet, spices and a great quantity of garlic. The mixture was made up in 'the largest gut you can find', smoked with sawdust for a week or ten days, and dried in the air: after which the sausages would keep for a year. 'They are very good boiled in pease porridge, and roasted with toasted bread under it, or in an omelette.'[61]

Andouilles were still occasionally mentioned during the seventeenth and eighteenth centuries; but they were a country dish and usually received the country name of chitterlings. An account of their preparation, published in 1750, emphasized how thoroughly both great and small guts had to be washed and scoured with salt and water to make them palatable. 'Others boil sage in their water to take off their hogoo [*haut gout*, i.e. strong flavour], for the preparation of chitterlings will prove the cleanliness or sluttishness of a housewife as much as any meat whatsoever will.'

Both black and white puddings were well liked in Tudor and Stuart times, and several versions of the meatless white pudding were developed. The breadcrumbs might be replaced with oatmeal groats (and the result was then sometimes called 'eisands' or 'essings'); or with rice, which was steeped in new milk overnight and then mixed with cream, egg yolks and the usual spices and fruits. The cream and eggs in the recipes served to moisten and lighten what would otherwise have been a very dense, solid mixture. These puddings, like their predecessors, were stuffed into guts and boiled; 'and as they swell, prick them with a great pin or small awl, to keep them that they burst not; and when you serve them to the table (which must be not until they be a day old) first, boil them a little, then take them out and toast them brown before the fire, and so serve them, trimming the edge of the dish either with salt or sugar'.

In some later recipes white puddings were made up in links like sausages ('and tie them up like beads, being about the bigness and length of an egg, or something longer'). Black puddings 'with some white puddings made with beef suet' were claimed to be 'a very good service for a common diet, especially at night'.[62]

Although guts were useful as containers in which puddings could be boiled in water, they had their disadvantages, for they were awkward to clean and inconvenient to fill. Moreover, as they were only available at pig- or sheep-killing time, they remained closely associated with the kind of pudding that was composed in part of liver, lights or blood; even though they were on occasion used for puddings from which those ingredients were absent.

Experiments were made in fitting puddings into other receptacles. Hollowed carrots, turnips and cucumbers were filled with mixtures of shredded liver, grated bread, dried fruits (in the case of cucumbers, fresh grapes or gooseberries, since this was a summertime dish), sugar and spices, according to recipes recorded in the Elizabethan period. Confections of this kind were forerunners of the poor man's pumpkin pie of the seventeenth century, and the other stuffed vegetables such as cabbage and cucumbers which remained in the canon of cookery all through the seventeenth and eighteenth centuries; but they did not lead to any real development in pudding making.

The future of the boiled suet pudding as one of England's national dishes was assured only when the pudding-cloth came into use. It received one of its earliest mentions in a recipe of 1617 for Cambridge pudding (also called college pudding, for it was served to the students in their college halls). The ingredients were sieved breadcrumbs, flour, minced dates, currants, pepper, shredded suet, fine sugar, eggs, all mixed with warm new milk. The paste was kneaded and then divided into two equal rounds. 'Then take butter and put it in the midst of the pudding, and the other half aloft. Let your liquor boil, and throw your pudding in, being tied in a fair cloth: when it is boiled enough, cut it in the midst, and so serve it in.'

The invention of the pudding-cloth or bag finally severed the link between puddings and animal guts. Puddings could now be made at any time, and they became a regular part of the daily fare of almost all classes. Recipes for them proliferated. Some, like the shaking or quaking pudding, a favourite during the seventeenth century, were not even suet puddings:

> To make a quaking pudding. Take a pint and somewhat more of thick cream, ten eggs, put [aside] the whites of three, beat them very well with two spoonful of rose-water, mingle with your cream three spoonful of fine flour, mingle it so well, that there be no lumps in it, put it altogether, and season it according to your taste, butter a cloth very well, and let it be thick that it may not run out, and let it boil for half an hour as fast as you can, then take it up and make sauce with butter, rose-water and sugar, and serve it up. You may stick some blanched almonds upon it if you please.[63]

In other boiled puddings suet was replaced or supplemented by bone marrow. Ground almonds were often an ingredient. Dried fruit was added liberally in some recipes to make a 'plum pudding' (plums were a portmanteau name for such fruits at this time; but plum pudding had not yet become associated with Christmas fare). Mace, nutmeg, cinnamon, ginger were the spices most often employed for seasoning. For cream-based puddings the spices were often boiled whole in the cream as a preliminary step and then removed, and further flavouring was added in the form of rosewater or orangeflower water and even musk and ambergris for those who liked a really rich pudding. The mixture in each case was put into a well-flavoured or buttered cloth, bound up 'like a ball' and dropped into boiling water to be cooked.

The household books of the day described the puddings eaten by the well-to-do. But puddings were becoming an important part of the diet in humble homes too. The reason is not immediately apparent from most contemporary recipes. But one which appears in *The True Gentlewoman's Delight* of 1653 hints at it. This describes an elegant pudding of spiced cream, ground almonds, eggs, rosewater and sugar, and goes on to say: 'then take a thick napkin, wet it and rub it with flour, and tie the pudding up in it, boil it where mutton is boiled, or in the beef pot. . . .'

The great advantage of the pudding wrapped in its pudding-cloth was that it could be simmered along with the meat by the poorer housewife whose principal means of cooking was still the cauldron suspended from a pot-hook over the fire, or the three-legged iron pot standing above the embers. A two-course meal could thus be prepared in a single container. This method of cooking was in regular use through the seventeenth and eighteenth centuries, and was still to be found in the nineteenth.

Different regions of the country developed their own puddings. In Sussex, for instance, the local pudding consisted of a paste of flour, milk, eggs and a little butter, with a big lump of butter in the middle, which was boiled in the meat-pot. 'When boiled enough, they find the butter run to oil, and so well soaked into the pudding, that they eat it with meat instead of bread, or without meat as a delicious pudding.'[64]

The puddings of country folk were often made from the meal of cheaper local grains such as oats or barley, though labourers could hope for something better at harvest time. 'We send to the mill for the folks puddings a bushel of barley', wrote Henry Best, an east Yorkshire farmer, in 1641, 'but never use any rye for puddings, because it maketh them so soft that they run about the platters; in harvest time they have wheat puddings.'

Economical puddings for poor families were made up with suet or a little butter, skim-milk and two or three eggs when they were plentiful. Powdered ginger, cheaper than other spices, was a usual flavouring. The addition of sugar was by no means general, but those who could afford it poured a sauce of milk and sugar, or melted butter and sugar, over their pudding before they ate it. The 'plum puddings' given to the harvest workers were sweetened with currants or raisins; and by the mid-eighteenth century it was claimed that such puddings could be made more cheaply if the eggs in the mixture were replaced by coarse sugar.[65]

The advent of the pudding-cloth was a vital factor in the great expansion in pudding eating. But Elizabethan cooks, in their attempts to release the pudding from its dependence on an animal-gut container, had also devised another method of treating the mixture. A 'pudding in a platter' was baked in the bread oven or a side-oven with a pastry crust over it like a tart. In the early part of the seventeenth century the pudding baked in a pot was still known as a 'pudding pie'.

The pie concept was continued in the arrangement whereby the baking dish was lined with a thin sheet of pastry before the pudding mixture went into it. This seems to have been an occasional practice in the seventeenth century, but a more frequent one in the eighteenth. Sometimes the pastry was simply used to garnish the brim of the dish, so that it looked elegant enough to be brought direct from oven to table.

Another baked pudding which emerged at an early stage was the whitepot, with ingredients that included a large quantity of cream mixed with eggs, breadcrumbs or rice soaked in milk, fruit and spices. The epithet 'Devonshire' was often applied to whitepots, which were a recognized speciality of that cream-producing county.

Soon recipes for baked puddings were appearing regularly in

the cookery books. They were often based upon rich ingredients and this, coupled with the fact that an oven had to be heated for their baking, made them confections for the well-to-do rather than the poor. Specially turned wooden baking dishes were sold in which they could be prepared. The same wooden dishes or basins with a cloth tied over them, could also be utilized for boiled puddings, in place of a pudding-cloth.

A typical seventeenth-century 'rice pudding to bake' was made as follows: 'Boil the rice tender in milk, then season it with nutmeg, mace, rosewater, sugar, yolks of eggs, with half the whites, some grated bread, and marrow minced with ambergrise, and bake it in a buttered dish.'

Baked puddings were given the same enrichments as boiled puddings in the form of ground almonds, dried fruits and spices; and indeed a number of the pudding mixtures were said to be equally suitable for either boiling or baking. Fresh fruits in season were substituted for the dried 'plums' in many recipes: and baked puddings containing apples, apricots, Seville oranges, lemons, and even carrots became common. The fresh fruits were less usual in boiled puddings, probably because it was found that they lost more of their flavour and consistency when boiled than when baked. But Hannah Woolley describes one attractive pudding boiled in a cloth which was a version of the creamy quaking pudding made up with a pint or more of whole raspberries. 'You may sometimes leave out the raspberries, and put in cowslip flowers or gooseberries', she wrote.[66]

Heavier suet pudding mixtures could, as an alternative to boiling, be formed into small cakes or balls, which were fried or stewed in butter. New College puddings were made in this fashion. Green puddings were suet puddings mixed with sugar, nutmeg or some other spice, eggs, and finely grated sweet herbs. Spinach juice was used to colour them, and they too were often rolled up into little balls, and then boiled in hot water or broth like dumplings. Sometimes the balls of green pudding were eaten like forcemeat with 'roast or boiled poultry, kid, lamb, or turkey, veal or breasts of mutton'.[67]

One other possible treatment of pudding mixture, that of

boiling over direct heat, was little used, because most pudding mixtures were too thick, too rich and therefore too liable to stick and burn on the pan for this mode of cookery. The only exceptions were the occasional rice pudding and the 'pudding in haste'.

A wide range of successors to the cereal pottages of medieval times still existed in the form of sweetened cereal preparations such as frumenty, gruel, pap, and milk pottage of crumbled bread, barley, rice or sago. In their ingredients these closely resembled puddings (except for the absence of suet), but they were of a runnier consistency, and were cooked directly over the fire. Until the later seventeenth century milk pottages were eaten on fasting days. Eventually rice and sago treated thus became 'proper for a top dish for supper' among the gentry, but such dishes were never classed with puddings in the cookery books.

The only named pudding to be made by the pottage method was the 'pudding in haste' or 'hasty pudding' of southern and midland Britain. It was in effect a thicker form of bread and milk pottage. It was prepared by boiling milk or cream, adding breadcrumbs and some flour, with such enrichments as butter, eggs, raisins, currants, spices and sugar. The mixture was then brought again to the boil. It had to be stirred constantly as it cooked, but was soon ready: hence its name. The hasty pudding of northern England, Scotland and Wales, was however, quite a different matter, for it was simply the traditional oatmeal pottage and only in name resembled the newfangled puddings of southern Britain.[68]

Before the end of the seventeenth century the boiled pudding composed of a suet crust wrapped around a filling was in existence. Apple puddings made with 'great apples being pared whole, in one piece of thin paste . . . you may also put some green gooseberries into some' were established by the 1670s. 'The good housewives pudding', described a few years later, contained left-over veal, mutton, capon, chicken, rabbit or the like, 'not fit to come to table any more', minced small and mixed with milk, eggs, spice, salt and little sugar, all wrapped in a sheet of thin paste and boiled for two or three hours in water. It was to be served in slices, with butter and sugar. Steak puddings, made with beef or mutton steaks, came into the cookery books somewhat later.[69]

Puddings of a different kind which only became widely known in the eighteenth century were batter puddings, either baked in the oven or cooked under the spit in the dripping that fell from the roasting joint to form Yorkshire pudding. Another eighteenth-century discovery was the economical rice pudding, made by tying a quantity of rice and some raisins or currants loosely in a cloth, and boiling them all in plain water until the rice had swelled enough. This pudding was eaten with a sauce of melted butter and sugar.[70]

The enormous variety of puddings and the rapidity with which they were developed in the seventeenth and early eighteenth centuries show that they filled a real need in the diet of Britain. To a great extent they took over the role of the thick pottages of earlier days. Rich in fat and carbohydrates to keep out the cold, and in sugar and fruit to build up energy, the Englishman's pudding filled his stomach and satisfied his appetite.

Foreigners marvelled at the concoction, for they had no equivalent at home. M. Misson, a visitor in the 1690s, wrote:

> The pudding is a dish very difficult to be described, because of the several sorts there are of it; flour, milk, eggs, butter, sugar, suet, marrow, raisins, etc. etc. are the most common ingredients of a pudding. They bake them in an oven, they boil them with meat, they make them fifty several ways: BLESSED BE HE THAT INVENTED PUDDING, for it is a manna that hits the palates of all sorts of people; a manna, better than that of the wilderness, because the people are never weary of it. Ah, what an excellent thing is an English pudding! To come in pudding-time, is as much as to say, to come in the most lucky moment in the world. Give an English man a pudding, and he shall think it a noble treat in any part of the world.

Fifty years later pudding was 'so necessary a part of an Englishman's food, that it and beef are accounted the victuals they most love. . . .'

And even at the end of the nineteenth century pudding was still a mainstay in the diet of the English labouring man and his family:

> Meanwhile, at home, three or four different kinds of vegetables would be cooked, and always a meat pudding, made in a basin. No feast and few Sunday dinners were considered complete without that item, which was eaten alone, without vegetables, when a joint was to follow. On ordinary days the pudding would be a roly-poly containing fruit, currants, or jam; but it still appeared as a first course, the idea being that it took the edge off the appetite.[71]

Chapter 9

Fruit and salad vegetables

Prehistoric period

Fruits and nuts remained wild foods, still uncultivated long after cereals were sown and harvested in prehistoric Britain. The indigenous crab apple, gean or wild cherry, service-berry, sloe, elder and hazel trees all took some years to mature and bear fruit; and as long as the early farmers lived a semi-nomadic life, growing their patches of corn in forest clearings and moving on as soon as the soil lost its fertility, they had no incentive to plant fruit trees. In any case they would usually have been able to find and gather ripe woodland fruits and nuts in their season.

Most were probably eaten at once, but even in neolithic times some may have been preserved for winter use. Crab apples collected at Windmill Hill settlement are thought to have been sliced and dried (the resultant scattering of pips could have caused the apple-pip impressions found on clay pots made in the same working area). Hazel nuts keep well, and their shells are common on prehistoric habitation sites.

Soft fruits which would have been available to early food collectors included wild strawberries, raspberries, bilberries, blackberries, dewberries, sloes, elderberries, geans and serviceberries. They were distributed where the soil was most favourable to them, and, in the case of low-growing plants, where the dense forest was already beginning to recede. In the dry and sunny climate that prevailed from about 2500 BC until the late Bronze Age the fruits would have acquired a greater natural sweetness than their modern descendants.

Actual evidence of prehistoric man enjoying the fruits of the field comes from a burial, probably of late Bronze Age date, found at Walton-on-the-Naze. Where the deceased man's viscera had been lay the remains of about a pint of seeds, the greater part from blackberries, the rest from rose and goosefoot in equal proportions. Much later the inhabitants of Glastonbury lake village indulged themselves on the local sloes: almost a barrow-load of sloe stones was recovered when the first century BC village was excavated.[1]

Of the deliberate cultivation of fruit in Britain in pre-Roman times there is little evidence. But it is possible that Iron Age farmers, who had learned to improve the yield of their cereal crops by dressing their fields with dung and household waste, may sometimes have introduced wild fruiting plants in order to give them similar attention. The medieval custom of transplanting woodland strawberry plants into gardens may have its origins as early as this.

Green-leaved plants, like fruits, must often have been consumed raw, especially when they were young and tender. But although the Celts of the Iron Age could have eaten fresh herbs with salt, the true dressed salad was a Roman concept, unlikely to have been known in Britain until the full impact of Roman cuisine was felt there.

Vinegar could have arrived somewhat earlier. By the first century BC it was in use among the Celts along the Atlantic coast of France, whose diet included fish baked with salt, vinegar and cumin.[2] Thence it may have reached southern Britain by way of trade. If it did so, it may well have been employed as a condiment in cooking rather than a dressing.

Roman period

The Romans introduced new economic plants. They had already developed several apple varieties, with fruits smaller than those of today but larger and sweeter than those borne by Britain's indigenous wild crabs. The cultivated sweet cherry, which had reached Italy from the Black Sea region, was transferred to Britain soon after the Roman conquest.

Vines were raised in southern England in the early years of the occupation, and again from AD 277 onwards, after restrictions on local wine making had been lifted. Peaches, apricots, figs and almonds may have been grown in a few sheltered gardens in the south.

The Romans propagated fruit trees from seeds or suckers, or by grafting on to other stocks. Branches were pegged to the ground to make them root, or a perforated pot or basket of earth was attached to a small branch for two years, when the newly rooted growth could be cut off. Seedlings were raised in tree-nurseries, and then planted in prepared soil in orchards. The possible site of a large Roman orchard, containing a rectangular grid of closely spaced ditches which could have received fruit trees, has been traced near Grimsby; and similar smaller areas have been found attached to Roman settlements in the Fens.[3]

The Romans liked to preserve some of their fruit harvest. Their apple varieties included types good for keeping, and villa owners stored them spread out in rows in a dry, well-ventilated loft. Pears, grapes and service-berries could be sealed in earthenware jars which were buried underground; or put into honey, wine-must, or a brine and vinegar pickle. Service-berries picked before ripening were hung up to dry. Apples were sliced into two or three pieces with a reed or bone knife (since metal stained the fruit), and were put to lie in the sun.

Some Mediterranean fruits and nuts which could not be raised in a northerly climate were dried in their country of origin and exported to Britain. Such were figs and raisins (sweeter than any grapes that ripened in British sunshine). Almonds and stone-pine kernels also arrived from southern Europe.[4]

Other plant introductions of the Roman era were vegetables, roots and pottage and salad herbs. In the last category were garlic, garden onions, radishes and lettuce (eaten both raw and cooked). Cucumbers, marrows, garden asparagus and cardoons (a form of globe artichoke) may have been grown in Britain's villa gardens, but they were too tender to survive the end of the Roman occupation. New flowers with culinary uses included the Gallic rose of southern Europe and the garden poppy.

Further contributions to Britain's food plants may have been fungi, several of which were eaten by the Romans. Examples of one rare species, *lactarius cilicioides*, thought to have been introduced by them, were found in September 1967 growing near Stane Street, the Roman road which runs north from Chichester.[5]

Salads, cooked vegetables, fungi and some light egg or fish dishes supplied the *gustus* or *hors d'oeuvre* at a Roman meal. A first course followed comprising meat and poultry in various forms, and fruit or sweet confections were produced at the second course. Lettuce, cucumber, endive and very young roots were eaten as raw salads. But all vegetables, whether fresh or cooked, were inevitably accompanied by a seasoned sauce: hence arose the concept of the dressed salad. Cucumbers were served with *liquamen* or *oenogarum* (*liquamen* combined with wine) to make them more tender and less flatulent. Endives were dressed with *liquamen*, a little oil, wine and chopped onion. Lettuces were considered indigestible, and were given a more powerful dressing which included cumin, ginger, rue, pepper, honey and vinegar. Radishes were served with a pepper sauce. Wild herbs were dipped in a simple one of *liquamen*, oil and vinegar.

Boiled vegetables such as cabbages, turnips, leeks or cardoons were provided with similar sauces based on oil and vinegar, with the addition of aromatic herbs and sometimes onion. Apicius has several recipes for vegetable marrows, boiled, fried or mashed with appropriate seasonings; and for stewed mushrooms and fungi, to be eaten with peppered *liquamen* or more complex sauces. Leafy vegetables, including lettuce, were on occasion boiled with cooking soda to enhance their green colour. They could then be finely chopped and puréed with herbs, oil, *liquamen* and wine; or made into a *patina* with eggs.

Patinae of fruit, more suitable for the second course but sometimes eaten as *hors d'oeuvres*, were produced from such fruits as peaches, pears and elderberries. Some unusual mixtures were recorded, including a *patina* of service-berries and cooked brains with eggs; and quinces and leeks stewed together with honey. Rose petals, the white parts removed and the remainder pounded in a mortar, were combined with brains and eggs mixed with wine to form another *patina*. Scented violets were no doubt also used in Roman cookery, and both rose- and violet-flavoured wines were made. Poppy seeds supplied a garnish for enriched breads.[6]

A very important fruit product, used both as condiment and preservative, was vinegar. The Romans manufactured it from wine which had gone flat or been attacked by vinegar bacteria during fermentation, with additional yeast, salt and honey. Vinegar sharpened sauces and dressings, and was much used in the preservation of fruits, vegetables and even fish. Raw oysters were said to keep well if washed in it, and so were pieces of fried fish if plunged into hot vinegar immediately after cooking. Diluted with several times its volume of water, vinegar made a refreshing drink widely consumed in the Roman empire. It was included in the rations of soldiers on the march, and may thus have become known over much of Roman Britain.[7] Some of the country's vinegar supply may have been imported from Gaul or Spain; and it is possible that beer-based alegar was already coming into use in Roman times.

Early medieval period

Some of the cultivated fruits and salad vegetables of Roman Britain failed to survive the decay of the villa system and its gardens. But in due course the Germanic settlers of the eastern lowlands developed horticulture on their own account. Apple-tree enclosure (*apulder-tun*) was the Anglo-Saxon word for orchard, which suggests that apples were their commonest fruit. But they also knew plums, pears, quinces and medlars. In a few places the fruit trees may even have remained in continuous cultivation from Roman times; but elsewhere forest trees are likely to have provided seeds and seedlings for domestic gardens.

Better varieties and some more delicate fruits may have been brought again from mainland Europe in the form of cuttings or young plants. In later years others may have been introduced by visitors from religious foundations on the continent to daughter houses in Britain. St Benedict had decreed in his rule that the chief meal of the day should consist of two cooked dishes, followed by a third of fresh vegetables and fruit. The gardeners who produced the fruit for the brethren experimented and improved their stocks by grafting; and it was through their labours, especially in some continental monasteries, that many of the new varieties which came into fashion in the course of the Middle Ages were created.

Vines had disappeared from Britain with the decay of Roman horticulture, but were reintroduced in early Christian times. By 731 Bede was able to record the existence of vineyards as one of the notable features of the country. At the time of Domesday there were nearly forty vineyards in southern England, from Norfolk to Dorset and Gloucestershire. So thickly grew the vines on the slopes below the monastery at Ely that the Normans when they arrived christened the place the *isle des vignes*. The grapes yielded wine for the monks, and also verjuice in such quantity that it had to be sold off outside[8].

Verjuice was an early medieval invention devised to make use of the grapes which in northern Europe remained unripe at the end of the season. They were fermented to form a kind of sharp vinegar, used in cookery and pickling. People who had no green grapes at their disposal made their verjuice from crab apples.

In the Celtic west of Britain, gardens and orchards were fewer than in the lowland area. But though orchards were rare, wild woodland fruits and nuts were a usual part of the diet. And it is possible that individual forest trees were assigned to private owners. The laws of Hywel Dda set a value on a hazel grove of twenty-four pence, and on a crab apple tree of four pence until it bore fruit, and thereafter thirty pence, which implies such personal ownership. The same idea is to be found in the Brehon laws of Ireland.[9]

The semi-wild fruit tree was a familiar feature in northern Europe during the early Middle Ages. Owing to the nature of the open field system, with its two- or three-course rotation of crops and fallow, the peasants found it impracticable to grow slow-maturing fruit trees on their strips in the shared fields. The strips were frequently re-alloted; and in any case the fields were thrown open for grazing as soon as the harvest was in, when few fruits, other than cherries, could have ripened and been gathered. In Norman France cherry, apple, pear, plum, quince and medlar trees were set at the edge of the woodland so that the villagers could enjoy the fruits.[10] The same practice may have been usual in both Saxon England and Celtic Wales well before the Norman Conquest.

Little is known of how fruits were eaten at that period. Soft ones must often have been consumed raw, and hard or sharp ones stewed with honey.

Kitchen gardens also contributed to the domestic economy. Cabbages, leeks and other garden produce were to be well fenced in against wandering cattle, according to the Welsh laws. The same two vegetables figured in the Anglo-Saxon terms for kitchen garden, *leac-tun* and *wyrt-tun*, literally leek-enclosure and cabbage-enclosure (although the word *wyrt* also carried a wider meaning and could be applied to herbs in general). Wild plants were still gathered extensively, and for some herbs both wild and garden varieties were recognized. There are references in Anglo-Saxon leechdoms and vocabularies to *tun-cerse* (garden cress), *tun-minta* (garden mint, probably the Roman spearmint), *tun-melde* (garden orache). Many of the other aromatic plants known to the Romans were also grown.

A law of the year 985 records that the fasting diet on national days of penance comprised bread, butter and worts, which may have been uncooked herbs. Of greenstuff dressed as salads at this period we know nothing. But there is a hint of the eating of condiments with raw vegetables in a remedy from the *Lacnunga* (*c.* 1000). 'For heaviness in the belly: Give to eat radish with salt, and vinegar to sip; soon his mood will lighten.'[11]

Later medieval period

Fruit and vegetable gardening in Britain benefited from closer links with the continent after the Norman Conquest. New varieties of apple and pear which had been developed in France were now introduced. Of the latter, the most highly regarded were the St Règle, the Caillou (a hard Burgundy pear) and the Pesse-Pucelle, and cuttings of all three were purchased for the garden of Edward I, and later in the thirteenth century for that of the Earl of Lincoln. The fruits of the St Règle and Pesse-Pucelle were dear to buy, costing from two to three shillings a hundred in 1292, when the inferior Dreyes, Sorrells and Gold-knobs were no more than two or three pence a hundred.

Warden pears were hard, and so much larger than any of the other varieties that the phrase 'wardens and pears' was current, as though they were a distinct fruit. 'Apples and costards' were linked in the same way.

One of the earliest named apples was the pearmain, recorded soon after 1200. The costard, a very large apple, was popular from the thirteenth to the seventeenth centuries. It was sold in the streets of London by costermongers, whose wares later extended to fruit of many kinds and other goods. By the fifteenth century pippins, pomewaters, bittersweets and blanderelles had become fashionable apple varieties. Several of the medieval apples were good keeping types; indeed, apples were preferred when they had been kept awhile and allowed to mellow.[12]

Peach-tree and cherry-tree slips and gooseberry bushes were planted in the royal garden at Westminster at various times during the thirteenth century. Wild gooseberries already grew in Britain, and may have been the plants known to the Anglo-Saxons as 'thefe-thorns'; but there is no earlier record of their cultivation in gardens. Other garden or orchard fruit trees of medieval times were plums, damsons and bullaces, medlars, mulberries and quinces; and walnuts, sweet chestnuts and hazels were grown. The thirteenth-century writer Walter de Biblesworth mentions also hawthorn, sloe thorn, briar rose and cornel cherry in his list of fruit-bearing trees. The flowers of the first named and the fruits of the last three were among the foodstuffs of his day. They could be gathered in the woodlands, but the trees were on occasion brought into gardens and cultivated there. Strawberry plants were obtained from the same source.[13]

Vineyards were not uncommon in the first centuries after the Norman Conquest. But they were costly to maintain, and had little economic value once plentiful and cheap wines from the Bordeaux area had begun to reach Britain. By Elizabeth's reign home-grown English grapes were rare enough to be noted as a curiosity.

Roman methods of grafting were taken over into medieval horticulture. A treatise of *c.* 1440 by 'Mayster Ion Gardener' gave explicit details of how it was to be done (using 'hazel-tree rind' and clay in place of modern raffia and grafting wax), and recommended grafting pears on to hawthorn stocks. A hundred years later Anthony Fitzherbert confirmed that such was usual practice, with the alternative use of a crab-tree stock, when no pear stock was available.

These men had an empirical knowledge of grafting; but other writers were far more imaginative. Instructions for grafting vines on to cherry trees (in order to have grapes as early as cherries); apples on to elms or elders (to produce red apples); and for inserting dyes such as 'azure of Allemagne' into a hole in a tree-stock to make the tree bear blue and other coloured fruits, appeared in two fifteenth-century gardening manuals. But no one claimed to have eaten the results of such fanciful gardening.[14]

Strange and exotic fruits had begun to reach Britain, but they came not from bizarre grafts, but through trade with southern Europe where oranges, lemons and pomegranates were cultivated. The original home of the citrus fruits lay in northern India. They had been known to the Romans under the name of 'Median apples', having apparently arrived from Persia; and their juice had been used as a medicine, and occasionally also to sharpen the tang of vinegar. But by the time of the migrations they had almost ceased to be grown in the Mediterranean region. It was the Arabs who rediscovered citrus fruits, once more in Persia, and propagated them around the eastern Mediterranean and as far west as Sicily and Spain. They adopted Persian methods of cultivation, planting the trees in gardens irrigated by water channels, so that they could be induced to bear fruit in a hot, dry climate.

The first Englishmen to enjoy oranges, lemons and 'Adam's apples' or shaddocks, were probably the crusaders who wintered with Richard Coeur-de-Lion in the fruit groves around Jaffa in 1191–2. About a hundred years later citrus fruits had begun to arrive in England itself. Fifteen lemons and seven oranges, together with two hundred and thirty pomegranates and some dried fruits were bought from a Spanish ship at Portsmouth in 1289 for Queen Eleanor (a former princess of Castile). The following year thirty-nine lemons were purchased for the queen at the time of her last illness for 'the astonishing price of 20/-'. Southern European fruits were very expensive at that time. Pomegranates cost Bogo de Clare sixpence each in 1284, an enormous sum in relation to the price of other foods.[15]

The oranges which reached England in those days were always bitter, of the type of the Seville orange. From the end of the fourteenth century the consignments became more frequent, coming in from Spain or Portugal, or on the Italian spice ships. Not only were the citrus fruits themselves imported, but also confectionery made from them. Seven jars of 'sitrenade' (probably succade made with lemons) were delivered by an Italian galley at the Port of London in 1420, along with a large consignment of oranges and lemons. A stiff marmalade of quinces, a luxury article imported in boxes usually from Portugal, was made subject to customs duty. In due course English housewives learned to make their own succade from fresh oranges and lemons, and marmalade from home-grown quinces.[16]

Also on the spice ships from southern Europe came great raisins, 'raisins of Corinth' or currants (for the latter word was simply a corruption of 'Corinth'), prunes, figs and dates. All were consumed in vast quantities by the well-to-do, for the sweetness of dried fruits was greatly appreciated while sugar was still rare and expensive. Poorer people ate them principally in festive pottages and pies during the twelve days of Christmas, but the rich enjoyed them at other times too, and especially on fasting days and in Lent. After Easter the demand fell off; and we hear of a Bristol merchant, who had commissioned a return load of figs and raisins from southern Spain, refusing to accept delivery of the cargo because the ship bearing it was badly delayed by storms and did not reach port until Lent was past[17].

Almonds too, were imported on an enormous scale. The royal household consumed no less than 28,500 pounds of them in 1286, and 19,696 pounds in 1287. Even Dame Alice de Bryene, with a relatively small household, bought forty pounds in the year 1418–19.[18] Pine nuts and walnuts also arrived from southern Europe, but in much smaller numbers.

Fresh fruits and raw salads were less medically acceptable than were dried fruits. But plums, damsons, cherries and grapes were admitted at rich men's tables provided they were eaten at the beginning of the meal as appetizers to open the stomach. 'After meat, [serve] pears, nuts, strawberries, wineberries and hard cheese, also blanderelles, pippins.' All were considered hard or astringent, and therefore suitable to close up the stomach again after eating. Even so, apples and pears when taken at the end of a meal were usually roasted, and eaten with sugar, comfits, fennel seed or aniseed 'because of their ventosity'.

Ordinary folk ate fruit as and when they could get it. The poor people in *Piers Plowman* sought to poison hunger with baked apples and 'ripe cherries many', along with peas, beans and onions; and cherry-feasts or cherry-fairs were held in the orchards when the crop was ripe. In London both strawberries and cherries were hawked in the streets in their seasons.[19]

Gluts of fruit led inevitably to that favourite medieval vice, gluttony. Harvests were uncertain from one year to another, so whenever any foodstuff was plentiful it seemed only prudent to eat it in the greatest possible amounts. But excessive indulgence in fresh fruit caused diarrhoea, and this was confused with the fluxes that accompanied fevers; so that the fruit itself was considered dangerous. No doubt it did carry infection when epidemics were abroad, but often the victim was simply paying the price for injudicious over-eating. 'I ate damsons yesterday', said the fifteenth-century schoolboy, 'which made my stomach so raw that I could eat no manner of flesh.'

The solution was to cook the fruit. 'Raw pears a poison, baked a medicine be', according to the *School of Salerno*; and quinces, wardens and hard pears were accordingly cored, filled up with sugar or honey and powdered ginger, and baked in pastry coffins. Apples were pulped in the mortar and then put into tarts; while boiled, sieved apples formed a well-loved pottage called 'appulmos'. Strawberries, cherries, mulberries, prunes and bullaces went into other pottages. The pulp was thickened with breadcrumbs or a cereal flour, sweetened and spiced. 'Murrey', the pottage made with mulberry juice, was sometimes reinforced with boiled and pounded veal, pork or capon. Evidently the colour rather than the fruit flavour was the significant feature of the dish, because in some 'murrey' recipes the mulberries are omitted and the colour supplied by sanders. Similarly, a pseudo-rose pottage of pulped chicken flesh was reddened with sanders in place of rose petals; while turnsole pottage could be tinted purple-blue either with turnsole flowers or blackberry juice.[20]

True rose pottage was also produced, using red or white rose petals pounded in the mortar as an ingredient. Primroses, violets and hawthorn flowers made other pottages. 'For to make spinée. Take the flowers of the hawthorn, clean gathered, and bray them all to dust, and temper them with almond milk, and allay it with amidon, and with eggs well thick, and boil it. And mess it forth; and flowers and leaves [laid] above on.'

The garnishing with petals of the same flower was part of the charm of flower pottages. In April and May, 'appulmos' was decorated with apple blossom. Clove gilliflower petals sometimes adorned other pottages, but they were often treated instead as a spice to flavour made dishes or wine. Elder flowers mingled with egg whites and curds formed the filling of a tart called 'sambocade'.

Fresh fruit was occasionally used to dress meat, as in the case of 'sauce madame'. But in most recipes dried fruit was preferred, and in particular currants, which went into many pottages and pies. Meatless pottages were made for Lent, such as 'figgey', of figs and bread, boiled in wine, mingled with raisins and pine nuts, and highly spiced. Such pottages were eaten in the same course as the fish dishes, since there was no separation of sweet from savoury at medieval meals. Indeed, 'rapey', another dried fruit pottage, was poured directly over fried fish to serve as a sauce.[21]

Dried fruits and nuts were also enclosed in batter and fried in oil as 'rissoles of fruit'; or were threaded on to long separate threads, which were wound together round a spit and basted with batter as they roasted to make a 'trayne roste'. The 'trayne' was afterwards cut into 'fair pieces of a span length' and eaten hot.

Pine nuts as well as dried fruits went into pies and pottages. Walnuts were eaten whole to close the stomach after a meal; or crushed with garlic as a sauce for stockfish.[22]

But the most versatile of all the nuts was the almond. Almonds were taken after sour meats as a digestive; and Boorde claimed that 'vi or vii eaten before meat preserveth a man from drunkenship'. In cookery almonds were added to certain dishes in their whole form; or they were blanched, fried, and scattered over the top of solid pottages as a decoration. But most often, they were pounded in the mortar, and thus brought to an entirely different consistency. In this form, they served as a thickening agent for a dish such as white mortrews.

Alternatively almond-milk was made first and then mixed with other ingredients. It could be sweet or savoury, depending upon how it was drawn. 'Take fair almonds and blanch them and grind them with sugar water into fair milk'; or, 'Take raw almonds and blanch them and grind them and draw them through a strainer with fresh broth and wine into good stiff milk'. Even, on occasion, 'Take almonds, and draw a good milk thereof with water'.

The great advantage of almond-milk was that it could be used as a substitute for cows' milk in fasting-day dishes. Drawn thicker, it became cream. And if it was boiled with a little wine or vinegar and strained through a canvas, the solid part could be eaten as almond-butter on fish days, especially in Lent. Poor people used bean-butter as a substitute.[23]

Marchpane or marzipan was a discovery of the later Middle Ages, dependent as it was upon the union of ground almonds with sugar. It may have been invented in Italy: at any rate its name is believed to have originated there, though it quickly spread into the other main languages of Europe. In thirteenth-century France it was made of pistachio nuts or almonds ground with sugar, and the latter type became the usual English marchpane.

One of the early uses for the paste was in 'subtleties'. These were figures of men, animals, trees, castles and so forth made from sugar paste and jelly, and placed before an admiring audience at the end of each course of a great medieval feast. Often the figures had an allegorical meaning, and bore written mottoes appropriate to the occasion. The 'subtleties' varied from simple depictions of a gilded eagle, or a swan upon a green stook, carrying mottoes in their bills, to such complexities as a portrayal of the Trinity in a sun of gold with a crucifix in His hand attended by saints and the kneeling figure of the new Archbishop of Canterbury, for whose enthronement feast the 'subtelty' had been made.[24] When they had been sufficiently applauded they were dismantled and eaten.

In the fifteenth century a 'marchpane' began to emerge as an object in its own right. And by Elizabeth I's reign, when the 'subtlety' was becoming archaic, a marchpane was regularly produced as the chief showpiece at the banquet or dessert course served to guests at the end of a meal.

It was made of ground almonds and sugar on a base of wafer biscuits, and was formed into a round (a hoop of green hazelwood sometimes helped shape it). 'Ye may while it is moist, strike it full of comfits of sundry colours, in a comely order', wrote John Partridge, '. . . the clearer it is like a lantern horn, so much the more commended. If it be thorough dried, and kept in a dry and warm air, a marchpane will last many years.'

The frosting of the marchpane with sugar and rosewater to make it 'shine like ice' was an important part of the preparation; and so was the gilding with decorative shapes in gold leaf. The marchpane, made and adorned after this fashion, enjoyed its individual fame for many years before it was finally united with the plum cake.[25]

Another medieval confection with origins in southern Europe was marmalade, called after the Portuguese *marmelo* (quince). It was copied in England, at first under the Anglo-Norman name of 'charedequynce'. According to one recipe thirty quinces and ten wardens were brayed in a mortar, strained with wine and boiled thick with honey; and the result was spiced with an ounce each of powdered ginger, galingale and cinnamon, and boxed for long keeping. Marmalade maintained its popularity, but by the later sixteenth century the heavy spicing had been dropped, and the quinces were boiled with sugar and water, with sometimes a little rosewater for extra flavour.[26]

The pomegranates imported from Mediterranean lands were

used mainly for decoration. Pottages were garnished with the whole fruits, or sprinkled with the grains or seeds.

The citrus fruits had two distinct roles in France, where their sharp juice supplied a sauce that could be used in place of verjuice, while their peels were candied and eaten as sweetmeats. The appetite-provoking quality of bitter orange juice was soon recognized in England too. During the fifteenth century oranges were bought as a treat by solicitous husbands and friends for pregnant wives. So usual was this custom in the Paston family that the youngest John Paston felt he had to apologize when he asked for some to be sent to Elizabeth Calthorpe who 'longeth for oranges, though she be not with child'.

Cooked oranges appear in the menu for the enthronement feast of Archbishop Warham held at Canterbury in 1505. The lords spiritual and temporal were given in the second course 'quince and orange baked'; but the lower orders had to make do with simple 'quince baked'. The next day orange fritters were served, again only to the nobility.[27]

At a light supper Archbishop Warham and the other lords 'sitting at a board at night' enjoyed dishes which included more baked quince and orange, marmalade and succade. Succade in its early days was made of either orange or lemon peels, soaked and boiled in plain water to take off their bitterness and then reboiled in honey or a sugar and water syrup. Like marmalade it was at first imported from southern Europe, often as a moist preserve with the rinds or sometimes whole fruits stored in their syrup, for we read of it being sold by the pot or little barrel.

When citrus fruits became more plentiful in England housewives learned how to make their own succade; and they presently extended the method to the roots and stalks of several plants which were thought to have medicinal properties, but were too bitter to eat raw.

As Andrew Boorde observed: 'There is no herb, nor weed, but God hath given virtue to them, to help man'. His words sum up the all-embracing attitude towards living plants that had prevailed through the Middle Ages and was still current in his own day. For this reason the medieval garden was stocked with a vast and varied array of plants, most of them intended for use either in food or in physic; though a few were 'strewing herbs', to be spread over floors, while a small number of flowers were cultivated simply for the sake of their beauty or their scent.

Contemporary lists and recipes show that the majority of the plants grown were regarded as potherbs, suitable for cooking in stews and sauces. Of these, a few doubled as salad herbs, to be eaten raw with a dressing. The names of some of them appear in our earliest salad recipe, recorded about 1393:

> Salad. Take parsley, sage, garlic, chibols, onions, leek, borage, mints, porray, fennel, and garden cresses, rue, rosemary, purslain; lave and wash them clean; pick them, pluck them small with thine hand, and mingle them well with raw oil. Lay on vinegar and salt and serve it forth.

The herbs were among those grown regularly in England, and were but few compared with the total number to be found in a well-stocked English medieval garden. An early fifteenth-century list (Sloane MS 1201) of 'herbs necessary for a garden' gives over a hundred, arranged in the first place alphabetically, and afterwards in classified order according to their usage for pottage, for sauces, for the cup (i.e. to flavour drinks), for distilling, and so forth. There are nearly twenty 'herbs for a salad': 'Buds of "stanmarche" [alexanders], violet flowers, parsley, red mints, cress of Boleyne, purslane, ramsons, calamints, primrose buds, daisies, rampions, dandelion, rocket, red nettle, borage flowers, crops of red fennel, "selbestryve", chickenweed.'[28]

Some of them look very strange to modern eyes; and lettuce in the fifteenth century was a pottage, not a salad plant. The medieval delight in coloured foods is well catered for. The purple violets and blue borage flowers would have made a striking contrast with the red mints, nettle and fennel, and with the paler buds of primrose and alexanders, and the various green leaves. The mixed herb and flower salad was so popular that it continued in fashion all through the Tudor and Stuart era.

Early modern period

The sixteenth century saw an upsurge of interest in fruit and vegetables, both in varieties long known in Britain, and in new species now introduced for the first time. The country was at last enjoying peace after prolonged civil war, so that men had the leisure and inclination to look after their gardens. Contacts with continental Europe increased again, and English gardeners acquired new ideas as well as new stock from France and the Low Countries, where fruit and vegetable cultivation was in a more advanced state of development.

The market gardens of Flanders were well established by the beginning of the fifteenth century, and Flemish garden produce was exported regularly to south-east England. Eventually the gardeners themselves came too, for in the middle years of the sixteenth century some arrived both from Flanders and France as refugees from religious persecution. They settled in East Anglia and south-east England, and set up gardens where they grew produce for sale in neighbouring towns. At the same time many of the English nobility and gentry began to take an interest in horticulture, and their gardeners too were kept busy nursing up new varieties of fruit and vegetables for their masters' delectation.

Market gardening proved lucrative, especially around London. Gardeners who worked within a six-mile radius of the city formed themselves into a guild, which obtained a charter in 1605. Twelve years later they claimed to be employing 'thousands of poor people, old men, women and children in selling of their commodities, in weeding, in gathering of stone, etc.'. Individual gardens were not big, but many people were put to work, the earth was dressed with the street soil of the city, and the resultant crops were heavy.[29]

Garden produce was sold traditionally near the gate of St Paul's and in the neighbouring streets. But that area now became too congested, and in the mid-seventeenth century some traders moved out to Covent Garden. Here the garden and orchard, which had once supplied fruit and vegetables for the convent of St Peter at Westminster, had come into the possession of the Earls of Bedford. Inigo Jones laid out the Piazza, a square with a portico on two sides, for the fourth Earl. The market gardeners gathered on the south side in such numbers that in 1670 the fifth Earl of Bedford obtained an official licence to hold a market within the Piazza; and by levying tolls on the traders, he made a fortune for himself and his family. Thereafter Covent Garden was London's fruit market.

Smaller towns had less problem in accommodating sellers of fruit and vegetables, and the ordinary market place usually sufficed. Fruit could also be bought from itinerant traders. In the towns it was cried through the streets and sold from barrows by costermongers, orange wives and other hucksters. Wild fruits were gathered locally in country places and offered for sale at fairs, or peddled from house to house.

By Elizabethan times a wide range of fruits was being grown in southern and midland Britain. Thomas Tusser drew up a list of twenty-seven different fruit trees and bushes for the gardener to set. All the medieval favourites were there, and many had burgeoned out into several new varieties, either home bred or imported as seeds or stocks from the continent. By 1629 John Parkinson could name no fewer than fifty-seven kinds of apple besides 'twenty sorts of sweetings and none good'; sixty-two cultivated pears and wardens; sixty-one different plums (including bullaces); thirty-five cherries and twenty-two peaches.[30]

Other familiar soft fruits on Tusser's list were gooseberries, grapes, mulberries, whortleberries (bilberries) and strawberries. In his day strawberry plants were still brought in from the wilds to be cherished by the careful housewife.

> Wife into thy garden, and set me a plot,
> with strawberry roots, of the best to be got:
> Such growing abroad, among thorns in the wood,
> well chosen and picked, prove excellent good.

But the woodland strawberry, like other fruits, was soon improved. It was crossed first with the slightly larger, musky flavoured hautbois strawberry brought from the continent. Then later it was interbred with a better flavoured variety from Virginia, cultivated in Europe by 1642. But the berries were still small, and it was only later in the eighteenth century that larger ones were produced through further crossing with a Chilean strawberry noted for big, but whitish and rather flavourless fruits. Finally in 1806 a plant was produced which bore large, red, well-flavoured strawberries, comparable with those we know today.[31]

Tusser's list also included some relatively recent arrivals. Among them was the apricot, still very rare in 1548 when William Turner had wished to call it 'an hasty peach tree' on the grounds that 'it is like a peach and it is a great while ripe before the peach trees'. The Elizabethans preferred the name 'apricock' which they derived from the Portuguese *albricoque*. Nectarines were not apparently raised, or at any rate recognized as a separate species, until the early seventeenth century.

Raspberries too were first recorded as garden fruits in England in 1548. They had been in cultivation in French gardens for some time.[32]

Wild red and black currants had likewise been bred up into garden plants by continental gardeners. In Tusser's list they appear under their early name of 'raisins'; and they were also known as 'bastard corinths', for there was at first some confusion in people's minds as to whether they were the originals of the well-known dried currants. Another sixteenth-century name for them was 'beyond sea gooseberry', since they were rightly recognized as belonging to the gooseberry family.

Barberries, the fruits of the common berberis, had long been an apothecaries' drug; but in Tudor times they took on a new role as a condiment for meat and fish, and they began to be grown regularly in gardens. Nut trees were also raised, and Tusser named chestnuts, filberts, small nuts (perhaps hazel) and walnuts on his list.

Several different species of gourd now became prominent.

The coarse gourds of medieval times had been stewed in pottage, for 'gourds raw be unpleasant in the eating'. A new cooking gourd introduced from France was the pompion or pumpkin. Poor folk removed the seeds and pith from pumpkins, stuffed them with apples and baked them. The well-to-do enjoyed them in elaborate pies.

Also from France came the more delicate melon. At first the fruits alone were imported as a rarity, 'only eaten by great personages'; but in due course the plants were cultivated on a limited scale in England, and melons became more common. The Elizabethans greatly admired musk melons. A recipe of 1597 suggested soaking melon seeds in sugar water flavoured with musk and cinnamon in order to produce 'such melons as the like hath not been seen . . . and thus you may do the seeds of pompions and cucumbers'; but there is no evidence that this particular piece of magic was ever made to work.

The cucumber was still little known in England in the fifteenth century, when it appeared on a garden list with the annotation, 'cucumber, it beareth apples', as though it were necessary to explain that the plant was raised for the sake of its fruit, and not for its leaves or roots. The cucumbers illustrated in early printed books are pear shaped or nearly round, unlike their modern counterparts. They began to be grown on a considerable scale during the sixteenth century when they were not only eaten fresh in summer, but also pickled for winter use. There was a brisk trade, too, in 'the pickled cucumbers that come from beyond sea'.[33]

Several food-plants were still valued for their flowers. Violets, primroses and borage flowers were candied or put into tarts. Marigolds supplied a vegetable dye used in cheese and butter making, and were found spicy enough to add to meat stews. Roses were the source of rosewater, much used as a flavouring in sixteenth- and seventeenth-century cookery. They took their place along with the fruit bushes in a well-planned kitchen garden.

The gooseberry, raspberry, and roses, all three,
With strawberries under them trimly agree.[34]

New gardening techniques were introduced from Europe too. By the later sixteenth century apricots and quinces were being grown against south-facing walls, a practice which probably stemmed from Italy. Even figs sometimes ripened in sheltered gardens in southern England.

Further north the climate imposed limitations. In Yorkshire the best fruits to set were: 'apples, pears, cherries, filberts, red and white plums, damsons and bullaces. . . . We do not meddle with apricocks nor peaches nor scarcely with quinces, which will not like our cold parts.' In northern England fruit was raised principally in the gardens of the gentry. There were parts of Lancashire and the north-west where even apples and plums were hardly known among ordinary people before the eighteenth century.

In Scotland too, fruit was grown on a limited scale. During medieval times apple, pear and plum trees were to be found only in monastic or castle gardens. Exceptionally vines were planted against orchard walls at the border monasteries of Melrose and Jedburgh, and even further north at Balmerino in Fife; and there is a rare record of cherry orchards at Ballencrief in Midlothian in 1524. It was some time before soft fruits were in regular cultivation. They were gradually introduced on gentlemen's estates during the seventeenth century, when the gardening enthusiasm of the English had had time and opportunity to spread to north Britain.[35]

On oranges and lemons Tusser's verdict was: 'These buy with the penny/Or look not for any'. From his day onwards they were shipped from Portugal and other southern countries in ever-increasing numbers. Both bitter and sweet oranges were now obtainable. Sweet oranges of an inferior flavour had been grown in east Mediterranean lands in the Middle Ages, but had hardly been known further west. But during the sixteenth century the Portuguese brought back from Ceylon a superior sweet orange, which soon spread into the other orange-growing countries of southern Europe. A hundred years later it was superseded in popularity by the still more delectable China orange, 'a sort lately had from Portugal, whither it came not many years since from China. This hath the rind so pleasant and free from bitterness that it may be eaten as well as the meat which is sweet, and it is the best kind to preserve whole.'

A few wealthy and enthusiastic garden owners purchased orange and lemon trees on the continent and tried to persuade them to fruit in the English climate. Sir Francis Carew is said to have grown the first orange trees in the country on his estate at Beddington in Croydon sometime before 1562; and Lord Burghley was another early possessor of an orange, a lemon and also a pomegranate tree. They were still rare when Pepys first saw oranges growing in Lord Brooke's garden in Hackney in 1666, 'some green, some half, some a quarter and some full ripe, on the same tree', and secretly purloined a tiny green one which he ate.

Citrus trees needed careful tending, and the additional warmth of a stove in the cold months for 'no tent or mean provision will preserve them'. They were sometimes planted in boxes on wheels that could be trundled out into the sunshine in summer, and kept indoors in winter. By such methods oranges, and eventually even the more delicate lemons and citrons, were occasionally made to fruit in England.[36]

Other citrus fruits, the lime and the shaddock which had been naturalized in several West Indian islands by the Spanish, became known in Britain somewhat later. Limes were particularly successful in Jamaica, and by the 1680s their juice was extracted there by means of presses and exported in casks to Europe. It was used in the making of punch, a drink newly popular in England.

Shaddocks, large citrus fruits the size of a man's head with thick peel and very little pulp, were for long known as Adam's apples or the forbidden fruit because of the 'toothmarks' on their skins. They were native to the Malay archipelago, and received a further introduction into the West Indies when a Captain Shaddock, commander of an East India ship, left some seeds at Barbados where he touched in the course of a voyage to England from the Far East. Subsequently the trees flourished in Jamaica, and there some time during the eighteenth century a variety with small thin-skinned fruits evolved. Early in the following century it acquired the name of grapefruit.

The new world had native fruits, too, hitherto unknown in Europe, which were discovered by the early explorers. One that was known for many years before it won acceptance as a food in Britain was the tomato. The Spaniards encountered it in Mexico, and had begun to cultivate it in southern Europe by the mid-sixteenth century.

Tomatoes in their original unimproved form were 'fair and goodly apples, chamfered, uneven and bunched out in many places; of a bright shining red colour and the bigness of a goose egg or a large pippin'. They were usually called 'apples of love', because of their supposed aphrodisiac properties. A yellow variety also existed to which was given the alternative name of 'golden apples'.

But whereas even in Gerard's day foreigners 'in Spain and those hot regions . . . do eat the apples with oil, vinegar and pepper mixed together for sauce to their meat, even as we in these cold countries do mustard', in England the fruits were viewed with great circumspection. Because 'the whole plant is of a rank and stinking savour', and because it was known to be of the same family as the deadly nightshade, tomatoes were considered a dangerous food. Gerard said that they yielded 'very little nourishment to the body, and the same naught and corrupt', and this view was held generally for many years. Tomatoes were cultivated in gardens only as a curiosity, 'and for the amorous aspect or beauty of the fruit'.[37] It was not until the later eighteenth century that they were admitted cautiously to English cuisine.

'A certain delicious fruit called a *pina*', discovered in the new world and christened by the Spanish settlers, won more approbation from the English. The first example was brought to Britain in Cromwell's time; and a queen pine from Barbados presented to Charles II in 1661 excited great interest.

'In Jamaica and Brasilia, grows the fruit *ananas*', wrote John Worlidge in 1676, 'on a stalk of a foot long, surrounded with sixteen sharp leaves, between which is the fruit like a pineapple, but much bigger; the innermost pulp whereof melts on the tongue, and is of so delicious a taste, that it exceeds all other dainties'. The curious phrase 'like a pineapple' in fact refers to a pinecone, then usually known as a pineapple. The name was later transferred to the new fruit, partly through association with the Spanish *pina*.[38]

English gardeners began to grow pineapples on hot-beds early in the eighteenth century. For many years thereafter pineries were a fashionable adjunct to those great estates that had their own hot houses, and wealthy hosts liked to offer home-grown pineapples to their guests But rearing them was a tedious, costly business, for they took two or three years to mature, depending upon the variety chosen. When eventually improved sea communications made it possible to bring fresh pineapples regularly from the West Indies, the pineries were no longer kept up.

Bananas had been discovered by Europeans as early as the fifteenth century, growing as food plants near the west African coast. They had already spread westwards across India and through central Africa from an original home in south-east Asia. They were then propagated in the Canary Islands and subsequently in the West Indies. In the latter region the fruits were roasted or baked and eaten with orange juice and sugar; and were said to be excellent stewed with sugar and a little cinnamon. The first bunch of bananas ever seen in England arrived from Bermuda in 1633; and was hung up to ripen and be admired in the shop of a herbalist named Thomas Johnson on Snow Hill in London. But bananas were very rare in Britain for many years after that, for they were too perishable to form a regular article of trade, even from the Canaries, until the coming of fast steamships in the nineteenth century.[39]

One of the latest garden fruits to be cultivated in England was rhubarb. Medicinal rhubarb, the rhubarb grown in China from the third millennium BC onwards for the sake of its root, a powerful purgative, had been traded to the west since Roman times. There was more than one variety, and the names Turkey rhubarb and Barbary rhubarb were given to two of them, denoting the countries through which passed the medieval spice routes whereby they travelled.

In the Tudor period the plants themselves were introduced into English herb gardens, and medicinal rhubarb became a garden crop in Britain. The Duke of Atholl had a famous plantation of Turkey rhubarb on his estate at Blair Castle in Perthshire in the 1770s, and sold the roots to an Edinburgh druggist.

The rhubarb now eaten as a fruit arrived in the seventeenth century, when John Parkinson received seeds from Italy and planted them in his garden. He described the leaf stalks, some two feet long and the thickness of a man's thumb, and thought a syrup might be made from the juice which would purge more gently than rhubarb from the East Indies or China. The cultivation of garden rhubarb spread in Britain in the eighteenth century, with encouragement during the later years from the Royal Society of Arts.[40]

The medieval fear and suspicion of uncooked fruit died hard. It was fostered by the medical men. 'And all manner of fruit generally fill the blood with water, which boileth up in the body as new wine doth in the vessel, and so prepareth and causeth the blood to putrefy, and consequently bringeth in sickness', according to Thomas Cogan.[41] Its dangers were greatest when epidemics raged. The sale of fruit in the streets was forbidden in 1569, a year of pestilence, and soft fruits were again suspect during the great plague of 1665. Fruit was often blamed at other times when any person fell into a sudden and unaccountable fever. It was only in the eighteenth century that fresh fruit began to be regarded as a safe and even, under some circumstances, health-giving food. In the meantime plenty of people ate it, of course, and survived.

But all through the sixteenth and seventeenth centuries the prudent way to eat fruit was to cook it first with sugar and spices or to condite it in sugar. Apples, pears, wardens and quinces were baked long in pies (six hours for a quince pie, in a recipe of 1588). Soft fruits were boiled and pulped to form tartstuff, or to be mingled with cream in a fool or similar creamy dish. They became an ingredient of puddings; and they were preserved in numerous ways with the aid of sugar.

Apple pies, and especially pippin and codlin pies, were in high favour in Tudor and Stuart times. Pippins were sometimes baked with candied orange peels, as well as cloves, cinnamon and dates to give them more flavour, and rosewater was a usual addition to both apple and quince pies. The medieval combination of citrus fruits with those of the apple and pear families was continued in the mid-seventeenth-century taffety tarts, with their layers of sliced apple strewn with sugar, fennel seed and finely cut lemon peel; and crystallized orange and lemon peel went into other apple tarts of the period. By Georgian times fresh lemon juice and raw shredded peel were used to season the apples.

Quinces, pears and wardens for Tudor and Stuart pies were often precooked in a syrup of red wine and sugar or honey which dyed them 'orient red'. Quinces were sometimes boiled in a similar syrup and preserved for winter use. More sinister was the greening of apples for pies by stewing them beforehand in a brass or copper pan. The addition of vine leaves enhanced the effect. The resultant 'fine green' owed more to the interaction of the acid fruit with the metal than to nature; but the practice seems to have been common in the eighteenth century. Elizabeth Raffald inveighed against it in *The Experienced English House-keeper* and then included two recipes for greening codlins by this method elsewhere in the book![42]

The pumpkin pies enjoyed by people of substance were in the tradition of the earlier rich pies of mixed ingredients. The pumpkin was first sliced and fried with sweet herbs and spices, sugar and beaten eggs. Then it was put into a pastry shell with alternate layers of apples and currants.[43] Pumpkin pie made on similar lines has become a national dish in America, having been introduced there by the early colonists. In England, however, it went out of fashion in the course of the eighteenth century.

During Elizabeth's reign and thereafter sweet potato tubers (*Ipomoea batatas*) were imported from Spain during the late summer. The plant was a South American one, cultivated successfully in Spain, but not able to withstand the climate of northern Europe. The sweet potato first appeared in print in England in a recipe of 1596 for 'a tart that is a courage to a man or woman'. As well as 'a potato root', the tart contained borage roots, quinces, dates, egg yolks, wine, sugar, spices and 'the brains of three or four cock sparrows'. Both sparrows' brains and sweet potatoes enjoyed a great reputation as aphrodisiacs at the time.

For the next hundred years potatoes (either Spanish or Virginia), artichoke bottoms and skirrets were baked in rich pies which, in true medieval fashion, contained also dried fruits, spices and animal marrow. Soon the dried currants, raisins and dates were being reinforced, and later often replaced, by crystallized oranges or lemons, preserved barberries, cherries, eringoes or other candied fruits or roots.

Gervase Markham gave an account of a magnificent pie of this genre. It comprised a raised coffin of the best pastry filled with a bottom layer of soles of artichokes, a second one of thickly sliced boiled potatoes, and a topping of 'candied eringo-roots mixed very thick with the slices of dates', the different levels being separated by pieces of beef marrow, spices, currants and raisins. After baking the pie was filled up with a liquor of white wine, rosewater, sugar, cinnamon and vinegar mixed together, and its lid was iced.

More usually artichoke bottoms, skirrets or potatoes alone provided the basis, though the additions were equally rich. In a recipe of 1690 for 'a potato or secrets pie', the slices of potato are described as 'secrets', their identity apparently lost among the array of preserved fruits which overlaid them.[44]

In the years that followed, sweetmeat pies began to lose their appeal, and artichoke bottoms, potatoes (now usually of the Virginia variety) and skirrets were more commonly baked with savoury seasonings, and such accompaniments as hard-boiled eggs, chestnuts, brains or cockscombs. Standing fruit pies, other than pasties, also went out of favour, and pies or tarts of fruits were now prepared regularly in dishes or patty pans.

Tarts had indeed always been baked thus, being made from short pastry which required a much briefer sojourn in the oven than the paste of the standing pie. The Elizabethan fruit tart was often filled with a kind of purée which ensured that the fruit had been well and truly cooked.

> To make all manner of fruit tarts. You must boil your fruit, whether it be apple, cherry, peach, damson, pear, mulberry or codlin, in fair water, and when they be boiled enough, put them into a bowl, and bruise them with a ladle, and when they be cold, strain them; and put in red wine or claret wine, and so season it with sugar, cinnamon and ginger.

Tartstuff of prunes was made in the same way, with the same seasonings. In a later version the prunes were boiled, strained, and reboiled with sugar, cinnamon and rosewater 'till it be as thick as marmalade'.[45]

The distinctive features of tartstuff were its consistency and its seasonings. This may explain why spinach, which could be cooked to the same sort of pulp as the strained fruits, was so popular as a filling for tarts. In that role it was flavoured sweet, not only with sugar and spice, but also with currants, and later in the seventeenth century with candied orange and lemon peel too.

Uncrushed strawberries, cherries or gooseberries were also put into tarts, and they received the same high seasoning as tartstuff. Only in the eighteenth century did the spicing yield to simple sweetening with sugar. Whole fruits were preserved too, for winter tarts. They were boiled rapidly in sugar and water, and then sealed in their syrup in gallipots.

Some tart fillings of Tudor and Stuart times are strange to modern tastes. Medlars or rosehips were pulped into tartstuff. Closed tarts of young peas were well liked, flavoured with saffron, salt, sugar and butter. A little verjuice was added for piquancy, and the pastry cover was topped with sugar icing. Tarts of flowers were prepared during spring and summer.

Cowslips, primroses or marigold petals were beaten small and combined with eggs and cream or curds.

The pineapple tarts in seventeenth-century recipe books contained not the recently discovered tropical fruit, but pine kernels, which were ground up with the pulp of two or three pippins and then mingled with cream and egg yolks. Almond tarts were popular, whether they took the form of cheesecakes, or were filled with ground almonds scented with rosewater or later with orangeflower water.[46]

In the eighteenth century fruit pies and tarts were enjoyed increasingly in the north of England. The development of the canal system allowed apples and plums to be carried there from Kentish and other southern orchards. In the south poor housewives chopped apples thriftily along with their cores and skins to make them go further in pies and pasties; or mixed them with sliced pumpkin or onions. Country folk made use of wild blackberries, bilberries and crab apples (saved until Christmas to take off some of their sharpness).

Garden rhubarb was a new acquisition for tarts. A recipe which appeared in the 1790s advocated slicing the stalks, and then treating them in the manner of gooseberries.[47]

Fruit fools and creams succeeded the medieval fruit pottages. They were based on the pulp of cooked fruits beaten together with cream and sugar. Gooseberries, and later orange juice combined with beaten eggs, were made up into fools. Recipes for almond cream abounded; and even artichoke bottoms were cooked and incorporated with egg yolks and cream to produce artichoke cream to eat cold. Codlin cream was not only made directly from apple pulp and cream, but could also be produced inside a codlin pie, by removing the lid, adding boiled cream and mashing the codlins into it at a late stage in the baking.

Fruit creams, like fruit pies, were usually served in the second course. The eighteenth century saw the invention of a new type of second course dish comprising such fruits as melons, peaches and pineapples made from flummery set in moulds. Spinach juice was used to dye the melon a delicate green, and cochineal to redden the peaches, while the pale yellow Dutch

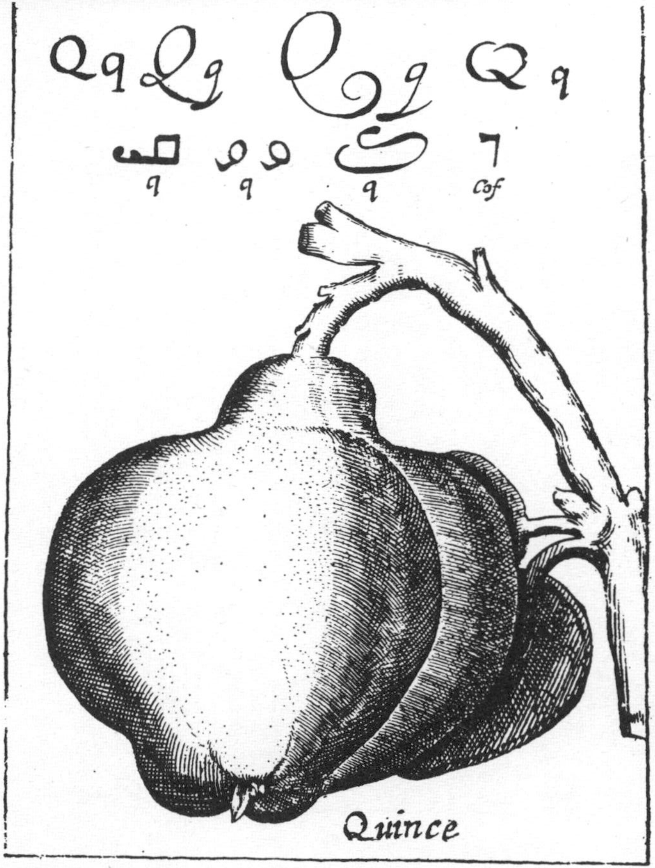

Quince

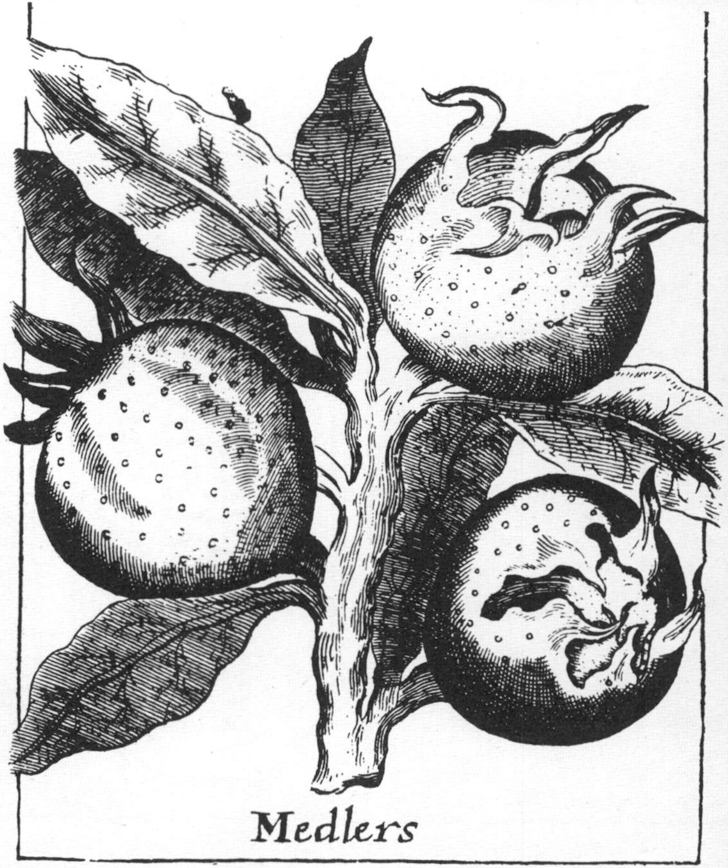

Medlars

From *A book of fruits and flowers*, 1653

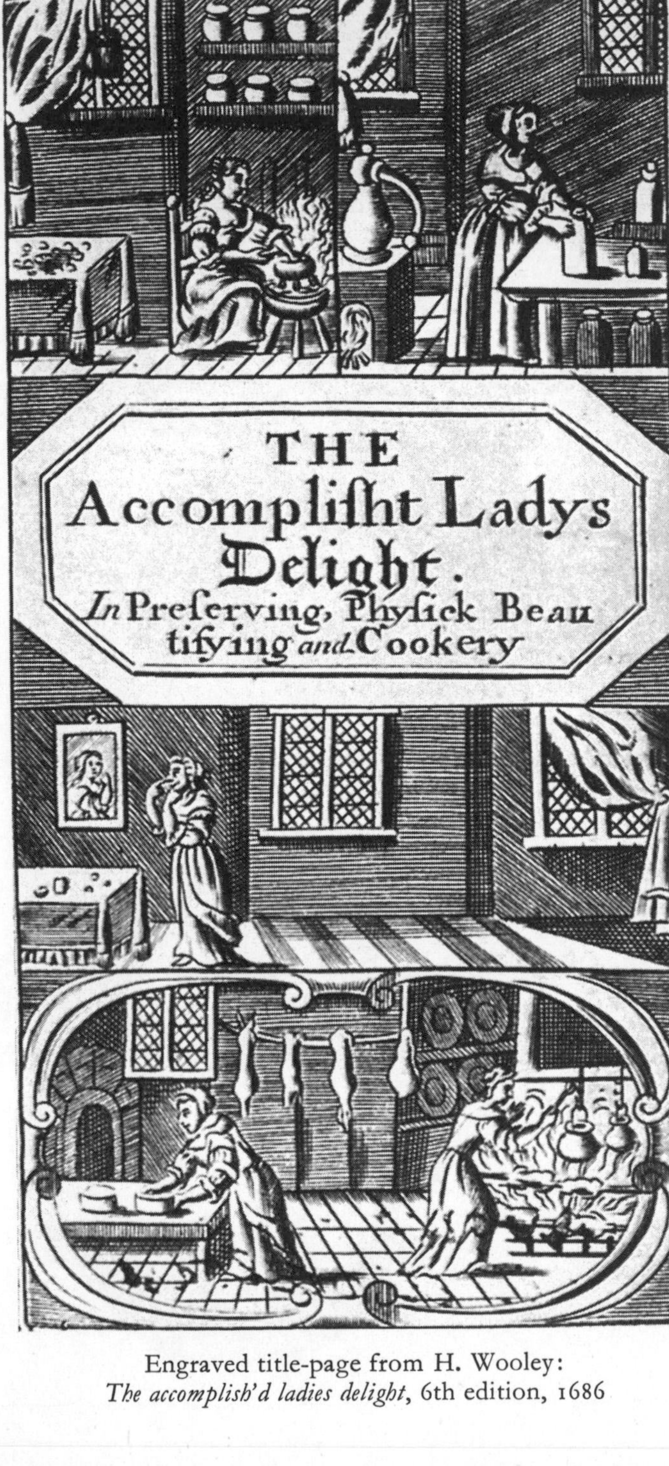
THE
Accomplisht Ladys
Delight.
In Preserving, Physick Beau
tifying and Cookery

Engraved title-page from H. Wooley:
The accomplish'd ladies delight, 6th edition, 1686

flummery pineapple had its leaves coloured green after it was turned out of the mould for a final touch of realism.[48]

Attempts were sometimes made to preserve soft berries in stoneware bottles, warmed first, in a recipe of the 1690s, to 'draw out as much of the air as may be'; but they had no great success. All the usual methods of conserving fruit involved processing it with sugar.

Sucket candy, beloved since its first arrival on the spice ships from southern Europe in the form of candied orange and lemon peel, was now made by English housewives. Citrus fruits or their peels alone were soaked in water and then boiled in sugar syrup to take away their bitterness. The same treatment was extended to the roots and stalks of certain native plants, especially those noted for their health-giving properties. 'The roots of borage and bugloss sodden tender, and made in a succade, doth engender good blood, and doth set a man in a temperance', wrote Andrew Boorde. The roots of elecampane, alexanders, parsley and fennel similarly prepared had other virtues. Those of eringo or sea-holly, which grows in sandy places on the east coast, were famed as an aphrodisiac; and the local eringo candying industry of Colchester, which was in existence by the late sixteenth century, survived into the middle of Victoria's reign. Candied roots were either kept in their syrup to be eaten as wet sucket, or put to dry on papers strewn with sugar.[49]

The stalks of lettuce and angelica were also candied, as were green walnuts. Unripe apricots, peaches, damsons and pear-plums were boiled directly in syrup without prior soaking, a practice which made use of the fruit that failed to mature in a poor summer. An addition of the eighteenth century was the preserved green pineapple, laid unripe in salted water for five days before being boiled and stored in sugar syrup.

Ripe soft fruits were less easy to candy whole. A recipe of 1587 told how to 'preserve all kind of fruits, that they shall not break in the preserving of them' by laying them between layers of sugar on a flat platter, covering them with a dish, and steaming them over a boiling pot. Later it was more usual to boil the fruits briefly in sugar syrup, and then reduce the latter to a thick consistency before pouring it over them in glass or stoneware jars. Alternatively the fruits, like the candied roots, were sugared ('strew them over with seasoned sugar, as you would do flour upon fish to fry them'), and slowly dried in a warm oven. By the mid-eighteenth century recipes appeared for the 'brandy fruits', peaches, nectarines, apricots, cherries and grapes, which were put up in jars containing brandy with a little sugar syrup, and sealed closely.[50]

Candied fruits, together with other dry and wet sweetmeats, were set out in little dishes at the banquet of Tudor and Stuart days, and thereafter were eaten as dessert at the end of the second course. They were also offered as refreshments to callers at other times of day. The dry sweetmeats included thick peach or quince marmalades divided into separate lumps, printed with moulds and sugared; pastes of fruit juice and sugar, similarly printed; and candied fruit chips. Stiff jellies were made from strawberries, raspberries or mulberries crushed in a mortar with sugar, boiled with water, rosewater and isinglass and sieved. They were boxed and would keep a year. For other jellies soft fruits were strained through a linen cloth or jelly-bag, and the juice was boiled until it would set with its own pectin. Pippins were also used for jelly of the latter type.[51]

Quince marmalade was still much loved, made by a variety of methods sometimes to look white and sometimes red. But there were now many other marmalades. For marmalade of damsons or prunes the fruit was boiled soft, coarsely sieved as for tart-stuff, and then reboiled with sugar. 'This wise you may make marmalade of wardens, pears, apples and medlars, services, checkers or strawberries, every one by himself, or else mix it together as you think good.'

Bitter orange and lemon marmalade soon followed, made like the others from the fruit pulp after it had been boiled tender, often with the addition of stewed apple as a stiffener. An innovation of the mid-seventeenth century was to 'slice the peel in long slits as thin as you can', and add it with the juice of two lemons and half an orange to the mingled orange and apple pulp. Marmalade was still dense and solid, to be cut with a knife rather than lifted up on a spoon, even during the eighteenth century.

The many other conserves, preserves and codiniacs were made on similar lines to marmalade. Sometimes soft fruits were simply bruised and boiled quickly in sugar syrup without any sieving or straining, and the resultant sweet compressed mass became known vulgarly as 'jam'. The word did not reach the printed cookery books until 1718, but thereafter both the name and the method of preparation became common, gradually replacing some of the earlier fruit preserves. As a filling for tarts in winter, jam superseded the earlier fruits boiled in syrup, which indeed it closely resembled.[52]

Flowers, like fruits, were confected with sugar and preserved by housewives of Elizabethan and Stuart times; and they must have looked very pretty. 'To rough-candy sprigs of rosemary. Lay your rosemary branches one by one upon a fair sheet of paper, then take sugar-candy beaten small like sparks of diamonds, and wet it with a little rosewater in a silver spoon, and lay it as even as you can upon every branch.' The sprigs were dried slowly, were candied likewise on the other side, and could then be boxed and kept for a year. 'They will appear to the eye in their natural colour, and seem to be covered with sparks of diamonds.'

It was claimed that 'all manner of flowers' could be preserved in this way. Blue borage flowers and purple violets were two of the favourites because of their rich colours. Marigolds were candied 'in wedges, the Spanish fashion'. Clove gilliflowers were made into conserves, or preserved in wine or vinegar to garnish winter salads.

But best loved of all the flowers was the rose, which had both its colours and scent to recommend it, and was esteemed by the physicians as a cordial. So rose petals were boiled in sugar and water to make restorative syrups, or were beaten fine with sugar-candy and formed into lozenges, or were turned into conserves.

> To make conserve of red and damask roses. Take of the purest and best coloured buds you can get, and clip off the whites from them, and to every pound of leaves you must take three pound of Barbary sugar and beat them together, till they be very fine, and then with a wooden spatter take it up and set it on the fire till it be through hot and then presently [i.e. immediately] put it up, and it will be of an excellent colour.[53]

Last but not least, rose petals in vast quantities were distilled to produce rosewater, a favourite condiment in Tudor and Stuart cookery. It was constantly added to herbal remedies too, and to cosmetics.

The perfuming of food was a custom borrowed from French cuisine, where it enjoyed a great vogue through the sixteenth and seventeenth centuries. It was never carried to the same lengths in England, nor was the range of scents employed so wide. The exotic musk and ambergris were added only occasionally to the foods of the well-to-do. But rosewater was ubiquitous, called for in sweet confections of every kind: cakes, puddings, creams and bakemeats.

Towards the end of the seventeenth century orangeflower water, another food perfume much used in France, was substituted in some dishes. Although one or two English recipes were published for making orangeflower water, there were few English gardens where fallen orange blossoms could be gathered, and the scented water was usually imported ready-made from France or Portugal. It became an alternative to rosewater, particularly in rich seed cakes, almond cakes and biscuits, and dessert creams. There is even a recipe of 1727 for orangeflower brandy.[54] Both rosewater and orangeflower water continued as food flavorants all through the eighteenth century, though neither was in such constant use as rosewater had been during the century before.

Flowers went into the composition of syrups for medicinal purposes, but fruit syrups were rare, other than those based on the juice of oranges, lemons and citrons: the sweet sugar syrup was a convenient medium for conveying the virtue of these sharp fruits. During the seventeenth century, when the efficacy of oranges and lemons against scurvy had been recognized, their juice was added to the earlier remedy of the fluid expressed from garden scurvy-grass, brooklime and watercresses in order 'to make an excellent syrup against the scurvy'.

Lemonade was a French invention. The first English recipe, translated from the French, describes lemon juice mixed with water and sugar, in which a whole sliced lemon was allowed to infuse. Orangeade could be made in the same way. The earliest native English account of lemonade included sack and brandy, as well as lemon juice. By the beginning of the eighteenth century lemonade was being prepared and bottled to keep, with the addition of sulphur to preserve it. By this time non-alcoholic lemonade had come into general use; but for many years thereafter English drinkers were inclined to add an equal quantity of white wine to their lemonade, to make it into something rather more heady.

Fresh orange juice was occasionally drunk. Pepys encountered it at the house of his cousin in 1669: '. . . here, which I never did before, I drank a glass, of a pint, I believe, at one draught, of the juice of oranges, of whose peel they make comfits; and here they drink the juice as wine, with sugar, and it is a very fine drink; but, it being new, I was doubtful whether it might not do me hurt.'[55]

The increasing use of citrus and other sharp fresh fruits in meat and fish cookery led eventually to a decline in the amount of dried fruit added to such dishes. But the latter was retained in some pies, stews and hashes, and was a feature of large cakes and the newly popular puddings. When in 1610 there was possibility that Greece would reduce her exports of currants, the Venetian ambassador in London wrote home:

> Such a thing cannot take place without discontenting the entire population of England, which consumes a greater amount of this fruit than all the rest of the world; being

> accustomed to the luxury and loving it so dearly that individuals have been found who, from lack of money to purchase it on certain high days and holy days when it is customary fare, are said to have gone out and hanged themselves.

Four years later another Italian described how 'English pies and puddings were literally stuffed with them [dried fruits], and no one who had not seen it with his own eyes could possibly believe what an incredible number of such pies and puddings the average Englishman was capable of eating'.[56]

Citrus and fresh garden fruits in Elizabethan meat or fish dishes were often mollified with sugar or honey. Thus a recipe of 1584 for a capon boiled with three bitter oranges or lemons has the broth seasoned twice with 'sugar a good deal', and thickened with wine and the yolks of eggs. Contemporary instructions for making a chicken and gooseberry pie are curiously titled 'To bake chickens without fruit'. The missing fruit was, of course, the dried currants, raisins and prunes then still closely associated with meat pies.

Elizabethan chickens were also baked with barberries, fresh or pickled, or with grapes; and both fruits, as well as gooseberries, were put into meat or fish stews during the seventeenth century.[57] Orange or lemon juice was often wrung into broths and bakemeats in place of verjuice. Orange and lemon slices supplied colourful garnishes, as did bunches of red barberries or red currants. The versatile barberries were also boiled with sugar to make winter tartstuff. They continued both as garnish and preserve, though in less frequent demand, all through the eighteenth century.

That century saw a swing in favour of more savoury meat and fish dishes. The sharp-flavoured seasoning fruits were still retained, with lemon, whether in the form of juice, grated peel or lemon pickle, gradually predominating. It was the principal garnishing fruit of the age, too. Seville oranges still appeared occasionally in the context of meat dishes; but China or sweet oranges were now the kind most often imported into Britain, and they were found too sweet to accompany savoury foods. Instead they flavoured some of the puddings, cakes and biscuits of the period, while orangeflower water, carrying its own version of the orange tang, was added to others.

A change had at last taken place in people's attitude to raw fruit. Fresh fruit was actually accepted by medical men as a harmless and even beneficial food. For centuries the physicians had handed on their inherited lore, deriving ultimately from Greek writers of the later Roman empire, of the dangers of uncooked fruit. But now new scientific theories of diet were evolved, which depended upon the supposed acidity or alkalinity of individual foodstuffs, and the need to strike a balance between them. Most fruits were held to be 'acescent' and therefore helpful in counteracting the alkaline properties of meat, cheese, eggs and other 'alkalescent' foods.

But moderation was still recommended, for gluttony was as much a vice of the age as it had been in earlier days. Eighteenth-century schoolboys, too, were no less greedy than their fifteenth-century predecessors. One such boy wrote home from Sedbergh about a fellow-pupil known to his parents who had been

> eating trash; his late sickness was occasioned by three pints of black currants, he has been very sufficiently cautioned against fruit and I believe he eats little or none at present. He lay four hours in most violent fits, there were six to hold him and they all proved too weak. His teeth were several times set and Mr Saunders [the headmaster] was out of all hopes of his recovery. He is now very well . . .[58]

Raw salads had never come under the same sort of disapproval as fresh fruit, partly because so many salad plants were thought to have helpful medicinal properties. Moreover, in a skilfully mixed salad, aromatic herbs noted for their warm, dry qualities, could counteract the coldness of other kinds, such as lettuce, purslane or endive.

The colourful medieval herb and flower salads continued to

be eaten in summertime for many more years. By Elizabeth's reign they were being further elaborated by the addition of new fruits and vegetables and hard-boiled eggs. They were first course dishes, and were also popular for suppers.

> To make a salad of all kind of herbs [in 1596]: Take your herbs and pick them very fine into fair water, and pick your flowers by themselves, and wash them clean, then swing them in a strainer, and when you put them into a dish, mingle them with cucumbers or lemons pared and sliced, also scrape sugar, and put in vinegar and oil, then throw the flowers on the top of the salad, and of every sort of the aforesaid things and garnish the dish about, then take eggs boiled hard, and lay about the dish and upon the salad.

Such a mixture formed a compound salad, forerunner of the complex grand salad of the seventeenth century, which was suitable for the table of a great house, or to be offered to special guests. Sometimes an egg and herb salad was further enhanced by the addition of sliced cold roast capon, anchovies and other meat or fish delicacies. Late in the seventeenth century the name of salmagundi was applied to mixtures of this type, and was subsequently corrupted to 'Solomongundy'. Simple everyday salads comprised merely one or more vegetables, dressed with vinegar, oil and sugar, or vinegar alone.[59]

During the sixteenth and seventeenth centuries the range of of salad vegetables was still wide. The greenstuff included lettuce, purslane, cornsalad, sorrel, dandelion, buds of alexanders, mustard, cresses, and the young leaves of radishes, turnips, spinach and lop lettuce (lettuces grown from seed which had never hearted). The many small-leaved plants were often known jointly as salading or small salad.

Improved gardening methods turned endive into a winter salad vegetable, for it was earthed up to blanch its leaves. Succory or chicory received like treatment. So also did celery, introduced in the course of the seventeenth century from Italy, where it had been developed as a variety of smallage. John

Evelyn commended both the tender leaves and the blanched stalks, peeled and slit longwise, in salads. Hannah Woolley favoured a winter salad of 'good hard cabbage, and with a sharp knife shave it so thin you may not discern what it is', dressed with oil and vinegar.

Cibols, chives and scallions or shallots were eaten raw. 'Onions boiled, and stripped from their rind, and served up with vinegar, oil and pepper is a good simple salad.' But garlic, universally appreciated in medieval times, for it appeared in the pottages of the wealthy and was one of the hot spices of the poor, now began to go out of favour. The Elizabethans called it the poor man's physic, of special value to seafaring men because 'it pacifieth the disposition to vomit'. A hundred years later it was no longer acceptable in polite circles, and Evelyn proscribed it from his salading, beyond 'a light touch on the dish, with a clove thereof, much better supplied by the gentler rocambole'.[60]

The Elizabethans enjoyed a salad of lemons, which comprised a dish of the fruits thinly sliced, well sugared and garnished with strips of their own peel. Orange and lemon slices were a decoration for grand salads all through the seventeenth century. John Parkinson had a charming salad addition to suggest. 'The kernels or seed [of oranges] being cast into the ground in the spring time, will quickly grow up . . . and when they are of a fingerlength high, being plucked up, and put among salads, will give them a marvellous fine aromatic or spicy taste, very acceptable.'[61]

The flowers for salads were still violets, primroses, borage, together with others which had a markedly attractive scent, such as cowslips, rosemary, elder, broom and above all clove gilliflowers. For winter use they were preserved, packed between layers of sugar in gallipots which were then topped up with vinegar. Evelyn thought that fresh flowers, too, gave 'a more palatable relish' if they were first infused in vinegar. Sometimes sugar-candied flowers were added to winter salads.

An exciting new plant received from the West Indies was the nasturtium or Indian cress, which delighted English gardeners with its gaudy flowers. It had a threefold salad potential. The flowers were a gay, edible decoration; the leaves were crisp and pungent among the greenstuff; and the unopened buds and young seed cases, put into vinegar, became a pickle. The flowers continued in salads during the eighteenth century, when most of the other blossoms had been abandoned.

The kidney bean was another new world vegetable, native to Peru and grown in other parts of South America: Gerard described the Brazil kidney bean. It was established in France earlier than in England, hence its alternative name of French bean. There were several varieties, including climbers.[62]

The 'Virginia' potato had been introduced to both England and Ireland before the end of Elizabeth's reign. French explorers of Canada brought back to Europe the Jerusalem artichoke, known as the 'potato of Canada'.

Further new vegetables reached England from France and Italy about this time. They included the red or Roman beet, of which the root was eaten; the white or Italian beet which was a kind of chard; the globe artichoke; garden asparagus and the cauliflower.

The edible parts of these new plants could rarely be enjoyed in their raw state. It was of course possible to add them to pottage, but the Elizabethans usually preferred to boil and butter them, or to eat them in boiled salads.

The earliest vegetable to be given individual treatment of this kind was spinach, which was held in special regard because it had reached the western world much later than the other greenstuff of medieval cookery. It came from Persia, through the Arabs, and was first recorded in the west by St Thomas Aquinas. It arrived too late to acquire any traditional medicinal merits. 'Spinach is an herb fit for salads, and for divers other purposes for the table only; for it is not known to be used physically at all.'

On account of its novelty spinach was from the first often cooked by itself. A late fourteenth-century recipe has it parboiled in water, drained, fried in clean oil and served with no more than a little spice powder on it. The Elizabethan boiled salad of spinach was not dissimilar. The boiled chopped leaves were put into 'a little pipkin with currants, sweet butter, vinegar and sugar, and boil them all together'. The salad was laid in a dish, strewn with sugar, and served. Another sixteenth-century recipe stresses that spinach should be 'fried with its own juice, without water'.

Many more boiled salads were devised, though spinach remained a great favourite. John Murrel described it in the 1630s and added:

> So you may serve borage, bugloss, endive, succory, cauliflowers, sorrel, marigold-leaves, water-cresses, leeks boiled, onions, asparagus, rocket, alexanders. Parboil them, (then set them on a chafingdish of coals) and season them all alike: whether it be with oil and vinegar, or butter and vinegar, cinnamon, ginger, sugar (and currants). Eggs are necessary, or at least very good for all boiled salads.[63]

Boiled and buttered vegetables were a simpler version of the boiled salad, usually eaten hot. 'The fruits and cods of kidney beans', explained Gerard, 'boiled together before they be ripe, and buttered and eaten with their cods, are excellent delicate meat and do not engender wind as the other pulses do'. Carrots, turnips and skirrets were sliced, boiled and buttered, or alternatively roasted in the embers and eaten with melted butter. Sweet or Virginia potatoes, similarly roasted, were sauced with sack and sugar.[64] But red beetroot was boiled and eaten, as in its native Italy, with oil and vinegar, or often with vinegar alone. It made a boiled salad on its own, and 'carved and sliced' it supplied a richly coloured garnish for other salads.

Vinegar was a condiment much beloved by the English. An Italian named Castelvetro who spent sixteen or seventeen years in England during the reign of Elizabeth complained that the salads there were served up swimming in vinegar, without benefit of either salt or oil. A hundred years later Evelyn still remembered the days when sugar and vinegar were 'the constant vehicles (without oil), but now sugar is almost wholly banished from all, except the more effeminate palates, as too much palling, and taking from the grateful acid now in use'. The dressing that Evelyn favoured was artfully compounded of three parts of olive oil, one of vinegar (or lemon or orange juice), dry mustard and the mashed yolks of hard-boiled eggs.

As a garnish for fresh salads and as a wintertime alternative to boiled ones, pickled vegetables were prepared. Mushrooms, broom buds (used as a substitute for capers), ash-keys and tops of young greenstuff were preserved in vinegar, stale beer or verjuice. Cucumbers were boiled in vinegar with salt, pepper, fennel, dill and mace, or similar seasonings, to give them more flavour. Barberries, grapes, red or white currants were put up in white wine or wine and vinegar.

Samphire grew in many places around the coast of Britain. It was pickled in brine or vinegar, and served as a condiment for cooked meat and fish dishes, as well as for salad. It was sometimes greened in the same dubious manner as apples, being boiled in vinegar in a brass pan. A more healthy pickle was red cabbage in claret-wine vinegar with boiled beetroots and turnips: 'it will all serve both for garnishing and salad; for your turnips thereby shall be dyed into a crimson colour, a handsome garnishing to the eye'.[65]

Beetroot and red cabbage, barberries and nasturtium flowers added the glow of red to fresh and pickled salads, but the tomato was still conspicuously absent. When it began to gain acceptance as a food in England in the second half of the eighteenth century, it was usually cooked and pulped for soups, or made into a sharp pickle with vinegar, garlic and ginger. At first golden tomatoes were often used, and Alexander Hunter's 'mock tomato sauce', for those who could not obtain the genuine article, was based upon sharp apples mixed with enough turmeric to produce the right shade of yellow. After a few decades cooked tomatoes were widely accepted, and still later candied tomatoes and tomato jam enjoyed some vogue. But more than three hundred years elapsed before the Elizabethan apples of love became the salad tomatoes of twentieth-century Britain.[66]

Chapter 10

Drinking in Britain

Prehistoric period

The picture of drinking in Britain before the era of written records is a shadowy one. Water was the beverage most readily to hand. With the arrival of the neolithic farmers the milk of domesticated cows, ewes and she-goats became available; while another new source of fluid was the liquid part of stews and pottages.

The successive groups of immigrants who reached Britain from about 2000 BC onwards have been named by archaeologists the Beaker Folk, on account of their most characteristic food vessels. Their deep, narrow beaker-like pots, often somewhat concave below the brim must often have held milk, now more plentiful as open pasture increased. Thin soups could have been drunk from them, too; and at times they may have contained fermented liquor.

The earliest invention in that field was almost certainly mead. Honey, if left for a time, will ferment of itself; and honey and water left together in a container would have produced an alcoholic drink. This discovery must have been made very far back in history, and in Britain probably well before the advent of farming. There may have been some increase in mead drinking during the later Bronze Age, when there is indirect evidence that more honey was used than formerly. The drink may sometimes have been flavoured with wild fruits and herbs. Traces of such a beverage, composed from cranberries, bog-myrtle and honey, were found in a birch-bark pail in a Bronze Age burial in Denmark.[1] Cereals may also have been added, and the Celts who later employed honey in their beer making could have been influenced by a tradition of drinks based on cereals with honey.

True brewing was practised in Mesopotamia and Egypt in the third millennium BC, and may have been developed independently in Europe too. But the earliest evidence for it in Britain and north-western Europe goes back no further than the Celtic Iron Age. Ungerminated cereals yield a drink of very low alcohol content. Beer results when the grain is first allowed to germinate in a warm atmosphere until it develops an enzyme, diastase, which converts its starch into fermentable sugars. Further germination must then be checked by heat, and the sugars left to ferment.

Celtic beer attracted the attention of several classical writers from the time of Pytheas, the Greek explorer who circumnavigated Britain about 300 BC, onwards. Its name, *curmi*, has survived in the Welsh *cwrw* and the Irish *cuirm*. Barley beer was the kind most often mentioned, but British beer brewed from wheat was noted in the first century AD.

True grape wine began to reach south-east England several decades before the Roman occupation. The arts of viticulture and wine making, known in the Greek world since Mycenean times, had been brought west in the seventh century BC by the Greek colonists of Marseilles. They traded their wine northwards up the Rhône and the Saône, and found eager purchasers among the Celtic aristocracy of northern France and the Rhineland. When in due course the Etruscans and the Romans learned the same arts, they took over the northbound wine trade. In Gaul wily Italian merchants found they could barter a single amphora of wine for a slave. The Celts drank the wine undiluted. 'And since they partake of this drink without moderation, by reason of their craving for it, they fall into a stupor or a state of madness', wrote Diodorus Siculus.

The same enthusiasm for wine came to be shared by the Belgic tribes of Britain. They enjoyed it in life, and in their tombs three amphorae of wine per man (the equivalent of seven dozen modern bottles), together with Roman cups and bowls to drink it from, accompanied the Celtic princes to the next world. A coin-type bearing a vine leaf, issued by Verica, the ruler of the Hampshire Atrebates, shortly before AD 43 may even have announced to other Belgic communities that in his domain wine was now made from home-grown grapes.[2]

Roman period

With the Roman occupation came the beginning of more widespread viticulture in lowland Britain. But local wine making was checked for a couple of centuries after Domitian, anxious to encourage the sale of Italian wine, forbade the growing of vines in Britain and Gaul. The ban was lifted about AD 277. A few traces of Romano-British wine production have been found in the form of vines at Boxmoor villa in Hertfordshire, grape pips at Silchester and Southwark, and pips together with grape skins – probably the debris of wine-pressing – at Gloucester. But local output fell far short of the needs of the Romano-Britons and much wine was imported, in particular from Italy and Spain in the first centuries of Roman rule, and from the Bordeaux area and the Moselle valley thereafter.[3]

Wine was made in Roman times, as it is today, by crushing grapes and fermenting their sweet juice by means of the natural yeasts which form the bloom on their skins. But whereas the grapes of Campania and other favoured parts of Italy yielded full, generous, natural wines, there were many other regions within the empire where the thin local wines needed preservatives to help them to keep and seasonings to disguise off-flavours as they deteriorated. For 'Greek' wines, the must was mixed with some seawater or salt. Other wines were resinated, or flavoured with myrtle, juniper, several sorts of herbs or oriental spices. Some wines were taken as physic, like the medicated wine, suitable for chest complaints, that was provided for the men of the VI legion when it was based at Carpow on the Tay in the early third century AD.

Sweet wines were made by adding honey and rose or violet petals or citron leaves to the must; and sweet raisin wine was also popular. Vermouth was produced from spiced wine flavoured with wormwood.[4]

The wines were first stored in large globular earthenware jars (*dolia*), and then racked off into pottery amphorae coated with pitch. But in the north-western provinces wooden barrels or casks, also treated with pitch, became the usual containers for the storage and transport of wine.

Wine intended for use in cooking was reduced by boiling before it was stored, which concentrated its sugars and made it keep better. The boiled-down must or *defrutum* was added, too, to sharp new wines to help to mature them. Thus the fact that grapes raised in the British climate were apt to produce thin vinegary wine was no deterrent to wine making. Additives could change its flavour and increase its keeping properties; and those Romano-Britons whose villa estates would support vines at all were able to enjoy wine that had been grown and pressed on their own land.

Beer continued as the alcoholic beverage of the poorer Briton. But the rich did not despise it if, as is thought, the fine pottery mugs with a capacity of a quart or more that were produced by British potters in the third and fourth centuries

AD were used for beer drinking among the well-to-do.[5] Some of the British beer was no doubt the honey-sweetened kind in favour among the Celts of north-western Europe. Mead was still a prized drink for feasts and may have been less rare, especially in the north and west, than the imported wine.

The principal non-alcoholic drinks were, of course, milk and water. Milk was most plentiful in pastoral areas, and in those places where sheep were raised intensively for wool, as on Salisbury Plain in the third and fourth centuries AD.

Water was common enough everywhere. But a new phenomenon now arose in the gathering together of large numbers of people within the narrow confines of Roman towns or military barracks. To provide them all with water, aqueducts, conduits and fountains were constructed to bring the water from neighbouring springs or streams. So the town dweller and the soldier, no less than the country farmer, had his drinking water close at hand.

Early medieval period

The Germanic tribesmen who settled in eastern Britain from the latest years of the Roman occupation onwards were already accustomed to brewing with barley or wheat. They continued the practice in England, and the resultant drinks bore the names ale and beer. At first both terms were in use, and their significance is not clear, though beer may have been confected with aromatic herbs while ale was made from malt alone. But by the tenth century the word 'beer' was used for the sweet new wort which had barely begun to ferment – in one vocabulary of the period *beor* is glossed with *hydromel* (honey-water), a Greek name, which in Latin usage denoted mead. Thereafter 'ale' was the common term for malted liquor, while 'beer' which 'left us in sweetness returned in bitterness' when Britain later adopted the hopped beverage of the Flemings.

The Anglo-Saxons were great ale drinkers. Ale houses became a feature of every village, and wayside taverns were set up near the old Roman roads by which travellers still moved about the country. Apart from their everyday ale they had such special kinds as bright ale (its dregs well settled after long standing), mild ale, and extra strong twice-brewed ale. Ales made with such additions as rosemary, yarrow, betony, gale or bog-myrtle were taken medicinally, and the same or similar herbs may have been put into ordinary ales to flavour and preserve them. Mixed herbs known as *gruit* were added regularly to ale in Germany in early medieval times; and it was in this context that the hop finally emerged as the ideal ale-herb.[6]

Welsh ale or *cwrw* remained the drink of western Britain. It retained its individuality even at the end of the eighteenth century when it was still made from barley kilned so as to give the liquor a smoky taste and render it 'glutinous, heady and soporiferous'. Welsh ale had become known in Saxon England by the seventh century when it began to figure in food rents, often alongside the traditional clear ale.

A land rent paid to the church of Worcester in the time of Offa included three hogsheads of Welsh ale, one sweetened with honey. The hogshead of sweetened liquor may have been bragot, honeyed and spiced ale which was drunk at the courts of the Welsh princelings, and stood second in esteem to mead. A vat of mead was demanded in the winter food tribute rendered by townships under the laws of Hywel Dda; and, failing that, two of bragot or four of ale.[7]

Mead was a warrior's drink, the drink of the aristocracy both Celtic and Saxon. Not for nothing was the great hall of the Saxon palace called the mead hall. In the highland zone mead drinking had a special significance. The bodyguard who surrounded a Celtic chief or princeling consumed his mead, but in recompense fought in his battles, a service known as 'paying for mead'. When three hundred Celtic warriors met the English at Catraeth (probably Catterick Bridge) in the late sixth century, 'the pale mead was their feast and was their poison'; for all except one gave their lives in the battle in payment for their mead.

In later, more peaceful times mead was a celebratory beverage. It was drunk on church festivals at the richer monastic houses, and was more readily available there than wine until well after the Norman Conquest.[8]

Trade in wine did not cease with the departure of the Roman legions, but it was much diminished. From the mid-fifth to the late seventh century small quantities of east Mediterranean wine occasionally reached a few coastal settlements in south-west England and Wales. The trade between eastern England and Europe was hindered for a long time by piracy in the channel. But eventually it was re-established; and ports such as London, Hamwih (Southampton) and York received Rhenish wine transported in the huge, heavy relief-band amphorae manufactured near Cologne. Wine came from France, too, and by the year 982 enough was arriving from Rouen to make it worth Aethelred's while to charge a toll on it at London Bridge. This is perhaps the earliest example of customs duty paid on alcoholic beverages entering the country.[9]

Britain's own viticulture, which had died out in the early fifth century, was revived after the conversion of the Anglo-Saxons to Christianity. Vineyards were attached to monasteries, so that the wine for the mass might be made from home-grown grapes. Later some lay landowners in the south also planted vineyards and pressed their grapes for wine.

Spiced and honeyed wine in the Roman tradition was still produced in Carolingian France under the name of *piment*. This was occasionally imported, and in due course was imitated in England.

Perry and cider, drunk among poor folk in certain parts of France, seem hardly to have been known in Saxon and Celtic Britain, and ale remained the ordinary man's beverage. The sobering influence of Christianity failed to curb habits of heavy drinking. St Boniface wrote in the eighth century of drunkenness as 'an evil peculiar to pagans and to our race'. Moreover drinking became linked with the festivals of the church, and several ecclesiastical canons had to be issued inveighing against drunkenness at church-wakes (vigils on the eve of saints' days).

Of the non-alcoholic beverages the commonest were milk, buttermilk, whey and water. Bede quotes an example of royal initiative in the matter of water provision which took place about the year 628. King Edwin of Northumbria, having noticed clear water springs near the highway in a number of places, had posts erected beside them from which bronze drinking cups were hung. And the people held him in such awe and love that none dared lay hands on them except for their intended purpose.[10]

Later medieval period

In the life of Norman Britain ale maintained a vital role. All large establishments had their own brewhouses, and even in quite small households the housewife usually brewed at home. Taverns and village ale houses thrived, and in the towns ale wives sold their wares through the streets.

The importance of ale in the national diet was recognized in 1267 when it was subjected, like bread, to a sliding price scale based upon the seasonal cost of grain. The Assize of Ale was arranged so that four gallons of ale sold for a penny when a quarter of barley cost two shillings. Thereafter for each increase of sixpence on the price of a quarter of barley, the amount of ale which a penny would buy dropped by half a gallon. Furthermore it was stated that 'when three gallons are sold for a penny in a borough, then four gallons should be sold for a penny in country villages'.

Later price fixing shows that two and sometimes three grades of ale were recognized. In the reign of Edward III the strongest, made from the first strainings of the mash-vat, sold for a penny ha'penny a gallon, while the middling and third grades from the later washings were a penny and three farthings a gallon respectively. The weakest small ale was the drink of children and the very poor. At Leicester the brewers were specially enjoined to make 'good wholesome small drink for the poor people after ½d. a gallon'.[11]

In the city of London the actual measures in which the ale was sold, of the capacity of a gallon, a pottle or a quart, had to be inspected and sealed by an alderman. To control the quality of the brew, a new civic official was appointed who was known as the ale-conner or ale-taster. The brewer or brewster (for there were many women in the profession) who sold his wares in an ale house put out a long stake above his door to indicate his stock-in-trade. It now became obligatory for him, each time he brewed, to hang a 'bush', usually a bunch of ivy, on the end of his ale-stake to show that he required the services of the ale-conner to assess his ale and fix its price. Tradition has it that the ale-conner spilt a little of the liquor on a bench, sat on it for a time, and then made his assessment by whether his leather breeches had stuck to the seat or not. If they had, the ale had not fermented long enough, for it contained too much unconverted sugar and not enough alcohol; and it was judged accordingly. Brewers who failed to observe the prices set by the ale-conner were presented and fined.

In the south of England the best ale was made from barley malt; but in parts of northern and western Britain oats were malted for brewing. Elsewhere mixed cereals were common; and wheat, oats and sometimes even beans were added to the malt before it was mashed. Wheat, oats and barley together supplied the large pre-Christmas brewing of 1289 in the household of Bishop Swinfield of Hereford; while wheat and oats were combined for two big brewings during the following March. At the other side of the country Dame Alice de Bryene's East Anglian household brewed ale with equal parts of barley malt and drage (itself a mixture of barley and oats) every five or six days during 1412–13, except in January and February when barley malt was used alone.

Spices were often introduced to sharpen the taste of the ale, being tunned up with the liquor or put in when the time came for drinking it. Long pepper seems to have been the favourite, though nutmeg, cinnamon and other spices were also employed, and later grains of paradise became popular.

Herbs that went into ale included ground ivy, used in Wales and Cheshire, and rosemary. We learn of one city brewster who sold her liquor in an unsealed 'quart' measure with an inch and a half of pitch plastered over the bottom on the inside, and sprigs of rosemary laid upon it. 'Which measure was assayed by the standard of London; whereby it was found that six such quarts as this would not make a proper gallon of ale'; and the lady was punished in the pillory. Unhopped ale soon became sour, and both herbs and spices helped to conceal its ill taste when that happened.[12]

The ale was left to clear itself, and some records have survived of complaints made against brewers who delivered their liquors after only a few hours, before the dregs had had time to settle. The thick 'pudding-ale' mentioned in Langland's *Piers Plowman* as a drink of the poor must have been ale of this quality. London brewers were therefore ordered to let their ale stand working in the vessel for at least a day and a night, 'and that upon the second morning at the taking away thereof, it be well filled with good and clear ale'. But in noblemen's houses ale was not drunk under five days old.[13]

English ale 'good and stale' was universally commended. Even the French admired this 'most wholesome drink, clear of all dregs, rivalling wine in colour, and surpassing it in savour' when Thomas à Becket arrived in France on an embassy in 1158, and brought two wagon-loads of casks with him as a gift for his hosts. They came perhaps from Kent, already famed for producing the finest ale in England.

But ale in more distant parts of Britain was not always so attractive. Andrew Boorde described the ale of Cornwall in the sixteenth century as 'stark nought, looking white and thick as [if] pigs had wrestled in it, smoky and ropy'. The smokiness suggests some affinity with the Welsh *cwrw*. Boorde also thought the ale of lowland Scotland 'evil', with the exception only of Leith ale.[14]

The unhopped ale was naturally sweet, but it was often taken as the base for still sweeter drinks. Bragot continued to be popular for festive occasions. The menu for a 'feast for a franklin' in the mid-fifteenth century ended merrily with spiced cakes and wafers, accompanied by bragot and mead. The simplest kind of bragot was made from ale, honey and powdered pepper only. But a more complex fourteenth-century recipe had ten gallons of ale, three pottles of fine wort and three quarts of honey combined and flavoured with four ounces each of cinnamon and pepper, one ounce each of galingale and cloves, and two ounces of ginger.

Among the thicker drinks was posset, a rich spiced pottage of milk curdled with ale or wine, which was drunk, or rather eaten, for suppers. Caudles, too, were confected from ale mixed with sugar or honey, and strained egg yolks, and were held to be nourishing food for men with weak digestions. Also recommended for sick men was aleberry made 'with groats and saffron and good ale'.[15]

For hundreds of years ale remained at the heart of the diet of Britain. Then within a few generations it was supplanted, in the south at least, by the hopped version known as beer.

Hopped beer is said to have been made in Bavaria as early as the ninth century AD. The preservative advantages of hops were recognized, and beer brewing gradually spread across northern Europe. By the fourteenth century beer had become an important drink in Flanders, whence it was introduced into Britain. Flemish brewers settled in London, where the drink quickly gained ground. A record of 1418 shows that London beer cost only two-thirds as much as London ale.

In 1441 beer, like ale, was made subject to an assize. It was not to leave the brewery for eight days after brewing, when it was tested to prove that it was sufficiently boiled, well enough hopped and not sweet. 'Double coyt' (twice boiled and therefore more highly concentrated) beer was to sell at two shillings and eightpence for the barrel of thirty-six gallons while malt was three shillings and fourpence a quarter; and for each shilling on a quarter of malt the price of beer went up a farthing a gallon. 'Single coyt' beer, however, was to remain constantly at two shillings a barrel.[16]

Later in the century the London beer brewers formed their own guild, separate from the Mystery of Free Brewers in the city of London, the ale brewers' guild which had been in existence for some fifty years. During the sixteenth century, however, both were united into one company.

But despite its success in the metropolis beer was fairly slow to gain ground in many parts of Britain. In the north and west the bitter flavour of the hops was not liked. Ale was still described in 1548 by Andrew Boorde as 'a natural drink' for an Englishman, while beer was 'a natural drink for a Dutchman. And now of late days it is much used in England to the detriment of many Englishmen . . . for the drink is a cold drink: yet it doth make a man fat and doth inflate the belly. . . .'

Nevertheless it was the hopping of the beer which gave it its advantage over ale and eventually secured its acceptance. The hops were boiled with the wort, and then strained off before the beer was tunned up. They contained oils and resins which helped to fine the liquor during brewing, and to preserve it afterwards. Hops were imported at first, mainly from the Low Countries. But early in the sixteenth century Flemish settlers began raising them on a considerable scale in Kent, and thereafter English-grown hops were a requisite for the best English beer.[17]

By Elizabeth's reign even ale was beginning to be lightly hopped, to help it to keep better. Bitter well-hopped beer continued as the favourite drink in the south of England, while the sweeter, less heavily hopped ale was for long preferred in the north and in Scotland.

Beer was drunk at all times of day, as ale had been. Beer, manchet and fish or meat were the usual breakfast of the members of the Percy family, according to the *Northumberland Household Book* of 1512. The parents were served with a quart of wine as well as a quart of beer, but wine was evidently thought unwholesome for the children, who received beer alone.

The drink came in several different qualities. The beer drunk at noblemen's tables was commonly a year old or more and was brewed in March (March and October were the two favourite months for brewing in large establishments, but small householders had to brew more often, since they could not store great quantities of liquor). The beer in ordinary households was consumed 'not under a month's age, each one coveting to have the same as stale as he may, so that it be not sour'.

Drunkenness remained a national vice. At first church-wakes were occasions for indulgence. Then the practice arose of holding scot-ales at which each participant contributed a share of the liquor (foreshadowing the modern bottle party). By the thirteenth century these too had become a scandal, and the bishops of the period tried several times to prohibit the holding of such frolics in their dioceses. But scot-ales, bid-ales, bride-ales, church-ales, Easter-ales, lamb-ales, leet-ales, Midsummer-ales, tithe-ales, wedding-ales, Whitsun-ales and many more still took place. So also did the long drinking sessions in town taverns and village ale houses.

By Elizabeth's reign the brewers were making some very strong ales and beers, such as 'huffcap' and 'doble-doble'. And the 'ale-knights', who sat drinking 'from morrow to even . . . and either fall quite under the board, or else, not daring to stir from their stools, sit still pinking with their narrow eyes, as half sleeping, till the fume of their adversary be digested that they may go to it afresh', remained a feature of English life.[18]

Under Norman influence wine consumption in Britain increased. In southern and eastern England Norman landlords planted vineyards, and there are records of viticulture as far north as Lincoln and York. Monastic vine growing increased too, with the establishment of many new religious houses.

The finest of the English grapes grew in the vale of Gloucester, and there wines were made which William of Malmesbury claimed were equal in their sweetness and delicate bouquet to those of France. White wine was produced abundantly on some estates in the region. The vineyard at Ledbury belonging to Richard de Swinfield, Bishop of Hereford, yielded seven full casks of it and nearly one of verjuice in the year 1289–90. The eastern side of the country fared less well. At Ely a high proportion of verjuice was sold off from the produce of the vineyards, according to the surviving annual accounts. There are even sad entries such as: 'No wine but verjuice made, 9. Edw. IV. (1470)'.

When the cheap and plentiful wine of Gascony began to flow

in during the reign of Henry II, the English wine industry went into decline. Records of vineyards become fewer over the next two or three centuries. The upheavals of the Wars of the Roses were a great discouragement to a long-term project like vine growing, and the dissolution of the monasteries broke the link that had so long existed between religious houses and viticulture. By Elizabeth's reign English wine was largely a thing of the past.

At first the bulk of the imported wine came from the Moselle valley, the Rhineland and northern France. But after Henry II's marriage with Eleanor of Aquitaine wines from Gascony, Poitou, Burgundy and Languedoc were shipped in vast quantities from Bordeaux to England. Some also reached Scotland, where Alexander III so much enjoyed them that he finally owed no less than £2,000 to a Gascony merchant. For a time the trade was affected by the Hundred Years War, and by the loss of Gascony to the French in 1449. But it recovered again, and cheap, plentiful wine from the Bordeaux region was a feature of English life until well into the seventeenth century.[19]

The virtues demanded of the ideal Anglo-Norman wine were many, according to the lists drawn up by contemporary writers. It had to be clear as the tears of a penitent to the very bottom of the glass, and green as buffalo's horn. On drinking it was to descend as impetuously as thunder, sweet-tasted as an almond, creeping like a squirrel, leaping like a roe-buck, strong as a Cistercian monastery building, scintillating like a spark of fire, subtle as the logic of the school of Petit-Pont in Paris, delicate as fine silk, and colder than crystal.

In fact, most medieval wine was drunk raw and strong. The exact nature of fermentation was not understood until about a century ago. During the Middle Ages old wine was liable to attack by vinegar bacteria and fungus growths, and soon became undrinkable; and once it was over a year old, it was already regarded as being past its best, and was sold off cheaply.

The first produce of the vineyards was grape juice or must, and a little of this was shipped to England from continental ports as early as September. It fetched a lower price than true wine, and was either drunk neat or used in cooking. The new season's wines, which were called 'wines of the vintage', arrived from late October to December. They had already undergone some fermentation, but were still young and rough by modern standards, and far from being as clear as a penitent's tears. Towards the end of winter the wines remaining in store were racked off the lees, barrelled up and transported to Britain where they were known as 'wines of the rack'. They were of better quality than the vintage wines. They came in during April, May and June and sometimes even later; but the merchants preferred to sell them off before the hottest weather set in, lest they should turn vinegary.[20]

German wines were still imported during the thirteenth and fourteenth centuries, but they were rarer now than those from Gascony, and often sold for a higher price. A certain amount of wine also arrived from Spain and Portugal. Some of the Peninsula wines were sweet varieties, drunk as dessert wines and more expensive than the ordinary 'small wines'.

The luxury trade in sweet wines from southern Europe and the eastern Mediterranean probably began at the time of the crusades. From the thirteenth century onwards it was constantly expanding, for, as the wines became better known, so their popularity increased. Their names show many provenances. There was wine of Crete (sometimes called wine of Candy); malvoisie (its name a corruption of Monemvasia in the Peloponnese, where it was first made: the English called this wine malmsey); Greek wine from southern Italy (so named because Greek influence was still strong in the region formerly known as Magna Graecia); romney of Modena, a resinated wine; vernage from Tuscany and other parts of Italy; wine from La Ribera in northern Spain; wine from Provence; and many more.

To increase supplies of sweet wine the malvoisie vines were propagated in other parts of the eastern Mediterranean. They did well in Crete, which produced a very good malmsey; and rather less well in Cyprus. In 1421 the island of Madeira was colonized by the Portuguese, and four years later its natural forest cover was burnt off and the land was planted with malvoisie grapes from Crete and sugar cane from Sicily. Thereafter Madeira malmsey was also available to meet the demands of northern Europe. Malmsey was a favourite wine in England all through the fifteenth and sixteenth centuries. The sweet southern wines were described by Andrew Boorde as 'hot wines [which] be not good to drink with meat; but after meat, and with oysters, with salads, with fruit, a draught or two may be suffered'.[21]

Also for consumption after meals were the sweetened and spiced wines, descendants of the *piment* already appreciated in Anglo-Saxon England. There were several kinds: the most usual were hippocras and clary.

Hippocras took its name from the bag through which it was strained, said to resemble Hippocrates' sleeve, and more probably shaped like the gown-sleeve of a medieval medical man. Red wine was the basis, sometimes further coloured with turnsole. The spices varied, but ginger, cinnamon and grains of paradise figured most often in its composition. Poor folk used pepper in place of grains while the latter were still expensive, and they sweetened their hippocras with clarified honey. But that of the nobility was made with triple-refined sugar or sugar-candy. Clary tended to be sweeter still, being based upon sweet southern wines with additional sugar or honey and a wide range of drugs and spices, some distinctly medicinal in character.

Numerous other herb- or spice-flavoured wines were drunk for pleasure or for reasons of health. The Normans introduced wine made with clove gilliflowers. King Henry III is said to have had wine prepared for him in Gascony which was *floreata et rosata*, flavoured with scented flowers and roses; and to have had two sesters of wine confected with zedoary, two with nutmegs, and two with cubebs as part of his Christmas cellar for 1244. His son, Edward I, had a taste for sage wine. Sage was also recommended to help restore ill-smelling wines, while inferior imported ones were doctored regularly with honey and aromatics.[22]

Ordinary wines, like ale, were incorporated in possets, caudles and other thick drinks. In the kitchens of the well-to-do wine was in constant use in cookery.

New possibilities for alcoholic drinks were opened up by the invention of distillation. The art is thought to have been developed by apothecaries at Salerno about 1100. The method employed to obtain the essence or spirit of wine, or any other liquid, was to heat it in a vessel of earthenware or, later, glass. The vapour rising from it was allowed to condense on the surface of an alembic or still-head placed over the container, and to run down through a tube into a receptacle outside.

For some hundreds of years the principal object of distillation was to produce medicines; so it was practised mainly by apothecaries and by the monks who distilled the juices of the healing plants in their physic gardens. They evaporated them with water, so as to release the essential oils, or with wine combined with sugar and spices. In the latter case, the end-products were the forerunners of the liqueurs for which some religious houses later became famous. They were taken medicinally, to relieve digestive and other bodily complaints.

In the early days of distilling, wine or wine-lees were the usual source-materials. When the distillation contained enough alcohol to burn, it was called *aqua ardens* or *aqua vitae*. A stronger spirit, produced by repeated distilling, was known as the *quintessence*.

Aqua ardens or *brandewijn* ('burnt wine': its name in the Low Countries) was soon being made throughout Europe. By the fourteenth century professional distillers were beginning to take over from the apothecaries; and before long corn spirits, such as the rye spirit so well beloved in Germany, became rivals to *brandewijn*. The spread of the new strong alcoholic beverages appears to have followed very closely in the wake of the Black Death. Because they gave a temporary feeling of warmth and well-being, they were prescribed by doctors in cases of plague or other fevers.

It was about this time that spirits began to be imported into England, at first by the Genoese and later by the Dutch. For a while they were regarded as something of a novelty, and their chief use, other than as medicine, was in order to produce flaming food as a party-trick for guests. A recipe of the early fifteenth century tells how to pour *aqua ardens* on to slices of rich mawmeny, 'then light it with a wax candle, and serve it forth burning'.

Home-production of spirits was still on a small scale, and was mainly concerned with the distillation of plant juices. But after the dissolution of the monasteries in the 1530s certain displaced monks found a new vocation as apothecaries and distillers, and the products of distillation became more widely known. It was, however, the English soldiers returning from the Dutch wars of Elizabeth who did most to spread the taste for strong liquors among the ordinary people.[23]

The traditional mead and metheglin still held their own in country places. Metheglin, confected from honey with warm aromatic herbs, was a particular drink of the Welsh. It was imitated elsewhere, not always successfully.[24] In wine-drinking circles mead was gradually eclipsed by the sweet southern wines.

The Anglo-Saxons had had some knowledge of 'apple-wine', but there is nothing to suggest that it was either made or drunk to any extent in England before the Norman Conquest. Cider making was introduced from Normandy about the middle of the twelfth century, and was at first confined mainly to Kent and Sussex. Sometimes Normandy cider itself was imported: large quantities were arriving at Winchelsea around 1270. The new beverage soon spread to other parts of the country. 'Wine of pearmains' formed part of a rent paid in Norfolk in 1205; and in 1296 one Simon de Monte was fined at Wakefield because he had failed to collect crab apples for the lord of the manor, who thereby lost two hogsheads of cider.

Cider could be made from apples mixed with pears, but if the drink was prepared largely or entirely of pears, it was usually called perry. In the fourteenth century a cheap version of perry known as 'piriwhit' was mixed with penny-ale at taverns and sold to labourers and lowly folk who lived by themselves (and therefore could not brew their own drink). But medical opinion was opposed to both beverages. Sir Thomas Elyot claimed that people in cider-drinking districts looked pale, and had 'the skin of their visage rivelled, although that they be young'.[25]

Both cider and perry helped to save the grain for brewing, as did other country drinks. Birch tree wine was fermented from the spring sap tapped from tree trunks in Sussex and in the Scottish highlands. The sap could also be brewed as ale with only a quarter of the normal allowance of malt. Mountain ash berries yielded a juice which was fermented alone or brewed in ale in Wales, especially in the region about Snowdon. These drinks had a long tradition in their own localities, but only became more widely known during the seventeenth century.

In addition, all sorts of flowers, herbs and berries were boiled in ale or beer, or infused in water to make medicinal drinks for the many physical ailments in which medieval life abounded. Even whey became a vehicle for herbal tonics.[26]

Milk, whey and buttermilk were prominent among the non-alcoholic drinks in the diet of the Middle Ages, the last two being the great standby of the country peasant and his family through most of the period. But the drink to be avoided at all costs, except under great necessity, was water. It had an evil reputation, less on account of the constant danger of contamination to supplies from rivers, wells or conduits than because it was thought medically unsound, being 'cold, slow and slack of digestion'.

The poor often had no alternative but to drink it. Other people partook of it only after processing, in the form of pottages or brewed drinks. The distinction is made clear in a complaint brought to the authorities of the City of London in 1345

> that whereas of old a certain conduit [probably the Cheapside conduit constructed in Henry III's reign] was built in the midst of the City of London, so that the rich and middling persons therein might there have water for preparing their food, and the poor for their drink; the water aforesaid was

> now so wasted by brewers . . . that in these modern times it will no longer suffice for the rich and middling, nor yet for the poor.

The brewers were supposed to draw their water supplies from the Thames at low tide, and as a result of the complaint were sent back to the river, and forbidden the use of the conduit water. So the poor regained their humble drink.

Among the rich and middling sort the feeling against plain water was still strong in the sixteenth century. Andrew Boorde said flatly in 1542: 'Water is not wholesome, sole by itself, for an Englishman'. And he recommended that those who drank their table wine diluted should use only water that had been strained and boiled, or, better still, herb-flavoured distilled water.[27]

Early modern period

Despite some competition from wine and spirits, beer and ale remained the basic beverages of Britain from Elizabeth's reign until the mid-eighteenth century. Initially brewing was still a small-scale operation, carried on by housewives at home or by individual ale-house keepers. But a royal edict of 1637 forbade ale-house keepers, taverners, cooks and victuallers to brew their own beer, and obliged them to obtain supplies from a common brewer. The object was to make it easier to levy a tax on brewing. Then in the civil war conditions of 1643, the Parliamentarians also imposed a beer duty, which was two shillings when the beer was valued at over six shillings a barrel (this included home-brewed beer) and sixpence a barrel if its value was under six shillings. The tax on domestic brewing was removed ten years later; but beer brewed for sale has paid excise duty ever since.

In the eighteenth century some of the common brewers built up their businesses into larger concerns, and a number of the brewing companies of modern times, such as Allsopp, Bass, Charrington, Courage, Tetley, Whitbread, Worthington

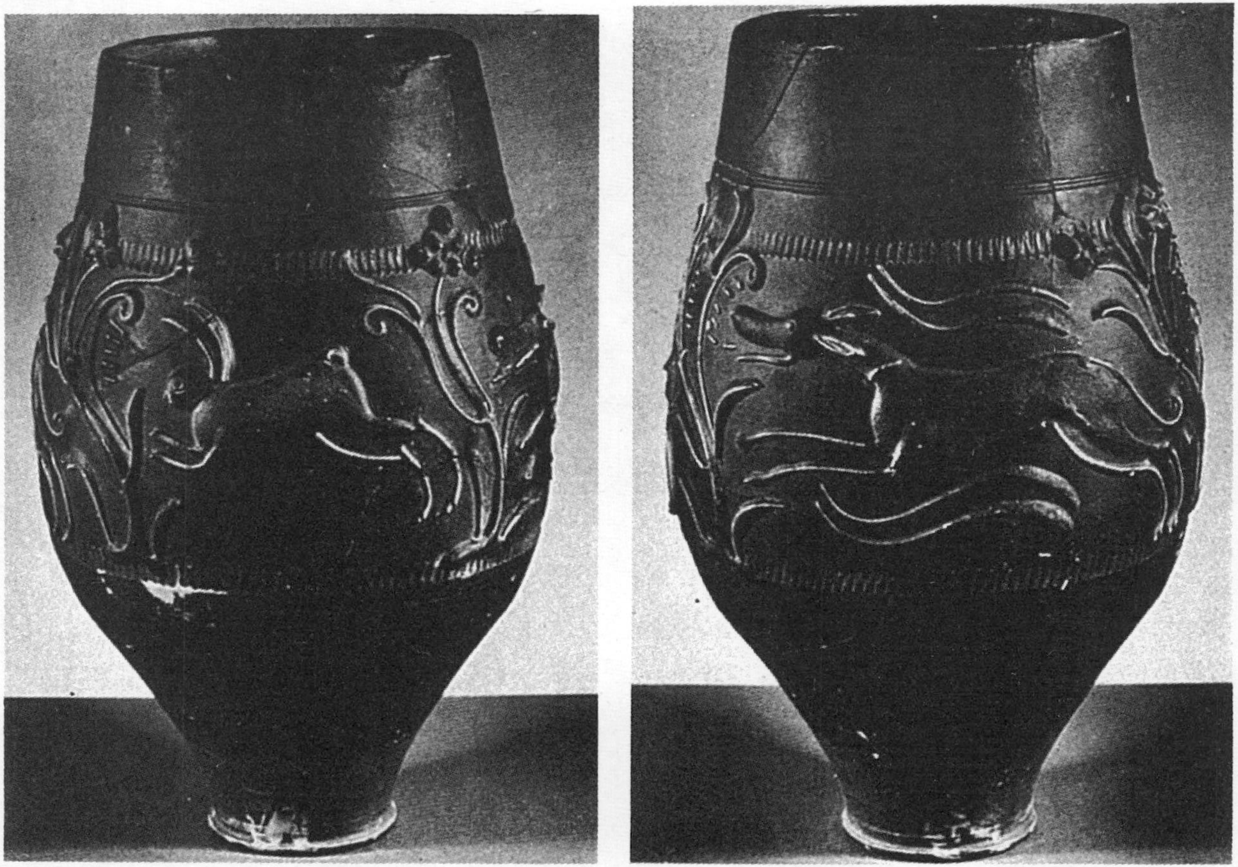

Castorware hunt cup. 3rd century AD

Cider presses
From J. Worlidge:
Vinetum Britannicum,
3rd impression, 1691

Distilling apparatus
From N. Lémery:
New curiosities of art and nature,
1711

and some others were founded at that period. The system of tied public houses arose about the same time.

But even in 1800 it is probable that at least half of the total amount of beer consumed was home-produced. Most larger households and institutions still found it worth while to brew their own. In the south cottage wives ceased to brew in the later eighteenth century as they ceased to bake, because fuel was dear or unobtainable. In addition, the equipment needed was too costly for people living near subsistence level. William Cobbett estimated that in his day the price of the vats, mash-tuns, pails and barrels for home-brewing would have come to about £10.

In the north of England where coal was available, in Scotland, and in wooded areas of south-western Britain, the practice survived longer than it did in the south and east. 'In several of the northern counties of England, where they have good barley, coke-dried malt, and the drink brewed at home, there are seldom any bad ales or beers', wrote the author of *The London and Country Brewer*, first published in 1738, 'because they have the knowledge in brewing so well, that there are hardly any common brewers amongst them. In the west, indeed, there are some few, but in the south and east parts there are many.'[28]

The beer of the wetter upland regions of the west, of such parts as Cheshire, Lancashire, Derbyshire, Devonshire and Cornwall, was for long brewed from malted oats because of the scarcity of barley. Elsewhere malts were mixed for brewing purposes, and even in Kent a combination of half oat-malt and half barley-malt was usual in the early eighteenth century.

Derbyshire ale was already renowned in London in Elizabeth's reign; and London ale itself had long had a high reputation. By 1630 Burton ale too was being sold in London. Seven years later John Taylor, the 'water-poet', picked out the ales of York, Chester, Hull, Nottingham and Derby for special praise, but also added a word in favour of the North Down and Gravesend ales of Kent. Yorkshire ale was drunk stale and strong, and was often called stingo. The best was said to come from Northallerton. Hull had a particularly powerful brew known to travellers as 'Hull cheese'. When beer became subject to excise duty, some brewers were no longer prepared to keep up the strength of their product by a generous use of malt; and after a few decades the efficacy of Derby, Nottingham and other strong ales was achieved by the addition of distilled spirits of ale and beer.[29]

The flavour, quality and colour of ale and beer depended upon the ingredients used – the mineral content of the water, whether the malt was lightly or heavily roasted, the degree to which the brew was hopped – as well as the particular methods of each brewer. Hard water with a high gypsum content, such as that in the vicinity of Burton on Trent, was best for pale ales, made with light-coloured malt that had been very slowly dried and kilned. London brewers in the eighteenth century were still using the soft waters of the Thames and the New River. With these and with well-toasted brown malt they made the rich dark porters and stouts that became famous throughout the country.

Porter, a beer that was almost black in colour, heavily hopped, and fermented long so that it had a high alcoholic content, was first brewed in London in the 1720s. It became very popular, and was soon copied in provincial towns. For a time London porter was even exported to Ireland, but the Irish version had come to rival the English by the end of the century, and the trade then moved in the opposite direction. Arthur Guinness of Dublin, who was largely responsible for this state of affairs, eventually bequeathed his name to the Irish form of porter.[30]

The eighteenth century saw changes in brewing techniques, and some improvements. During its opening years isinglass had come into use for fining beers. Even newly brewed beers, which had formerly remained hazy for some time, could now be served very soon in a clear, bright condition. The isinglass was sometimes added direct, dissolved in a small quantity of the liquor and mixed with the rest. It could also be incorporated into 'excellent balls for fining, feeding, preserving, relishing, and colouring malt drinks, wines and ciders'. The balls included calcined and powdered marble, oyster shells and chalk, with horse-bean flour, treacle and selected spices. They were added to beer at the rate of six to a barrel, and were well stirred in.

The fact that such balls were needed is a reminder that brewing methods were still based on rule of thumb. Brewers knew nothing of the micro-organisms that could attack their liquors, and failed to understand why some beers quickly became sour, foxy or ropy. The balls would have been effective in that the marble, oyster shells and chalk would have neutralized excess acidity, the spices would have disguised the resultant earthy taste, while the bean flour and isinglass would have caused impurities to sink to the bottom of the cask.

But there was only a narrow line between the addition of such balls as preservatives and the barefaced use of adulterants such as cocculus indicus (which is highly poisonous), capsicum, quassia, aloes, grains of paradise, ginger and other spices to sharpen the drink; tobacco, treacle and licorice to colour it; and copperas, alum or extra yeast beaten into the brew to give it a frothy head. All these substances, and several more, were regularly employed by common brewers in the later eighteenth century.

In their defence it may be said that they were only following a long tradition in the use of herb or spice additives to help ale or beer to keep better. But in their desire to make extra profit on weak or flat beers, they showed complete indifference to the possible effect on the health of their customers. The malpractices of adulteration, not only of beer but also of many other foodstuffs, continued for nearly another century before they were finally stamped out by the Sale of Food and Drugs Act of 1875.

There were however some improvements in techniques of brewing in the late eighteenth century, which helped towards producing beers of better quality. The thermometer had come into use by the 1780s. It allowed the brewer to control the temperature of his wort exactly, whereas hitherto he had been in the habit of allowing the water in his mash-tun to cool until he could see his face in it, or of testing it with his finger before he added the malt. The saccharometer, a type of hydrometer, was another new piece of equipment, which could record the specific gravity, and thus the strength, of both wort and beer.[31]

The traditional herb- and spice-flavoured ales were still occasional drinks long after the establishment of plain hopped ales and beers. Sir Hugh Platt warmly commended sage ale 'made by mingling two or three drops of the extracted oil of sage with a quart of ale, the same being well brewed out of one pot into another. . . . The like is to be done with the oil of mace or nutmegs.' Indeed, a whole range of herb, fruit or spice essences could be made and added to simple ale as required. 'And so, at all times, with one good tub of ale in your house, and other materials, you may make forty several changes, to pleasure yourself, and make your friends wonder how you came by such variety of liquors.'[32]

John Taylor duly recorded his astonishment when he visited a Manchester man who had nine different ales on his table at once, among them ones flavoured with hyssop, sage, wormwood, rosemary, betony and scurvy-grass. The continuing popularity of herbal ales in the north of England was partly due to the fact that ale there was for long much more lightly hopped than in the south.

But herb-flavoured 'physical ales' and diet drinks were in universal demand as remedies until late in the eighteenth century. Scurvy-grass ale was a usual springtime beverage once scurvy had been recognized in England as a definite disease. Its unpleasant symptoms developed after people had gone through the winter on a diet in which all fruit and vegetables were heavily overcooked. The most efficacious cure was pure juice of scurvy-grass put into ale or beer. In more complex recipes the leaves of scurvy-grass, mingled with those of cresses, brook-lime, sage or other herbs, and with sliced oranges and spices, were inserted into a small bag to be hung in the ale as it stood in the barrel.

Purging drinks of many varieties were made in like fashion from other combinations of herbs and spices. Cock-ale was believed to cure consumption: the bird was parboiled and steeped in sack, and then put into ale for a few days along with raisins, dates and spices.

'Covent-garden purl' was initially a purging ale made with senna, coriander seeds, rosemary and sage flowers and much Roman wormwood. Later the flavourings were adjusted to include several more spices and omit the senna, and hot purl remained a favourite morning drink with Londoners until well into the nineteenth century. Brunswick mum, a heady and potent herbal ale matured for two years before drinking, was popular in the later seventeenth century, and for a time was retailed at special mum-houses. Pepys recorded a visit in 1664 to 'the Fleece, a mum-house in Leadenhall'.[33]

Flower and fruit ales were usually brewed at home. The juice of elderberries or blackberries, combined with ordinary wort and fermented, made fruit-flavoured ales. A spiced version of elderberry ale called 'ebulum' was much admired, and was said to be 'often preferred to port-wine for its pleasant taste and healthful quality'. For cowship ale the flowers were merely left in barrelled ale for a fortnight, after it had done working. It was then drawn off and put up in bottles.

Bottled ale went back at least to Elizabethan times; but in those days, when liquors were not properly fined, particles of yeast continued to work in the brew. 'And this is the reason why bottle ale is both so windy and muddy, thundering and smoking upon the opening of the bottle, because it is commonly bottled the same day that it is laid into the cellar', wrote Sir Hugh Platt. He recommended bottling only when the beer was ten or twelve days old.[34]

The thickened aleberries, ale caudles, possets and similar drinks, which had been a feature of medieval diet, were still enjoyed, and indeed only began to go out of fashion in the later eighteenth century. Mild beers, lightly hopped, were the usual foundation. These warm drinks were taken early in the day as a morning draught, or in the evening in lieu of supper. Buttered ale was a favourite version of the thickened ale drink during the seventeenth century. To make it, mild beer or ale was boiled with some butter, sugar, nutmeg, or other spice, and was thickened with beaten eggs or egg yolks. Mulled ale was not dissimilar, for although it was prepared without butter it often contained eggs. It had to be poured back and forth between pan and bowl many times, in order to achieve the right consistency. The version known as lambswool, made with sugar, spices and the pulp of roasted apples, was a traditional beverage for Halloween, Christmas eve and Twelfth Night. Hot spiced ales were served with a brown toast floating on the surface.

Aleberry survived under its original name in Scotland, where it was one of several drinks thickened with oatmeal. Another was ale crowdie, or uncooked meal and ale, fortified with treacle and whisky, and consumed at the harvest home celebrations. But in the southern parts of Britain the thickened ale caudles and possets began in the later eighteenth century to take on the role of invalid foods.[35]

In the made dishes of cookery beer played a less direct part than ale had done in medieval cuisine. But alegar, made from wort, was more important than ever as a condiment, and increasingly took the place of verjuice in pickles and sauces. It gradually usurped the name vinegar, formerly applied only to the wine-based product. There were alternatives, such as brown sugar vinegar, gooseberry vinegar, and the white wine vinegar demanded by the more genteel recipes; but malt vinegar, which was cheap and simple to make, was the type in most general use.

English grapes still yielded verjuice more readily than wine. The experts recommended training the vines against protective walls, and cutting and processing the ripest fruit separately, 'by which means some have had wine comparable with the best French wines that are pressed from the grapes promiscuously'. But the making of grape wine in England remained the hobby of a very small minority.[36]

At the end of Elizabeth's reign imported table wines were still arriving in bulk from France and in lesser quantities from the Moselle and Rhineland regions. During the seventeenth century the pattern changed. Excise duties were increased on both the English and French sides of the channel; prohibitions were laid at various times on the Dutch carriers who brought most of the Rhineland and much of the French wine to British ports; and finally trade was affected by the Anglo-Dutch war with France of 1689–97.

It was no longer worth while to import the 'small wines' or *vins ordinaires* of France, and those who had formerly enjoyed them at home or in the taverns turned increasingly to beer or spirits. Later the sweetish beverage wines of Portugal gained in popularity, especially after 1690 when they were granted a preferential rate of taxation. But French wines of better quality still appealed to English connoisseurs, and those prepared to pay the new high prices could purchase some fine clarets. Pepys drank Château Haut Brion 'that hath a good and most particular taste' in 1663; and by the early eighteenth century wines from the now famous Châteaux Margaux, Lafite and La Tour were also reaching England. Some burgundy was imported too. It was usually dearer than claret, because the cost of transport within France was often as great as that of the wine itself.[37]

Champagne, first popularized at the English court at the time of the Restoration by Saint-Evremond, also won adherents among the rich, for it was the most expensive of the French wines. During the eighteenth century both red and white varieties were drunk, and they were often still, not sparkling. Hermitage wine from the Rhône valley and wine from Frontignan known as frontiniac were two others that enjoyed some contemporary vogue.

A notable corollary of the high import duties on French wines and on the brandies which the French now found it profitable to distil from their 'small wines' was the rapid growth of smuggling in both commodities. During the eighteenth century the smugglers added tea, silks and laces, all heavily taxed, to their stock-in-trade.

Another development was the new interest in southern beverage wines. Red and white Italian chianti was arriving in the late seventeenth century and was well liked for some fifty years before its quality deteriorated. After that the rough red chianti was used as a colorant for artificially concocted clarets and burgundies.[38]

The light 'red Portugal' from the Minho region deteriorated on the journey to England; but the fuller wines from the Douro valley were more successful, and their makers began to fortify them with a small measure of brandy to slow down fermentation and so preserve them longer. The trade with England gained from the preferential duties allowed to Portuguese wines in 1690 and afterwards under the Methuen treaty of 1703. And as relations with France worsened port drinking became a patriotic gesture, and to refuse to buy the dearer claret was no less than a patriotic duty. The sentiment was reversed across the border, however, and after the Act of Union of 1707, many Scotsmen looked back nostalgically to the auld alliance, and if they could afford it purchased claret in preference to the Englishman's port.

In England port was drunk all through the meal and all evening too by the three and four bottle men of the heavy drinking eighteenth century. But although fortified with brandy, the wine still could not survive unharmed for more than four years in cask and two in the squat, short-necked upright bottles of the period. The last step forward was the development, about the beginning of the 1770s, of cylindrical bottles which could be binned lying on their sides, thus ensuring that their corks remained moist from the wine and did not dry out and shrivel through contact with the air. Port could now mature for ten or fifteen years in the bottle, and could absorb a greater proportion of brandy than ever before to produce a rich, heavy mellow wine.[39]

The sweet wines of southern Europe had been popular since the later Middle Ages. A newcomer, hardly known before Henry VIII's reign, was sack, a dry amber wine from southern Spain. It was not at first sweet enough to satisfy the palates of the Elizabethans, who liked to drink it with sugar. Later imitations were shipped from other parts of south-west Europe, and were often sweetened before export to conceal their inferior flavour. 'Sack or Spanish wine hath been used of a long time to be drunk after meat', wrote John Gerard, 'to cause the meat the better to digest: but common experience hath found it to be more beneficial to the stomach to be drunk before meat.' The best sack came from Jerez, while the Canary Islands supplied a richer version. On the English side the centre of the trade was Bristol, and in Pepys' day the drink was already known as 'Bristol milk'. For many years sack was still sugared, as were other dry wines. As late as 1762 the wine list at Vauxhall Gardens included 'old hock with or without sugar' at five shillings a bottle, and 'rhenish and sugar' at two and six-pence.[40]

Madeira malmsey arrived in small quantities during the seventeenth century but thereafter became very popular, drunk not only in Britain but also among the American and West Indian colonists. In the same period some Spanish wines were in favour in England, among them malaga (known later as mountain), alicant and tent (*vino tinto*). The practice of fortifying wine with brandy, which had proved so successful in the case of port, was extended more widely. Marsala was strengthened by a two per cent addition of brandy to conserve it on the journey when it was first shipped to England from Sicily in 1773; and the same method was applied to several other sweet southern wines.

Some imported wines received more sinister treatment. In Elizabeth's reign the vintners of the Low Countries were said to counterfeit malmsey by mixing concentrated wine must with beverage wine, and it was hinted that London vintners did likewise. The Portuguese learned to doctor their port in bad years with elderberry juice and heavy sweet Spanish wine.

In England there was a long tradition, too, of 'curing' unsatisfactory wine by adding beaten oyster shells or powdered chalk to counteract sourness, or occasionally the highly poisonous sugar of lead to sweeten over-acid wine or cider. Powdered alum was used to fine ropy wines, and sulphur to check vinegary ferments; while aromatic herbs and spices were inserted to conceal the taste of the other substances. But when the price of French beverage and southern dessert wines increased, the procedure was carried still further and artificial wines were created which could be passed off as the real thing by unscrupulous wine merchants and innkeepers.

Artificial claret was made from distilled water of clary, red-streak cider, six pounds of Malaga raisins beaten in a mortar, old claret wine-lees, the juice of mulberries, blackberries or gooseberries, and of course water. The liquor was fermented for fifteen days, clarified with egg whites and isinglass, 'and it will refine down and be very rich, not distinguishable from right claret, unless by those very well skilled in wines, and of this there is great quantities sold'.

Artificial malaga was simpler: raisins and water fermented in an old malaga cask, and the liquor fortified with a pint of best *aqua vitae* and a quart of alicant wine to every twenty gallons. To turn it into canary-sack, it had only to be 'dashed with a little good white wine, or curious brisk pippin-cider'. White wine and rhenish were contrived from other ciders. The faking continued and increased during the eighteenth century.[41]

Counterfeiting was not confined to the wholesale industry. There are many recipes for homemade palermo, mountain, frontiniac and other European wines. They were usually raisin wines with some aromatic addition. Frontiniac was flavoured with elder flowers.

The later seventeenth century saw a new departure in home wine making; for the juice of garden fruits was now for the first time fermented directly to produce alcoholic beverages. Initially the juice was simply added to grape wine. Raspberry sack was one such amalgam, and in another, white wine was sweetened and flavoured with raspberry juice. But very soon, as sugar became cheaper and more plentiful, wines were made by fermenting crushed garden fruits with their own natural yeasts and no other addition than pure sugar. The latter was needed to bring the wine must to a level of sweetness at which it could develop into a well-rounded and properly alcoholic wine; for no other English fruits had the natural sweetness of ripe grapes. Among the fruits now pressed for wines were cherries, gooseberries, damsons, raspberries and garden currants (red-currant wine became known as 'English champagne'), and also wild elder and blackberries.[42]

Flower and herb wines were made too, though these were more akin to sugar beers, set working with brewer's yeast, in which the tops of the plants were steeped for a few days to impart some of their aroma. Cowslip was the favourite one, and balm and clary wine recipes also recur frequently in contemporary household books.

The traditional spiced and thickened wine drinks were adapted to the times. By the mid-eighteenth century wine caudle had become a wine-flavoured gruel often regarded as invalid food. But sweet wine possets, enriched with cream and spices, were elegant enough to be served at formal suppers.

Hippocras was still in vogue during the seventeenth century, when both red and white versions were current. An innovation was the addition of milk or cream, strained into the wine for white hippocras along with the sugar and spices, which improved its colour by making it more opaque. Red hippocras was now sometimes tinted with cochineal. But when the Tudor and Stuart banquet went out of fashion hippocras too disappeared, and during the 1720s it vanished from the recipe books. Those who regretted its passing had to be content with homemade ginger wine, fermented with yeast and sugar, and put up with a lump of sugar in each bottle so that it remained 'brisk'.[43]

The sixteenth century saw the emergence of a rival to wine in the form of spirits. In 1527 the first English translation of a continental manual for distillers, Hieronymus Braunschweig's *The Vertuose Boke of Distyllacion*, was published, and English versions of other similar handbooks followed. They contained descriptions of apparatus, as well as recipes for the extraction of alcohol from wine and the 'waters' from herbs, flowers and fruits.

Those in the distilling trade used wine-lees and broken wines (obtained cheaply from vintners and coopers) to produce *aqua vitae* which, as a result, was often very crude. To conceal the nauseous flavour of the raw spirit they added aromatic herbs and spices, and these in turn gave their supposed medicinal properties to the drink. *Aqua composita* was a name often given to such concoctions. Dr Steven's water and *rosa solis* (confected with large amounts of that herb) were two which found great favour in Tudor and Stuart times. All such warming drinks stimulated the action of the heart, and they became known as 'cordial waters'.[44]

The juice of juniper berries, valued both for its fresh taste and for its efficacy in several medical conditions, was often an ingredient of Elizabethan *aqua vitae* or *aqua composita*. In Holland where brandy-wine was already being ousted by corn spirits, it was used to flavour the latter; and soon this new Dutch drink was being imported into Britain under the name of genever or gin.

Wormwood, which provoked appetite and cured gripes, had been a flavorant of wines in Roman times and still kept that role. In England wormwood was put into both wine and ale; and wormwood water was produced by distillation. An Elizabethan recipe gives six gallons of strong and old ale, with appropriate spices, licorice, and a quantity of wormwood leaves as ingredients for the water.[45] Later, when it had become customary to fortify certain wines with spirits, the drinks now known as absinthe and vermouth were evolved from wormwood wine with an admixture of the more alcoholic water. The green leaves of wormwood, hyssop and mint were used to give absinthe its characteristic colour.

Spirits were widely drunk in the plague year of 1593, but achieved little success as prophylactics or cures. As a result, the distillers were discountenanced for a few years, but they were at work again before the end of Elizabeth's reign. Their equipment was cheaper than that of the brewers, and took up less space. And as spirits made in England carried a tax of only twopence a gallon before 1736, theirs was a lucrative business.

In London the Company of Distillers was incorporated in 1638 and remained in nominal control of the trade until the beginning of Queen Anne's reign. But in practice plenty of people engaged in distilling and sold their wares without the blessing of the Company, and without undergoing the due apprenticeship.

The handbook of the Distillers' Company was *The London Distiller*, first published in 1639. It makes clear that the raw materials of distillation were still very often beer dregs, lees of wine or cider, or 'damnified, dried fruits soaked and fermented in water. Extra yeast was added to set them working again, and large quantities of spirit could then be distilled from them. From the later years of the seventeenth century molasses fermented with barm and 'Rhenish tartar' was used to produce crude rum-spirits. Grains of paradise served to make the spirits 'hot, strong, and fiery in the mouth'. Small wonder that the more enlightened medical men recognized *aqua vitae* as more deserving of the name *aqua mortis*.

But the drink known as British brandy was true corn spirit, drawn either from newly fermented barley malt or from 'sound beer'. The consumption of home-produced corn spirit and spirits of cider was encouraged by parliamentary acts of 1690 and 1703, both designed to reduce the importation of French brandy and to curb smuggling. That of the latter year took away the monopoly of the Distillers' Company and officially threw open the trade to all comers.[46]

In England the 'low wines' of the first distillation were usually rectified once, twice or even thrice, partly to eliminate some of the flavour of the ingredients and, in the case of malt, a burnt taste which often arose from careless handling of the still, and partly to increase their alcoholic content. By the beginning of the eighteenth century rectifying had become almost a separate industry. The distillers prepared crude spirit and passed it on to the rectifiers, who added herbs and spices and redistilled it to provide the finished 'hot waters'.

Proof spirit was made by successive distillations, sometimes with the addition of Bay salt, which speeded up the process. It was proved with gunpowder. 'The proof of its goodness is thus known, put some grains of gunpowder in a spoon, or small silver-taster, and fill it with spirit, and hold it in cold water [while] being fired, but let not any water in, and if it is good, it will fire off the gunpowder.'

From proof spirit was made simple *aqua vitae*: four parts of spirit to one of water and some aniseeds for flavouring, all rectified together. The liquor was sweetened with sugar or sugar syrup, and was often coloured with a tincture of red roses, poppy petals or sanders infused in spirit. A more strongly flavoured aniseed water was made as 'an excellent water to strengthen the stomach'. Angelica water (proof spirit redistilled with the roots and green herb of angelica, aromatic seeds and water) wonderfully strengthened the heart; rosemary water was 'an excellent cephalic and stomachic'; clove, cinnamon, caraway, nutmeg, marjoram and spearmint waters all had their own special powers. Even lavender water, enriched with lilies of the valley and other herbal goodies, was taken internally against falling sickness, convulsions and infirmities of the brain.[47]

The cordials were sold as drams by distillers, and also by doctors and apothecaries, whose recipes were often much more complex. But distilling apparatus was within reach of any well-equipped household, and the compleat housewife had to be able to produce surfeit water, hysterical water, black cherry water, clary water, saffron cordial and a host of others. Surfeit water was distilled from *aqua vitae* in which poppies, raisins and aromatic spices were infused. A simpler way to make it was to immerse the remaining ingredients in good brandy which was left to stand in the sun. Other waters could be prepared with little labour in the same manner. The eighteenth-century ratafia (brandy flavoured with almonds or apricot kernels) was made by this method.

Less attractive was cock-water for a consumption. 'Take a running cock, pull him alive, then kill him, cut him abroad by the back . . . then put him into a rosewater still, with a pottle of sack', and with dried fruits, herbs and new milk. Cock broth had long been a specific for consumption, and no doubt it was felt that the distilled essence of cock would be even more effective. Snail-water was made for the same purpose. The mention of a rosewater still is a reminder that rosewater was home-produced for use as a flavorant and perfume until well into the eighteenth century.

Spirits made at home were usually more wholesome than those sold by the distillers: the best recipes were based on malaga sack, fine canary, French brandy, or at least white wine. They were thought of as nostrums, replacing the earlier treacle in that role; but, alas, the Englishwoman with a bottle of black cherry brandy ever at her elbow, and 'if ever so little qualm or disorder be on the stomach, or perhaps merely fancied, then away to the brandy bottle', became far too common.[48]

For drunkenness was on the increase in Restoration England; and when the acts of 1690 and 1703 threw open the distilling trade freely to all comers, it began to grow into a vast social problem. The town-dwelling poor drank as an escape from their drab lives. Their liquors were the cheap, crude spirits distilled in back-street basements from any fermentable material that came to hand, and flavoured with fiery drugs and spices. In London, especially, the gin shops multiplied, with their shameless signboards proclaiming 'Drunk for a penny; dead drunk for two-pence; clean straw for nothing', the same legend that appears over the doorway in Hogarth's well-known engraving of Gin Lane.

The cure came very gradually. The Gin Act of 1736, which prohibited the sale of gin in small quantities and increased the duty payable on it, did little good, since the same drinks, with perhaps a few extra herbal additions, were sold under new names, or offered by the apothecaries as colic- or gripe-water. And there was almost certainly an increase in the amount of smuggled spirit brought in from Holland and France. In 1751 an additional duty of £7–7–0 per tun was placed upon all corn spirits distilled in England. Again the effect was slight; but after that the duty was raised every few years until in 1783 homemade spirits paid excise at the rate of £61–19–9d. per tun and imported molasses spirits at £81–6–6d. per tun. The worst tyranny of Gin Lane was thus broken. Nevertheless drunkenness among the urban poor continued through much of the nineteenth century.

Heavy drinking was usual among the wealthy too, and their chosen liquor was grape brandy from France, especially that made about Cognac in Charente. Some of the more important distilleries, such as Martell, Gautier and Hennessy, were founded during the eighteenth century. For less discriminating palates, brandy was shipped from Spain, Portugal and the Canaries, while Spanish spirit was blended with French to be re-exported as 'cognac'.[49] Much brandy entered Britain illicitly through smuggling, as did Holland's gin, brought in along the east coast.

Arrack arrived via the East India trade. Distilled in the Indies from rice, sugar and dates, with spice and fruit juice flavourings, it was 'a kind of *aqua vitae*, much stronger and more pleasant than any we have in Europe'. Until 1736 it paid a higher duty than other foreign spirits.

Far more widely known, for it was sent in greater quantities, was the rum from the West Indian sugar islands, where the art of distillation had been introduced, perhaps by the Dutch. A mid-seventeenth-century account of Barbados observed: 'The chief fuddling they make in the island is rumbullion, alias kill devil, and this is made of sugar cones distilled, a hot hellish and terrible liquor'.[50] West Indian rum was exported to England, and much of it was both potent and crude. Its quality improved only after the bonding system was introduced by the Board of Customs in 1736. The rum was kept in bonded warehouses at the port of entry, and gradually removed and sold, the duty being paid off in instalments; and thus some at least gained the long period of maturation needed to produce a full, rounded spirit.

In the West Indies the rawness of the local rum caused the sugar planters to import French and Spanish brandy for their personal use. Brandy had become a favourite shipboard drink, for unlike beer it did not decay on long voyages in hot climates. Rum, which was positively improved by long keeping, even in heat, was now taken on board too, at first on West Indian voyages and later more generally. It remained the more plebeian drink. The seamen of the British navy were issued with rum, while their officers drank French brandy.

Molasses was traded to Britain, where some distillers made from it spirits that were no less crude than the West Indian rum. Others distilled the residue of the sugar refineries which now existed in several coastal towns. The product of the Scottish sugar houses of Glasgow and Leith was 'scarce to be discerned or known from the finest of the foreign brandy', according to its manufacturers in 1684. It was not only sold in Scotland, but for a time also shipped to London.[51]

Punch, 'compounded of brandy or *aqua vitae*, juice of lemons, oranges or such-like; very usual amongst those that frequent the sea', was a longer drink, with a tradition of some two thousand years behind it in India. Its name derived from the Hindu word for 'five', referring to its ingredients: sugar, spirits, citron juice, water, aromatic flavourings. The East India merchants introduced it to Britain, where a recipe of 1672 called for 'one quart of claret wine, half a pint of brandy, and a little nutmeg grated, a little sugar, and the juice of a lemon'. Milk punch, in which the wine was replaced by milk and a greater proportion of brandy and lemon juice, came into vogue early in the eighteenth century.

Punch was usually served in a bowl, with a toast, or toasted biscuits floating on top of it. When it first became fashionable in the later seventeenth century, it had political undertones, since it was favoured by the Whigs; the Tories, more conservative in their tastes, drank claret or the traditional sack.[52]

In the east arrack too was evidently made up into long beverages, for one English recipe for 'East-India arrack, as it is made here' describes a punch-like concoction of brandy, cider, fruit juice, water and sugar, with some spices. Shrub was another such drink, with an Arabic name denoting a middle eastern origin. It first became popular in the early eighteenth century, and was made with brandy, lemon juice and peel, sugar and white wine. Later rum-shrub became very usual; and there were also fancy shrubs flavoured with ground almonds or currant juice.[53]

Drinking in Scotland followed a pattern that was parallel to, but by no means identical with that of England. In the early years distillation appears to have been undertaken in religious houses. There spirits were made from barley-malt: an entry in the exchequer rolls for 1494–5 shows that a certain Friar John Cor was supplied in that year with eight bolls of malt for making *aqua vitae*.

Later Scottish distilling became more of a family affair. The surplus barley of the farm was malted, and with the aid of burn water, a peat fire and a pot-still was transformed into *usquebagh* or whisky. Most of it was consumed locally; what remained was sold in the nearest town. Whisky became an integral part of the Scottish economy, which explains the enormous amount of illicit distilling that went on, especially in the highlands, when the spirit became subject to English excise duties after the Union. As a Ross-shire minister explained in the *Statistical Account* of 1796: 'Distilling is almost the only method of converting our victual into cash for the payment of rent and servants: and whisky may, in fact, be called our staple commodity'.

In Ireland too, *usquebagh* (the Celtic word for 'water of life') was distilled from barley at an early date. In England it was preferred in the early seventeenth century to the English *aqua vitae* 'because the mingling of raisins, fennel-seed, and other things, mitigating the heat, and making the taste pleasant, makes it less inflame, and yet refresh the weak stomach with moderate heat, and a good relish'.[54]

In Scotland imported French brandy was a popular drink among gentlemen. During the seventeenth century the practice of distilling malt whisky in pot-stills spread into the highlands. Hitherto the highlanders' drinks had been spring water, milk, buttermilk and whey, for ale had never had the place in their diet that it held in lowland Scotland. When they took to whisky, they drank it like water, often from scallop shells which they carried with them to serve as tumblers.

The eighteenth century saw a great increase in distilling, much of it illegal; and even in the lowlands spirits began to oust ale as the everyday beverage. In England the poor drank gin most heavily in the period before its price was pushed up by taxation. In Scotland, by contrast, it was the excise duty (charged in a different way, at first upon the malt and later upon the capacity of the still, but no less an imposition for that reason) which increased the rate both of distilling and of drinking. The produce of the illicit stills had to be disposed of quickly and usually locally: the only solution was to drink it. Neat whisky became the drink of the poor, serving not only as a stimulant, but also as a meal-time drink, with bannocks or bread and cheese.

The traditional role of spirits as medicine, which had so strong a hold in England, also had its counterpart in Scotland. Highland 'bitters', made by infusing spices and bitter herbs in whisky, were drunk as a stomachic before meals, especially breakfast, until well into the nineteenth century.

Long drinks were based on whisky too, and highland gentlemen in the 1720s mixed it with water and honey, or milk and honey, or sugar and melted butter to make 'punch'. But toddy, which was whisky and boiling water with sugar, was the most usual long drink for convivial occasions in eighteenth-century Scotland. Whisky was put into hot ale with sugar and beaten eggs for the 'het pint', a drink for wedding eves and New Year mornings; and was added to oatmeal brose with honey and cream for the celebrated Atholl brose. Rum punch was sometimes drunk too, but mainly by gentlemen who aped English fashions and by the West India merchants and clubmen of Glasgow.[55]

In England the traditional mead and metheglin still survived, becoming less common as time went on, though both enjoyed a revival among the gentry after the Restoration. Sir Kenelm Digby collected no fewer than fifty-six different recipes from his friends. In some the liquor was set working with ale-barm or yeast, but the best meads, in his view, were those in which the honey fermented of itself. Originally mead had been the simple honey and water based drink, while metheglin had additional herb or spice flavourings, but the two names were already interchangeable by Elizabethan times. Sir Kenelm's white mead recipe, for instance, had a quarter of an ounce each of mace and ginger and half an ounce of nutmegs together with a handful of sweet marjoram, thyme and sweet-briar boiled in an amalgam of six gallons of water and six quarts of honey. Country folk who kept bees made their own versions of the drink from the washings of the honeycombs.

Mead drinking was on the wane in the eighteenth century, though cookery books still gave a few recipes. Sack mead (fortified with sack and brandy), cowslip mead and walnut mead were three variants recommended by Elizabeth Raffald. But what had once been the liquor of warriors was now no more than an occasional light refreshment, offered as an alternative to wine when ladies paid morning calls on one another.[56]

Cider and perry, however, maintained their popularity. When cider was made in small quantities, the apples were beaten in a wooden trough with pestles; for larger amounts they were crushed in a horse-mill. In the later seventeenth century a specially constructed cider mill came into use with a wooden cylinder that was rotated by hand. The pulp was then placed between straw in a screw-press to extract the juice. The new must or murc was fined with isinglass, and was fermented in a cask. After a time it was put up into bottles. It is interesting to read John Worlidge's claim, made in 1676: 'Therefore is laying the bottles sideways to be commended, not only for preserving the corks moist, but for that the air that remains in the bottle is on the side of the bottle where it can neither expire, nor can new be admitted, the liquor being against the cork. . . .' That was the method of storage destined to prove so successful in maturing port-wine in the following century.

The apple pulp mixed with boiled water and pressed a second time yielded water-cider. It was ready for consumption within a few days, was drunk at family tables in place of small beer, and could even be hopped like beer for longer keeping.

'But if your fruit be unripe or your cider small, and that you have a mind to strengthen it, especially if you live in the North-country, you may improve it', wrote John Mortimer. Raisins soaked in apple juice or brandy were to be pressed, and the fluid mixed into the cider. Or royal cider could be made, a potent liquor comprising the spirits distilled from one hogshead of cider added to the cider in a second hogshead. It could be made to 'drink like canary' with extra spirits and sugar. Perry was produced in the same fashion as cider; and could likewise be enriched by the addition of spirits of pear juice.[57]

No less noteworthy than the rise in spirit drinking was the phenomenal success of three new non-alcoholic drinks, coffee, chocolate and tea. Unlike beverages made from milk, whey or unfermented cereals, coffee and tea were stimulants, and their advocates were quick to point out their virtues in clearing the head and driving away alcoholic vapours.

Coffee came to Europe from the Moslem world. The tree now called *coffea arabica* is indigenous to Ethiopia and the Sudan, where the natives discovered how to parch the beans to make a foodstuff with useful keeping properties. People took coffee beans on long journeys, and chewed them both for nourishment and as a stimulant. An intoxicating drink may also have been produced by fermenting the thin, sweet pulp of the ripe fruits, and it was perhaps to this form that the Arabs gave the name *kahweh*, a word they used for wine. As Moslems they viewed the drink with disfavour; but by the fifteenth century an infusion of roasted coffee beans and water was known in Arabia, and this met with far greater approval. Coffee drinking spread through the Middle East, and by the 1530s had reached Turkey.

Individual travellers, such as Nathaniel Conopios whom John Evelyn saw drinking coffee in Balliol College in 1637, first brought the custom to England. The earliest English coffee house was also at Oxford, being established at the 'Angel' in the parish of St Peter in the East in 1650. Two years later London had its first coffee house in St Michael's Alley, Cornhill, and many others soon came into existence. As in the east, they had an all-male clientele who enjoyed the club-like atmosphere where they could read newspapers, chat or hold discussions on business, politics or literature.

Coffee remained expensive, for it was costly to import and within a few years was made liable to excise duty. In 1663 the coffee houses were turned into licensed premises. But they were able to sell the drink for no more than a penny a dish. The powdered coffee beans were three shillings a pound in 1685. Then customs duties were increased and the price was four shillings by 1690 and by 1693 had crept up to six.

The coffee houses did not at first increase their charges, but the strength of their brew was affected. Only an ounce of powdered coffee was normally used to a quart of water. Those who brewed it at home added one and a half to two ounces powder for medium strength and three for strong coffee to the same amount of water. The last type was said to be 'truly grateful both to palate and stomach, and wonderfully fortifies or strengthens it'.

Coffee, like other tropical crops, was soon transplanted by enterprising European colonists to new areas of the world. The Dutch began to cultivate it in their East Indian colonies at the end of the seventeenth century. Some years later it was introduced into the West Indies, several central American states and parts of South America. The French grew a variety which came to be known as Bourbon coffee on the island of Réunion.

In England the new drink spread from the coffee houses to the homes of the gentry. The Bedford family at Woburn Abbey bought coffee in very small quantities for several years after 1670. But by 1685, two or three pounds were bought in a year; and eight years later two or three pounds every month. Individual members of the family had their own personal coffee pots and china dishes from which to drink the beverage. A similar rise in coffee consumption took place in other gentry families; and coffee or chocolate succeeded ale and beer as their breakfast drink.[58]

The advocates of coffee praised it for its tonic effect. 'Moderately drunk [it] removes vapours from the brain, occasioned by fumes of wine, or other strong liquors; eases pains in the head, prevents sour belchings, and provokes appetite.' But it had its detractors too. 'In a word, coffee is the drunkard's settle-brain, the fool's pastime, who admires it for being the production of Asia, and is ravished with delight when he hears the berries grow in the deserts of Arabia, but would not give a farthing for an hogshead of it, if it were to be had on Hampstead-Heath or Banstead-Downs. . . .'[59]

The early idea that coffee must be made from specially prepared water (spring water with a little handful of sweet malt and bayberries tied in a rag and boiled in it) was abandoned after a time. By the mid-eighteenth century,

> The right way to make coffee, is to heat the berries in a fire-shovel, till they sweat a little; and then grind them, and put the coffee-pot over the fire with water; when hot, throw the water away, and dry the pot by the fire, then put the powder into it, and boiling water immediately over the same; let it stand three or four minutes, and pour off the clear. By this means the hot water meets the spirit of the coffee; whereas if you boil coffee, as the common way is, the spirit goes away, so that it will not be so strong nor quick to the taste.

William Ellis, who supplied the above recipe, also claimed that 'coffee poured on one or two yolks of eggs, and then just boiled up over a fire, will, with sugar, drink a little like chocolate'. And following on the success of chocolate-flavoured cream desserts, coffee-flavoured variants were developed.

There are several contemporary references to artificial coffee made from burnt wheat or barley, or toast. It was perhaps this last notion that led to the invention of the beverage known as 'toast and water'.[60]

Coffee grew in popularity until the Georgian era, when it began to feel the competition from tea. It remained a drink of the gentry and middling sort of people, and never made much progress with the artisan and labouring classes who preferred tea. Unlike tea leaves, coffee beans could not easily be faked or adulterated, so coffee remained relatively pure, and consequently expensive: for it was far less economical in use than tea. The worst that could happen to it was that West India coffee (which in 1750 retailed at three shillings and sixpence a pound) might be sold to the unwary as Turkish coffee (then four and six a pound); or at least mixed in with the Turkish.[61] But it was only in the last quarter of the eighteenth century, after the import duties on Jamaican and American coffee had been greatly reduced, that coffee consumption in Britain began once more to rise.

In the American colonies the situation developed rather differently. The British colonists took the coffee-house habit with them to Virginia, and coffee drinking was introduced thence into other parts of America. But the coffee houses degenerated into taverns where alcoholic drinks were also on sale, and they became too rough to be visited by gentlefolk.

At the time of the Boston Tea Party, coffee was the obvious alternative to the hated tax-bearing tea, and it was then that it became a favourite household beverage. But its emergence as the national drink of the United States was probably due less to late eighteenth-century patriotism than to the fact that in after years so many immigrants arrived from the coffee-drinking countries of continental Europe.

Chocolate, by contrast, came from the new world; and like coffee it was first made and sold commercially in Britain in the 1650s. The cacao tree, indigenous to the Amazon and Orinoco forests, had been carried thence to central America. There the Aztecs gathered the beans, dried and roasted them, and crushed them with stones to a paste which they mingled with maize flour and pimento and formed into cakes. From these they made a sort of bitter porridge by breaking off a piece and beating it up in water with a whisk. When the Spaniards came into contact with the Aztec way of life, they recognized the nourishing properties of cocoa beans, but preferred to flavour their version of the paste with the local vanilla, and to add other spices and sugar. They, and soon afterwards the Portuguese, began to make up chocolate cakes in large moulds and to send them home. Chocolate was thus introduced into the Iberian Peninsula; but for a long time its method of manufacture was a strictly guarded secret. Some chocolate eventually reached other European countries, but the price was kept high and at first the new drink was hardly known except in aristocratic circles.

A little chocolate was coming into England by the middle of the seventeenth century, and a direct trade in cocoa beans became possible after 1655 when the British captured Jamaica, where the Spaniards had already made considerable plantations of cacao trees. In 1657 the proprietor of a house in Queen's Head Alley in Bishopsgate, London, was advertising 'an excellent West India drink called chocolate to be sold, where you may have it ready at any time, and also unmade at reasonable rates'. Several more chocolate houses were shortly established. Like the coffee houses they assumed the nature of clubs. And, like both coffee and tea, liquid chocolate was made subject to an excise duty in 1660, at the rate of eighteenpence a gallon.

The cocoa beans or nibs themselves were now often dried and sent whole to England and other European countries. Recipe books began to contain instructions on how to transform them into

> chocolate cakes and rolls. Take cacao-nuts gently dried in an iron pan, and then peel off the husks, powder them very small, so as to be sifted; then to every pound so prepared, add of white sugar six ounces, cinnamon half an ounce, one nutmeg, one vanilla [pod] of the best; ambergris or musk each four grains, if for high price or Spanish chocolate, but in the English it is left out.

All these ingredients were worked together with an iron roller on an iron plate over gentle heat, 'and while it is warm it may be made into rolls or cakes, or cast into moulds, or what form thou pleasest'.[62]

Drinking chocolate was made by scraping or grating chocolate powder from one of the cakes and adding a liquid. Early versions of the drink resembled wine caudle. 'To make chaculato. Take half a pint of claret wine, boil it a little, then scrape some chaculato very fine and put into it, and the yolks of two eggs, stir them well together over a slow fire till it be thick, and sweeten it with sugar according to your taste.'

Soon milk or milk and water chocolate became quite usual. Eggs were still added to help to incorporate the drink; 'then mill it with a mill for that purpose till it becomes thick and proper for drinking: This mill is a stick, with an head at the end full of notches, which you must, at the little end, hold in your hand, and hastily twirl it about.'

William Salmon in the 1710 edition of his *Dictionary* describes three types of chocolate drink then current: that made with water alone (but fortified with a little brandy); that made with milk; and 'wine chocolate' in which the liquid element was supplied by three quarters of a pint of water and half a pint 'choice red port or rather choice sherry'.[63]

The chocolate from which these beverages were made was richer than present-day drinking chocolate, for it contained the full measure of cocoa butter from the beans. All three of William Salmon's recipes include a little flour and salt. The flour (replaced in recipes of a later date by arrowroot) took up some of the fat as the drink thickened, and thus helped to make it more digestible.

In the West Indies chocolate was heated and defatted, so that the cocoa butter could be used for cosmetic and medicinal purposes; but it was not until the early nineteenth century that chocolate factories in England and other European countries developed processes for defatting cacao. From the cocoa butter mixed with natural cacao and finely ground sugar 'eating chocolate' was then manufactured, which was sold in the form of chocolate bars.

But this was not the earliest eating chocolate. Chocolate almonds, which could be purchased from French confectioners in the 1670s, were soon copied by English housewives. Flavoured at first with musk and ambergris and later with orangeflower water, the almonds were served for dessert along with crystallized fruits and candies. Chocolate itself flavoured other confectionery, notably chocolate puffs (little light cakes of sugar and beaten eggs). Chocolate cream was a second course dish, for which thick cream, eggs and melted chocolate were milled together 'that it may go up with a froth'. The more solid part was put into little dishes, and the froth, which had been reserved on a sieve, laid over it. Later smooth chocolate cream, analogous to tea and coffee creams, became more usual.[64]

Drinking chocolate enjoyed its greatest popularity in the late seventeenth and early eighteenth century. At that time either chocolate or coffee was the normal breakfast drink among the gentry, accompanying a light meal of wigs, spice-bread or buttered toast. Fifty years later chocolate at breakfast-time was growing rare, for it had been superseded by tea and, to a lesser extent, coffee. The chocolate houses closed down or took on another role, like White's in St James', London, which became a club. Thereafter raw chocolate served to produce the more plebeian cocoa and the new chocolate bars.

Tea was the other important new drink of the seventeenth century, and it arrived in England during the decade when the earliest coffee and chocolate houses opened. Not surprisingly, it was at first sold in the former. 'That excellent and by all physicians approved drink called by the Chineans *Tcha*, by other nations *Tay* alias *Tee* is sold at the Sultaness Head a coffee-house in Sweetings Rents by the Royal Exchange London', ran an advertisement published in *Mercurius Politicus* in September 1658.

Tea had been known for many hundreds of years in China, but it had not always been brewed as a drink. In the fifth century AD the leaves were made into cakes and boiled with rice, spices, nuts and other ingredients. Later dried tea leaves were powdered and whipped up in hot water. The infusion of tea leaves in hot water only came into fashion in the fifteenth century.

In the middle of the following century the Portuguese founded a trading station at Macao, and were able to send a little tea back to Portugal from time to time. When the Dutch had acquired a foothold in Java and Sumatra, they too obtained small quantities, brought to them by trading junks from China: and it was from this source that tea first reached Holland. From there it was occasionally sent into France and England.

In 1664 the East India Company began bringing small amounts direct to England. At first they were dependent for supplies on Chinese traders who visited their entrepôts in Malaya, but later the Company was allowed to trade direct with Amoy and Canton, and more tea became available. The contemporary English pronunciation, 'tay', came from the Amoy dialect: in Canton the beverage was called 'ch'a'.

In England the tea was initially sold 'in the leaf for six pounds, and sometimes for ten pounds the pound weight'. Thomas Garway, reporting this in his celebrated broadsheet of about 1660, went on to claim that he had been the first person publicly to sell tea 'in leaf and drink, made according to the directions of the most knowing merchants and travellers into eastern countries', and that he was now offering it at from sixteen to fifty shillings the pound. The price was soon enhanced by an excise duty, payable at first on the liquid as supplied at coffee houses. The rate was eightpence a gallon in 1660, raised to two shillings a gallon in 1670. By 1680 enough leaf tea was being bought privately to require a different mode of taxation, and the duty was changed to five shillings a pound, irrespective of price or quality of the tea.

Among the varieties imported were Bohea, 'which is a little leaf inclining to black, and generally tinges the water brown, or of a reddish colour'; Singlo of two kinds, one of them of bluish-green colour with a flavour that could survive three or four changes of water; and Bing or Imperial, a large-leafed green tea of very pleasing aroma, which was costly but would only take two waters.

The eighteenth century added Congou, Souchon and Pekoe to the black teas, while the green ones now included Singlo, Twankay, Hyson and Gunpowder. The last named had a tiny leaf, but was strong enough to 'draw four or five waters'.[65]

During the seventeenth century tea remained expensive. Three guineas a pound was a usual price for the finest ones, though inferior teas might cost well under £1 a pound, duty paid. But the drink was made very weak, with no more than a small pinch of tea leaves infused in boiled water for two or three minutes. It could be edulcorated with sugar, but was not yet drunk with milk.

An alternative recipe, brought by a Jesuit from China in 1664, was suggested by Sir Kenelm Digby.

To near a pint of the infusion, take two yolks of new-laid eggs, and beat them very well with as much fine sugar as is

> sufficient for this quantity of liquor; when they are very well incorporated, pour your tea upon the eggs and sugar, and stir them well together. So drink it hot. This is when you come home from attending business abroad, and are very hungry, and yet have not conveniency to eat presently a competent meal. . . . The water is to remain upon [the tea] no longer than whilst you can say the *Miserere* psalm very leisurely.

The same idea was carried forward into the eighteenth century in the form of tea caudle. The ingredients were a quart of strong green tea, boiled with a pint of white wine and the beaten yolks of four eggs, with grated nutmeg and sugar to taste.[66]

Despite the high cost of the leaf the tea-drinking habit gathered momentum. Its domestic success was ensured when Catherine of Braganza, the Portuguese wife of Charles II, who was already familiar with tea and the ritual of its preparation, encouraged tea drinking at the court. The East India Company soon followed up its first imports of tea by bringing in genuine china tea cups or 'dishes' – small, wide, handleless cups – and china tea pots. A bowl for sugar and a salver to hold all the items completed the set. Copper or silver urns were made which could be heated in the drawing-room over a small brazier fuelled by spirits of wine. Early in the eighteenth century tea tables came into fashion, on which the equipage could be assembled; while the urn was succeeded by the tea kettle.

The hostess could thus brew and serve tea herself in the presence of her guests, a ceremony which had great appeal. The wives of the nobility and gentry eagerly acquired the new possessions, and served tea to their friends, who reciprocated. The very costliness of the tea itself gave an extra cachet to the person who offered it at her entertainments – a psychological advantage which in due course helped to spread tea drinking further and further down the social scale.

Social tea drinking was further encouraged when Thomas Twining opened the first tea shop for ladies (coffee houses by contrast were male preserves) in Devereux Court, London, in 1717. Fifteen years later came another new departure, for the

Vauxhall pleasure gardens were developed as a tea garden. Their success led to the establishment of many more such gardens on the outskirts of London and other towns: at one time there were more than thirty in the vicinity of London. Members of both sexes could forgather there to drink tea and to enjoy a variety of concerts, sports or spectacles provided by the proprietors.

Tea gardens were open to people of every class, to servant-girls no less than their mistresses, and they helped to spread the tea-drinking habit still further. By the 1740s the buttered toast or bread which made the English middle-class breakfast was almost invariably accompanied by tea; and now, as Per Kalm noted, 'most people pour a little cream or sweet milk into the teacup when they are about to drink the tea. The servants in London also commonly get such a breakfast, but in the country they have to content themselves with whatever else they can get.'[67]

Tea was also drunk after dinner; and when the fashionable dinner hour had gradually advanced from two or three o'clock at the beginning of the eighteenth century to six or even seven by the closing years, a new light meal of afternoon tea was established to help bridge the gap between a late breakfast and dinner.

Finally, for the true enthusiast, a tea-flavoured dessert cream was developed in the first part of the eighteenth century, following on the earlier success of chocolate cream. To make tea cream, a quarter of an ounce of the best green tea leaves were stewed with a little sugar in a quart of cream until they had yielded up their taste. The gizzards of two or three fowls were chopped small, warmed and melted in a cupful of cream which was added to the rest to 'velvet' it (in later recipes rennet was substituted). It was gently heated again, and then cooled before serving. For a time tea cream enjoyed quite a vogue, but it was eventually superseded by coffee cream.[68]

Tea grew ever more popular, but it was not without enemies. Jonas Hanway was one, and in 1757 he strongly condemned its growing use among the lower orders. Other objections were raised on grounds of health. At first the drink was thought wholly beneficial, for it contained enough caffein to act as a slight stimulant, and to clear headaches and giddiness. Then over-indulgence was found to 'hurt the nerves (Bohea especially) and cause various distempers, as tremors, palsies, vapours, fits, etc.' So milk or cream was put to it, to counteract the effect of the tannin.

Some people used more bizarre methods. 'I know a gentlewoman who in her last dish of tea puts six or more lavendar drops, to prevent the rise of vapours. Others boil archangel flowers in milk, to drink with their tea.' In parts of Scotland the last cup of tea was always qualified with a little whisky; and highlanders often added cinnamon to their tea, to provide extra piquancy. For tea drinking became widespread in Scotland too, and by the 1740s tea had very generally replaced ale or spirits as the morning draught.[69]

Consumers in both countries mollified the drink with sugar. The English were already accustomed to sugaring wine which was not sweet enough for their palates, and were quite ready to do the same for other imported drinks that lacked sweetness. The habit persisted, and was largely responsible for the rising sugar consumption of Britain during the eighteenth century.

Although more and more tea was being drunk, the price of the leaf, inflated by customs duties, kept the finer varieties well in the luxury class for most people. But cheaper tea could be obtained. An enormous amount was smuggled in from the continent, and there was no difficulty in finding a market for it, even among the most respectable people. Parson Woodforde wrote in his diary for 29 March 1777: 'Andrews the Smuggler brought me this night about 11 o'clock a bag of Hyson tea 6 pound weight. He frightened us a little by whistling under the parlour window just as we were going to bed. I gave him some Genever and paid him for the tea at 10s. 6d. per pound.'[70]

And much more was produced by the art of the counterfeiters, who made imitation teas to be mixed in varying proportions with the genuine China article (Indian tea was not imported until the end of the 1830s, and Ceylon tea followed still later in the 1870s). Leaves of hawthorn, sloe, ash and other native trees were dried, rolled and curled, and coloured with verdigris for green tea, and logwood or copperas for black. In the trade this product was known in the later eighteenth century as 'smouch', and since it sold for a few pence a pound, it brought in big profits. Other dealers purchased used tea leaves from the cooks or kitchen maids of the wealthy, and dried and tinted them for resale.

Small wonder that members of the medical profession recommended balm, sage or other herb teas as a safe alternative to the 'deleterious product of China' – and of the tea fakers. Small wonder too that the gentry and middling class, when they had obtained fine teas for their own use (in 1776 it was possible to pay anything from two shillings and sixpence to twenty shillings a pound, with the average around five shillings), kept the leaves in locked caddies, out of reach of unscrupulous servants. But the servants themselves soon had to be considered; and during the second half of the eighteenth century it became usual to stipulate tea twice or more times a day in the terms under which maid-servants were hired, or to offer them an additional payment for tea and sugar.

In 1784 high grain prices were affecting the cost and also the quality of beer. And the duty on tea was at last lowered to a nominal sum on the grounds that 'tea has become an economical substitute to the middle and lower classes of society for malt liquor, the price of which renders it impossible for them to procure the quantity sufficient for them as their only drink'. In these circumstances the government, though eager as ever to raise revenue, could no longer continue to tax tea as a luxury article. By the end of the century tea was well on the way to becoming the national drink of Britain, or at least of its southern half.

The south country labourer could not afford to buy milk or often sugar to put to his tea; nevertheless he drank vast amounts, brewed from cheap, crude, adulterated blends.

> Exclusive of beer, when he can afford it, and spirits, the quantity of water, which with tea forms a beverage which is seldom qualified with milk or sugar, poured down the throats of a labourer's family is astounding. Any person who will give himself the trouble of stepping into the cottages of

Middlesex and Surrey at meal times, will find that in poor families tea is not only the usual beverage, in the morning and evening, but is generally drunk in large quantities even at dinner.[71]

Tea was a necessity for such people. High food prices, enclosure and their general poverty had reduced them to a monotonous diet of bread, cheese and occasionally bacon. Through lack of fuel they had lost the art of making warm soups and pottages, and indeed had lost the taste for them too. Tea was not simply their sole liquid to wash down their dry meals; it was also the only warm and comforting element in their diet.

In the north of England and Scotland 'besides water the general drink of the labouring classes is whey or milk, or rather milk and water, or at best very meagre small beer', even in 1797. Water was thus still especially the drink of the poor, whether taken neat or in the form of weak tea or beer.

Among the wealthy there was new interest in water of a particular type. Early in the seventeenth century mineral waters were found to be helpful in cleansing systems that had taken in too much rich food, wine and spirits. And so the watering places grew up, the 'spaws', called after the prototype Spa in Belgium. And those who had drunk too heavily all through the year travelled many miles to do penance, in company with others of their ilk, by taking the waters for a few weeks.

Chapter 11

The nineteenth century and after

From the end of the eighteenth century Britain's diet has continued to change, and the innovations have been closely linked with the advancement of technology. Improved transport has allowed fresh foods to be brought quickly from distant regions. The growth of the railway system in the middle decades of the nineteenth century meant that meat, fish and milk could be conveyed rapidly to markets in the large towns. Not long afterwards steamships began to import perishable fruits from overseas, such as the bananas of the Canaries and the West Indies, and also, as freezing techniques were improved, frozen meat from America and Australasia. Ice-making machines strong enough to keep meat fresh even in tropical conditions were developed in the 1870s.

The most significant result of closer contacts with other countries and other continents was that there were no more famine years. Failure of crops in Britain, and even in Europe, no longer spelt starvation when cereals and other foodstuffs could be brought from America or Australia.

Nevertheless preservation methods were further developed, partly for storage purposes, and partly to make the fullest possible use of foods which were seasonally plentiful and cheap. Nicholas Appert, at the end of the eighteenth century, discovered how to conserve meat, fruit, vegetables and even milk, by sealing the foodstuff in glass bottles which thereafter were boiled in water. In England the idea was adapted to foods heated and then sealed in tinned iron containers. Although this arrangement soon produced excellent results, canned meats during the first part of the nineteenth century were regarded primarily as rations for the navy, the army and the colonial service. But the late 1860s saw the arrival in Britain of tinned mutton from Australia; and in the decade that followed there was a huge expansion in the canning of meat in Australia, New Zealand and America for the British market. Tinned American fruits and tomatoes followed soon afterwards.

At home milk was sweetened, condensed and canned, and sold cheaply enough to become a regular substitute for the genuine article among poor people. Fresh milk profited from the experiments of Louis Pasteur in France, though it was the 1890s before pasteurization became common in British dairy practice.

Drying techniques made some progress, but here the greatest advances came in the twentieth century. An innovation from North America, popularized in Britain in the 1920s, was dried or toasted breakfast cereals to be eaten in the place of porridge. The latter had become a usual middle-class breakfast dish throughout Britain during the nineteenth century. A later and more considerable advance has been the recent invention of accelerated freeze drying, by which vegetable foods, dehydrated at very low temperatures, retain a greater part of their flavour than is possible through simple air or heat drying. Packages of dried mixed ingredients, which can quickly be turned into mealtime dishes, are also prominent among today's convenience foods.

Food additives in the early nineteenth century followed the

pattern already established, and were often of a pernicious nature. Adulteration of beer, tea, bread, pickles, and indeed most other processed foods continued and increased until the passing of the 1872 'Adulteration of food, drink and drugs act', further amended by the 'Sale of food and drugs act' of 1875. Thereafter additives had to be named, so that the consumer could know the components of food mixtures; and public analysts were appointed to analyse doubtful samples, and if necessary to prosecute the makers.

This was not the end of food additives, for many chemical substances were, and still are, employed to colour and flavour foods and to reduce bacterial growth. One of the more recent introductions is monosodium glutamate, tasteless in itself, which acts on the taste-buds to enhance the flavours already present in food. Artificial flavourings may not always be pleasing to the palate, but most are at least harmless.

Another serious threat to Britain's diet was the development of manufactured foods which, in their early days, gave very little nutrition. Margarine, invented in the 1870s as a cheaper substitute for butter, was made at first from emulsified beef suet, but later from vegetable oils. Factory jam, based on sugar, vegetable pulp and artificial flavourings and colourings, was another unnourishing product of the late nineteenth century much used by the poor in place of butter.

The danger of such foods when they formed a substantial part of the diet was recognized once the importance of vitamins had been established about 1912. Dieticians had already discovered the role of proteins, fats, carbohydrates and mineral salts in foodstuffs; and they subsequently learned how to fortify such manufactured foods as margarine and tinned condensed milk with the missing vitamins which were present in their natural counterparts. Bread, too, lost much of its vitamin content when flour was produced by roller-milling; but it has never been thought necessary to reintroduce the absent vitamins into flour as a matter of national policy. Today, however, even those who have the lowest incomes can afford to eat a balanced diet, although it may be a monotonous one.[1]

Foodstuffs have changed, and so too have attitudes to food.

The trend towards a simpler, less highly spiced diet was already becoming apparent at the end of the eighteenth century, and it continued during the nineteenth. In the Victorian era there was a belief that high thinking should be coupled with plain living, and that a simple diet was morally healthier, and in particular more suitable for children.

During the present century overeating has been recognized as a definite health hazard. Nowadays the well-to-do cultivate slimness and choose diets rich in protein foods, fruit and vegetables, but low in starch and sugar; and they no longer eat to excess. This is a new attitude. Until the last few decades, prosperity has always been equated with hearty eating and a well-rounded figure. Our forebears favoured conspicuous consumption; and their physique displayed their enthusiasm for their food.

Abbreviations

Quotations from classical authors are based upon the translations in the Loeb Classical Library, except where otherwise attributed.

The following abbreviations have been used (fuller details appear in the Bibliography, pages 453–9).

BD	Boorde: *Dyetary* (*A compendyous regyment,* etc.)
BGG	*Be gesceadwisan gerefan*
CC	*Compleat Cook* (1655)
E.E.T.S.	Early English Text Society
EHI	*England's Happiness Improved*
FC	*Forme of Cury*
FSB	*Fifteenth Century School Book,* ed. Nelson
HDL	*Hywel Dda: Laws* (*Book of Blegwryd*), trans. Richards
LCC	*Liber Cure Cocorum*
MA	*Myvyrian Archaiology*
MCB	*Munden's Chantry, Bridport: Account book, 1453–60* (*A Small Household of the Fifteenth Century*, etc.)
MHE	*Manners and Household expenses*
MIG	Mayster Ion Gardener: 'The feate of gardeninge'
NHB	*Northumberland Household Book*
PNB	*A Proper Newe Booke of Cokerye,* ed. Frere
PP	Power & Postan (eds.): *Studies in English Trade in the Fifteenth Century*
QCO	*The Queen's Closet Opened*, by M. (W.)
VCH	*Victoria County History*
VV	*A Volume of Vocabularies*, ed. Wright
WDW	*The Whole Duty of a Woman*
WHH	Walter of Henley: *Husbandry*

Suggestions For Further Reading

Brears, P. *The Gentlewoman's Kitchen: Great Food in Yorkshire 1650-1750.* Wakefield, England 1984.

_________*Traditional Food in Yorkshire.* Edinburgh, 1987.

Burnett, J. *Plenty and Want: A Social History of Diet in England, 1815 to the Present Day*, 3rd ed. London, 1979.

Culinary Historians of Boston, *Current Research in Culinary History: Sources Topics and Methods.* Hingham, MA, 1986.

David, E. *English Bread and Yeast Cookery.* London, 1977.

Davidson, A. *On Fasting and Feasting.* London, 1988.

Driver, C. *The British at Table, 1940-1980.* London, 1983.

Fenton, A. and Myrdal, J., eds. *Food and Drink and Travelling Accessories.* Edinburgh, 1988.

Freeman, B. *First Catch your Peacock.* Griffithstown, Gwent,Wales, 1980.

Heal, F. *Hospitality in Early Modern England.* Oxford, 1990.

Henisch, B.A. *Fast and Feast: Food in Medieval Society.* University Park, PA, and London, 1976.

Hess, K.,ed. *Martha Washington's Booke of Cookery.* New York, 1981.

Hieatt, C.B. *An Ordinance of Pottage: an Edition of the Fifteenth-century Culinary Recipes in Yale University's MS Beineke 163.* London, 1988.

Hieatt, C.B. and Butler, S., eds. *Curye on Inglysch: English Culinary Manuscripts of the Fourteenth Century.* Early English Text Society, S.S.8, London 1985.

Hope, A. *The Caledonian Feast: Scottish Cuisine through the Ages.* London,1989.

Hutchins, S. *Grannie's Kitchen: Recipes from East Anglia.* London, 1980.

Kurti, N. and Kurti G. eds. *But the Crackling is Superb: an Anthology on Food and Drink by Fellows of the Royal Society*. Bristol, England, and Philadelphia, PA, 1988.

McGee, H. *On Food and Cooking: the Science and Lore of the Kitchen*. New York, 1984.

Oddy, D. and Miller D., eds. *The Making of the Modern British Diet*. London, and Totowa, NJ, 1976.

Rance, P. *The Great British Cheese Book*. London, 1982.

Wilson, C.A., ed. *The Appetite and the Eye: Visual Aspects of Food and its Presentation within their Historical Context*. Edinburgh, 1991.

________. *"Banquetting Stuffe": the Fare and Social Background of the Tudor and Stuart Banquet*. Edinburgh, 1991.

________. *The Book of Marmalade: its Antecedents, its History and its Role in the World Today*. London, 1985, and New York, 1986.

References

Chapter 2

1 J. G. D. Clark, 'The development of fishing in prehistoric Europe', *Antiq. J.* (1948), 28, pp. 45–63, 81, 84–5; A. H. Bishop, 'An Oronsay shell-mound – a Scottish pre-Neolithic site', *Proc. Soc. Antiq. Scotland* (1913), 48, p. 102; H. L. Movius, 'A Neolithic site on the river Bann', *Proc. Roy. Irish Acad.* (1935), 43C, pp. 17–40; J. G. D. Clark, *Prehistoric Europe* (1952), pp. 63–5.

2 S. Piggott, *Ancient Europe* (1965), p. 171; F. T. Baker, 'The Iron Age salt industry in Lincolnshire', *Lincs. Archit. & Archaeol. Soc., Rep. & pap.* (1959), n.s.8, pp. 26–31, 34.

3 Clark, *Antiq J.* (1948), 28, p. 80; S. S. Frere, *Britannia* (1967), p. 299; Tacitus, *Agricola*, 21.

4 Apicius, *The Roman Cookery Book*, ed. B. Flower and E. Rosenbaum (1958), pp. 12–15. Hereafter cited as Apicius.

5 J. Liversidge, 'Roman kitchens and cooking utensils', Apicius, pp 29–36; Pliny, *Historia naturalis*, XXXI, xliii, 93–4; *Geoponica*, XX, 46.

6 Apicius, X, i, 5; X, iii, 2; IX, vi.

7 Athenaeus, *Deipnosophistae*, III, 116f.

8 F. L. Attenborough, *The Laws of the Earliest English Kings* (1922), Ine c.70.

9 D. Knowles, *The Monastic Order in England, 914–1216* (1949), pp. 459–60.

10 Aelfric, *Colloquy*, ed. G. N. Garmonsway, 2nd ed. (1947), p. 46. Hereafter cited as Aelfric. C. L. Cutting, *Fish Saving* (1955), p. 54. Hereafter cited as Cutting. N. J. M. Kerling, *Commercial Relations of Holland and Zeeland with England* (1954), p. 59. Hereafter cited as Kerling.

11 Clark, *Prehistoric Europe*, pp. 89–90; A. M. Samuel, *The Herring* (1918), p. 71.

12 L. F. Salzman, *English Industries of the Middle Ages* (1923), p. 259. Hereafter cited as Salzman (1923). MA, p. 1041; Clark, *Prehistoric Europe*, p. 63; A. J. Robertson, *The Laws of the Kings of England from Edmund to Henry I* (1925), IV Aethelred c. 5.

13 L. Alcock, *Dinas Powys* (1963), p. 40; Bede, *Ecclesiastical History*,

ed. B. Colgrave and R. A. B. Mynors (1969), p. 15. Hereafter cited as Bede. R. R. Clarke, *East Anglia* (1960), p. 171; Aelfric, p. 29.

14 P. H. Blair, *An Introduction to Anglo-Saxon England* (1956), p. 263; Aelfric, p. 27.

15 E. H. Rudkin and D. M. Owen, 'The mediaeval salt industry in the Lindsay marshland', *Lincs. Archit. & Archaeol. Soc., Rep. & pap.* (1959), n.s.8, pp. 76–82; H. P. R. Finberg, *The Early Charters of the West Midlands* (1961), p. 86.

16 Egil, *Saga*, trans. E. R. Eddison (1930), p. 30.

17 BD, p. 269; *A Collection of Ordinances and Regulations for the Government of the Royal Household* (1790), p. 38.

18 W. de Worde, *Boke of Kervynge*, ed. F. J. Furnivall (1868), p. 116; R. Warner, *Antiquitates Culinariae* (1791), pp. 98–9. Hereafter cited as Warner. *Two Fifteenth Century Cookery Books*, ed. T. Austin (1888), p. 51. Hereafter cited as Austin.

19 BD, p. 269; FSB, no. 30.

20 Salzman (1923), p. 260; Kerling, pp. 89, 92.

21 P. Heath, 'North Sea fishing in the fifteenth century: the Scarborough fleet', *Northern History* (1968), 3, pp. 61–2; Samuel, *The Herring*, p. 71; J. S. Dodd, *An Essay towards a Natural History of the Herring* (1752), p. 61; T. Nashe, *Works*, ed. R. B. McKerrow (1958), 3, p. 179.

22 C. Bonnier, 'List of English towns in the fourteenth century', *Eng. Hist. Rev.* (1901), 16, p. 502; L. F. Salzman, 'Industries', *VCH: Sussex* (1907), 2, p. 267; Heath, *Northern History* (1968), 3, pp. 60–1.

23 E. M. Carus Wilson, 'The Icelandic trade', PP, pp. 172–4; Cutting, p. 121.

24 Clark, *Prehistoric Europe*, p. 63; MHE, p. 14, etc.; Salzman (1923), p. 266.

25 J. Russell, *Boke of Nurture*, ed. F. J. Furnivall (1868), p. 55. Hereafter cited as Russell. Warner, p. 94; M. Martin, *A Description of the Western Islands of Scotland circa 1695*, ed. D. J. McLeod (1934), p. 135. Hereafter cited as Martin.

26 MHE, p. 561.

27 M. W. Labarge, *A Baronial Household of the Thirteenth Century* (1965), p. 80; C. C. Trench, *The Poacher and the Squire* (1967), p. 60. Hereafter cited as Trench. Dame J. Berners, *Treatyse of Fysshynge with an Angle* (1885), pp. 34–5, 30.

28 F. E. Zeuner, *A History of Domesticated Animals* (1963), p. 480. Hereafter cited as Zeuner. MHE, p. 563; T. Pennant, *British Zoology* (1776), 3, p. 310. Hereafter cited as Pennant.

29 E. M. Carus Wilson, 'The overseas trade of Bristol', PP, pp. 197–8.
30 L. von Rozmital, *Travels*, trans. M. Letts, *Hakluyt Soc.*, 2nd ser. (1955), 108, p. 58; Warner, p. 120.
31 Pliny, VIII, xlvii, 109; E. Topsell, *The History of Four-footed Beasts* (1658), p. 36.
32 D. Rough, *Register*, ed. K. M. E. Murray, *Kent Archaeol. Soc. Rec.* (1945), 16, p. x.
33 Salzman (1923), p. 280; S. Thrupp, 'The grocers of London', PP, pp. 278–9; Cutting, pp. 40–1; W. J. Passingham, *London's Markets* (1935), p. 43.
34 R. Holinshed, *Chronicle, 1577*, new ed. (1807), 4, p. 255; J. Leland, *Itinerary*, ed. L. T. Smith (1909), 4, p. 10; M. Sellers, 'Industries', *VCH: Durham* (1907), 2, p. 293.
35 A. R. Bridbury, *England and the Salt Trade in the Later Middle Ages* (1955), pp. 98–9; Kerling, p. 98; NHB, p. 57.
36 A. Neckam, *De Utensilibus*, VV, pp. 97, 102. Hereafter cited as Neckam. Austin, pp. 103, 110.
37 MHE, p. 50; Russell, pp. 58–9; Austin, p. 102.
38 Warner, p. 49.
39 Austin, p. 103; PNB, p. 23.
40 Austin, pp. 23, 105.
41 BD, p. 268; FSB, no. 31.
42 Russell, p. 44; Salzman (1923), p. 260, FC, no. 167.
43 Austin, pp. 26, 95; *A Noble Boke off Cookry*, ed. Mrs A. Napier (1882), p. 42. Hereafter cited as Napier.
44 Dame A. de Bryene, *The Household Book, Sept 1412 – Sept 1413* (1931), p. 48. Hereafter cited as Bryene. Warner, p. 69; Austin, p. 90.
45 Napier, p. 74; Austin, p. 106; Warner, pp. 107–21.
46 FSB, no. 22; Russell, p. 42.
47 Salzman (1923), p. 266; Bryene, Appendix III, pp. 135–6; Warner, p. 47.
48 Russell, pp. 41, 57; *The Goodman of Paris, c. 1393*, ed. E. Power (1928), p. 328. Hereafter cited as *Goodman.*
49 T. Tusser, *Five Hundreth Pointes of Good Husbandrie* (1590), p. 103. Hereafter cited as Tusser (1590).
50 *Goodman*, p. 273; F. G. Emmison, *Tudor Food and Pastimes* (1964), p. 45.
51 BD, p. 269; Russell, pp. 38–9, 45, 57.
52 NHB, pp. 73, 80–1.
53 T. Cogan, *The Haven of Health* (1612), p. 138. Hereafter cited as Cogan. Cutting, p. 32.
54 F. G. Emmison, *Tudor Secretary* (1961), p. 143. Hereafter cited

as Emmison (1961). S. Pepys, *Diary*, ed. R. Latham and W. Matthews (1970), 2, p. 37.

55 H. Glasse, *The Art of Cookery* (1747), pp. 76–118. Hereafter cited as Glasse (1747).

56 Cutting, pp. 203–4; 132–5.

57 T. Moufet, *Health's Improvement* (1746), p. 257. Hereafter cited as Moufet. Pepys, *Diary* (1970), 3, p. 71.

58 Sir H. Platt, *Jewell House of Art and Nature* (1594), no. 88; J. C. Shenstone, 'Industries', *VCH: Essex* (1907), 2, p. 438.

59 G. S. Thomson, *Life in a Noble Household, 1641–1700* (1940), p. 159. Hereafter cited as Thomson. D. Defoe, *A Tour through the Whole Island of Great Britain, 1724–5* (1927), 2, p. 499.

60 Defoe, *Tour*, 2, p. 684; Cutting, p. 216.

61 C. Fiennes, *Journeys*, ed. C. Morris (1949), pp. 49, 224, xxi; Defoe, *Tour*, 1, p. 261.

62 Cutting, p. 103; Defoe, *Tour*, 1, p. 123.

63 EHI, pp. 142–3, 146.

64 *The Good Hous-wives Treasurie* (1588), A5; PNB, p. 21; *The Second Part of the Good Hus-wives Iewell* (1597), p. 22.

65 C. Hole, *English Home Life, 1500–1800*, 2nd ed. (1949), pp. 22–3.

66 R. May, *The Accomplisht Cook*, 2nd ed. (1665), pp. 328, 361. Hereafter cited as May. *Complete Cook*, new ed. (1710), p. 123; Sir K. Digby, *The Closet Opened, 1669*, ed. A. Macdonnell (1910), p. 193. Hereafter cited as Digby.

67 See p. 247 and p. 358; see also E. Raffald, *The Experienced English Housekeeper*, 2nd ed. (1771), pp. 23–5. Hereafter cited as Raffald. M. Smith, *The Complete Housekeeper* (1772), p. 67. Hereafter cited as Smith (1772). Glasse (1747), p. 94.

68 *The Second Part of the Good Hus-wives Iewell*, p. 28.

69 J. Murrel, *Murrels Two Books of Cookerie and Carving* (1638), pp. 61, 75, 129, 135. Hereafter cited as Murrel (1638). Sir H. Platt, *Delightes for Ladies* (1605), C15. Hereafter cited as Platt (1605).

70 Murrel (1638), pp. 9–10; May, B6–B8.

71 CC, pp. 91, 97; May, p. 109; Raffald, pp. 74, 95, 110; E. Smith, *The Compleat Housewife* (1727), p. 61. Hereafter cited as Smith (1727).

72 May, p. 403; A.W., *A Booke of Cookry* (1584), f. 17. Hereafter cited as A.W. (1584). Raffald, pp. 37, 242. W. Rabisha, *The Whole Body of Cookery Dissected* (1673), p. 210. Hereafter cited as Rabisha.

73 G. Markham, *The English House-wife*, 4th ed. (1631), pp. 110–11. Hereafter cited as Markham (1631). May, pp. 339, 358, etc.

74 May, p. 343; Glasse (1747), p. 88.
75 Platt, *Jewell House*, no. 4; Salzman (1923), p. 281; Digby, pp. 184–5.
76 J. Cooper, *Art of Cookery* (1654), p. 131; Fiennes, *Journeys*, pp. 192–3.
77 May, p. 331; Defoe, *Tour*, 2, p. 660; Raffald, p. 31, 350; Platt (1605), C17; Apicius, I, ix, 1.
78 Sir F. M. Eden, *The State of the Poor* (1928), p. 106. Hereafter cited as Eden. H. Glasse, *The Art of Cookery*, 6th ed. (1758), pp. 379–81. Hereafter cited as Glasse (1758). Raffald, p. 17.
79 Glasse (1747), p. 90; Cutting, pp. 168–70.
80 Glasse (1758), p. 380; Cutting, pp. 87, 239–41; J. Burnett, *Plenty and Want* (1966), pp. 101, 147.

Chapter 3

1 Clark, *Prehistoric Europe*, pp. 35, 65; and *Excavations at Star Carr* (1954), pp. 15, 18–20, 168; Tacitus, *Germania*, 22; Homer, *Odyssey*, XVIII, 44–5.
2 Sir L. Scott, 'Gallo-British colonies: note on food preservation', *Proc. Prehist. Soc.* (1948), 14, pp. 124–5.
3 Piggott, *Ancient Europe*, p. 40.
4 Clark, *Prehistoric Europe*, p. 125; E. Burt, *Letters from a Gentleman in Scotland*, new ed. (1815), 2, p. 109.
5 Sir R. E. M. Wheeler, *Maiden Castle, Dorset* (1943), pp. 366–7; W. F. Grimes, 'Neolithic Wales', *Prehistoric and Early Wales*, ed. I. L. Foster and G. Daniel (1943), p. 60.
6 M. J. O'Kelly, 'Excavations and experiments in early Irish cooking-places', *J. R. Soc. Antiq. Ireland* (1954), 84, pp. 105–55; Burt, *Letters*, 2, pp. 252–3.
7 Bede, p. 19; R. Trow-Smith, *A History of British Livestock Husbandry to 1700* (1957), p. 15. Hereafter cited as Trow-Smith (1957). Wheeler, *Maiden Castle*, p. 118.
8 C. F. C. Hawkes and M. A. Smith, 'On some buckets and cauldrons of the Bronze and early Iron Ages', *Antiq. J.* (1957), 37, pp. 137–98; S. Piggott, 'Firedogs again', *Antiquity* (1948), 22, pp. 21–8.
9 J. J. Tierney, 'The Celtic ethnography of Posidonius', *Proc. R. Irish Acad.* (1960), 60C, pp. 247, 250; Cato, 162.
o S. Applebaum, 'Agriculture in Roman Britain', *Agric. Hist. Rev.* (1958), 6, p. 71; Columella, VI, iii, 24; Strabo, IV, v, 1–2; Frere, *Britannia*, p. 100.
11 Applebaum, *Agric. Hist. Rev.* (1958), 6, pp. 74–5; Columella, VII, vi–vii.

12 A. Bulleid and H. St G. Gray, *The Glastonbury Lake Village* (1917), 2, p. 641.
13 Varro, *Res Rusticae*, III, xii, 3, xv, 1–2; Zeuner, pp. 412–14, 415–16; Apicius, VIII, ix.
14 Varro, III, xiv, 4–5; Apicius, VII, xviii.
15 Liversidge, in Apicius, pp. 31–2; Apicius, VII, v, 5; VIII, vii, 3–4, 8; VIII, v, 1.
16 Apicius, VIII, ii, 4, 7, 8; VII, xii, 1, ix–x; Columella, XII, lv, 4.
17 B. H. Slicher van Bath, *The Agrarian History of Western Europe* (1963), p. 68; Alcock, *Dinas Powys*, p. 36; Trow-Smith (1957), p. 80.
18 MA, p. 1015; F. W. Grube, 'Meat foods of the Anglo-Saxons', *J. Eng. & Germ. Philol.* (1935), 34, pp. 518–19; F. Moryson, *Itinerary* (1617), 3, p. 162.
19 K. Branigan, *Latimer* (1971), p. 165; Aelfric, pp. 23–4; J. E. Harting, *British Animals Extinct within Historic Times* (1880), p. 20; MA, p. 1020.
20 Grube, *J. Eng. & Germ. Philol.* (1935), 34, p. 514.
21 T. Tusser, *A Hundreth Good Pointes of Husbandrie, 1557* (1810), p. 9.
22 H. P. Finberg, 'An early reference to the Welsh cattle trade', *Agric. Hist. Rev.* (1954), 2, p. 12; F. J. Fisher, 'The development of the London food market, 1540–1640', *Econ. Hist. Rev.* (1935), 5(2), p. 51; NHB, p. 5.
23 WHH, p. 29; *Seneschaucie*, in WHH, p. 97.
24 Moufet, pp. 143–5; Emmison (1961), pp. 144, 308–14.
25 J. G. Millais, *Mammals of Great Britain and Ireland* (1906), 3, p. 109; W. Harrison, *Elizabethan England*, 1587, (1902), pp. 206, 172. Hereafter cited as Harrison. E. M. Veale, 'The rabbit in England', *Agric. Hist. Rev.* (1957), 5, pp. 86–8; G. Turbervile, *Booke of Hunting, 1576* (1908), pp. 219, 148; W. Fitzstephen, *Description*, ed. S. Pegge (1772), pp. 26, 61; Warner, p. 93.
26 Turbervile, *Booke of Hunting*, p. 79; FSB, no. 100; Trench, p. 87; P. E. Jones, *The Worshipful Company of Poulters of the City of London*, 2nd ed. (1965), p. 86. Hereafter cited as Jones. BD, p. 275.
27 Zeuner, p. 413; Warner, p. 77; Moufet, p. 159.
28 See p. 253.
29 Napier, pp. 64–8; Austin, pp. 38, 80–1; FC, no. 174; Warner, p. 89; Russell, p. 36.
30 Neckam, p. 102; Austin, pp. 40, 83, etc.; Warner, p. 74.
31 WHH, p. 13.
32 Warner, pp. 57–8, 43; FC, no. 11–13, 185; Austin, pp. 47–55; Napier, p. 58.

33 Apicius, I, vii, 1; LCC, p. 33; J. Partridge, *The Widowes Treasure* (1585), B4.
34 W. Ellis, *The Country Housewife's Family Companion* (1750), p. 108. Hereafter cited as Ellis. LCC, p. 6; BD, p. 271; Austin, p. 69; T. Webster, *Encyclopaedia of Domestic Economy* (1844), p. 376.
35 See p. 204; see also Austin, p. 32; Tusser (1590), p. 25.
36 W. Langland, *Piers Plowman*, ed. W. W. Skeat (1886), 1, p. 220; H. D. Renner, *The Origin of Food Habits* (1944), p. 246; BD, p. 273; Cogan, p. 150.
37 W. de Biblesworth, *Treatise*, in VV, p. 173; Napier, p. 4; Warner, pp. 79, 98; Austin, pp. 11–12; Tusser, p. 35; Moufet, p. 147.
38 Harrison, p. 158
39 Tusser (1590), p. 56; Neckam, p. 104; MHE, p. 211.
40 Pliny, XXVIII, xxxix; Austin, p. 6.
41 Austin, pp. 51, 54–5; Napier, p. 53; BD, p. 276.
42 FC, no. 101–2; Warner, pp. 44, 61; Austin, p. 87.
43 Trench, p. 65; Harrison, p. 207; FSB, no. 25; BD, pp. 274–5.
44 R. de Swinfield, *Roll of the Household Expenses . . . 1289 and 1290, Camden Soc.* (1853–4), 59 and 62, pp. cvii, cxcvi, ccxxii. Hereafter cited as Swinfield. Warner, pp. 44–5.
45 Russell, pp. 37, 25; Austin, pp. 7, 40.
46 FC, no. 13; Austin, pp. 10, 51, 70, 73; Napier, pp. 53; 103, A.W. (1584), f. 23.
47 Worde, *Boke of Kervynge*, p. 151; Austin, p. 80; Warner, pp. 38, 59; Russell, p. 31.
48 G. Markham, *The English Hus-wife* (1615), p. 54. Hereafter cited as Markham (1615); May, p. 198; Pennant, 1, p. 32.
49 F. M. Misson, *Memoirs*, trans. J. Ozell (1719), pp. 313–14.
50 P. Kalm, *Account of his Visit to England . . . in 1748*, trans. J. Lucas (1892), pp. 14–15. Hereafter cited as Kalm.
51 *Ibid.*, p. 173; Count B. Rumford, *Essays*, new ed. (1802), 3, pp. 67–9; C. Clair, *Kitchen and Table* (1964), pp. 197–9.
52 Markham (1615), p. 52; J. Mortimer, *The Whole Art of Husbandry* (1707), p. 180. Hereafter cited as Mortimer. Glasse (1747), pp. 4, 9.
53 WDW, pp. 468–9; Glasse (1747), p. 69.
54 CC, p. 78.
55 A.W. (1584), f. 35; Markham (1615), p. 63.
56 A.W. (1584), f. 30; Rabisha, p. 90; P. Lamb, *Royal Cookery* (1710), pp. 34–5.
57 Raffald, pp. 70, 72, 116.
58 Burt, *Letters*, 2, p. 109.
59 Ellis, pp. 109f, 223; Platt (1605), C18; Glasse (1758), p. 366.

60 Glasse (1747), p. 161; Raffald, pp. 259–60.
61 Ellis, pp. 69–70; Burt, *Letters*, 1, p. 113.
62 CC, pp. 101–2; May, p. 122; A. Blencowe, *The Receipt Book, A.D. 1694* (1925), p. 21. Hereafter cited as Blencowe. Glasse (1747), p. 252; Raffald, p. 253.
63 Raffald, p. 129.
64 A.W. (1584), f. 36; May, p. 204; Smith (1727), p. 149; Raffald, pp. 162, 174.
65 May, pp. 201, 205; Smith (1772), pp. 279–81.
66 Trench, pp. 116–28; Moufet, p. 158; Mortimer, p. 188; A. Harris, 'The rabbit warrens of east Yorkshire in the eighteenth and nineteenth centuries', *Yorks. Arch. J.* (1971), 42, pp. 429–43.
67 G. C. F. Forster, 'York in the seventeenth century', *VCH: York* (1961), p. 199; PNB, pp. 19–21; Markham (1615), p. 59; May, p. 144; Rabisha, p. 117; WDW, p. 334.
68 Markham (1615), pp. 66–7; Pepys, *Diary* (1970), 1, p. 9.
69 May, p. 231; Smith (1727), p. 25; Glasse (1747), p. 8.
70 May, pp. 45, 147; M. Kettilby, *A Collection of above 300 Receipts* (1714), p. 20. Hereafter cited as Kettilby. G. Hartman, *The True Preserver and Restorer of Health* (1682), 2, p. 17; Smith (1727), p. 52.
71 See p. 102; see also A.W. (1584), f. 6; May, p. 223; Rabisha, p. 26; H. Woolley, *The Queen-like Closet*, 2nd ed. (1672), p. 203. Hereafter cited as Woolley (1672). Digby, pp. 207–8.
72 May, pp. 228, 415–17; F. P. de La Varenne, *The French Cook*, 3rd ed. (1673), p. 76. Hereafter cited as La Varenne.
73 CC, p. 43; La Varenne, pp. 70–1; J. Nott, *The Cook's and Confectioner's Dictionary* (1723), S86–91; Woolley (1672), p. 17; Blencowe, p. 52; Smith (1727), p. 247.

Chapter 4

1 Clark, *Prehistoric Europe*, pp. 37–41; Burt, *Letters*, 2, p. 252; Martin, pp. 230, 439.
2 Zeuner, pp. 443–52; Caesar, *De Bello Gallico*, V, 12.
3 Columella, VIII, vii; Pliny, X, xxix.
4 Apicius, VI, ix, 14, v, 6, ii, 2–3; Anthimus, *De Observatione Ciborum* (1963), p. 12. Hereafter cited as Anthimus.
5 Clarke, *East Anglia*, p. 171.
6 Knowles, *The Monastic Order in England, 914–1216*, p. 458.
7 HDL, p. 86.
8 Aelfric, p. 31.
9 Dame J. Berners, *The Boke of St. Albans* (1881), D3–4; HDL, p. 32; Pennant, 1, p. 167.

10 Pennant, 1, p. 242.
11 NHB, p. 106; Jones, pp. 72, 130–43; Austin, p. 79.
12 *Hosebonderie*, WHH, p. 73; Swinfield, p. ccxxx; Bryene, Appendix III, pp. 125, 135.
13 Pennant, 2, p. 477; 'A relation . . . of the Island of England', trans. C. A. Sneyd, *Camden Soc.* (1847), 37, p. 10.
14 Bryene, p. 62; FSB, no. 26.
15 PNB, pp. 3–5, 9.
16 Warner, p. 37; Austin, p. 78; BD, pp. 270–1; Sir T. Elyot, *The Castel of Helth* (1541), p. 21. Hereafter cited as Elyot.
17 Neckam, p. 102; Moufet, p. 169.
18 FC, no. 30, 48; Russell, pp. 36–7; Austin, p. 81.
19 Worde, *Boke of Kervynge*, p. 151; Russell, p. 28.
20 H. T. Riley, *Memorials of London* (1868), p. 426.
21 Austin, pp. 18, 78; Warner, p. 54; Moryson, *Itinerary*, 3, p. 155.
22 Austin, pp. 9, 109, 74; Napier, p. 53; Cogan, p. 122.
23 Austin, p. 79; Warner, p. 63; BD, p. 270.
24 NHB, p. 108; Austin, p. 61.
25 Bryene, p. 28; Tusser (1590), p. 138.
26 Austin, p. 40.
27 Cogan, p. 132; Emmison (1961), p. 224.
28 Pennant, 1, p. 324; 2, pp. 386, 501–3; G. E. Fussell and C. Goodman, 'Eighteenth century traffic in livestock', *Econ. History* (1934–7), 3, p. 235; Raffald, p. 52.
29 Martin, pp. 378, 416; F. M. McNeill, *The Scots Kitchen*, 2nd ed. (1963), p. 71. Hereafter cited as McNeill.
30 EHI, p. 139; E. Smith, *Compleat Housewife*, 14th ed. (1750), p. 7; Pennant, 1, p. 241; R. Briggs, *The English Art of Cookery* (1788), p. 11.
31 Pennant, 2, p. 558.
32 Mortimer, p. 196; M. Plant, *The Domestic Life of Scotland in the Eighteenth Century* (1952), p. 110. Hereafter cited as Plant.
33 Emmison (1961), p. 35.
34 Warner, p. xviii; Jones, p. 139; H. Buttes, *Dyets Dry Dinner* (1599), K5; Moufet, p. 168; Mortimer, p. 199.
35 Mortimer, p. 198; Smith (1727), p. 29.
36 Tusser (1590), p. 57; Pennant, 2, p. 284.
37 Fussell and Goodman, *Econ. History* (1934–7), 3, pp. 235–6; Ellis, p. 157; Digby, p. 233.
38 R. Seymour, April 25, 1670, *Roy. Comm. Hist. Mss.* (1968), 58, p. 294; Burt, *Letters*, 1, p. 114.
39 Jones, pp. 134–42.
40 T. Tryon, *The Way to Get Wealth*, 2nd ed. (1702), 2, pp. 93–6.

41 Markham (1631), p. 88; May, p. 148; Moufet, p. 167.
42 A.W. (1584), f. 2; Glasse (1747), pp. 34–6; PNB, p. 9; Smith (1772), pp. 98–9.
43 May, pp. 27–8; Glasse (1747), p. 50; Digby, p. 211.
44 A.W. (1584), f. 8; PNB, p. 51.
45 See p. 227; see also A.W. (1584), f. 12; E. Grey, *A Choice Manual of Rare and Select Secrets* (1653), p. 16.
46 Digby, p. 128.
47 Apicius, VI, ii, 3; T. Dawson, *The Good Huswifes Iewell* (1596), f. 9. Hereafter cited as Dawson. May, p. 72; Glasse (1747), p. 41.
48 Raffald, p. 108; S. MacIver, *Cookery and Pastry*, 3rd ed. (1782), p. 91.
49 Digby, p. 209; Glasse (1747), p. 130.
50 Digby, p. 211; Smith (1727), pp. 61, 112.
51 CC, p. 100; Glasse (1747), p. 72; Raffald, p. 129.
52 A.W. (1584), f. 20; Glasse (1747), p. 73.
53 Scott, *Proc. Prehist. Soc.* (1948), 14, pp. 124–5; Martin, p. 434.
54 Apicius, VII, xix, xiii, 8; IV, ii, 1, 9, 35.
55 Robertson, *Laws*, IV Aethelred c. 11.
56 *Hosebonderie*, WHH, p. 73; Jones, pp. 130–4; Riley, *Memorials of London*, p. 426.
57 Bryene, pp. 45–57; Worde, *Boke of Kervynge*, p. 160; Napier, p. 37.
58 NHB, p. 78; Emmison, *Tudor Food*, p. 48.
59 Warner, pp. 69, 82–3, 89; Austin, pp. 11, 24, 91, 94; FC, no. 90.
60 FC, no. 172; *Goodman*, p. 274; Austin, pp. 20, 45.
61 Russell, p. 33; FC, no. 150–1; BD, p. 264.
62 W. Salmon, *The Family Dictionary*, 2nd ed. (1696), p. 137; Mortimer, pp. 191, 193; Martin, p. 434; Ellis, pp. 152, 168.
63 BD, p. 265; Cogan, p. 150; May, pp. 169, 443–6; E. Cromwell, *The Court & Kitchin of Elizabeth* (1664), p. 104. Hereafter cited as Cromwell.
64 May, p. 430; Raffald, p. 249, 141; Markham (1615), p. 43; Blencowe, p. 13.
65 Markham (1615), p. 45; Glasse (1747), p. 82; Kettilby, p. 57; Raffald, p. 149.
66 See p. 412.
67 PNB, p. 37; H. Woolley, *The Accomplish'd Ladies Delight*, 6th ed. (1686), p. 146. Hereafter cited as Woolley (1686). Kettilby, p. 55.
68 PNB, pp. 24–5; Platt (1605), C29; CC, p. 73; Raffald, p. 170.
69 QCO, p. 260; G. Rose, *A Perfect School of Instruction for the Officers of the Mouth* (1682), pp. 171–4, 254. Hereafter cited as Rose. F. Massialot, *The Court and Country Cook* (1702), p. 153.

Chapter 5

1 Clark, *Prehistoric Europe*, p. 126; Pliny, XXVIII, xxxv; Tacitus, *Germania*, 23; Columella, VII, viii.
2 V. Cheke, *The Story of Cheese-making in Britain* (1959), p. 66. Hereafter cited as Cheke.
3 Columella, VII, viii; T. Oswald, 'The *mortaria* of Margidunum and their development', *Antiq. J.* (1944), 24, pp. 45–6.
4 Apicius, IV, i, 2, ii, 13, 17; Pliny, XVIII, xxvii.
5 T. Wright, *A History of Domestic Manners and Sentiments* (1862), p. 26. Hereafter cited as Wright (1862).
6 Trow-Smith (1957), p. 61; Aelfric, pp. 35–6; MA, p. 1027.
7 Trow-Smith (1957), pp. 180, 94, 107.
8 WHH, pp. 27, 77, 79; Sir A. Fitzherbert, *The Book of Husbandry, 1534*, ed. W. W. Skeat (1882), p. 61. Hereafter cited as Fitzherbert. Tusser (1590), pp. 86–7; Harrison, p. 157.
9 T. Lodge and R. A. Greene, *A Looking-glass for London and Englande, 1594, Malone Soc.* (1932), B4; BD, p. 267.
10 Partridge, *Widowes Treasure*, B2, Warner, p. 40; Kettilby, p. 71.
11 Neckam, p. 102; BD, p. 267.
12 Markham (1631), pp. 200, 206; Austin, p. 36.
13 Markham (1631), pp. 201–2; Cheke, p. 73.
14 *Goodman*, pp. 257, 331; Tusser (1590), p. 83.
15 Bryene, p. 103.
16 BD, p. 266; Russell, p. 6; Moufet, p. 219; Elyot, f. 23; FC, no. 166; Warner, p. 70; *Seneschaucie*, WHH, p. 113; Markham (1631), p. 206.
17 BD, p. 266; Russell, p. 7; R. Bradley, *The Country Housewife*, 6th ed. (1736), p. 76.
18 MHE, pp. 29, 37; FC, no. 166; Warner, p. 70; Austin, pp. 48, 75, 39.
19 Ellis, pp. 309–11, 319–22.
20 Markham (1631), pp. 195–9; Bridbury, *England and the Salt Trade*, p. xv; *Goodman*, p. 309.
21 Cogan, p. 156; Sir J. C. Drummond and A. Wilbraham, *The Englishman's Food* (1939), p. 83.
22 Moufet, p. 217; 'A relation . . . of the Island of England', *Camden Soc.* (1847), 37, p. 11; BD, pp. 265–6; Russell, p. 44.
23 Cogan, p. 156; NHB, pp. 73–4, 78–81; Emmison (1961), pp. 142–3. For almond butter, see p. 336.
24 Lord Ernle, *English Farming Past and Present*, 6th ed. (1961), p. 202; Ellis, p. 341; Plant, pp. 101–2.

25 G. E. Fussell, *The English Dairy Farmer, 1500–1900* (1966), p. 301. Hereafter cited as Fussell. Raffald, p. 270, etc.
26 Eden, p. 108; Lady G. Baillie, *Household Book, 1692–1733* (1911), pp. 278–9, 287. Hereafter cited as Baillie. Fussell, p. 149.
27 Austin, p. 37; Platt (1605), A59; E. Grey, *A True Gentlewomans Delight* (1653), p. 10. Hereafter cited as Grey. Smith (1727), p. 153.
28 Blencowe, pp. 14, 20; Glasse (1747), p. 147; Raffald, pp. 158–60.
29 Dawson, f. 23; Markham (1631), p. 112; May, p. 292; Woolley (1672), p. 39; Glasse, *Art of Cookery*, 4th ed. (1751), p. 285; *In an Eighteenth Century Kitchen* (1968), p. 20.
30 *The Accomplished Ladies Rich Closet of Rarities* (1687), p. 195.
31 Platt (1605), A23; Digby, p. 120; Grey, p. 105; May, p. 284; Woolley (1672), p. 39.
32 N. Bailey, *Dictionarium Domesticum* (1736), 'I'; Glasse (1758), p. 332; Smith (1772), p. 296.
33 May, p. 284; CC, p. 111; Salmon, *Dictionary*, 2nd ed., p. 330; Fiennes, *Journeys*, p. 23; Glasse (1747), p. 99.
34 *The Good Huswives Handmaid* (1597), f. 42; Raffald, p. 270.
35 Plant, pp. 101, 94; Martin, p. 242.
36 Moryson, *Itinerary*, 3, p. 163; Grey, pp. 124, 105; *Good Houswives Treasurie*, B4; Markham (1615), p. 73; May, p. 292.
37 CC, p. 25; Kettilby, p. 55; Smith (1727), pp. 116, 122.
38 May, p. 425; CC, p. 51; Smith (1727), p. 155; MacIver, *Cookery and Pastry*, p. 46.
39 Fiennes, *Journeys*, p. 112; Bradley, *Country Housewife*, p. 76.
40 Blencowe, p. 4; Cheke, pp. 44–5; Ellis, p. 343.
41 Fiennes, *Journeys*, p. 177.
42 Pepys, *Diary* (1970), 2, p. 191; Defoe, *Tour*, 1, p. 53.
43 Cogan, p. 159; B. Googe and S. Hartlib quoted in Fussell, p. 223; Moufet, p. 220; Smith (1727), p. 56.
44 Defoe, *Tour*, 1, p. 278; Bailey, *Dictionarium Domesticum*, 'O'.
45 Ellis, p. 232; Bradley, *Country Housewife*, p. 82.
46 Defoe, *Tour*, 2, p. 509.
47 Fussell, pp. 242, 251; Cheke, p. 125.
48 T. Fuller, *English Worthies: Wales* (1662), p. 5; Ellis, p. 74.
49 M. Dods, *The Cook and Housewife's Manual* (1826), p. 343. Hereafter cited as Dods.
50 Lord P. Ruthven, *The Ladies Cabinet Enlarged* (1654), p. 198; Digby, p. 223.
51 Moufet, p. 221; CC, p. 76; Kettilby, p. 73.
52 Woolley (1672), pp. 176, 343.
53 Bradley, *Country Housewife*, p. 80; Ellis, p. 341.

54 Kalm, p. 16.
55 May, pp. 432, 441, 445; Cogan, p. 160; Digby, p. 228; *Complete Cook* (1710), p. 110; Glasse (1747), p. 97; Smith (1727), p. 123.
56 PNB, p. 41; *Goodman*, p. 254; CC, p. 64.
57 May, pp. 82–4, 89; WDW, p. 452.
58 Ellis, pp. 306, 309; Fussell, pp. 209–11, 271–8.
59 Cogan, pp. 33, 45.
60 Grey, p. 108; Misson, *Memoirs*, p. 314.
61 Kalm, p. 13; C. P. Moritz, *Travels*, in *The British Tourists*, ed. W. Mavor, 2nd ed. (1800), 4, p. 14.
62 Platt (1605), C21; Salmon, *Dictionary*, 2nd ed., p. 45.
63 Markham (1615), p. 58; Glasse (1747), p. 158; Ellis, p. 365.

Chapter 6

1 K. Jessen & H. Helbaek, 'Cereals in Great Britain and Ireland in prehistoric and early historic times', *K. danske Vidensk. Selsk. Biol. skr.* (1944), III, 2, p. 62; G. Bersu, 'Excavations at Little Woodbury, Wilts.', *Proc. Prehist. Soc.* (1940), 6, p. 53.
2 Martin, p. 243.
3 McNeill, p. 231; D. and P. Brothwell, *Food in Antiquity* (1969), p. 177.
4 A. Keiller, *Windmill Hill and Avebury Excavations* (1965), pp. 40–2.
5 G. Petrie, 'Notice of ruins of ancient dwellings at Skara Brae', *Proc. Soc. Antiq. Scotland* (1869), 7, p. 213; A. Maurizio, *Histoire de l'alimentation végétale* (1932), p. 139.
6 P. V. Glob, *The Bog People* (1969), pp. 33, 57–8, 91; Jessen and Helbaek, *K. danske Vidensk. Selsk. Biol. skr.* (1944), III, 2, p. 60; H. Helbaek, 'Studying the diet of ancient man', *Archaeology* (1961), 14, p. 99.
7 See p. 276; see also Pliny, XVIII, xiv.
8 H. Helbaek, 'Early crops in southern England', *Proc. Prehist. Soc.* (1952), 18, p. 211; Bulleid and Gray, *Glastonbury Lake Village*, p. 628.
9 Apicius, IV, iv, 2; VIII, vi, 2.
10 Cato, 87.
11 F. E. Zeuner, 'Cultivation of plants', *A History of Technology*, ed. C. Singer and others (1954), 1, p. 355; Cato, 156–8; Pliny, XIX xl–xli; Apicius III, *passim*.
12 Pliny, XIX, xxv–xxviii; Applebaum, *Agric. Hist. Rev.* (1958), 6, p. 70.
13 Pliny, XVIII, xliv; Jessen and Helbaek, *K. danske Vidensk. Selsk.*

Biol. skr. (1944), III, 2, p. 62; R. U. Sayce, 'Need years and need foods', *Montgomeryshire Coll.* (1953), 53, p. 60.
14 Jessen and Helbaek, *K. danske Vindensk. Selsk. Biol. skr.* (1944), III, 2, p. 64; T. O. Cockayne, *Leechdoms, Wortcunning and Starcraft* (1866), 2, pp. 220, 230, 236, 315; MA, p. 1061.
15 Cockayne, *Leechdoms*, p. 276; J. H. G. Grattan and C. Singer, *Anglo-Saxon Magic and Medicine* (1952), p. 121.
16 Anthimus, p. 4.
17 BD, p. 262.
18 FC, no. 116; *Goodman*, p. 275.
19 Austin, pp. 6, 10, 112; FC, no. 3; Warner, p. 75.
20 Anthimus, p. 26; Warner, pp. 62, 74; Labarge, *A Baronial Household*, p. 98; Byrene, Appendix III, pp. 120, 137; FC, no. 9.
21 Fitzherbert, p. 21; LCC, p. 46; Bryene, Appendix III, pp. 126–7.
22 W. Turner, *The Names of Herbes, 1548* (1881), p. 47; Neckam, p. 96; *Goodman*, p. 252; Napier, pp. 83–4; FC, no. 70.
23 MIG, pp. 163–4; W. Caxton, *Dialogues in French and English*, E.E.T.S. (1900), e.s. 79, p. 13; Napier, p. 84.
24 Tusser (1590), p. 80; Austin, p. 14.
25 Cogan, p. 45; MIG, p. 164; FC, no. 6; Warner, p. 80.
26 Hon. A. M. T. Amherst, *A History of Gardening in England*, 3rd ed. (1910), p. 66. Hereafter cited as Amherst. LCC, p. 47; *Goodman*, p. 255.
27 G. E. Fussell, 'History of cole (brassica sp.)', *Nature* (1955), 176, p. 48; FC, no. 5.
28 E. H. M. Cox, *A History of Gardening in Scotland* (1935), p. 24; R. Higden, *Polychronicon* (1865), 1, p. 405.
29 FC, no. 25–6, 39–40; Warner, pp. 73, 88; Austin, pp. 13, 14, 18.
30 Austin, pp. 85, 71, 80; Warner, pp. 54–5, 79; FC, no. 21, 66.
31 FC, no. 45–6.
32 Warner, pp. 75–6; Austin, p. 84. For chardequince, see p. 337.
33 FC, no. 36; Austin, pp. 21, 114. For caudel ferry, see p. 141.
34 Warner, p. 45.
35 Russell, p. 36.
36 FC, no. 140, 144; Austin, pp. 77, 109–10.
37 FC, no. 135, 137, 143; Austin, pp. 108, 110.
38 Russell, pp. 36, 57–8; A.W. (1584), ff. 4–6, 10.
39 Eden, pp. 101, 106, and *passim* for workhouse diets.
40 CC, p. 59; May, p. 420; Ellis, p. 214; Cromwell, p. 116.
41 Anthimus, p. 24; *Goodman*, p. 293; *Good Huswives Handmaid*, f. 42; Markham (1631), p. 22.
42 QCO, p. 128; Rose, p. 386; Nott, *Dictionary*, O 68; W. A.

Henderson, *The Housekeeper's Instructor*, 5th ed. (1795), p. 302; Digby, p. 137; Raffald, p. 379.
43 Markham (1631), p. 242; May, p. 428; Ellis, p. 214.
44 CC, p. 61; May, p. 297.
45 Grey, p. 85; Glasse (1747), p. 112.
46 Digby, p. 137; Ellis, p. 213; J. Lucas, *Studies in Nidderdale* (1882), p. 15; Eden, p. 101; McNeill, p. 213
47 Markham (1631), p. 241.
48 Digby, p. 131; Blencowe, p. 33; Baillie, p. 282.
49 Kettilby, p. 77; Nott, *Dictionary*, S 37; Smith (1727), p. 152.
50 Markham (1631), p. 85; Digby, p. 131; S. Switzer, *The Practical Kitchen Gardener* (1727), p. 148.
51 La Varenne, p. 25; Ellis, p. 224; Kalm, pp. 15–16; Eden, p. 102.
52 J. Evelyn, *Acetaria* (1699), p. 72; Rabisha, p. 55.
53 R. N. Salaman, *The History and Social Influence of the Potato* (1949), pp. 146–7, 445, 452. Hereafter cited as Salaman. Murrel (1638), p. 58; Cromwell, pp. 80, 85, 89; Blencowe, p. 24; Eden, p. 102; Ellis, p. 228.
54 *Adam's Luxury and Eve's Cookery* (1744), pp. 164–7; Kalm, p. 15; Cutting, p. 240.
55 Markham (1615), p. 47; La Varenne, p. 24; May, pp. 78, 115; Glasse (1747), p. 65.
56 La Varenne, p. 160 etc.; Digby, p. 152.
57 May, p. 140; Moritz, *Travels*, in *The British Tourists*, ed. Mavor, 2nd ed. 4, p. 14; C. Mason, *The Lady's Assistant*, 2nd ed. (1775), p. 325. Hereafter cited as Mason.
58 Rabisha, p. 56; Digby, p. 133, WDW, p. 178, Glasse (1747), pp. ii, 54.
59 Blencowe, pp. 24, 33, Glasse (1747), p. 64, Mrs Nourse, *Modern Practical Cookery*, 2nd ed. 1811, p. 291.
60 Kalm, p. 14.
61 Blencowe, p. 23.
62 Glasse, *Art of Cookery*, 4th ed. (1751), p. 331; 6th ed. (1758), p. 340.
63 *Good Huswives Handmaid*, f. 16; Dawson, f. 29; Austin, p. 61; Rabisha, A2; May, pp. 297–300; Rose, pp. 373–4; Massialot, *Court and Country Cook*, p. 69; A. Haslemore, *The Economist* (1823), p. 377; Mrs Dalgairns, *The Practice of Cookery* (1829), p. 305.
64 A.W. (1584), f. 6; Cromwell, p. 70; Woolley (1672), pp. 195, 225, 276; Baillie, p. 279; Dods, 1, p. 50.
65 Warner, p. 57; *Good Hous-wives Treasurie*, A4; Markham (1615), p. 48; Baillie, p. 282; Dods, 1, p. 58.

Chapter 7

1 Maurizio, *Histoire de l'Alimentation végétale*, p. 441; Helbaek, *Proc. Prehist. Soc.* (1952), 18, p. 212.
2 Cato, 74.
3 Helbaek, *Proc. Prehist. Soc.* (1952), 18, pp. 198, 211; Bersu, *Proc. Prehist. Soc.* (1940), 6, pp. 30–111.
4 Pliny, XVIII, xxviii and xii; R. J. Forbes, 'Culinary arts' *History of Technology*, ed. C. Singer and others (1954), 1, p. 275.
5 Helbaek, *Proc. Prehist. Soc.* (1952), 18, pp. 213–14.
6 Columella, II, xx; L. A. Moritz, *Grain-mills and Flour in Classical Antiquity* (1958), p. 116; Frere, *Britannia*, pp. 259–60, 298.
7 Pliny, XVIII, xx, xxvii; Moritz, *Grain-mills*, pp. 153, 177.
8 Apicius, VII, xiii, 3; Cato, 75–6.
9 G. C. Boon, 'A Roman pastrycook's mould from Silchester', *Antiq. J.* (1958), 38, pp. 237–40.
10 Apicius, VII, xiii, 6; VI, v, 6.
11 BGG, p. 571; E. C. Curwen, *Plough and Pasture* (1946), pp. 136–7.
12 M. T. Hodgen, 'Domesday watermills', *Antiquity* (1939), 13, pp. 266–8.
13 F. W. Grube, 'Cereal foods of the Anglo-Saxons', *Philol. Quart.* (1934), 13, pp. 154–7.
14 MA, p. 1044; N. K. Chadwick, *Celtic Britain* (1963), p. 88.
15 Sir W. Ashley, *The Bread of our Forefathers* (1928), pp. 137–44, 67–76; Columella, II, ix, 13.
16 WHH, p. 71; G. Markham, *Farewel to Husbandry*, 5th ed. (1653), p. 40; Tusser (1590), p. 34; H. Best, *Rural Economy in Yorkshire in 1641*, *Surtees Soc.* (1857), 33, p. 42. Hereafter cited as Best.
17 Fitzherbert, p. 29.
18 Curwen, *Plough and Pasture*, p. 115.
19 *Liber Albus*, ed. H. T. Riley (1862), 3, pp. 266–7; H. E. Salter, 'The assize of bread and ale, 1309–1351', *Oxford Hist. Soc.* (1919), 73, p. 137; Harrison, p. 97 and note.
20 A. C. S. Ross, 'The assize of bread', *Econ. Hist. Rev.*, 2nd ser. (1956), 9, p. 334.
21 NHB, p. 58; Russell, pp. 4, 23.
22 'A relation . . . of the Island of England', *Camden Soc.* (1847), 37, p. 25.
23 Giraldus Cambrensis, *Descriptio*, I, 10; Higden, *Polychronicon* (1865), 1, p. 405; Sir J. Froissart, *Chronicles*, trans. T. Johnes (1852), 1, p. 18.
24 *Liber Albus*, 3, p. 267; Langland, *Piers Plowman*, 1, p. 220.

25 Markham (1631), p. 251; N. S. B. Gras, *The Evolution of the English Corn Market* (1915), p. 36. Hereafter cited as Gras.
26 Harrison, p. 96.
27 Ashley, *Bread of our Forefathers*, pp. 45, 95; Gras, pp. 82–9; Langland, *Piers Plowman*, 1, p. 222.
28 Gras, p. 452; R. Sheppard and E. Newton, *The Story of Bread* (1957), p. 71.
29 Neckam, p. 97; *Goodman*, p. 223; LCC, p. 53.
30 *Liber Albus*, 3, p. 58; MHE, p. 20; Austin, p. 35.
31 Warner, p. 46.
32 Renner, *Origin of Food Habits*, p. 222; BD, p. 211; FC, no. 82; Napier, p. 76; Warner, p. 88. For pokerounce, see p. 291.
33 May, p. 176; *The Pilgrim's Sea-voyage*, ed. F. J. Furnival, E.E.T.S. (1867), o.s. 25, p. 39.
34 Apicius, VII, xiii, 3; Austin, pp. 42, 98; FC, no. 159; Napier, p. 45; A.W. (1584), f. 37.
35 Ross, *Econ. Hist. Rev.* (1956), 9, p. 333; Sheppard & Newton, *Story of Bread*, p. 41.
36 Moufet, p. 341.
37 Russell, p. 55; *The Church Book of St. Ewen's Bristol, 1454–1584*, ed. B. R. Masters and E. Ralph, *Bristol & Glos. Arch. Soc., Rec. Sect.* (1967), 6, p. 106; Partridge, *Widowes Treasure*, D1.
38 F. Seager, *The Schoole of Vertue, 1557*, ed. F. J. Furnivall, E.E.T.S. (1868), o.s. 32, p. 231; Langland, *Piers Plowman*, 1, p. 402; *Goodman*, pp. 305, 329; Austin, p. 39.
39 Austin, pp. 97, 15; Napier, p. 57; FC, no. 92; Raffald, p. 242.
40 Riley, *Memorials of London*, p. 426.
41 Austin, pp. 47–56; FC, no. 189.
42 Tusser (1590), p. 57; FC, no. 195–6; Austin, p. 50; Napier, p. 47; A.W. (1584), f. 26; Murrel (1638), pp. 144–6, Russell, p. 32.
43 Moufet, p. 339; Markham (1631), p. 249; *Good Huswives Handmaid*, p. 51; Ruthven, *Ladies Cabinet*, p. 194; Smith (1727), p. 131; Raffald, p. 237.
44 Harrison, p. 97; Markham (1631), p. 250.
45 A. Young, *A Six Months Tour through the North of England*, 2nd ed. (1770), 3, *passim*; Eden, p. 103; Ellis, pp. 196–7.
46 I. C. Peate, 'The pot-oven in Wales', *Man* (1943), 43, pp. 9–11; R. U. Sayce, 'Food through the ages', *Montgomeryshire Coll.* (1946), 49, p. 278; Plant, p. 101.
47 *Fiennes*, Journeys, pp. 188–94; Eden, p. 104.
48 Lucas, *Studies in Nidderdale*, p. 16; McNeill, pp. 47, 183.
49 Markham (1631), p. 251; Ellis, p. 11.

50 Best, p. 104; Ellis, p. 22; Mortimer, p. 99; Sayce, *Montgomeryshire Coll.* (1953), 53, p. 71; Eden. p. 208.
51 Gras, pp. 449, 38; Fiennes, *Journeys,* pp. 190–1; Eden, p. 208; Moryson, *Itinerary,* 3, p. 149; *Annals of Agriculture* (1796), 25, p. 580.
52 Best, p. 99; Ellis, pp. 18, 194.
53 F. Accum, *A Treatise on Adulterations of Food* (1820), p. 133.
54 Smith (1727), p. 82; Markham (1615), p. 46; CC, p. 119; WDW, p. 493.
55 See p. 336 for marzipan and p. 305 for baked gingerbread; see also J. Murrel, *A Daily Exercise for Ladies and Gentlewomen* (1617), no. 49–50. Heareafter cited as Murrel (1617). May, p. 275; Blencowe, p. 6; Glasse (1747), p. 139.
56 CC, p. 63; Glasse (1747), p. 76; Raffald, pp. 42–3, 59.
57 Mason, p. 463.
58 A.W. (1584), ff. 36, 34; E. Russell, *Complete Family Cook* (1800), pp. 275–6.
59 Grey, p. 68; Kettilby, p. 76.
60 Smith (1727), p. 127; Pepys, *Diary* (1970), 2, p. 50; Ellis, p. 75; Raffald, p. 232; Smith (1772), p. 263; A. Murray, *The Domestic Oracle* (1826), p. 438.
61 Glasse (1747), p. 151.
62 Markham (1615), p. 72; Platt (1605), A19; May, p. 274; M. Eales, *Receipts* (1718), p. 78.
63 Kettilby, p. 90; Raffald, p. 374.
64 Platt (1605), A56; Raffald, p. 236; Murrel (1617), no. 54.
65 Dawson, f. 12; A.W. (1584), f. 37; CC, p. 119; Digby, p. 221; Woolley (1672), p. 49; Markham (1615), p. 72.
66 See p. 227; see also CC, p. 14; Wooley (1672), p. 113; *In an Eighteenth Century Kitchen*, p. 31.
67 Dawson, f. 13; Markham (1631), p. 132; Kettilby, p. 88; Smith (1727), p. 141.
68 Glasse (1747), p. 138; Raffald, p. 226.
69 Markham (1615), p. 75; CC, p. 109; Baillie, p. 279.
70 PNB, p. 29; *Second Part, Good Huswives Iewell*, p. 16; *Good Huswives Handmaid*, f. 17; Markham (1615), p. 64; Best, p. 104.
71 PNB, pp. 37–45; *Good Hous-wives Treasurie,* A8.
72 Dawson, f. 24; Platt (1605), A24; Massialot, *Court and Country Cook*, p. 174.
73 A.W. (1584), f. 17; Glasse (1747), p. 74.
74 May A7–8.

Chapter 8

1 J. G. D. Clark, 'Bees in antiquity', *Antiquity* (1942), 16, pp. 208–15.
2 A. P. Conolly, 'Report of plant remains at Minnis Bay', *New Phytologist* (1941), 40, p. 299.
3 Pliny, XII, xiv, xliii and lix.
4 Apicius, VII, xiii; I, i–iii and xiii.
5 Pliny, XII, xvii, 32; Varro, III, xvi; Columella, IX; S. S. Frere, *Surrey Arch Coll.* (1960), 57, p. 57, note.
6 H. M. Fraser, *History of Beekeeping in Britain* (1958), p. 13.
7 Apicius, I, xii, 4, 8; Columella, XII, lvii; Palladius, *De Re Rustica*, VIII, 9.
8 Cuthbert's letter, in Bede, p. 585.
9 A. R. Lewis, *The Northern Seas* (1958), pp. 129–31; J. Brutzkus, 'Trade with eastern Europe, 800–1200', *Econ. Hist. Rev.* (1943), 13, p. 33; Robertson, *Laws,* IV Aethelred c. 2; J. Lestocquoy, 'The tenth century', *Econ. Hist. Rev.* (1947), 17, p. 7; BGG, p. 575.
10 Fraser, *History of Beekeeping,* pp. 17–19.
11 R. Fabyan, quoted in E. M. Carus Wilson, *The Overseas Trade of Bristol in the Later Middle Ages, Bristol Rec. Soc.* (1937), 7, p. 118.
12 Swinfield, p. 115, note; Cogan, p. 110; N. Deerr, *The History of Sugar* (1949), 1, pp. 78–9. Hereafter cited as Deerr.
13 S. Thrupp, 'The Grocers of London', PP, pp. 248, 258–9, 274–6; Riley, *Memorials of London,* p. 120; Bryene, Appendix III, p. 120; H. S. Bennett, *The Pastons and their England* (1951), p. 57.
14 MCB, p. xxviii; Bryene, Appendix III, p. 137.
15 E. A. Bowles, *A Handbook of Crocus and Colchicum,* rev. ed. (1952), p. 33; MIG, p. 166.
16 H. S. Redgrove, *Spices and Condiments* (1933), p. 281; M. S. Giuseppi, 'The wardrobe and household accounts of Bogo de Clare, A.D. 1284–6', *Archaeologia* (1920), 70, p. 32.
17 Cogan, p. 108; Swinfield, pp. 64, 68, 115–16; Bryene, Appendix III, pp. 120, 137.
18 MCB, p. 32.
19 Neckam, p. 97; MHE, p. 28.
20 Warner, p. 76; Austin, pp. 6, 29.
21 Russell, pp. 36–7, 58; Warner, pp. 52, 60; FC, no. 98.
22 Austin, p. 30; Warner, pp. 41–2, 47; Russell, pp. 50, 52.
23 MIG, pp. 165–6; Tusser (1590), pp. 74–7.
24 Langland, *Piers Plowman,* 1, p. 159; Bryene, Appendix III, p. 137; Russell, pp. 36, 58–9; *Goodman,* p. 286; FC, no. 145.

25 G. Benson *Later Mediaeval York* (1919), pp. 41–2; *Goodman*, pp. 241, 246.
26 L. F. Salzman, *English Trade in the Middle Ages* (1931), p. 417. Hereafter cited as Salzman (1931): H. Johnstone, 'The wardrobe and household of Henry, son of Edward I', *Bull. J. Rylands Lib.* (1922), 7, pp. 411–14.
27 Deerr, 1, p. 109; *Goodman*, p. 287; Austin, p. 7.
28 Warner, pp. 81, 78; FC, no. 97; Austin, p. 30.
29 *Goodman*, pp. 295–8; FC, no. 100, 59; Napier, p. 100; Austin, pp. 12, 41, 87; MHE, p. 192.
30 R. H. Tawney and E. Power, eds. *Tudor Economic Documents* (1924), 2, p. 19.
31 R. W. K. Hinton, *The Eastland Trade* (1959), p. 91.
32 Cogan, p. 109
33 P. McGrath, ed., *Merchants & Merchandise in Seventeenth Century Bristol, Bristol. Rec. Soc.* (1955), 19, p. 284.
34 Rose, p. 480; Mason, p. 321; Briggs, *English Art of Cookery*, p. 296; Platt (1605), A71; Woolley (1672), p. 142.
35 Rabisha, A4; Digby, p. 130; La Varenne, p. 15.
36 Evelyn, *Acetaria*, pp. 102–3.
37 Smith (1772), p. 95; Evelyn, *Acetaria,* Appendix; Mason, p. 349; Blencowe, p. 34; Glasse (1747), p. 52.
38 R. Price, Ms. recipe book, 1681, in the possession of Mr A. J. L. Vaughan, p. 142; Raffald, pp. iii, 2.
39 May, p. 114.
40 Deerr, 1, pp. 100–28; 2, pp. 458–66; T. S. Willan, *Studies in Elizabethan Foreign Trade* (1959), pp. 315, 320.
41 J. T. Fowler, 'The account book of William Wray', *Antiquary* (1896), 32, p. 78.
42 Deerr, 2, pp. 427–30; Willan, *Studies in Elizabethan Foreign Trade*, pp. 316, 325.
43 P. Hentzner, *Travels in England*, new ed. (1894), p. 47; Markham (1631), p. 13; Murrel (1617), no. 83; *A Book of Fruit and Flowers* (1653), pp. 7–8, 20; Partridge, *Widowes Treasure,* A3.
44 Murrel (1638), pp. 94–7; Markham (1631), p. 115.
45 B. Winchester, *Tudor Family Portrait* (1955), p. 142.
46 *Ffor to Serve a Lord*, ed. Furnivall, E.E.T.S. (1868), o.s. 32, p. 355; Harrison, p. 92; Winchester, *Tudor Family Portrait*, p. 104.
47 Platt (1605), A54; Murrel (1617), no. 78; *A Closet for Ladies and Gentlewomen* (1608), p. 16; Partridge, *Widowes Treasure,* F3.
48 Rose, pp. 128–31; F. Massialot, *New Instructions for Confectioners* (1702), pp. 1–4.

49 T. S. Ashton, 'Changes in standards of comfort in eighteenth century England', *Proc. Brit. Acad.* (1955), 41, p. 182.
50 Salmon, *Dictionary* 3rd ed. (1705), p. 104; *Complete Cook* (1710), p. 47; Eden, p. 101.
51 Best, pp. 67–8; C. Butler, *The Feminine Monarchie* (1634), pp. 159–60; Digby, p. 8; Carus Wilson, *Bristol Rec. Soc.* (1937), 7, p. 107; J. Hill, *The Virtues of Honey* (1760), p. 12.
52 Butler, *Feminine Monarchie*, pp. 172–5; May, p. 423.
53 Hill, *Virtues of Honey*, pp. 13–25; *The Accomplished Housewif* (1745), p. 292.
54 Apicius, II, iv, i, 4 and iii, 2; Sir R. E. M. and T. V. Wheeler, *Verulamium* (1936), p. 92.
55 VV, p. 286.
56 Neckam, p. 104; *Goodman*, p. 308; FC, no. 160.
57 *Goodman*, p. 248; Langland, *Piers Plowman*, 1 p. 390; Austin, p. 41; A.W. (1584), f. 12; Tusser (1590), p. 56.
58 Austin, p. 130; Warner, p. 39, LCC, p. 36; A.W. (1584), f. 12; *Good Hous-wives Treasurie*, B3–4.
59 Markham (1631), p. 78; May, p. 37; Rabisha, p. 83; Ellis, pp. 83–6; Grey, p. 15, Kettilby, p. 35; Mason, p. 186.
60 CC, p. 15; Smith (1727), p. 46; Ellis, p. 86.
61 Platt (1605), C12; Rabisha, p. 82; May, p. 127; Glasse (1758), p. 370.
62 Ellis, p. 93; A.W. (1584), f. 13; Markham (1631), p. 74; Rabisha, pp. 80–2.
63 A.W. (1584), ff. 13–14; J. Murrel, *A New Booke of Cookerie* (1617), pp. 57–8; CC, p. 25.
64 Grey, p. 23; Woolley (1672), p. 252; Ellis, p. 147.
65 Best, p. 104; Ellis, p. 33.
66 *Good Hous-wives Treasurie*, A8; Markham (1631), p. 122; May, p. 182; Woolley (1672), p. 150.
67 *Good Huswives Handmaid,* f. 50; Smith (1727), p. 98; CC, p. 28; May, p. 179.
68 Raffald, p. 272; May, p. 179.
69 Woolley (1672), p. 252, and her *Queen-like Closet*, 5th ed. (1684), supp. p. 71; Glasse (1758), p. 132.
70 See p. 99; see also WDW, p. 476.
71 Misson, *Memoirs,* p. 315; Ellis, p. 33; F. Thompson, *Lark Rise to Candleford,* new ed. (1954), p. 13.

Chapter 9

1 Keiller, *Windmill Hill*, p. 41; S. H. Warren, 'On a prehistoric interment near Walton-on-the-Naze', *Essex Naturalist* (1911), 16, pp. 201–2; Bulleid and Gray, *Glastonbury Lake Village*, p. 73.
2 Athenaeus, IV, 152.
3 Pliny, XV, xxx, 102; XVII, xxi–xxviii; Cato, 51–2, 133; Frere, *Britannia*, p. 279.
4 Cato, 7; Pliny, XV, xviii; Apicius, I, xii; Columella, XII, xiv; W. H. St J. Hope, 'Excavations . . . at Silchester, Hants, in 1907', *Archaeologia* (1908), 61, p. 213.
5 *Daily Telegraph*, 23 Sept. 1967.
6 Apicius III, *passim*; VII, xv, IV, ii.
7 Columella, XII, v; Pliny, XIV, xix, 131; Apicius, I, ix.
8 Knowles, *The Monastic Order in England, 914–1216*, p. 462; Bede, p. 14; Amherst, p. 23.
9 Giraldus Cambrensis, *Descriptio*, I, 17; M.A, p. 1056; J. G. D. Lamb, 'The apple in Ireland', *Econ. Proc.* R. *Dublin Soc.* (1951), 4, p. 2.
10 C. Parain, 'The evaluation of agricultural technique', *Cambridge Econ. Hist. Europe,* 2nd ed. (1966), 1, p. 168.
11 MA, p. 1061; Robertson, *Laws,* VII Aethelred, c. 1; Grattan and Singer, *Anglo-Saxon Magic,* p. 173.
12 T. H. Turner, 'Observations on the state of horticulture in England in early times', *Archaeol. J.* (1848), 5, pp. 300–3; Amherst, pp. 20, 34–7; Elyot, f. 26.
13 Wright (1862), p. 296; Turner, *The Names of Herbes, 1548*, p. 305; Biblesworth, *Treatise*, VV, p. 162.
14 MIG, p. 161; Fitzherbert, p. 88; Wright (1862), pp. 302–3; *Goodman*, p. 27.
15 Apicius, p. 53, note; S. Tolkowsky, *Hesperides* (1938), pp. 71–111, 298; Salzman (1931), p. 413; Giuseppi, *Archaeologia* (1920), 70, p. 32.
16 See p. 338 for succade; see also N.S.B. Gras, The early English customs system (1918), pp. 514, 700; Austin, p. 106.
17 Carus Wilson, *Bristol Rec. Soc.* (1937), 7, p. 147.
18 Salzman (1931), p. 411; Bryene, Appendix III, p. 120.
19 Russell, pp. 8, 6; BD, pp. 284–5; Langland, *Piers Plowman*, 1, p. 220; Wright (1862), p. 299.
20 FSB, no. 44; *School of Salernum*, trans. Sir J. Harington, new ed. (1922), p. 160; Austin, p. 19; Warner, pp. 48, 55, 84.
21 Warner, pp. 42, 89; FC, no. 171; Napier, p. 119; Austin, p. 113. For sauce madame, see p. 122.

22 Austin, pp. 97, 109; Russell, p. 6; Buttes, *Dyets Dry Dinner*, D5.
23 BD, pp. 285, 267–8; Austin, pp. 85, 19; Warner, p. 69; LCC, p. 15.
24 W. E. Mead, *The English Mediaeval Feast* (1931), p. 164; Napier, p. 4; Austin, p. 68.
25 Warner, p. xxxvii, J. Partridge, *The Treasurie of Commodious Conceites* (1584), c. 9–10. For marzipan on plumcake, see p. 271.
26 Austin, p. 106; A.W. (1587), ff. 42–3.
27 *Goodman*, pp. 288, 307; BD, p. 286; Bennett, *The Pastons and their England*, p. 58; Warner, pp. 114–21.
28 BD, p. 282; FC, no. 76; Amherst, pp. 66-8.
29 Fisher, *Econ. Hist. Rev.* (1935), 5, p. 54.
30 Tusser (1590), p. 62; J. Parkinson, *Paradisi in Sole Paradisus Terrestris* (1629), pp. 571-93. Hereafter cited as Parkinson.
31 Tusser (1590), p. 35; M. Hadfield, *Gardening in Britain* (1960), p. 284.
32 Turner, *The Names of Herbes, 1548*, pp. 56, 68. *Goodman*, p. 196.
33 FC, no. 8; Elyot, f. 24; Parkinson, pp. 524–6; *Second Part Good Hus-wives Iewell*, p. 41; Amherst, p. 66.
34 Tusser (1590), p. 35.
35 Amherst, pp. 127 and 125 quoting W. Lawson, *New Orchard*, 1618; Cox, *History of Gardening in Scotland*, pp. 11, 18.
36 Tolkowsky, *Hesperides*, p. 245; Sir T. Hanmer, *Garden Book, 1659* (1933), p. 132; Parkinson, p. 584; Pepys, *Diary* (1972), 7, p. 182.
37 J. Gerard, *Herball* (1597), p. 275. Hereafter cited as Gerard. Parkinson, p. 380.
38 *Jamestown Voyages under the First Charter*, ed. P. Barbour, *Hakluyt Soc.* 2nd ser. 136 (1969), 1, p. 100; J. Evelyn, *Diary*, ed. E. S. de Beer (1955), 3, p. 293; J. Worlidge, *Vinetum Britannicum* (1676), p. 4.
39 D. Quélus, *The Natural History of Chocolate*, 2nd ed. (1730), p. 84. Hereafter cited as Quélus. Amherst, p. 149.
40 Boorde's third letter, 1535, in E.E.T.S. (1870), e.s. 10, p. 56; Tusser (1590), p. 77; Plant, p. 71; Parkinson, p. 484.
41 Cogan, p. 89.
42 *Good Hous-wives Treasurie*, A7; Markham (1631), pp. 114–15; Raffald, pp. 126, 297, 300.
43 CC, p. 14.
44 Dawson, f. 20; Murrel (1638), p. 132; Markham (1615), p. 68; M. Tillinghast, *Rare and Excellent Receipts* (1690), p. 13.
45 Dawson, f. 17; Markham (1631), p. 119.

46 May, pp. 245, 287; Rabisha, p. 181; CC, p. 82; Smith (1727), p. 122.
47 Ellis, pp. 46, 246, Henderson, *Housekeeper's Instructor*, p. 203.
48 Grey, p. 6; Woolley (1672), p. 152; Markham (1631), p. 116; Smith (1772), p. 291; Raffald, pp. 162–3. For flummery, see p. 168.
49 Tryon, *Way to Get Wealth*, 2 p. 79; BD, p. 278; J. C. Shenstone, 'Industries', *VCH: Essex* (1907), 2, p. 371; Gerard, p. 1000.
50 Woolley (1672), p. 98 and (1686), p. 55; A.W., *A Book of Cookrye*, new ed. (1587), f. 43; QCO, pp. 200, 241; Raffald, pp. 189, 333; Glasse (1758), p. 307.
51 Platt (1605), A29; *Closet for Ladies*, p. 47; Murrel (1617), no. 46–7.
52 Partridge, *Treasurie of Commodious Conceites*, c. 18; QCO, p. 247; Eales, *Receipts*, p. 16.
53 Murrel (1617), no. 61; BD, p. 281; *Closet for Ladies*, p. 54.
54 Smith (1727), p. 232.
55 Woolley (1686), p. 38 and (1672), p. 135; La Varenne, p. 284; Tryon, *Way to Get Wealth*, 2, p. 61; Pepys, *Diary*, ed. H. B. Wheatley (1920), 8, p. 255.
56 K. T. Butler, 'An Italian's message to England in 1614', *Ital. Stud.* (1938), 2, p. 10.
57 A. W. (1584), ff. 6; 19; PNB, p. 31; Murrel (1638), pp. 89, 103.
58 Drummond and Wilbraham, *The Englishman's Food*, pp. 273–81; E. Hughes, *North Country Life in the Eighteenth Century: the North-east 1700–1750* (1952), p. 356.
59 Dawson, f. 25; Markham (1615), p. 39.
60 Gerard, p. 221; Woolley (1672), p. 304; Markham (1615), p. 39; Buttes, *Dyets Dry Dinner*, H5; Evelyn, *Acetaria*, pp. 63, 28.
61 Parkinson, p. 586.
62 Gerard, p. 1040.
63 Parkinson, p. 496; FC, no. 180; A.W. (1584), f. 15; Buttes, *Dyets Dry Dinner*, F5; Murrel (1638), p. 40.
64 Gerard, p. 1042; Parkinson, p. 518.
65 Butler, *Ital. Stud.* (1938), 2, p. 6; Evelyn, *Acetaria*, pp. 34, 96–105; May, p. 163; Rabisha, p. 5.
66 P. Miller, *The Gardener's Dictionary* (1752) Lycopersicon; A. Hunter, *Culina Famulatrix Medicinae* (1804), pp. 128, 193; Webster, *Encyclopaedia*, p. 479.

Chapter 10

1 H. Shetelig and H. Falk, *Scandinavian Archaeology* (1937), p. 149.
2 R. J. Forbes, *Studies in Ancient Technology* (1955), 3, pp. 63–70, 126; Athenaeus, IV, xxxvi, 152; Dioscorides, *De Materia Medica,* II, 88; Diodorus Siculus, *Bibliotheca Historica,* V, 26; Piggott, *Antiquity* (1948), 22, p. 22.
3 Frere, *Britannia,* p. 293; M. H. Callender, *Roman Amphorae* (1965), p. 56.
4 A. Birley, *Life in Roman Britain* (1964), p. 53; Cato, 24; Columella, XII, xx; Apicius, I, i–iii.
5 Frere, *Britannia,* p. 294.
6 Tacitus, *Germania,* 22; Forbes, *Studies in Ancient Technology,* 3, pp. 127–8. VV, p. 27; J. Bickerdyke, *The Curiosities of Ale and Beer* (1886), p. 152. Hereafter cited as Bickerdyke.
7 R. V. French, *Nineteen Centuries of Drink in England* (1884), p. 24, note. Hereafter cited as French. Attenborough, *Laws,* Ine c. 70; Bickerdyke, p. 30; HDL, p. 72.
8 K. H. Jackson, *The Gododdin: the Oldest Scottish Poem* (1969), pp. 35–7; Knowles, *The Monastic Order in England, 914–1216,* p. 465.
9 Robertson, *Laws,* IV Aethelred c. 2.
10 French, pp. 28, 37; Bede, p. 192.
11 *Fleta, 2,* ed. H. G. Richardson and G. O. Sayles, *Selden Soc.* (1955), 72, p. 118; Bickerdyke, p. 154; Salzman (1923), p. 293.
12 Cogan, p. 109; Gerard, p. 707; Riley, *Memorials of London,* p. 319.
13 Langland, *Piers Plowman,* 1, p. 149; *Liber Albus,* 3, p. 139; Russell, p. 12.
14 H. A. Monckton, *A History of English Ale and Beer* (1966), p. 40. Hereafter cited as Monckton. Giraldus Cambrensis, *Autobiography,* ed. H. Butler (1937), p. 71; A. Boorde, *Fyrst Boke of the Introduction of Knowledge, 1547,* ed. F. J. Furnivall, E.E.T.S. (1870), e.s. 10, pp. 123, 136.
15 Russell, p. 55; J. Strutt, *Horda Angel-cynnan* (1776), 2, p. 74; LCC, p. 53.
16 Forbes, *Studies in Ancient Technology,* 3, p. 127; Kerling, p. 114; Salzman (1923), pp. 295–6.
17 BD, p. 256; Harrison, p. 102; Bickerdyke, p. 70.
18 NHB, pp. 73–8; Harrison, pp. 93–103; French, pp. 81–3.
19 A. L. Simon, *The History of the Wine Trade in England* (1906), 1, pp. 10–16, 112. Hereafter cited as Simon (1906). Swinfield, pp. xliii, xlvi; Amherst, p. 24.

20 Neckam, p. 102; G. Ordish, *Winegrowing in England* (1953), pp. 20–1; Simon (1906), 1, pp. 265–7.
21 Simon (1906), 1, p. 282; 2, p. 217; Deerr, 1, p. 100; BD, p. 255.
22 Russell, pp. 9–12; Warner, p. 90; Salzman (1923), pp. 404–5; Markham (1631), pp. 157–61.
23 R. J. Forbes, *Short History of the Art of Distillation* (1948), pp. 90, 95; Warner, p. 76; NHB, p. 371.
24 Elyot, f. 36; Harrison, p. 103.
25 Salzman (1923), p. 300; Swinfield, p. xlvi, note; Langland, *Piers Plowman*, 1, p. 148; BD, p. 256; Elyot, f. 34.
26 J. Evelyn, *Sylva* (1679), pp. 70, 68; *Good Huswives Handmaid*, f. 42.
27 Bickerdyke, p. 123; BD, p. 253.
28 Monckton, pp. 115–17, 137, 148; Burnett, *Plenty and Want*, pp. 4–5; *The London and Country Brewer*, 6th ed. (1750), p. 69.
29 Markham (1631), p. 235; Mortimer, p. 278; Bickerdyke, p. 335; J. Taylor, *Drinke and Welcome, 1637, Spenser Soc.* (1873), 14, p. 9; *In Praise of Yorkshire Ale* (1685), p. 6; G. C. F. Forster, 'Hull in the sixteenth and seventeenth centuries', *VCH: Kingston upon Hull* (1969), p. 166; Mortimer, p. 589.
30 Monckton, pp. 144–9.
31 EHI, p. 103; *London and Country Brewer*, pp. 74, 292; Monckton, pp. 140–2.
32 Platt (1605), C32; EHI, p. 101.
33 J. Taylor, *Works* (1630), p. 126; Gerard, p. 325; Hartman, *True Preserver and Restorer of Health*, p. 175; EHI, p. 98; J. Houghton, *A Collection of Letters for the Improvement of Husbandry and Trade* (1681), 2, p. 93; Pepys, *Diary* (1971), 5, p. 142.
34 Smith (1727), pp. 216, 225; *London and Country Brewer*, pp. 194–5; Platt (1605), C27.
35 May, p. 423; Raffald, p. 268; Ellis, p. 72; McNeill, pp. 214, 254; Glasse (1747), p. 119.
36 Parkinson, pp. 563, 566; Worlidge, *Vinetum*, p. 124.
37 Thomson, pp. 197–200; Pepys, *Diary* (1971), 4, p. 100; A. L. Simon, *Bottlescrew Days* (1926), pp. 153, 172–3. Hereafter cited as Simon (1926).
38 Sir E. Barry, *Observations, etc.* (1775), p. 442.
39 S. Bradford, *The Englishman's Wine* (1969), pp. 35–6, 54–7; Simon (1926), pp. 236, 252.
40 Gerard, p. 736; Simon (1906), 2, p. 210 and (1926), p. 75; Markham (1631), p. 162; Pepys, *Diary* (1920), 8, p. 47; J. Hart, *Klinike* (1633), p. 24.
41 Gerard, p. 730; Bradford, *The Englishman's Wine*, p. 47; EHI, pp. 33–5.

42 Smith (1727), pp. 218–24; QCO, p. 215; E. Smith, *Compleat Housewife*, 6th ed. (1734), pp. 200–1.
43 *The Accomplished Housewife*, p. 274.
44 Platt (1605), B6, B8.
45 Platt (1605), C33; NHB, p. 371; Partridge, *Widowes Treasure*, B8.
46 W. Yworth, *The Compleat Distiller*, 2nd ed. (1705), pp. 9–10, 29; Hart, *Klinike*, p. 193.
47 W. Yworth, *A New Treatise of Artificial Wines* (1690), p. 29; *The London Distiller*, new ed. (1652), pp. 9, 56; Yworth, *Compleat Distiller*, pp. 64–5, 87.
48 QCO, pp. 283, 14; Smith (1727), pp. 235–8; Woolley (1672), p. 19; T. Tryon, *Healths Grand Preservative* (1682), p. 9.
49 Simon (1926), pp. 19–26, 34.
50 Worlidge, *Vinetum*, p. 10; Sir A. Burns, *History of the British West Indies* (1954), p. 218.
51 Yworth, *Compleat Distiller*, p. 17; Simon (1926), p. 29; T. C. Smout, 'The early Scottish sugar houses, 1660–1720', *Econ. Hist. Rev.* (1961), 14, pp. 241–52.
52 Worlidge, *Vinetum*, p. 10; Woolley (1672), p. 134; Kettilby, p. 113.
53 EHI, p. 99; Smith (1727), p. 210; Raffald, p. 292.
54 Forbes, *Short History of the Art of Distillation*, p. 101; D. Daiches, *Scotch Whisky, its Past and Present* (1969), p. 36; Moryson, *Itinerary*, 3, p. 162.
55 Burt, *Letters*, 2, pp. 39, 243–5; Dods, *Cook and Housewife's Manual*, p. 337; McNeill, pp. 250–1.
56 Digby, pp. 23, 72; Best, p. 68; Raffald, pp. 288–9.
57 Worlidge, *Vinetum*, pp. 80–91, 108, 119; Mortimer, pp. 588–9.
58 Evelyn, *Diary* (1955), 2, p. 18; A. E. Haarar, *Modern Coffee Production* (1962), pp. 4–9; Thomson, pp. 168–9; Salmon, *Dictionary*, 4th ed. (1710), pp. 104–5.
59 EHI, p. 95; T. Tryon, *The Good Hous-wife Made a Doctor*, 2nd ed. (1692), p. 213.
60 EHI, p. 94; Ellis, p. 300. For toast and water, see p. 265.
61 Ellis, p. 299.
62 Quélus, pp. 63–7; Yworth, *New Treatise of Artificial Wines*, p. 56.
63 Woolley (1672), p. 90; EHI, p. 96; Salmon, *Dictionary*, 4th ed., pp. 104–5.
64 Quélus, pp. 74–9; Thomson, p. 173; Eales, *Receipts*, pp. 67, 91; Smith (1727), p. 186; *The True Way of Preserving, Candying, etc.* (1681), p. 145; Raffald, p. 212.
65 Brothwell, *Food in Antiquity*, p. 172; J. M. Scott, *The Tea Story*

(1964), pp. 16–17, 24–5; T. Garway, *An Exact Description of . . . the Leaf Tea* (*c.* 1660); J. Ovington, *An Essay upon the Nature & Qualities of Tea* (1699), pp. 9–14.

66 Thomson, p. 170; Worlidge, *Vinetum*, p. 140; Digby, p. 132; Smith (1727), p. 151.

67 Kalm, p. 13.

68 V. La Chapelle, *The Modern Cook* (1736), 3, p. 220.

69 J. Hanway, *Journal of an Eight Days Journey . . . to which is added An Essay on Tea*, 2nd ed. (1757), 2, p. 272; Ellis, p. 294; Plant, p. 115.

70 J. Woodforde, *The Diary of a Country Parson*, ed. J. Beresford (1924), 1, p. 201.

71 J. B. Botsford, *English Society in the Eighteenth Century as Influenced from Oversea* (1924), p. 66; Eden, pp. 106–7.

Chapter 11

1 Material for this chapter has been drawn from Sir J. C. Drummond and A. Wilbraham, *The Englishman's Food*; J. Burnett, *Plenty and Want*; and T. C. Barker, J. C. McKenzie and J. Yudkin, eds., *Our Changing Fare* (1966).

Bibliography

Place of publication is London, unless otherwise stated.

1. General works

AELFRIC: *Colloquy*, ed. G. N. Garmonsway, 2nd ed. 1947.

AINSWORTH-DAVIS, J. R.: *Cooking through the Centuries*. 1931.

AMHERST, HON. A. M. T.: *A History of Gardening in England*, 3rd ed. 1910.

ASHLEY, SIR WILLIAM: *The Bread of our Forefathers*. Oxford, 1928.

BAILLIE, LADY GRISELL: *The Household Book, 1692–1733*, ed. R. Scott-Moncrieff. Edinburgh, 1911.

BARKER, T. C., MCKENZIE, J. C. and YUDKIN, J. (eds.): *Our Changing Fare*. 1966.

'*Be gesceadwisan gerefan*', in CUNNINGHAM, W.: *Growth of English Industry and Commerce*, 4th ed., 1, p. 571. Cambridge, 1905.

BEDE: *Ecclesiastical History of the English People*, ed. B. Colgrave and R. A. B. Mynors. Oxford, 1969.

BEST, H.: *Rural Economy in Yorkshire in 1641*, Surtees Society, 33, 1857.

BICKERDYKE, J. (C. H. COOK): *The Curiosities of Ale and Beer*. 1886.

BOORDE, A.: *A Compendyous Regyment, or A Dyetary of Helth, 1542*, ed. F. J. Furnivall, Early English Text Society, e.s. 10, 1870.

BRADFORD, S.: *The Englishman's Wine*. 1969.

BRIDBURY, A. R.: *England and the Salt Trade in the Later Middle Ages*. Oxford, 1955.

BROTHWELL, D. and P.: *Food in Antiquity*. 1969.

BRYENE, DAME ALICE DE: *The Household Book of Dame Alice de Bryene, of Acton Hall, Suffolk, Sept. 1412–Sept. 1413*, trans. M. K. Dale and ed. V. B. Redstone. Ipswich, 1931.

BURNETT, J.: *Plenty and Want*. 1966.

BURT, E.: *Letters from a Gentleman in the North of Scotland*, new ed. 2 vols. 1815.

CHEKE, V.: *The Story of Cheese-making in Britain*. 1959.

CLAIR, C.: *Kitchen and Table*. 1964.

CLARK, J. G. D.: *Prehistoric Europe: the Economic Basis*. 1952.

COGAN, T.: *The Haven of Health . . . Augmented*. 1612.

CUTTING, C. L.: *Fish Saving*. 1955.

DEERR, N.: *The History of Sugar.* 2. vols. 1949.
DEFOE, D.: *A Tour through the Whole Island of Great Britain, 1724–5.* 2 vols. 1927.
DODD, J. S.: *An Essay towards a Natural History of the Herring.* 1752.
DRUMMOND, SIR JOHN C. and WILBRAHAM, A.: *The Englishman's Food.* 1st ed. 1939.
EDEN, SIR FREDERIC M.: *The State of the Poor, 1797,* abridged A. G. L. Rogers. 1928.
ELYOT, SIR THOMAS: *The Castel of Helth . . . Augmented.* 1541.
EMMISON, F. G.: *Tudor Food and Pastimes.* 1964.
—: *Tudor Secretary: Sir William Petre at Court and Home,* 1961.
ERNLE, LORD (R. E. PROTHERO): *English Farming Past and Present,* 6th ed. 1961.
EVELYN, J.: *Acetaria.* 1699.
FIENNES, C.: *Journeys,* ed. C. Morris. 1949.
FISHER, F. J.: 'The development of the London food market, 1540–1640', *Economic History Review,* 5, 1935, pp. 46–54.
FITZHERBERT, SIR ANTHONY: *The Book of Husbandry, 1534,* ed. W. W. Skeat, English Dialect Society, D37, 1882.
FORBES, R. J.: *Short History of the Art of Distillation.* Leiden, 1948.
—: *Studies in Ancient Technology,* 3. Leiden, 1955.
FRASER, H. M.: *History of Beekeeping in Britain.* 1958.
FRENCH, R. V.: *Nineteen Centuries of Drink in England.* 1884.
FRERE, S. S.: *Britannia.* 1967.
FUSSELL, G. E.: *The English Dairy Farmer, 1500–1900.* 1966.
GERARD, J.: *The Herball.* 1597.
GLOB, P. V.: *The Bog People.* 1969.
The Goodman of Paris, c. 1393 (Ménagier de Paris), ed. E. Power. 1928.
GRAS, N. S. B.: *The Evolution of the English Corn Market.* Cambridge, Mass., 1915.
GRATTAN, J. H. G. and SINGER, C. J.: *Anglo-Saxon Magic.* 1952.
GRUBE, F. W.: 'Cereal foods of the Anglo-Saxons', *Philological Quarterly,* 13, 1934, pp. 140–58.
—: 'Meat foods of the Anglo-Saxons', *Journal of English and German Philology,* 34, 1935, pp. 511–29.
HADFIELD, M.: *Gardening in Britain.* 1960.
HANMER, SIR T.: *The Garden Book, 1659,* intro. E. S. Rohde. 1933.
HARRISON, W.: *Elizabethan England,* ed. F. J. Furnivall and L. Withington. Scott Library (1902).
HARTLEY, D.: *Food in England.* 1954.
HELBAEK, H.: 'Early crops in southern England', *Proceedings of the Prehistoric Society,* 18, 1952, pp. 194–233.
HOLE, C.: *English Home Life, 1500–1800,* 2nd ed. 1949.

Household books of John, Duke of Norfolk, & Thomas, Earl of Surrey, 1481–1490, ed. J. P. Collier. Roxburghe Club, 1844.

HUNTER, A.: *Culina Famulatrix Medicinae*. York, 1804.

HYWEL DDA: *Laws (Book of Blegywryd)*, trans. M. Richards. Liverpool, 1954.

JESSEN, K. and HELBAEK, H.: 'Cereals in Great Britain and Ireland in prehistoric and early historic times', *K. danske Videnskabernes Selskab, Biol. skr.*, III, 2. Copenhagen, 1944.

JONES, P. E.: *The Worshipful Company of Poulters of the City of London a Short History*, 2nd ed. 1965.

KERLING, N. J. M.: *Commercial Relations of Holland and Zeeland with England from the Late Thirteenth Century to the Close of the Middle Ages*. Leiden, 1954.

LABARGE, M. W.: *A Baronial Household of the Thirteenth Century*. 1965.

LEWIS, A. R.: *The Northern Seas: Shipping and Commerce in Northern Europe, A.D. 300–1100*. Princeton, 1958.

The London and country brewer, 6th ed. 1750.

The London distiller, new ed. 1652.

Manners and Household Expenses of England in the Thirteenth and Fifteenth Centuries (Household roll of Eleanor, Countess of Leicester, 1265; and: The expenses of Sir John Howard, 1462–1469). Roxburghe Club, 1841.

MARTIN, M.: *A description of the Western Islands of Scotland circa 1695*, and *A Late Voyage to St. Kilda*, ed. D. J. McLeod. Stirling, 1934.

MAURIZIO, A.: *Histoire de l'Alimentation végétale*, trad. F. Gidon. Paris, 1932.

MAYSTER ION GARDENER, 'The feate of gardeninge', ed. Hon. A. M. T. Amherst, *Archaeologia*, 54, 1894, pp. 157–66.

MEAD, W. E.: *The English Medieval Feast*. 1931.

MONCKTON, H. A.: *A History of English Ale and Beer*. 1966.

MORITZ, L. A.: *Grain-mills and Flour in Classical Antiquity*. Oxford, 1958.

MORTIMER, J.: *The Whole Art of Husbandry*. 1707.

MORYSON, F.: *An Itinerary*. 1617.

MOUFET, T.: *Health's Improvement*, ed. C. Bennet. 1746.

Myvyrian Archaiology of Wales: Laws of Howell the Good, trans. A. Owen. Denbigh, 1870.

NECKAM, A.: *De Utensilibus*, in *A Volume of Vocabularies*, ed. T. Wright. Liverpool, 1857.

NELSON, W. (ed.): *A Fifteenth Century School Book*. Oxford, 1956.

NICHOLSON, B. E. and others: *The Oxford Book of Food Plants*. 1969.

Northumberland Household Book. The Regulations and Establishment of the Household of Henry Algernon Percy . . . 1512. New ed. 1905.

Our English home. 1860.

OVINGTON, J.: *An Essay upon the Nature & Qualities of Tea*. 1699.

PARKINSON, J.: *Paradisus in Sole, Paradisus Terrestris*. 1629.

PASSINGHAM, W. J.: *London's Markets*. 1935.

PENNANT, T.: *British Zoology*, 4th ed. 4 vols. 1776–7.

PIGGOTT, S.: *Ancient Europe from the Beginnings of Agriculture to Classical Antiquity*. Edinburgh, 1965.

PLANT, M.: *The Domestic Life of Scotland in the Eighteenth Century*. Edinburgh, 1952.

PLATT, SIR HUGH: *Jewell House of Art and Nature*. 1594.

POWER, E. and POSTAN, M. M. (eds.): *Studies in English Trade in the Fifteenth Century*. 1933.

QUÉLUS, D.: *The Natural History of Chocolate*, trans. R. Brookes, 2nd ed. 1730.

REDGROVE, H. S.: *Spices and Condiments*. 1933.

RENNER, H. D.: *The Origin of Food Habits*. 1944.

RILEY, H. T.: *Memorials of London, 1276–1419*. 1868.

ROSS, A. C.: 'The assize of bread', *Economic History Review*, 2nd series, 9, 1956, pp. 332–42.

RUSSELL, J.: *Boke of Nurture*, in *Early English Meals and Manners*, ed. F. J. Furnivall, Early English Text Society, o.s. 32, 1868.

SALAMAN, R. N.: *The History and Social Influence of the Potato*. Cambridge, 1949.

SALZMAN, L. F.: *English Industries of the Middle Ages*, new ed. Oxford, 1923.

—: *English Trade in the Middle Ages*. Oxford, 1931.

SAYCE, R. U.: 'Need years and need foods', *Montgomeryshire Collections*, 53, pp. 55–80. Welshpool, 1953.

SCOTT, J. M.: *The Tea Story*. 1964.

SHEPPARD, R. and NEWTON, E.: *The Story of Bread*. 1957.

SIMON, A. L.: *Bottlescrew Days*. 1926.

—: *The History of the Wine Trade in England*. 3 vols. 1906.

SLICHER VAN BATH, H.: *The Agrarian History of Western Europe, A.D. 500–1850*. 1963.

A Small Household of the Fifteenth Century, Being the Account Book of Munden's Chantry, Bridport, 1453–60, ed. K. L. Wood-legh. Manchester, 1956.

SWINFIELD, R. DE: *Roll of the Household Expenses of Richard de Swinfield, Bishop of Hereford, during Part of the Years 1289 & 1290*, ed. J. Webb. 2 vols. Camden Society, 59, 62, 1853–4.

SWITZER, S.: *The Practical Kitchen Gardener*. 1727.

TANNAHILL, R.: *The Fine Art of Food*. Folio Society, 1968.

THOMPSON, F.: *Lark Rise to Candleford*. World Classics, 1954.

THOMSON, G. S.: *Life in a Noble Household, 1641–1700.* Bedford Historical Series, 8, 1940.
TOLKOWSKY, S.: *Hesperides.* 1938.
TRENCH, C. C.: *The Poacher and the Squire.* 1967.
TROW-SMITH, R.: *A History of British Livestock Husbandry to 1700.* 1957.
TURNER, W.: *The Names of Herbes, A.D. 1548.* English Dialect Society, D34, 1881.
TUSSER, T.: *Five Hundreth Pointes of Good Husbandrie . . . Newlie Augmented.* 1590.
—: *A Hundreth Good Pointes of Husbandrie, 1557*, new ed. 1810.
WALTER OF HENLEY: *Husbandry*, trans. E. Lamond. 1890.
WEBSTER, T.: *An Encyclopaedia of Domestic Economy.* 1844.
WILSON, C. A.: 'The Preston Collection of English Cookery Books', *University of Leeds Review*, 9, 1964, pp. 58–70.
WINCHESTER, B.: *Tudor Family Portrait.* 1955.
WORDE, W. DE: *Boke of Kervynge*, in *Early English Meals and Manners*, ed. F. J. Furnivall, Early English Text Society, o.s. 32, 1868.
WORLIDGE, J.: *Vinetum Britannicum.* 1676.
WRIGHT, T.: *A History of Domestic Manners and Sentiments in England during the Middle Ages.* 1862.
— (ed.): *A Volume of Vocabularies.* Liverpool, 1857.
YWORTH, W.: *The Compleat Distiller*, 2nd ed. 1705.
—: *A New Treatise of Artificial Wines.* 1690.
ZEUNER, F. E.: 'Cultivation of plants', *A History of Technology*, ed. C. Singer and others, 1, pp. 353–75. Oxford, 1954.
—: *A History of Domesticated Animals.* 1963.

2. *Cookery books*

The Accomplished Housewife. 1745.
The Accomplished Ladies Rich Closet of Rarities. 1687.
Adam's Luxury and Eve's Cookery. 1744.
ANTHIMUS: *De Observatione Ciborum*, ed. E. Liechtenhan. Berlin, 1963.
APICIUS: *The Roman Cookery Book: a Critical Translation of the Art of Cooking*, by B. Flower and E. Rosenbaum. 1958.
AUSTIN, T. (ed.), *Two Fifteenth-century Cookery Books: Harleian MS 279 & 4016*, Early English Text Society, o.s. 91, 1888.
BAILEY, N.: *Dictionarium Domesticum.* 1736.
BLENCOWE, A.: *The Receipt Book, A.D. 1694.* 1925.
A Book of Fruits and Flowers. 1653.
BRADLEY, M.: *The British Housewife.* 2 vols. 1756.
BRADLEY, R.: *The Country Housewife and Lady's Director*, 6th ed. 1736.

BRIGGS, R.: *The English Art of Cookery*. 1788.
BUTTES, H.: *Dyets Dry Dinner*. 1599.
A Closet for Ladies and Gentlewomen. 1608.
The Compleat Cook. 1655.
—: new ed. 1710.
COOPER, J.: *Art of Cookery Refin'd and Augmented*. 1654.
CROMWELL, E.: *The Court & Kitchin of Elizabeth*. 1664.
DAWSON, T.: *The Good Huswifes Iewell . . . with Additions*. 1596.
DIGBY, SIR K.: *The Closet Opened, 1669*, ed. A. Macdonnell. 1910.
DODS, M. (C. I. JOHNSTONE): *The Cook and Housewife's Manual*. Edinburgh, 1826.
EALES, M.: *Receipts*. 1718.
ELLIS, W.: *The Country Housewife's Family Companion*. 1750.
England's Happiness Improved, 2nd ed. 1699.
The Forme of Cury, in *Antiquitates Culinariae*, ed. R. Warner. 1791.
GLASSE, H.: *The Art of Cookery Made Plain and Easy*. 1747.
—, 6th ed. 1758.
The Good Hous-wives Treasurie. 1588.
The Good Huswives Handmaid, for Cookerie in her Kitchin. 1597.
GREY, E., COUNTESS OF KENT: *A True Gentlewomans Delight*. 1653.
HENDERSON, W. A.: *The Housekeeper's Instructor*, 5th ed. 1795.
HILL, J.: *The Virtues of Honey*, 3rd ed. 1760.
In an Eighteenth Century Kitchen, ed. D. Rhodes. 1968.
KETTILBY, M.: *A Collection of above Three Hundred Receipts in Cookery, Physick and Surgery*. 1714.
KITCHENER, W.: *Apicius Redivivus*. 1817.
LA CHAPELLE, V.: *The Modern Cook*. 3 vols. 1736.
LA VARENNE, F. P. DE: *The French Cook (Cuisinier françois)*, 3rd ed. 1673.
LAMB, P.: *Royal Cookery*. 1710.
Liber Cure Cocorum . . . Sloane MS 1986, ed. R. Morris. Berlin, 1862.
M., W.: *The Queens Closet Opened*. 1655.
MACIVER, S.: *Cookery and Pastry*, 3rd ed. Edinburgh, 1782.
MCNEILL, F. M.: *The Scots Kitchen*, 2nd ed. 1963.
MARKHAM, G.: *The English Hus-wife*. 1615.
—, 4th ed. 1631.
MASON, C.: *The Lady's Assistant*, 2nd ed. 1775.
MASSIALOT, F.: *The Court and Country Cook (Cuisinier roial et bourgeois)*. 1702.
—: *New Instructions for Confectioners (Nouvelle instruction pour les confitures)*. 1702.
MAY, R.: *The Accomplisht Cook*, 2nd ed. 1665.
MURREL, J.: *A Daily Exercise for Ladies and Gentlewomen*. 1617.

—: *Murrels Two Books of Cookerie and Carving*, 5th ed. 1638.
NAPIER, MRS A. (ed.): *A Noble Boke off Cookry*. 1882.
NOTT, J.: *The Cook's and Confectioner's Dictionary*. 1723.
PARTRIDGE, J.: *The Treasurie of Commodious Conceites*. 1584.
—: *The Widowes Treasure*. 1585.
PLATT, SIR HUGH: *Delightes for Ladies*. 1605.
A Proper Newe Booke of Cokerye, ed. C. F. Frere. Cambridge, 1913.
RABISHA, W.: *The Whole Body of Cookery Dissected*. 1673.
RAFFALD, E.: *The Experienced English Housekeeper*, 2nd ed. 1771.
ROSE, G. (trans.): *A Perfect School of Instruction for the Officers of the Mouth* (*Escole parfaite des officiers de bouche*). 1682.
RUNDELL, E.: *A New System of Domestic Cookery*. 1806.
RUTHVEN, LORD PATRICK: *The Ladies Cabinet Enlarged and Opened*. 1654.
SALMON, W.: *The Family Dictionary*, 2nd ed. 1696.
—, 3rd ed. 1705.
—, 4th ed. 1710.
The Second Part of the Good Hus-wives Iewell. 1597.
SMITH, E.: *The Compleat Housewife*. 1727.
SMITH, M.: *The Complete Housekeeper and Professed Cook*. Newcastle, 1772.
Stere Hit Well (*Pepysian ms. 1047*, Magdalene College, Cambridge). 1972.
TILLINGHAST, M.: *Rare and Excellent Receipts*. 1690.
The True Way of Preserving, Candying and Making Several Sorts of Sweetmeats. 1681.
TRYON, T.: *The Way to Get Wealth*, 2nd ed. 1702.
W., A.: *A Booke of Cookry Very Necessary for All Such as Delight Therein, Gathered by A.W.* 1584.
— (Another ed.). 1587.
WARNER, R. (ed.): *Antiquitates Culinariae*. 1791.
WHITE, F.: *Good Things in England*, 2nd ed. 1962.
The Whole Duty of a Woman. 1737.
WOOLLEY, H.: *The Accomplish'd Ladies Delight*, 6th ed. 1686.
—: *The Queen-like Closet*, 2nd ed. 1672.

Index

For ingredients in regular usc in cookery, see also recipes in text.